PRACTICUM AND INTERNSHIP

PRACTICUM AND INTERNSHIP

Textbook and Resource Guide for Counseling and Psychotherapy

John C. Boylan, Ph.D.
Patrick B. Malley, Ph.D.
and Eileen Petty Reilly, M.Ed.

USA	Publishing Office:	BRUNNER-ROUTLEDGE
		A member of the Taylor & Francis Group
		325 Chestnut Street
		Philadelphia, PA 19106
		Tel: (215) 625-8900
		Fax: (215) 625-2940
	Distribution Center:	BRUNNER-ROUTLEDGE
		A member of the Taylor & Francis Group
		7625 Empire Drive
		Florence, KY 41042
		Tel: 1-800-634-7064
		Fax: 1-800-248-4724
UK		BRUNNER-ROUTLEDGE
		A member of the Taylor & Francis Group
		27 Church Road
		Hove
		E. Sussex, BN3 2FA
		Tel: +44 (0) 1273 207411
		Fax: +44 (0) 1273 205612

PRACTICUM AND INTERNSHIP: Textbook and Resource Guide for Counseling and Psychotherapy

1 2 3 4 5 6 7 8 9 0

Printed by George H. Buchanan, Co., Philadelphia, PA, 2001
Cover design by Joe Dieter.

A CIP catalog record for this book is available from the British Library.
∞   The paper in this publication meets the requirements of the ANSI Standard
Z39.48-1984 (Permanence of Paper).

Library of Congress Cataloging-in-Publication Data
Boylan, John Charles.
      Practicum and internship : textbook and resource guide for counseling and psycho-
therapy / John C. Boylan, Patrick B. Malley, Eileen Petty Reilly.— 3rd ed,
        p. cm
      Includes bibliographical references and index.
      ISBN: 1-58391-088-3 (alk. paper)
      1. Psychotherapy—Study and teaching (Internship)—Outlines, syllabi, etc. 2.
Psychotherapy—Study and teaching—Supervision—Outlines, syllabi, etc. 3. Psychotherapy—Study and teaching (Intership)—Forms. 4. Psychotherapy—Study and
teaching—Supervision—Forms. I. Malley, Patrick B. II. Reilly, Eileen Petty. III. Title.

RC459 .B68 2001
616.89'14'0711–dc21   2001018459

CONTENTS

CHAPTER 2
Preparation for Practicum

John C. Boylan and Judith Scott

CHAPTER 3
Practicum Content Issues

John C. Boylan

CHAPTER 4
Practicum Process Issues

John C. Boylan

CHAPTER 5
Monitoring the Professional Development of Practicum Students   73

Judith Scott and Eileen Petty Reilly

PART II
ETHICS AND THE LAW

CHAPTER 6
Ethical Issues

93

Patrick B. Malley and Eileen Petty Reilly

CHAPTER 7
Legal Issues

129

Patrick B. Malley and Eileen Petty Reilly

PART III
THE INTERNSHIP EXPERIENCE

CHAPTER 8
Guidelines for Interns Working With Special Populations

145

Patrick B. Malley and Eileen Petty Reilly

x / CONTENTS

ABOUT THE AUTHORS

John C. Boylan, Ph.D., is assistant chair of the Counseling and Psychology Department in the Graduate Program of Counseling and Psychology at Marywood University, Scranton, Pennsylvania, where he is also professor. In addition, Dr. Boylan maintains a private practice in Scranton and Clarks Summit, Pennsylvania, specializing in individual, marital, and sex therapy. He received his bachelor's degree from the University of Scranton and his M.Ed. and Ph.D. from the University of Pittsburgh. He also completed a postdoctoral residency in sex therapy at Mount Sinai Medical School, New York City.

Dr. Boylan is a certified school counselor, a licensed psychologist, a certified sex therapist, and a diplomat of the American Board of Sexology. During his 29 years at Marywood University, he has served variously as director of Career Planning and Placement and as chairperson of the Department of Counseling and Psychology.

Dr. Boylan has also served as a consultant to the Pennslyvania Department of Education's Adult Education Section and has conducted many adult education workshops throughout Pennsylvania. In addition, he has been the director of several major grants in the area of adult education counseling and has written several resource guides for adult educators.

Dr. Boylan is married to Jean McCann Boylan, and the couple has two children, Meghan and John.

Patrick B. Malley, Ph.D., is a licensed psychologist and professor emeritus in the Department of Psychology at the University of Pittsburgh. At the university, Dr. Malley served as associate chairperson of the Psychology Department and taught the required ethical courses in the program.

In addition to teaching coursework in the subject area, Dr. Malley has done extensive work on the topics of legal and ethical considerations in mental health. He is the first author of *Legal and Ethical Dimensions for Mental Health Professionals*, published in 1999 by Accelerated Development. He has also served as a consultant in legal and ethical issues for counseling centers, corporations, and a number of governmental agencies.

In addition to this third edition of *Practicum and Internship*, Dr. Malley's latest book, *The Selfish Spirit*, will also be published in 2001.

Eileen Petty Reilly, M.Ed., is a school counselor. She earned her B.A. from Carnegie-Mellon University and her M.Ed. from the University of Pittsburgh. She is the coauthor of *Legal and Ethical Dimensions for Mental Health Professionals*, published in 1999 by Accelerated Development.

ACKNOWLEDGMENTS

The authors gratefully appreciate the efforts of the following individuals, who were instrumental in the development of this textbook.

Judith Scott, Ph.D., licensed psychologist and counselor, Pittsburgh, PA. Dr. Scott was a co-author of the first two editions of this textbook. The authors appreciate Dr. Scott's permission to use her materials from the first two editions.

Graduate students in the Master's degree program in counseling and psychology at Marywood University. A special thank you for your invaluable feedback and suggestions for the development of the forms used in the textbook.

Mrs. Mary Kay Vesko, Departmental Secretary, Marywood University. Mrs. Vesko's dedicated service to the faculty of the Counseling and Psychology Department at Marywood University is greatly appreciated. Mrs. Vesko's energy, time commitment, and considerable computer skills have made the writing of this textbook possible.

PREFACE

The purpose of this text is to assist supervisors, practicum students, and interns in their practicum and internship training. This third edition of *Practicum and Internship: Textbook for Counseling and Psychotherapy* contains theoretical components that are valuable and essential to the training of student counselors and psychotherapists. In addition to the theoretical aspects presented, training activities germane and necessary to the development of applied counseling skills are explicated.

This edition represents a major revision of previous editions. The text has been divided into chapters specific to practicum activities and internship activities. Within the text, excerpted professional guidelines and contributed articles from other sources appear as separate items. These can be used to reinforce discussions of the topics. To provide easy access, all forms referenced in the text are compiled in duplicate at the end of the book and as files on the accompanying disk.

The first part of the text is designed to focus specifically on the activities needed for a successful practicum experience. The student is introduced to the definitions, terms, and standards of the counseling profession as well as the required activities of a practicum experience. In addition, the authors provide examples of the variety of data gathering and precounseling methods that are essential to the structuring of an initial counseling session. Similarly, a step-by-step process guides the student from his or her philosophical and theoretical orientation toward actual assessment, diagnosis, case conceptualization and treatment planning. Methods and techniques for monitoring the development of the student in practicum are highlighted.

The second part emphasizes ethics and the law. Ethical codes, principles, and virtues are defined and discussed at length. Emphasis is directed toward the implementation of ethical principles. The counselor and his or her relationship with special populations are explored in light of the counselor's ethical requirements.

The third part of the text is directed toward the preparation for internship as well as the internship experience itself. Students are provided with a variety of preinternship activities aimed at helping them choose an appropriate placement. Additionally, students are presented with examples of models and methods of supervision and helpful hints for becoming comfortable with the supervision process. Further, students become familiar with crisis intervention strategies, models of brief therapy, and basic psychopharmacological terms commonly used in internship and agency settings. This part also references specific practicum and internship evaluation forms that are used throughout the practicum and internship experience.

In summary, this third edition of *Practicum and Internship* provides a wealth of new information that is essential for successful practicum and internship experiences. This revision has allowed the authors to add new areas to the text, including a new chapter on the practicum experience, to include updated and relevant ethical and legal guidelines, and to extend their discussion of case conceptualization and treatment planning techniques, crisis intervention, and brief therapy strategies. The new organization and revision has resulted in a fully updated format that is more "reader-friendly" and thus more useful for students preparing for practicum and internship experiences.

THE PRACTICUM EXPERIENCE

The first five chapters of this textbook focus on the essential components of a practicum experience. Chapter 1 provides the student with the essential definitions, phases, and standards of practicum training. The education and training requirements of several national accreditation agencies are included. Chapter 2, "Preparation for Practicum," provides guidelines for choosing a practicum site, as well as practical questions that will help the student in selecting an appropriate placement. The roles and responsibilities of both the intern and the supervisor are discussed. This chapter also provides forms to be used in the critical prepracticum data gathering activities, as well as forms that the practicum student can use to record preliminary practicum activities. Chapter 3, "Practicum Content Issues," addresses procedures for assisting the client, monitoring the client's progress, and case reporting. This chapter also includes forms that students may use in their work with clients as they begin the practicum experience. Chapter 4, "Practicum Process Issues," takes the student through the steps of assessing, diagnosing, conceptualizing, and treating the client. Chapter 5, "Monitoring the Professional Development of Practicum Students," stresses the importance of understanding the function of supervision in the practicum and provides the student with an overview of the variety of approaches used in counseling supervision. Attention is also given to the monitoring of the student's cognitive and performance skills. Forms that can be used for the purpose of self and peer assessment and rating, as well as other evaluation tools, are also referenced and can be found at the end of the book.

John C. Boylan
Judith Scott

Definitions, Phases, and Standards

The focus of this book is on fostering the development of qualified, competent practitioners of the helping professions. It is written for students registered in graduate programs in counselor education, mental health counseling, and psychology. It is our intent to aid both the student and the support personnel through the practicum and internship experiences. To this end we have devoted part I (chapters 1 through 5) to the practicum experience, part II (chapters 6 and 7) to the legal and ethical issues pertinent to both the practicum student and intern, and part III (chapters 8 through 12) to the internship experience.

Practicum and internship experiences are required in a broad variety of preparation programs in the helping professions. Counselor education and psychology training programs, national associations, and the accrediting bodies related to these specializations continue to clarify and solidify the definitions of practicum and internship, along with their field experience requirements. They also specify activities, experiences, and knowledge base requirements that are appropriate to each component of training. A review of Hollis and Dodson (2000) suggests that the number of clinical hours required for practicum and internship experiences is increasing. Similarly, national accrediting bodies specify the qualification and levels of experience of both field- and campus-based supervisors.

▇ Prepracticum Considerations

All individuals involved in the applied training components of counseling and psychology need to carefully examine the expectations they bring to the practicum and internship. The practicum professor, practicum student, site supervisor, and professional accreditation agencies all have expectations about practicum and internship that may vary. The following list of questions provides examples of those types of questions that could be directed toward each source. Students should modify and adapt this list in keeping with their own training program and specific practicum situations.

Questions for the Practicum Professor

Following is a list of important questions for the practicum student to ask his or her practicum professor.

- How do students define the knowledge, skills, and activities appropriate to a practicum?
- What are the basic skills and content areas that are necessary to begin a practicum experience?
- What are the concepts that provide a foundation for the practicum experience?
- Does the professor have an established relationship with the field site?
- Does the professor serve as a liaison between the practicum course activities and the field site?
- How does the professor provide for field site–based and on campus–based supervision?
- How is the student expected to demonstrate identified competencies and how are they to be evaluated?
- Will the student be retained in practicum until minimal competencies are demonstrated?
- Will the student be responsible for audio- or videotaping at the field site?
- How much time will be spent in direct service activities with individual clients? With groups?
- How does the professor view the responsibility for site placement? Is the student's responsibility clearly stated?
- What is the role of the professor in the field site experience? Instructional leader? Evaluator? Liaison? Role model? Resource person?

Questions for the Practicum Student

Following is a list of questions for practicum students to ask themselves before beginning the practicum experience.

- What kinds of experiences are expected and needed by the student? Are they clearly defined by both program and field site?
- What models, methods, or approaches are employed in a practicum?
- Will practicum experiences lead to the appropriate certification and licensing from the state and/or national certification and licensing boards?
- How do the experiences afforded in a practicum reflect the depth and breadth of professional counseling and psychology?
- Will both individual and group counseling or therapy be part of the practicum experience?
- With what range and diversity of client can the student expect to work? Are these clients representative of the client population with whom the student expects to work when employed?
- Who are the other practicum students? With what kinds of experiences and points of view might they add to group supervision sessions?
- How will the students be evaluated? With what frequency? What kinds of records of counseling or therapy practice (written or taped) will be expected?
- What are the guidelines and procedures for practicum placement?
- What field site placements are recommended and available? Is there a list of approved field sites?
- Are practicum students expected to have their own malpractice insurance?
- Does the field site have materials that describe its program goals and objectives?

Questions for the Practicum Site Supervisor

Following is a list of useful questions for the student to ask a potential practium site supervisor.

- What are the credentials and supervisory experience of the site supervisor?
- What are the supervisor's views on counseling and psychology?
- Is the supervisor active or inactive in professional organizations?
- What model or method of supervision is employed?
- How does the site supervisor define the role of the practicum student? How much time is expected for record keeping, report writing, and case conferences?
- How much time each week will the supervisor devote to supervision and/or interaction with the student? To individual supervision? To group supervision?
- How does the site supervisor communicate with the university training program?

- Has the site had previous experience with practicum students from my program? From other programs?

Questions About the Standards Set by Professional Organizations, Certifying Boards, Accrediting Agencies, and University Programs

Following is a list of questions about professional standards that the practicum student should consider:

- How many hours of practicum are required in the program, and what number of these hours is spent in direct service? What is the ratio of direct service to supervision?
- What kinds of supervisory support are required? Are both individual and group supervision required or recommended? How many hours of supervision are needed?
- What kinds of procedures have been established for the protection of clients?
- How are the clients informed about practicum students working with them?
- What are the prerequisites for the practicum? Where in the program is it placed?
- What number of credit hours are devoted to the practicum? Do practicum hours include class on campus?

Definitions

Throughout this textbook the words *counselor, student, site supervisor,* and *practicum professor* are used to describe individuals involved in counseling and psychology training. A few terms must be defined to promote a clear understanding of the meanings intended in this text.

Counselor: Typically an advanced graduate student in counseling or psychology who has fulfilled the necessary program requirements and who requires field-based training experiences as part of the program.

Practicum Student: A student in training who is enrolled in a specific practicum course and field work experience.

Intern: A student in training who has completed the academic and experiential prerequisites for an internship in counseling or psychology and is enrolled in the internship component of the program.

Student: A term used in certain places in the text to refer to the person enrolled in either practicum or internship.

Practicum Site Supervisor: The person at the field site who shares or has primary responsibility for supervision of the practicum student at the site.

Practicum/Internship Professor: The agent of the university (generally a university faculty member) who is directly responsible for the university course in practicum or internship to which the student is assigned.

Practicum Site: The place where the practicum experiences occur. The site may be within the university, such as a counseling practicum clinic or counseling center. Alternatively, the site may be within a school or community agency, for example, a correctional clinic, diagnostic center, mental hospital, employment agency, pastoral counseling agency, or rehabilitation agency.

Internship Site: The place where the internship experience occurs. The site meets the university training programs standards for internship experiences and provides the intern with the opportunity to perform all the activities that a regularly employed staff member who occupies the professional role to which the intern is aspiring would be expected to perform. The site may be within a school, university, or community agency.

Internship Site Supervisor: A clearly designated professional staff member at the internship site who is directly responsible for providing systematic, intensive on-site supervision of the intern's professional training activities and performance. The internship supervisor has professional credentials appropriate to the role to which the intern aspires.

■ Phases of Practicum

The phases of practicum can be described from a variety of perspectives. For example, one might describe the practicum from the categories of level of skill, such as beginning, intermediate, or advanced. Another way of categorizing phases of practicum might be according to functions, such as structuring, stating goals, acquiring knowledge, and refining skills and interventions. We prefer to describe practicum phases from a developmental perspective.

Several principles regarding development can be identified within practicum:

1. **Movement is directional and hierarchical.** Early learning in the program establishes a foundation (knowledge base) for later development in the program (applied skills).

2. **Differentiation occurs with new learning.** Learning proceeds from the more simplistic and straightforward (content) toward the more complex and subtle (process).

3. **Separation or individuation can be observed.** The learning process leads to progressively more independent and separate functioning on the part of the counselor or therapist.

These developmental principles can be identified within the specific program structure, the learning process, and the supervisory interaction encountered by the student.

Development Reflected in the Program Structure

Students in a counseling or psychology training program can expect to proceed through a well-thought-out experiential component of their programs. Generally experiences are orderly and sequentially planned. A typical sequence would be as follows:

Foundations of Counseling

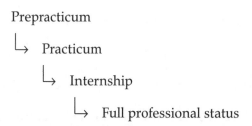

Some variations exist in counseling and psychology programs regarding the number of credit hours required in each component of training. Some variations also exist in training programs regarding the range and depth of expected skills and competencies that are necessary before a student can move to the next component in the program. Generally programs begin with courses that orient the student to the field. The history of the profession and its current status might well be a beginning point. Early courses tend to be more didactic and straightforward. As the student enters the prepracticum phase of the program, he or she can generally expect more interaction, and active participation with the professor. In this stage, the focus is on basic skill development, role playing, peer interaction and feedback and observation activities in a classroom or counseling laboratory. In the practicum component, the student is likely to be functioning at a field site with supervision and on campus in a practicum class with university faculty. The focus in both of these settings is on observation by functioning professionals as well as on initial interactions with clients. As time progresses, the student becomes more actively involved with a range of clients and is given increased opportunities to expand and develop the full range of professional behaviors. At the internship end of the continuum, the student is expected to be able to participate in the full range of professional counseling activities within the field site under supervision of an approved field site supervisor.

Development Reflected in the Learning Process

As practicum students progress in their training, they tend to progress across several stages or steps of learning. Initially, counselors often lack confidence in their skills and tend to imitate the type of supervision they receive. Counselors look to others for an indication of how they should function in the setting. Counselors tend to question their level of skill development. As time passes, they tend to fluctuate between feeling competent and professional and feeling inadequate. At this point, most counselors see the need to develop an internalized theoretical framework, to give them a sense of "grounding" and to help them to develop their own approach to counseling. Further learning helps counselors to develop confidence in their skills and an awareness of their strengths, weaknesses, and motivations. Finally, counselors develop a sense of self-confidence in their skills and can internalize and integrate their counseling behavior.

At the beginning stage of learning, the counselor's role and professional behaviors are viewed as being taken in and learned from the outside. At the higher level of learning, the trainee integrates the role of counselor or therapist into his or her personal identity and becomes the one who knows. New methods, interventions, and techniques are reflected upon, considered, and tried rather than merely read about and applied.

Development Reflected in Supervisor Interaction

Supervisory interaction between supervisor and student begins with a high level of dependence upon the supervisor for instruction, feedback, and support. This interaction is modified as skill, personal awareness, and confidence increase for the student. The student becomes more likely to explore new modes of practice that reflect his or her own unique style. The interaction continues to move more gradually toward a higher level of independent judgment by the student and a more collegial and consultative stance on the part of the supervisor. The reader is directed to the chapters on the internship experience (chapters 8–12) for a fuller discussion of the supervisor-supervisee interaction.

Standards in Accreditation and Certification for Practicum and Internship

Accreditation of counselor preparation programs in the United States is a voluntary process; the accreditation bodies are independent from federal and state governments. In most cases, the accreditation body was initially established by a professional association. For example, the American Personnel and Guidance Association (now the American Counseling Association) established the Council for Accreditation of Counseling and Related Educational Programs (CACREP), the American Association for Marriage and Family Therapy (AAMFT) established the Commission on Accreditation for Marriage and Family Therapy Education (COAMFTE), the American Association of Pastoral Counselors (AAPC) become the accrediting body for pastoral counselors, and the Council on Rehabilitation Education (CORE) became the accrediting body for rehabilitation counselors (Hollis & Dodson, 2000, p. 21). Each accreditation body established criteria to be met by programs before accreditation. If a department offers more than one program, each program must be evaluated separately for accreditation. Thus a department may have some programs that are accredited and others that are not.

Graduation from an accredited program has a number of significant advantages for students. For example, accreditation programs

- assure applicants and all concerned that the program meets high professional standards;
- maintain periodical review of the program;
- provide a base of pride for faculty, students, and the college or university as they become contributors to and involved in a nationally recognized program
- offer graduates of the program the advantage of having graduated from an accredited program (Hollis & Dodson, 2000, p. 21).

The five accreditation bodies, the American Psychological Association (APA), CACREP, COAMFTE, CORE, and AAPC, have published standards that influence state certification and licensing of psychologists and counselors. These standards also encourage academic units to develop preparation programs that meet national standards. More and more hiring officials are recognizing what accreditation may mean in terms of a graduate's choice of programs. This trend has caused students to seek admission to accredited programs, thus giving accreditation significantly more meaning in the last few years. The acceptance of national standards is not universal; however, standards are accepted widely and influence what is offered in counselor preparation programs (Hollis & Dodson, 2000).

The major experiential components in counselor preparation—practicum and internship—have undergone three major changes in the recent past: (a) the amount of time spent in practicum and internship has increased; (b) the setting in which the experience occurs has changed; and (c) the specifications for qualifications of the supervisor doing the clinical supervision of the practicum or internship student have become more stringent. These three aspects—clock hours spent, setting, and supervisor qualifications—could make major differences in the job opportunities, types of practice, clientele, philosophical orientation, and techniques emphasized throughout the student's professional life. For these reasons, as well as others (e.g., personalities involved, practicum and internship sites available), each student needs to give considerable attention to where he or she does practicum and internship, under whose clinical supervision, and for what period of time.

Each of the accreditation bodies, or national organizations, have established separate and somewhat different standards. Even though your interest may be in only one accreditation body, understanding the requirements of the other bodies will assist you in obtaining knowledge about the qualifications of other individuals in the helping professions.

Professional Counselors

The Council for Accreditation of Counseling and Related Educational Programs (CACREP) is an independent council that was created in 1981 by the American Personnel and Guidance Association (now the American Counseling Association). It is the accrediting body for the world's largest association of counseling. At its inception, the council agreed to honor all previous accreditation decisions rendered by the Association for Counselor Education and Supervision (ACES) and those previously made by the California Association of Counselor Education and Supervision (CACES).

CACREP accredits entry level programs at the master's degree level in five areas:

- community counseling (48 semester hours);
- marriage and family therapy/counseling (60 semester hours);
- mental health counseling (60 semester hours);
- school counseling (48 semester hours); and
- student affairs practice/counseling in higher education (48 semester hours).

Within the community counseling program, further specializations in gerontological counseling (48 semester hours) and career counseling (48 semester hours) are provided.

At the entry level, CACREP statements related to practicum and internship are as follows:

> The program must provide curricular experiences and demonstrated knowledge and skill in different specialization areas so that the student may gain experience in the professional setting where the student intends to practice. The direct service hours required should include work with the population with whom the student intends to work. . . .
>
> Practica will extend over a minimum of one academic year and should provide for the development of individual and group work skills. Individual and group supervision by approved faculty and field site supervisors should be provided on a weekly basis and include ongoing evaluation as well as a formal evaluation at the end of practicum. . . .
>
> A supervised internship that provides opportunities for students to engage in both individual and group work is recommended. The internship provides an opportunity for the student to perform, under supervision, a variety of activities that a regularly employed staff member in the setting would expect to perform. A regularly employed staff member is defined as a person occupying the professional role to which the student is aspiring. . . .
>
> Ordinarily, internships will be full time of a work week extended over a minimum of one academic term or halftime of a work week extended over two academic terms. Individual and group supervision by approved faculty and field site supervisors should be provided on a weekly basis. Formal evaluation of the student's performance during the internship by faculty and site supervisors is required. (CACREP, 2001)

The following descriptions provide summary information about the three primary aspects of practicum and internship in each of the counseling specializations:

Community Counseling

Setting: Community agency.
Clock hours
   Practicum: 100 hours, with 40 hours of direct client contact.
   Internship: 600 hours, with 240 hours of direct service to client, including but not limited to using preventive, developmental, and remedial interventions with appropriate clientele and community interventions consistent with the program.
Supervisor: National certified counselor (NCC) certification or a degree in a counseling-related field. A minimum of 2 years of pertinent experience.

Gerontological Specialization in Community Counseling

Setting: Community agency serving older individuals (50 years of age or older).
Clock hours
   Practicum: 100 hours, with 40 hours of direct contact working with older persons.
   Internship: 600 hours, with 240 hours of direct contact with clients (which is defined as older persons, their families, and caregivers).
Supervisor: NCC certification or a degree in a counseling-related field. A minimum of 2 years of pertinent experience.

Career Counseling Specialization in Community Counseling

Setting: A setting where career counseling regularly occurs.
Clock hours
>*Practicum:* 100 hours, with 40 hours of direct client contact, including work with clients seeking career counseling.
>*Internship:* 600 hours, with 240 hours of direct client contact.

Supervisor: NCC certification or degree in a counseling-related field. A minimum of 2 years of pertinent professional experience.

Mental Health Counseling

Setting: A setting where the applicant is provided with opportunities to develop skills relevant to the practice of clinical mental health counseling.
Clock hours
>*Practicum:* 100 hours, with 40 hours of direct client contact, including individual and group work.
>*Internship:* 900 hours, with a minimum of 360 hours of direct client contact.

Supervisor: 300 clock hours of supervised experience must be under the direct supervision of a qualified mental health professional (Certified clinical mental health counselor [CCMHC], licensed psychologist with clinical credentials, or licensed clinical social worker).

Marriage and Family Counseling or Therapy

Setting: A setting that regularly offers counseling services to couples and families.
Clock hours
>*Practicum:* 100 hours, with 40 hours of direct client contact, including work with couples and families.
>*Internship:* 600 hours, with 240 hours of direct client contact, defined as work demonstrating systematic approaches and completed primarily with couples and families.

Supervisor: NCC certification or degree in a counseling-related field. A minimum of 2 years of pertinent clinical experience.

School Counseling

Setting: A school setting.
Clock hours
>*Practicum:* 100 hours, with 40 hours of direct client contact.
>*Internship:* 600 hours, with 240 hours of direct service, including but not limited to individual counseling, group work, developmental classroom guidance, and consultation.

Supervisor: NCC certification or degree in a counseling-related field, or certified school counselor. A minimum of 2 years pertinent counseling experience.

Student Affairs Practice in Higher Education, College Counseling Emphasis

Setting: Postsecondary setting.
Clock hours
>*Practicum:* 100 hours with 40 direct service.
>*Internship:* 600 hours with 240 hours of direct service, including but not limited to individual

counseling, group work, career planning, consultation, student advisement, leadership training, and developmental programming.

Supervisor: NCC certification or counseling-related degree. Two years of pertinent counseling experience.

CACREP also accredits counselor education programs at the Ph.D. and Ed.D. levels. The statement applicable to practicum and internship at this level is as follows:

Doctoral students are required to participate in a supervised advanced practicum in counseling. Doctoral students are required to complete at least one doctoral level counseling internship of 600 clock hours. The 600 hours may include supervised experience in clinical settings, teaching, and supervision and includes most of the activities of a regularly employed professional in the setting. (CACREP, 2001)

For more specific information on CACREP certification, contact:
Council for Accreditation of Counseling and Related Educational Programs (CACREP)
5999 Stevenson Ave.
Alexandria, VA 22304-3302
Tel: (703) 823-9800, ext. 301
Fax: (703) 823-0252
E-mail: cacrep@aol.com

Counseling Psychologists

The APA has for several years accredited programs for the preparation of counseling psychologists at the doctoral level only. Additionally, the APA has developed guidelines and requirements for accrediting doctoral level internships. The trend is for employers and state licensing boards to require completion of an APA-approved internship or its equivalent. Accreditation criteria for practicum and internship are as follows:

Setting
Practicum: Setting not specified but implied within a clinical setting.
Internship: An APA-approved site or its equivalent.
Clock hours
Practicum: 300 hours (division is currently considering raising this to 600 hours), 150 of these hours in direct service, with 75 hours of formally scheduled supervision.
Internship: Full time for 1 academic or calendar year or part time for 2 years, with a minimum of 2 hours per week for formally scheduled individual supervision.
Supervisor: Psychologists who are licensed or certified in the state in which they work and who have completed an internship in the appropriate speciality. Collaborative work with representatives of other disciplines is desirable.

More specific information on accreditation and standards can be accessed by visiting the APA's website at www.apa.org.

Marriage and Family Therapists

COAMFTE (Commission on Accreditation for Marriage and Family Therapy Education) was established by the AAMFT and is recognized by the Department of Education as the accrediting agency for clinical training programs in marriage and family therapy. The major statements pertaining to practicum and internship are as follows:

Clinical training must integrate didactic with clinical material. A practicum is a part time clinical experience completed concurrently with didactic coursework. A practicum typically results in 5–10 direct client contact hours per week; it also includes such activities as supervision, staff meetings, community relations, and record-keeping. . . .

Students are required to spend a minimum of 500 face to face hours with clients. Although students may treat individual clients, at least 50 percent of the 500 direct client hours must be completed with couples or families physically present in the therapy room. (COAMFTE, 1991)

In summary form, the following requirements are applicable:

Setting: clinical setting implied.

Clock hours

Supervised clinical practice: 500 direct contact hours, 50% of which are with couples or families; a minimum of 100 hours of supervision required

Internship: Required at the doctoral level, 9 to 12 months of no fewer than 30 hours per week comprising at least 500 client contact hours, and a minimum of 100 hours of supervision.

Supervisor: AAMFT-approved supervisor or supervisor in training. Alternate supervision may be approved by AAMFT on a case-by case basis.

Rehabilitation Counselors

The Council on Rehabilitation Education (CORE) is the accrediting body for master's degree programs in rehabilitation counseling. The statements pertinent to practicum and internship are as follows:

Practicum must be done under supervision with disabled person and include case conferences, client staffing, plan development, client evaluation, referral, case recording and case management. . . .

Internship is a fieldwork experience in an accredited rehabilitation agency or facility, supervised by a certified rehabilitation counselor for a minimum of one hour per week. The intern must be involved in tasks performed by a regularly employed rehabilitation counselor. (Council on Rehabilitation Counseling Certification, 1999)

In summary, the requirements for this accreditation are as follows:

Setting: An accredited rehabilitation agency or facility.

Clock hours

Practicum: 100 hours of supervised rehabilitation counseling experience.

Internship: 600 hours of supervised rehabilitation counseling experience.

Supervisor: Certified rehabilitation counselor or rehabilitation counselor education faculty member.

For more information regarding CORE requirements and standards, contact:

Council on Rehabilitation Education, Inc. (CORE)
1835 Rohlwing Road, Suite E
Rolling Meadows, IL 60008
Tel: (850) 878-4966
Fax: (850) 878-3183
E-mail: patters@polaris.net

Pastoral Counselors

The American Association of Pastoral Counselors (AAPC) was founded in 1993 in response to the need for leadership and standards for involvement of religious organizations in mental health care (Hollis & Dodson, 2000, p. 22). Institutions can be accredited as training centers, service centers, or both. As of June 1998, 5 training programs and 28 service center training programs were certified. The following are statements that relate to supervised practice:

> Educational preparation for certified membership should contribute to the pastoral counselor's training and develop a broad experience related understanding of people. This should take place in a setting in which both the school and practical situation are in mutual relation. . . .
>
> 375 hours of pastoral counseling together with 125 hours of supervision of that counseling are required with one third of such supervision to have been with an AAPC approved Center for training in Pastoral Counseling or from a Diplomat of the Association. (AAPC, 2000, p. 7)

In summary form, the following requirements are applicable:
Setting: Not specified.
Clock hours: 375 hours of pastoral counseling with 125 hours of supervision.
Supervisor: One third of supervision hours with AAPC-approved center or a diplomat of the association.

For more information on AAPC requirements, contact:

American Association of Pastoral Counselors (AAPC)
9504 A. Lee Highway
Fairfax, Va. 22031-2302
Tel: (703) 385-6967
Fax: (703) 352-2302
E-mail: info@aapc.org

Counselor Certification

Certifying bodies, in addition to accreditation organizations, are stipulating what is expected within the preparation program and are being more specific about practicum and internship experiences. As a result, counselors in training need to keep abreast of what these requirements and trends are, so as to obtain those practicum and internship experiences that will enable them to be eligible for the certificate(s) they may seek after graduation.

The National Board of Certified Counselors (NBCC) awards the designation of national certified counselor (NCC) to those applicants who successfully fulfill certain criteria. Applicants graduating from CACREP accredited programs may sit for the National Counselors Examination (NCE) immediately upon completion of their master's degree program.

Those who successfully pass the examination are awarded NCC status. Effective July 1, 1995, applicants graduating from programs that are not CACREP approved will need to complete a minimum of 48 semester or 72 quarter hours of graduate study in the practice of counseling or a related field. This requirement includes a master's degree from a regionally accredited counselor preparation program in which coursework in eight identified areas and a minimum of two academic terms (3,000 hours) of supervised field experience in counseling at the post-master's level under the weekly supervision (100 hours face to face) of a NCC (or the equivalent as determined by the board), in addition to successful completion of the National Counselor's Examination.

The NBCC also awards specialty counseling credentials in career, gerontological, school, clinical mental health, and addictions counseling. The requirements for specialty certification require additional coursework and experience as well as the passing of an examination. With any NBCC specialty certification, the requirements for the general practice certification (NCC) are a prerequisite.

The Academy of Clinical Mental Health Counseling provides and implements standards for the independent practice of mental health counseling. Applicants for the certified clinical mental health counselor (CCMHC) credential must meet or exceed Academy requirements in each of the following four areas: (a) academic preparation, (b) clinical experience and supervision, (c) examination, and (d) clinical skill. Preapplication requirements include completion of a CACREP-accredited 60 semester hour master's degree program in mental health counseling or its equivalent and 2 years of clinical practice after the master's degree. This experience must include 3,000 hours of direct client contact in a supervised clinical setting. Applicants also must have documented 100 hours of face-to-face supervision by an Academy-approved supervisor.

The Commission on Rehabilitation Counseling Certification (CORE) provides and implements standards for qualification as a certified rehabilitation counselor (CRC). Applicants who have completed a CORE-accredited master's degree program are eligible to take the CRC examination upon graduation. Those who have graduated from a rehabilitation master's degree program that is not fully accredited by CORE must complete a 600-hour internship supervised by a CRC and/or additional acceptable employment experience under the supervision of a CRC. Those not supervised by a CRC must complete a Provisional Supervision Contract in addition to passing the examination.

The American Association for Marriage and Family Therapy (AAMFT) provides a professional credential entitled clinical member status. The eligibility criteria requires a master's or doctoral degree in marriage and family therapy or an equivalent degree, including a supervised practicum as defined by the AAMFT. In addition, a minimum of 2 years of post-master's degree experience in clinical work supervised by an AAMFT supervisor or supervisor-in-training is required. This post-master's degree experience includes 1,000 hours of face-to-face marriage and family therapy with individuals, couples, and families, and at least 200 hours of supervision completed concurrently.

The AAPC has established certification guidelines delineated by membership status in the organization. Categories of membership are member, fellow, and diplomat. Each category of certified membership requires explicit levels of education and supervised practice, an oral examination, and an endorsement from a recognized religious body.

(The above-listed requirements for the five-certification bodies was summarized and adapted from Hollis and Dodson, 2000.)

Implications

Implications for students in preparation are becoming quite clear. In addition to requirements for practicum and internship as stipulated by the counselor preparation program, each student will need to give careful consideration to (a) the selection of sites where practicum and internship is experienced, (b) a review of required supervisory credentials, (c) a determination of the amount of supervisory time available, (d) the identification of a site that provides opportunities to work with one's chosen population, and (e) an understanding of the credentialing requirements of organizations with which the student hopes to affiliate.

As they develop, professional certification requirements are increasingly being established with more rigorous requirements than the standards set for graduation from the training program. Thus, when planning their future careers in counseling or psychotherapy, students must look beyond their college or university requirements and must consider trends in certification by professional organizations as well as state licensure and certification requirements.

Summary

In this chapter, we have provided the basic definitions, phases, and standards that apply to students in a variety of counseling and psychology training programs. Specific attention was directed to the CACREP guidelines; the APA, COAMFTE, CORE, and AAPC guidelines were also presented. In addition, the specific requirements of counselor certification were discussed. We hope that the information in this chapter will help the beginning counseling student to gain a fuller understanding of the professional training and certification requirements for counseling specializations.

Suggested Readings

American Association for Marriage and Family Therapy. (1999). *Membership requirements and applications.* Washington, DC: Author.

American Psychological Association Committee on Accreditation. (1993). *American Psychological Association accreditation handbook.* Washington, DC: Author.

Bradley, R. (1989). *Counselor supervision: Principles, process, practice* (2nd ed.). Philadelphia, PA: Accelerated Development.

Delaney, D. J. (1978). Supervising counselor in preparation. In J. Boyd (Ed.), *Counselor supervision: Approaches, preparation, practices* (pp. 341–374). Muncie, IN: Accelerated Development.

Drapela, V. J., & Drapela, G. B. (1986). The role of the counselor in intern supervision. *The School Counselor, 92–99.*

Granello, P. E., & Witmer, M. (1998). Standards of care: Potential implication for the counseling profession. *Journal of Counseling and Development, 76,* 371–380.

Kitchener, K. S. (1984). Intuition, critical evaluation and ethical principles. The foundation for ethical decisions in counseling psychology. *Counseling Psychologist, 12*(3), 43–55.

Lamb, D. H., Baker, L., Jennings, M., & Yams, E. (1982). Passages of an internship in professional psychology. *Professional Psychology, 13*(5), 661–669.

National Board of Certified Counselors. (1994). *Specialty certification.* Greensboro, NC: Author.

References

American Association of Pastoral Counselors. (1999). *General information on individual membership/affiliations.* Fairfax, VA: Author.

Commision on Accreditation for Marriage and Family Therapy Education. (1991). *Manual on accreditation.* Washington, DC: Author.

Council for Accreditation of Counseling and Related Educational Programs. (2001). *CACREP accreditation standards and procedures manual.* Alexandria, VA: Author.

Council on Rehabilitation Counseling Certification. (1999). *CRC Certification Guide.* Rolling Meadows, IL: Author.

Hollis, J. W., & Dodson, T. A. (2000). *Counselor preparation. 1999–2001, Program, Faculty, Trends* (10th ed.). Philadelphia, PA: Accelerated Development.

CHAPTER

2

John C. Boylan
Judith Scott

Preparation for Practicum

In chapter 1, we reviewed the definitions and summarized the professional standards that are currently influencing the applied practice components (practicum and internship) of counseling programs.

Chapter 2 has as its focus the process of selecting and negotiating a practicum site placement. The specific guidelines of CACREP and the APA are followed in the format presented. Students are reminded that adaptations in the format may need to be made to meet the particular and specific needs of the training institution and the internship site.

Guidelines for Choosing a Practicum Site

The practicum placement is often the first opportunity that the student has to gain the experience of working with a client population. Prior counseling experience usually occurs in prepracticum or practicum lab situations with volunteers or peer counseling interactions. Many counselor preparation programs offer the student an opportunity to have some say in determining practicum placement. In addition, the practicum student may be able to gain experience at more than one practicum site. The university practicum supervisor has the responsibility for deciding where the practicum student might gain the best experience for professional development based on his or her personal needs and professional goals. The practicum site personnel are responsible for selecting practicum students who they believe will benefit from the placement and who will best serve the needs of the site's client population. The practicum student can select sites of interest to him or her and then, with the university supervisor's approval, visit and apply for placement. A list of approved sites may be provided by the student's training program.

The selection and application process of practicum sites can be confusing and at times overwhelming. To alleviate some of the frustration it is often helpful to have a set of criteria in mind. The criteria should stem from the following categories:

- Professional staff and supervisor
- Professional affiliations of the site
- Professional practices of the site
- Site administration
- Training and supervision values
- Theoretical orientation of the site and supervisor
- Client population

In the sections that follow, we list questions pertaining to these categories that may be helpful in determining selection of a practicum site:

Professional Staff and Supervisor

- What are the professional credentials of the site personnel?
- Do their credentials meet the standards of your professional credentialing body?
- What are the educational backgrounds and ranges of experience of the director and practicum supervisor?

We have noted in chapter 1 that the professional organization to which the practicum student aspires to be a professional member often requires the therapeutic supervisor to hold the appropriate credentials to perform such supervision. For example, a mental health professional who does not have the recommended and necessary credentials may not be recognized as an appropriate supervisor. Each practicum student benefits from a supervisor who holds the credentials specific to his or her profession. For example, a person who is training to be a school counselor is best served by a supervisor who has the experience and credentials appropriate for a school setting (National Certified School Counselor [NCSC]). Similarly, school psychologists are trained in assessment, placement, and program planning of students, and although the trainee benefits from understanding the role of the school psychologist, he or she must realize that the primary responsibility is to meet the developmental needs of schoolchildren. Thus, the skills learned from supervision should be appropriate to the standards set by the trainee professional organization.

Professional Affiliations of the Site

- In what association does the site hold membership?
- Does the site hold approval of national certifying agencies?
- What is the reputation of the site among other organizations?
- Does the site have affiliations or working cooperations with other institutions?

Memberships in state and national certifying agencies carry with them specific guidelines for the operation and management of agency activities. Agencies that accredit counseling facilities include the Commission on Accreditation of Rehabilitation Facilities (CARF), the International Association of Counseling Services (IACS), and the Joint Commission on Accreditation of Health Care Agencies (JCAHO). Generally, agencies and schools that carry state and national certification have rigid standards for membership. Similarly, the reputation of the site among other organizations and cooperations with other institutions are important considerations for prospective practicum students. A practicum experience carried out at a well-recognized and respected facility provides the student with the best chance of having a worthwhile and professionally fulfilling experience.

Professional Practices of the Site

- Does the site follow the ethical guidelines of the appropriate profession (APA, ACA, etc.)? Which code(s) of ethics is followed?
- What kinds of resources are available to personnel (for example, library, computer programs, ongoing research, professional consultation)?
- What are the client procedures, treatment modalities, and staffing and outreach practices? How are these practices consistent with the goals of the practicum?

- How are client records kept?
- What are the policies and procedures regarding taping (audio/video) and other practicum support activities?
- Do the staff members regularly update their skills and participate in continuing education?
- Are continuing education opportunities available to interns?

Each professional organization requires that professionals have a minimum number of hours in order to maintain their credentials as a practicing member of the organization. If professionals do not adhere to these requirements they may be excluded from the profession and not permitted to practice under the auspices of the title they once had. If the professional is licensed and does not satisfy these requirements and continues to practice as a professional, he or she may be considered to be in a breach of legal duty and obligation. Membership in professional organizations carries with it the requirement that members adhere to the ethical guidelines of that organization. Agencies may follow several ethical guidelines depending on the specialization of the therapist; for example, counselors would follow the ethical guidelines established by the American Counseling Association (ACA), while psychologists would adhere to those of the APA.

It is also important for beginning practicum students to consider the types of resources available to personnel at the site. A well-managed school or agency should have a variety of resources available for the professional use of the intern. In addition, it is important for the practicum student to understand the practices used by the site for the treatment of clients, as well as the site's staffing and outreach practices. Knowledge of these essential practices is of the utmost importance to the beginning practicum student, as familiarity with the agency's or school's operation enables the student to make a positive transition from the educational environment to the practicum. The student should consider whether these practices are consistent with his or her goals. The degree of "fit" experienced by the practicum student is directly related to the consistency between the site practices and the student's particular goals.

The student should also make certain that he or she is familiar with the site's procedures and guidelines regarding keeping client records. Ethical guidelines mandate specific practices to ensure the confidentiality and security of client records. Particular attention should be paid to the policies regarding audio- and videotaping of clients, and other support activities. Practicum students need to have a complete understanding of the site's procedures regarding taping to ensure that appropriate ethical guidelines are followed.

It is important, as well, for the practicum student to consider what opportunities exist for continuing education. Continual professional development is essential for the maintenance of quality treatment for clients. The student can determine if the site encourages this level of professional development by determining if the staff members who work at the site regularly update their skills through continuing education. It is our experience that well-run placement sites provide students with in-service programming and permit them to participate in programming that is provided for full-time staff members.

Site Administration

- What resources if any, are directed toward staff development?
- Does the administration of the site provide "in-house" funds for staff training or reinforcement for college credit?
- How is policy developed and approved (corporate structure, board of directors, contributions)?
- How stable is the site? (Does the site receive hard money or soft money support? What is the length of service of the director and staff? What is the site's mission statement or purpose?)

Staff development and training are typically provided for employees in most cases. Thus it is important for the practicum student to consider this aspect of site administration. The availability of such opportunities should be an important preplacement consideration, and a lack of staff development and training opportunities for the staff should be weighed carefully in relation to the other opportunities provided.

Another important consideration in determining if a site is a good "fit" is the method of policy development and approval. Knowledge of how policy is developed helps the student to understand the "chain of command" within the organization. In addition, the stability of the site is obviously of critical concern to the student. A quality practicum experience assumes that the student is placed in an established, well-organized, financially stable environment that effectively addresses the needs of its client population.

Training and Supervision Values

- What values regarding training and supervision are verbalized and demonstrated?
- Will the supervisor be available for individual supervision for a minimum of 1 hour per week?
- Will practicum students have opportunities for full participation?
- Are adequate facilities available for practicum students?

Practicum students should be aware that there are a variety of approaches to the supervision of counseling practice. Although there is no evidence to support claims that one training methodology is better than another, student practitioners may have experience with a particular method of supervision that they prefer. For example, if the counseling sessions are taped, some supervisors prefer to listen to the entire tape, whereas others may ask the practicum student to review the tape and make available several sequences of communication that exemplify work well done or work the student has questions about. Other supervisors may demand that students present work that demonstrates the area of competency that they consider essential to good counseling practice. For example, practicum students may be asked to demonstrate counseling skills of support and confrontation, an ability to work with thematic patterns that consistently surface in the client dynamics, and a capacity to relate to content and process and/or the facilitation of client decision making.

It is essential that the student and the supervisor reach a mutual understanding of their values regarding training and supervision. The roles, duties, and obligations of both parties should be clarified prior to the beginning of the practicum experience. In addition, it is important to recognize that individual supervision is a time-consuming process and that to address the task adequately the supervisor must have the time, motivation, and conscientiousness to do so. CACREP guidelines, as well as many program and university guidelines, insist upon a minimum of 1 hour of individual supervision per week. If the site is a popular and busy one, however, the supervisor may have many supervisees and so may not be able to find the time needed for this work. It is important to remember when selecting a site that weekly supervision is a requirement, not an option, in most training programs.

It is also important to determine the level of participation that practicum students will have at the site, as well as whether the available facilities are adequate for the student's particular needs. Generally, interns are provided with full participation in the professional activities of the site. However, participation is determined on the basis of the student's training and background and the agency's ability to provide adequate supervision for those activities.

Theoretical Orientation of the Site and Supervisor

- What are the special counseling or therapy interests of the practicum supervisor(s)?

Many therapists are eclectic in their counseling practice, but many may also favor a particular therapeutic approach over others. Thus, if students are exposed to a supervisor who favors and supports the use of a particular theoretical approach, it requires the student to have grounding in the knowledge base of that theory. Naturally the advantage of having one approach to counseling is that it affords the student the opportunity to become more proficient at it. Also, in mastering one approach, the student begins to develop a clearer, firmer professional identity regarding his or her goals in counseling practice. Conversely, the disadvantage of learning only one approach is that it limits the student's opportunity to measure other approaches that could be more in keeping with his or her own style and personality.

Client Population

- What are the client demographics in the placement site?
- Who is the client population served? For example, is it a restricted group or open? Is the age range narrow or wide? Are clients predominately of a low, middle or high socioeconomic level?
- Do clients require remedial, preventive, and/or developmental services?
- What opportunities exist for multicultural counseling?
- Does the site and its professional staff demonstrate high regard for human dignity and support the civil rights of clients?

Multicultural counseling skills have become increasingly important for the practicing school and mental health counselor. Constantine and Gloria (1999) noted that studies have suggested that interns' "exposure to multicultural issues may increase sensitivity to and effectiveness with racially and ethically diverse clients" (p. 43). In addition, the demographic composition of clients is and will be of a different nature than it was a few years ago. Statistics from the U.S. Bureau of Census (1992) indicated the multicultural makeup of the country will be quite different in the year 2050 than it is today. Between 1992 and 2050, the African-American population in the United States will grow from 32 million (or 12% of the population) to 62 million (16%). In the same period, the Hispanic population will grow from 24 million (9%) to 81 million (21%) and the American Indian, Eskimo, and Aleut population will grow from 2.2 million (0.8%) to 41 million (11%), while the non-Hispanic White population will grow at a much slower rate, from 191 million (75%) in 1992 to 202 million (52%) in 2050.

The counseling skills required of an effective multicultural counselor have been explored by Sue, Arredondo, and McDavis (1992). Some of the common beliefs and attitudes of culturally skilled counselors follow.

- They demonstrate sensitivity to clients' cultural heritage and how it effects their lives.
- They are comfortable with culturally different clients, are aware of their own negative emotional reactions, respect clients' religious or spiritual beliefs, recognize minority community efforts, and value bilingualism.
- They understand how their own cultural heritage may contribute to their biases and how racism may effect their personality and work.
- They have information about the group with whom they are working, the institutional barriers that client population may face, minority family structures, and pertinent discriminatory practices in the community.
- They can seek consultative help, are familiar with relevant research, and are actively involved with clients outside the counseling setting; they can send and receive verbal and non-verbal communications accurately and appropriately.

It is clear that many counselor education programs have responded to these multicultural imperatives by examining their curricular offerings and reacting positively to the need for multicultural training. For programs that have not met the challenge, Ponterotto, Alexander, and Grieger (1995) developed a multicultural competency checklist that counseling training programs can use to examine their comprehensiveness. This checklist includes 22 items organized around six major themes. A summary of the list follows:

Minority representation: African Americans, Hispanic Americans, Asian Americans, Pacific Islanders, and Native Americans constitute at least 30% of students, faculty, and program support staff.
Curricular issues: Multicultural issues are incorporated into all facets of the curriculum.
Counseling practice and supervision: All trainees have caseloads with at least 30% minority clients.
Research: At least one faculty member is interested in multicultural research.
Student and faculty competency evaluation: Multicultural issues are included in exams.
Physical environment: Multicultural art is actively displayed in the campus environment.

■ Negotiating the Practicum Placement

Having completed the initial stage of identifying, reviewing, and selecting a practicum site, the next step is to negotiate the practicum placement. This process works best when a written exchange of agreement is made so that all parties involved in the practicum placement understand the roles and responsibilities involved. With regard to written contracts, most counselor or psychology training programs have developed their own practicum contracts. Specific guidelines followed in the practicum are stated as part of the agreement. Guidelines identified by national certifying agencies are often used or referenced in formalizing the practicum placement. For example, in APA practicum guidelines, statements concerning the development of the following capacities are included:

- an understanding of and commitment to professional and social responsibility as defined by statutes of the ethical code of the profession (see chapter 6 in this text);
- a capacity to conceptualize human problems;
- an awareness of the full range of human variability among the dimensions of ethnicity, subculture, affirmative action, race, religion, sexual preferences, handicap, sex, and age;
- an understanding of one's own personality and biases and of one's impact upon others in professional interaction;
- skills in relevant interpersonal interactions such as systematic observation of behavior, interviewing, psychological testing, psychotherapy, counseling, and consultation;
- an ability to contribute to current knowledge and practice.

In CACREP guidelines, the development of individual and group work skills is recommended. Statements related to practicum activities include the following:

- experience in individual and group interactions (at least one fourth of the direct service hours should be in group work);
- opportunities for students to counsel clients representative of the ethnic, lifestyle, and demographic diversity of their community; familiarizing students with a variety of professional activities other than direct service work;
- use of a variety of professional resources such as measurement instruments, computers, print and nonprint media, professional literature, and research.

State licensing boards and state departments of education also may provide guidelines and set standards regarding field experience activities and minimum number of hours required in practicum. In addition, university and program faculty may have their own guidelines for practicum. We suggest that counselor preparation programs identify the guidelines that it follows and include the guidelines in the practicum contract.

An example of a formal contract between the university and the practicum field site is included in the "Forms" section at the end of the book for your review. The sample Letter to Practicum Site Supervisor (Form 2.1) and the Practicum Contract (Form 2.2) can be adapted to the specific needs of your training program. The contract includes a statement concerning guidelines to be followed, conditions agreed upon by the field site, conditions agreed upon by the counselor or psychologist preparation program, and a list of suggested practicum activities.

Role and Function of the Practicum Student

The practicum student who has been accepted to the field site will start as a novice in the counseling profession, but at the same time will be a representative of his or her university training program and of other student counselors and psychologists. The student is working in the setting as a guest of the practicum site. The site personnel have agreed to provide the student with appropriate counseling experiences with the clientele they serve.

Although the individual freedom of the student counselor is understood and respected, the overriding concern of the site personnel is to provide role-appropriate services to the client population. The role of the practicum student is to obtain practice in counseling or psychotherapy in the manner in which it is provided in the practicum setting. The student counselor is expected to adhere to any dress code or expected behaviors that are existent at the field site. In some instance, the student may disagree with some of the site requirements; however, the role of the student counselor is not to change the system but to develop his or her own abilities in counseling practice.

Occasionally tension or conflict may arise between the practicum student and site personnel. Although such events are upsetting to all involved, these events can provide an opportunity for the practicum student to develop personal insight and understanding into the problem. After all, practicum placement is real-life exposure to the realities of the counseling profession. However, should the tension or conflict persist, the student intern should consult with the faculty liaison who is available to assist the student in the process of understanding his or her role within the system and to facilitate the student's ability to function in the setting.

A Student Profile Sheet (Form 2.3) and a Student Practicum/Internship Agreement (Form 2.4) have been included in the "Forms" section. The profile sheet guides the documentation of the student counselor's academic preparation and relevant experience prior to practicum. The agreement form demonstrates the formal agreement being entered into by the student. Both of the forms can be a valuable resource for the site supervisor in assessing the student intern's preparation for practicum.

Concepts in Practicum

Concepts about the practicum experience influence the kinds and range of activities, the process of supervisory and consulting interaction, and the nature of the teaching contract between the practicum student and the university professor. Such concepts provide the foundation of this beginning experiential component of professional training. Although no one right way exists to develop a conceptual framework for practicum, the university professor has the obligation to articulate the framework employed by the university in practicum education.

The remainder of this section presents a typical conceptual framework for practicum training that can be used as a reference for the student who is beginning the practicum experience. Some concepts may be used as a point of departure for discussion and others may be modified and/or challenged.

1. **Practicum is a highly individualized learning experience in which the practicum student is met at a level of personal development, knowledge, and skills that he or she brings to the experience.** Initially it is crucial for the practicum to focus on the present developmental level of the student, leaving other concerns for future consideration. In any group of practicum students, one can expect a wide range of talents, unique perspectives regarding human behavior, and varying capacities to perceive accurately and engage emotional content. One of the functions of the practicum professor is to role-model the optimal facilitative behavior to support the growth and development of students in order to increase the level of role functioning. The process parallels the counseling or therapy process. Students should remember that they and their practicum professor are partners in learning. As a partner in learning, the professor demonstrates respect for the student as a learner with a unique set of meanings, capable of accepting responsibility for his or her own learning. The student has the responsibility to bring in material about his or her counseling practice and to share any concerns related to practice.

2. **Practicum facilitates an understanding of one's self, one's biases, and one's impact upon others.** Counseling or therapy is an enterprise that has as its core the assumption that individuals develop by a process of differentiating self from others. It may be viewed as the process of bringing more of one's experiences into the conscious domain. It may be viewed as being able to determine what is "my problem" and what is "your problem." It may be viewed as challenging patterns of thinking that are inappropriately imposed on experience. Whatever the theoretical orientation of counseling, practicum students must personally examine those qualities about themselves that may enhance or impede their counseling. The practicum experience provides the setting in which personal qualities related to counseling practice can be examined. Therefore, activities that help clarify the counselor's own feelings, values, background, and perceptions—in the context of the counseling work—are an appropriate and necessary part of the practicum experience. Focus in practicum is not only directed toward determining the dynamics and personal meaning of the client but also upon examining how the student views others and how his or her behaviors and attitudes affect others. Similarly, the internship experience, which this book discusses in later chapters, provides the student with the opportunity to examine his or her own values in an on-the-job environment.

3. **Each member of a practicum group is capable of and responsible for facilitating professional growth and development.** The practicum experience usually involves dyadic, individual, and group activities designed to enhance the quality of counseling practice. Frequently, peer counseling and peer feedback are selected training activities. Group interaction provides a forum in which practicum members can give and receive feedback regarding counseling techniques, interventions, and concerns. Each member of the practicum participates not only as a student but also as someone who is able to provide valuable feedback to others regarding the impact particular responses and attitudes can have upon clients. The practicum professor is not the only one among many whose responses can be examined. As a result, the practicum experiences tend to be more member centered than leader centered. High-quality interaction and feedback are essential for professional growth and development.

4. **Practicum is composed of varied experiences, which are determined by the particular needs, abilities, and concerns of the practicum group members and the practicum professor.** Two conditions contribute to the variety and kinds of learning activities that are part of the practicum. First, program considerations about how the practicum is placed within the overall curriculum are influential. In some programs, basic skills training is an integral part of practicum. In other programs, skill training activities are included in other courses. The Marywood University program, for example, has skill training activities very early in the student's program; there, a course entitled Applied Practice I focuses on basic skill development activities. Conversely, some training programs require more hours of field experience, with a practicum that is followed by an extensive internship, while in other training programs the practicum is the only experiential component of the program.

    A second condition influencing the kinds and variety of experiences included in practicum is the unique needs that the student brings to the group. These may be personal concerns of the student or concerns related to client needs brought back to the practicum class for discussion. Therefore, practicum, by necessity, must have a flexible and formative approach to planning learning activities.

All practicum experiences provide a wide range of activities such as:

- structured skill development exercises,
- unstructured group interactions,
- role playing,
- peer counseling, taping, and critiquing,
- selected assigned reading regarding special problem areas,
- keeping personal journals,
- videotaping and observing counseling sessions,
- giving and receiving feedback,
- preparing case presentations,
- supervisor-supervisee interaction.

5. **Supervision and consultation form the central core of the practicum experience.** Intensive supervision and consultation allow the student to move more quickly toward competence and mastery in counseling or therapy. The supervisory interaction can help make the student more aware of obstacles to the counseling process so that they can be examined and modified. The supervisory interaction also provides the opportunity for the role-modeling process to be strengthened. The student can usually expect both intensive one-on-one supervision and regular group supervision to be standard parts of the practicum. These supervision sessions not only provide skill development opportunities but also implicitly guide the counselor or therapist toward an openness and appreciation for collegial supervision and self-supervision.

6. **Self-assessment by student and practicum professor is essential.** Because of the flexible and formative nature of the practicum, regular reviews need to be made of how the practicum experiences are meeting the learning needs of the student. Self-assessment allows the student to be consciously aware of and responsible for his or her own development and also provides information for the practicum professor in collaborating on appropriate practicum activities.

   The format for this self-assessment can be structured in a variety of ways. One possible approach is to identify current strengths, current weakness, and current concerns or confusions. The assessment should be defined as concretely as possible. Once the assessment of current functioning is described, a contract can be made with the practicum professor and other group members regarding the particular aspects of counseling practice that have been targeted by the student for improvement or development. Ongoing self-assessment is needed to give direction to the practicum.

7. **Evaluation is an integral part and ongoing part of the practicum.** Evaluation in practicum provides both formative and summative information about how the counseling development goals of the student and professor are being reached. A variety of activities support this evaluation process. Among these are self-assessment, peer evaluations, regular feedback activities, practicum site supervisor ratings, and audio- and videotape review. The attitude from which evaluations are offered is characterized by a "constructive" coaching perspective rather than a "critical" judgmental perspective.

Suggested Course Requirements

The practicum has been described as a complexly interwoven set of counseling practices and support activities designed to promote skill development, personal growth, and application of knowledge on the part of the trainee. Activities entered into at the practicum site are directed and monitored by the practicum supervisor based upon site opportunities and student abilities. During the first week of activities, the usual emphasis is on orientation to site policies and practice, observation of professional activities, and review of client records and treatment plans in preparation for counseling practice. As the practicum progresses through the several weeks, activities gradually are expanded to include intake interviewing, testing, client orientation, coleading, and contacts with referral sources. Individual counseling sessions are increased, group work and outreach are added, and the student participates in in-service and case conferences. In the final weeks of practicum, experiences include individual and group counseling or psychotherapy, as well as consultation and referrals.

In addition to actual site-based counseling practice, course requirements are designed to support and monitor the evolving skill and knowledge base of the student.

Class Meetings

Practicum students generally are expected to spend a minimum of two hours per week in a group session with the university supervisor. This time can include didactic and experiential activities and usually includes some form of review of counseling practices. A typical class session would begin by addressing any specific concerns a student has regarding his or her practicum. After immediate concerns are addressed, the student counselor might engage in any of the following:

- role-playing situations encountered at the practicum site;
- listening to and discussing various recorded counseling sessions;
- reviewing previously taped counseling sessions made by class members;
- discussing theories and techniques related to common problems and client work of concern to group members; and/or
- giving and receiving feedback with peers regarding personal and professional interaction.

Counseling Sessions

In addition to the weekly group meetings, students are required to engage in a specified number of counseling sessions each week. These may be both individual and group sessions. Early in the course, the typical amount of required sessions would be fewer in number than at the middle and final phases of the course. A specific minimum number of sessions are required for the course. One-time sessions with clients as well as a continuing series of sessions with a client are specified.

Individual Supervision Sessions

The student is expected to spend one or more hours per week throughout the length of the course in individual supervision with the site and/or university professor. These meetings provide an intensive focus on the student's counseling and therapy work and are often regarded by the student counselor as one of the most valuable practicum components. Typical questions addressed during individual sessions include the following:

- Is the student counselor providing a facilitative interaction with the client?
- Is the student counselor accurately perceiving the needs of the client?
- What are the goals of the counseling process?
- Is the student counselor able to facilitate the desired growth or change in the client?
- What obstacles may be present in the counseling work?

Tape Critiques

If at all possible, practicum students are expected to tape (audio and video) their counseling sessions. Of course, permission must be obtained from each client prior to taping the session. The practicum site will have policies and procedures that must be followed in order to ensure the informed consent of the client (see Forms 3.1 and 3.2 in the "Forms" section at the end of the book). The tapes are to be submitted weekly to the practicum and/or university supervisor to allow for sharing and evaluation. Each tape should be reviewed by the student prior to submission and be accompanied by a written or typed critique. The critique should consist of the following information:

1. student counselor's name;
2. client identification and number of the session with the client;
3. a brief summary of content of the session and intended goals;
4. comments regarding the positive aspects of the counselor's work during the session;
5. comments regarding areas of the counselor's work that need improvement;
6. concerns, if any, regarding client dynamics; and
7. plans for further counseling with the client.

Every effort must be taken to ensure the confidentiality of the counseling session. When the tape has been reviewed and discussed with the student counselor, appropriate notes regarding counseling performance can be made for the student's records. The tape(s) should then be erased.

Blank copies of a Tape Critique Form (Form 2.5) have been included in the "Forms" section for students' use. This form can be used to guide the student in developing a written review and analysis of taped therapy sessions. An example of a completed Tape Critique Form is provided in Figure 2.1.

Documenting Practicum Activities

Because of national accreditation guidelines and state and university requirements, it is necessary procedure to document both the total number of hours spent in practicum and the total number of hours spent in particular practicum activities. Two forms are provided here for your use in tracking the time spent at various activities. The Weekly Schedule (Form 2.6) can be used in two ways. First, the weekly schedule can be used by the practicum student and the practicum supervisor to plan the activities in which the student will participate from week to week. Second, the weekly schedule can be used to document the weekly activities the student has already completed. An example of a completed *Weekly Schedule* is provided in Figure 2.2.

The Monthly Practicum Log (Form 2.7) provides a summary of the number of hours of work per month in which the student has engaged within the activity categories established in the practicum contract. A file should be kept for each student for the duration of the practicum experience.

◼ Summary

The information presented in this chapter is designed to assist the counseling student in the process of choosing and negotiating a practicum placement. Several aspects of the practicum experience need to be carefully considered by the student prior to making this important decision, and to this end, we have provided a number of questions that warrant attention. It is recommended that the student make an effort to answer these questions in order to understand fully the benefits and disadvantages of a particular site. Additional information concerning the role and function of the practicum student has been discussed. Finally, sample forms have been included for use in preselection planning and preliminary practicum activities, which the student can adapt to fit his or her own needs.

TAPE CRITIQUE FORM

Jane Smith
        Student counselor's name

Tom D. Session #3
        Client I.D. & no. of session

Brief summary of session content

Tom is citing his reasons for being unhappy in his job situation and reviewing all he has attempted to do to make his boss like and respect his work.

Intended goals

1. To help Tom explore all of his feelings and experiences related to the job situation.
2. To help Tom be able to assess and value his work from his own frame of reference, rather that his boss's.

Comment on positive counseling behaviors

I was able to accurately identify Tom's feelings and to clarify the connection of feelings to specific content.

Comment on areas of counseling practice needing improvement

I sometimes became hooked into Tom's thinking about how to please his boss and would work with him about problem solving in this way.

Concerns or comment regarding client dynamics

Plans for further counseling with this client

Continue weekly appointments; move focus back onto the client and try to identify other ways he worries about approval.

Tape submitted to   _____

Date   _____

FIGURE 2.1. Sample completed Tape Critique Form (Form 2.5).

WEEKLY SCHEDULE

Day of week	Location	Time	Practicum activity	Comment
Mon	UUC	9-10	Intake Interview	1st session
			John W.	Prob. exploration
		10-11	Ind. cnslg.	5th session, taped
			Jane D.	personal/social
		11-12	Ind. supervision	Reviewed reports
				Tape critique
		1-3	Group counseling	Eating disorder Group
			Co-lead	3rd Session
		3-4	Report writing	
		4-5	Testing	Interpreted
			Mary B.	Strong/Campbell
Wed	University	6-8	Group	Case Presentation
			supervision	Jane D.

Student Counselor Name _____

Week beginning _____ Ending _____

FIGURE 2.2. Sample completed Weekly Schedule (Form 2.6).

◼ Suggested Readings

American Psychological Association. (1986). *Accreditation handbook.* Washington, DC: Author.
Council for the Accreditation of Counseling and Related Educational Programs. (1995). *CACREP accreditation standards and procedures manual.* Alexandria, VA: Author.

◼ References

Constantine, M. G., & Gloria, A. M. (1999). Multicultural issues in predoctoral internship programs: A national survey. *Journal of Multicultural Counseling and Development, 27,* 42–53.
Ponterotto, J. G., Alexander, C. M., & Grieger, I. (1995). A multicultural competency checklist for counselor training programs. *Journal of Multicultural Counseling and Development, 23,* 11–20.
Sue, D. W., Arredondo, P., & McDavis, R. J. (1992). Multicultural counseling competencies and standards: A call to the profession. *Journal of Multicultural Counseling and Development, 20,* 64–88.
U.S. Bureau of Labor Statistics. (1992). Washington, DC: Author.

John C. Boylan

Practicum Content Issues

▮ Initial Interaction with the Client

This chapter is designed to assist the practicum student or intern in assessment and data gathering activities conducted prior to and during the initial stages of counseling.

The following materials have been included to assist the school counselor, the mental health counselor, and the psychologist in preparation for their initial interaction with a client. It is our belief that issues such as initial interaction with the client, structuring the interview, interview assessment, note taking strategies, and progress recording are essential elements that foster the development of a counseling relationship

The gathering of client data, a requirement of both practicum and internship experiences, can be a difficult task for the beginning counselor or therapist. The amount of client data required, as well as the manner in which data are to be recorded in a client's file, varies from institution to institution and from agency to agency. The practicum student or intern must first gain a working knowledge of the procedures that are followed and then develop his or her own framework and style of gathering data. Thus, care must be taken to ensure that the student can process and report data in a clear and concise manner. Generally, most settings have developed clear guidelines for the obtaining and recording of client data. A review of these guidelines is the first step in the preparation for counseling practice.

Initial Contact, Structuring, and Assessment

The initial contact with the client is a crucial point in the process of counseling. It provides the counselor with the opportunity to begin structuring the therapeutic relationship. Methods of structuring vary according to the counselor's style and theoretical approach to counseling. Ivey (1999) suggests a five-step process for the purpose of structuring the interview.

1. **Rapport and structuring** is a process that has as its purpose the building of a working alliance with the client in order to enable the client to become comfortable with the interviewer. Structuring is needed to explain the purpose of the interview and to keep the sessions on task. Structuring informs the client about what the counselor can and cannot do in therapy.

2. **Gathering information, defining the problem, and identifying client's assets** is a process designed to assist the counselor in learning why the client has come for counseling and how he or she views the problem. Skillful problem definition and knowledge of the client's assets gives the session purpose and direction.

3. **Determining outcomes** enables the counselor to plan therapy based upon what the client is seeking in therapy and to understand, from the client's viewpoint, what life would be like without the existing problem(s).

4. **Exploring alternatives and confronting incongruities** is the purposeful behavior on the part of the counselor to work toward resolution of the client's problems. Generating alternatives and confronting incongruities with the client assists the counselor in understanding more about client dynamics.

5. **Generalization and transfer of learning** is the process whereby changes in the client's thoughts, feelings, and behaviors are carried out in everyday life by the client.

In a similar fashion, Hutchins and Cole (1992) suggested that structuring includes explaining to the client the kinds of events that can be expected to occur during the process of helping, from the initial interview through the termination and follow-up process. Some aspects of structure will occur in the initial phase of the helping process (initial greeting, discussion of time constraints, roles, confidentiality), while other aspects of structure may take place throughout the remainder of the helping process (clarification of expectations and actions both inside and outside the interview setting) (Hutchins & Cole, 1992, p. 50).

Weinrach (1989) suggested as a valuable time saver the method of committing to the process of structuring. Weinrach advocated basing written guidelines on the issues most frequently raised by clients as well as the areas in which potential conflicts may exist. These guidelines include the following common client inquiries:

- How often can I expect to have an appointment?
- How might I reach you if I feel that it is necessary?
- What happens if I forget an appointment?
- How confidential are therapy sessions?
- What do I do in an emergency?
- When is it time to end treatment?
- What are my financial responsibilities?
- How often do I obtain reimbursement from insurance?

According to Hutchins and Cole (1992), structuring such concerns in writing makes for effective and efficient use of time and stimulates open discussion about a variety of concerns before they become problems. They further suggest that the helper think through the kinds of things that are expected to happen in the helping process. The following list of questions can serve as a starting point (Hutchins & Cole, 1992):

- Am I personally and professionally qualified to work with this client who has this particular concern or problem in this specific situation?
- Do I understand the unique personal, educational, social, and cultural aspects of this client enough to be able to assist in this situation?
- Should the client be referred to a helping professional who has more or different specialized training or skills, such as a licensed psychologist, social worker, marriage and family specialist, drug and alcohol specialist, or other type of helping professional?
- What is my role of helper in this relationship?
- What kinds of things do I see as important variables in the helping process?
- What kind of behavior (thoughts, feelings, actions) do I expect of the client both in and outside of the therapy setting?
- What kind of commitment do I expect of the client in terms of time, work, and responsibility?
- What about confidentiality in the setting in which I work?
- What legal, ethical, and moral considerations must be considered before working with this client? (p. 46)

These critical questions asked by the helper, counselor, or therapist, coupled with printed client concerns, can serve as a valuable asset and aid in the structuring of clinical interviews in the counseling or therapy process.

In summary, structuring the relationship entails defining for the client the nature, purpose, and goals of the therapeutic relationship. Critical to the structuring process is the therapist's ability to create an atmosphere that enables the client to know that the therapist is genuine, sincere, and empathic in his or her desire to assist the client. The therapist, in the process of preparing the client for data gathering and assessment activities, employs attending skills and facilitative therapeutic techniques.

It is important to remember that interviewing with the client and having the client engage in other assessment procedures are only part of the overall assessment process in counseling and psychotherapy. Equally significant are the therapist's own mental and covert actions that take place during the process. The therapist typically gathers great amounts of information from clients during this stage of counseling or therapy. However, data are of little or no value unless the counselor or therapist can integrate and synthesize the information.

The task of counselors and therapists during the assessment process requires that they know what information to obtain and how to obtain it, and that they have both the ability to put it together in some meaningful way and the capacity to use it to generate clinical hunches. Such hunches, or hypotheses about client's problems, can then allow counselors and therapists to develop tentative ideas for planning and treatment (Cormier & Cormier, 1998, p. 147).

■ Assessment Activities

The following is a description and format of typical assessment activities occurring prior to and during the initial stages of counseling or therapy.

Obtaining Authorizations

The first step in the process of counseling and psychotherapy is obtaining the appropriate authorizations prior to the start of therapy. Examples of authorization forms are included for this purpose in the "Forms" section at the end of the book; the Parental Release Form (Form 3.1) should be used when initiating counseling with a child, while the Client Release Form (Form 3.2) should be used when initiating counseling with adults. These forms should be adapted for use by the practicum student or intern according to the specific field site and university requirements.

Obtaining Information from the Client and Others

A practical method to use in obtaining client information from others (parents, therapists, teachers) is to develop a form that focuses upon the specific information to be obtained. For example, the Initial Intake Form (Form 3.3) tends to include more medical, psychological, and psychiatric data that focus upon the history and outcomes of treatment. Similarly, background and developmental data are obtained for the purpose of assessing the acuteness or chronicity of current complaints. The Initial Intake Form is designed to provide the counselor or therapist with initial identifying data about the client. Data about the client are obtained directly from the client at the initial interview.

In contrast, the Elementary School Counseling Referral Form (Form 3.4) and the Secondary School Counseling Referral Forms (Form 3.5) tend to include more data regarding the academic history of the student and his or her behavior and demeanor in school. Aptitude, attitude, and interest toward school are typically stressed. The Elementary and Secondary School Counseling Referral Forms are designed to obtain appropriate precounseling data from sources other than the client. Typically, the professional making a referral of a school-age child for counseling or therapy is asked to describe and comment on his or her perceptions and knowledge of the pupil's current academic and social standing.

Assessing the Client's Mental Status

Mental health exams are rarely used by school counselors. However, mental health counselors, counseling psychologists, and professional counselors routinely use the mental status examination. These professionals often find that, in order to gain insight into the client's presenting condition, that client's mental status may need to be assessed. The mental status examination is, therefore, designed to provide the therapist with signs that indicate the "functional" nature of the person's psychiatric condition. In addition, the mental status examination can be used to provide the therapist with a current view of the client's mental capabilities and deficits prior to and during the course of treatment and is beneficial to the beginning therapist who lacks the clinical experience to quickly assess the client's mental status.

Many formats can be used to obtain a client's mental status. However, all formats have common areas that are routinely assessed. The following is an example of items fairly typically covered, with an explanation of material generally included. The Mental Status Checklist (Form 3.6) can be used by students in evaluating these common areas of assessment.

Mental Status Categories of Assessment

Appearance and Behavior: This category consists of data gathered throughout the interview so that the person reading the narrative has a "photograph" of the client during the interview. Data is gathered by direct observation of the client. To assess a client's appearance and behavior, the counselor or therapist might employ the following questions: Is the client's appearance age appropriate? Does the client appear to be his or her stated age? Is the client's behavior appropriate to the surroundings? Is the behavior overactive or underactive? Is the behavior agitated or retarded? Is speech pressured? Retarded? Logical? Clear? What is the content of speech?

Attention/Alertness: Is the client aware of his or her surroundings? Can the client focus attention on the therapist? Is the client highly distractible? Is the client scanning the environment? Is he or she hypervigilant?

Affect/Mood: What is the quality of the client's affect? Is the client's affect expressive? Expansive? Blunted? Flat? Agitated? Fearful? Is the client's affect appropriate to the current situation?

Perception/Thought: Does the client have false ideas or delusions? Does the client experience his or her own thoughts as being controlled? Does the client experience people putting thoughts in his or her head? Does the client experience his or her own thoughts being withdrawn or taken away? Does the client feel that people are watching him or her? Out to get him or her? Does the client experience grandiose or bizarre delusions?

Sensory Perception: Does the client hallucinate? Does the client experience visual, auditory, tactile, or gustatory false perceptions?

Orientation: Is the client oriented to persons, place, and time? Does the client know with whom he or she is dealing? Where he or she is? What day and time it is?

Judgment: Can the client act appropriately in typical social, personal, and occupational situations? Can the client show good judgment in conducting his or her own life?

Attention/Concentration: Does the client have any memory disturbance?

Recent Memory: Can the client remember information given a few minutes ago? (For example, give the client three or four things to remember and ask him or her to repeat back after several minutes.)

Long-Term Memory: Can the client remember or recall information from yesterday? From childhood? Can the client concentrate on facts given to him or her?

Abstract Ability: Can the client recognize and handle similarities? Absurdities? Proverbs?
Insight: Is the client aware that he or she has a problem? Is he or she aware of possible causes? Possible solutions?

Recording Psychosocial History

The Psychosocial History (Form 3.7, see the "Forms" section at the end of the book) is a part of the pretherapy assessment procedure employed by most community mental health agencies. The psychosocial history provides the therapist with a comprehensive view of the client over time. In most instances, the psychosocial history provides more data than the initial intake and is invaluable in examining the acuteness or chronicity of the client's problem. Specific attention is directed toward the milestones or benchmarks in the client's developmental history that have implications for the treatment strategies to be employed in therapy.

■ Monitoring and Evaluating the Client's Progress

Monitoring of the client in therapy is a continuous process, beginning with the initial contact with the client and ending with therapy termination. Monitoring is an invaluable asset that allows the therapist to understand how the goals and objectives of the therapy are being met as well as the direction of the therapy and the progress taking place during therapy.

An adaptation of Kanfer and Schefft's (1988, pp. 255–256) discussion of monitoring and evaluating client progress suggests doing the following:

- monitoring and evaluating the client's behavior and environment session to session;
- assessing improvement in coping skills by noting the client's use of the skills in relation to behavior and other activities;
- evaluating any change in the client's status or in his or her relationships to significant others that resulted from treatment;
- utilizing available data to review progress, to strengthen gains, and to maintain the client's motivation for completing the change process;
- negotiating new treatment objectives or changes in methods or the rate of progress if the evidence suggests the need for such changes; and
- attending to new conditions that have been created by the client's change and that may promote or defeat further change efforts.

Further, Kanfer and Schefft (1988, pp. 257–258), in examining treatment effectiveness, suggested that therapists ask themselves the following questions:

- **Are the treatment interventions working?** The therapist should note the client's progress with respect to therapeutic objectives, as compared to the baseline data gathered at the beginning of treatment (initial assessment).
- **Have other treatment targets been overlooked?** By monitoring other changes and emergent problems, the therapist obtains cues for the necessity of renegotiating treatment objectives or treatment methods.
- **Is the therapeutic process on course?** Individuals differ with regard to their rate of progress; plateaus may occur at various phases of therapy, and these need to be scrutinized.
- **Are subsidiary methods needed to enhance progress or to handle newly emerged problems? Are there gaps in the client's basic skill level needed to execute the program?**
- **Are the client's problems and the treatment program being formulated effectively?** Monitoring and evaluating by the therapist in process is crucial to successful treatment. Consultation with other professionals and colleagues is recommended.

Building a Client Folder

A valuable adjunct to the monitoring process is the building of a folder for the client. When carefully and properly developed and organized, the file folder serves as a quick reference to review session-by-session developments and is used to assist in the summarization and evaluating of the course of treatment.

Additionally, practicum students and interns will also be responsible for contributing to the file folder maintained by the agency, institution, or school in which the counseling sessions are held. Each student needs to understand the format employed, the kinds of information desired, and the kinds of information to be added to the folder. In order to maintain effective client confidentialilty, students must understand the specific security procedures to be followed in the agency or school. The procedures to be followed will depend upon the policies of the agency, institution, or school.

The practicum or internship course objectives, in addition to those held by the agency, institution, or school in which the counseling is done, may necessitate a separate folder for the university supervisor. This folder should be maintained by the counselor and his or her school or agency site supervisor, and should be available for review.

The purposes for having a separate folder for each client may include the following:

- to teach the student counselor the procedures for building a folder for each client similar to what will be required on the job;
- to foster organizational skills in the managing of critical client data;
- to assist the student counselor in gathering pertinent data applicable to the treatment of the client;
- to provide a vehicle for reviewing client progress made during the course of treatment;
- to summarize the therapeutic activities that have been performed by the counselor and client;
- to serve as a format for the preparation and dissemination of summative data of all counseling activities that have taken place prior to and during treatment; and
- to provide essential information when writing a termination report regarding the client.

The development of a client folder, whether for meeting overall professional development or for continuing information to the agency, is an invaluable asset to the practicum/internship student

---

PROCESSING INTERVIEW NOTES*

Joseph W. Hollis

During or following each counseling/therapy session, the student counselor or therapist will make notes of what occurred and comments regarding plans for therapy. With the large number of clients seen in therapy and seen over an extended period of time, the Therapy Notes (Form 3.8), completed after each session with a client, are an invaluable asset to the therapist. Therapy notes can serve various purposes:

1. The record of the interview can reacquaint the therapist with what previously had transpired in contacts with the client as well as with his or her initial impressions of the therapeutic process.
2. Notes may serve as valuable aids in helping a different therapist (who may take over therapy) under-

*This material appeared in a chapter entitled "Counseling Techniques and Process," pp. 77–174, in K. Dimick and F. Krause, *Practicum Manual for Counseling and Psychotherapy,* 1980, Muncie, IN: Accelerated Development. Reprinted with permission. (Edited to make terminology consistent with the present volume.)

stand the development nature of the previous contacts and gain knowledge of the kind of treatment or methods employed in therapy.

3. Of great importance is the value that therapy notes have as a self-learning device. Notes can help us check ourselves against the tendencies to be restricted, preoccupied, or sterile in our contacts. Notes have a decided utility in promoting a greater psychological understanding of behavior as displayed by a variety of clients. Much of this understanding can be accomplished by attempting to put into words our impressions and our feelings about the client, which too often have been implicitly assumed.

4. Therapy notes can be utilized in research and evaluation. They can aid in acquiring more ideas regarding the process itself and movement by the individual when certain techniques are used.

5. Notes serve to keep each helping professional in contact with the work and methods of other professional workers in the same settings. The knowledge gained from what others are doing may serve to help one become more flexible and productive in therapy.

6. Notes may serve as a type of legal protection for professionals because reference to these notes clarified what actually occurred during the course of therapy.

Thus, note taking is an essential process in counseling. It has been our experience that very few programs have explicit training in note taking as part of the training program. All too often, it is assumed that everyone can take clinical notes. Furthermore, knowing what kind and type of content notes should be recorded requires considerable experience and training in its own right.

The counseling literature provides little assistance and few guidelines for proper note taking, yet the demand to document our accountability is an ever-present reality. The following article by Presser and Pfost has been included because it focuses on the clinician's attention to certain aspects of the counseling or psychotherapy process, enabling him or her to record appropriate case notes.

A FORMAT FOR INDIVIDUAL PSYCHOTHERAPY SESSION NOTES*

Nam R. Presser and Karen S. Pfost

The writing of case notes, although a necessary task, is one for which therapists often receive little or no training. Yet case notes can enhance the therapeutic process by enabling the clinician to assess the validity of conceptualization, to monitor progress toward goals, and to note patterns within and across sessions. In training institutions, case notes can serve an additional function: they provide the supervisor with another source of data regarding the supervisee, the client, and the client-therapist relationship. They provide a molar view of therapy that is a valuable precedent to a molecular analysis of events within a session. Case notes also indicate to the supervisor which aspects of therapy are most salient and most recordable to the supervisee; omissions may serve as cues to focus on areas in supervision, either because they are problematic or inadequately conceptualized. Thus, thorough case notes can enhance both the supervisory process and the quality of services delivered, and can serve as a safeguard for the supervisor as well.

In our experience, trainees' case notes were typically unfocused narratives of events within a session. Such notes often communicated little regarding the process and taught the trainee very little. The Individual Psychotherapy Session Notes (IPSN) form (see Figure 3.1 below) was developed for use within a training program. It was designed to focus the trainees' attention on important aspects of therapy sessions and to provide relevant information to the supervisor. Although the IPSN format is especially useful for fledgling clinicians, it is also appropriate for use

* This article appeared in *Professional Psychology: Research and Practice*, 1985, Vol. 16, No. 1, 11–16. Copyright©1985 by the American Psychological Association. Reprinted with permission.

by more experienced professionals. Its primary emphasis is on process, in contradistinction to the problem focus of other case note formats, most notably the Problem Oriented Medical Record (POMR) (Weed, 1968).

The development of the IPSN form was based on three principals. First, the form encourages therapists to attend to several specific, relevant aspects of the therapeutic process. Second, the form is, to the extent possible, atheoretical so that it can be adopted for use by therapists adhering to most theoretical positions. This feature is especially important for supervisors, who often train clinicians with various theoretical orientations. Third, it was important that the form not be excessively complex, cumbersome, or time-consuming to complete, so that after it has been learned it can be used easily after each session.

The initial version of this form was tested over the course of a year by master's-level clinical and counseling psychology trainees, and by doctoral-level psychology interns. They used the form to record several hundred client sessions occurring in a variety of settings. Systematic feedback from these trainees was used to determine the IPSN's usefulness and to make modifications.

Description of the IPSN Form

The Individual Psychotherapy Session Notes form, shown in Figure 3.1, is discussed in further detail below. Following is a description of each section of the form.

I. **Brief Summary of Session.** This section allows for a narrative overview of the session. Although it is perhaps the least noteworthy section, it allows for the kind of case notes with which many practitioners are familiar and with which they may not be ready to dispense. Entries in this section are most likely to be in the form of a sequential account of major events within the session. Its relative brevity necessitates discrimination among the session's events.

II. **Client.** This section (and the following two) forces a clear distinction between database and inference. The first subsection is provided for the recording of observations of the client's verbal and nonverbal behavior. Objectivity is the key to completion of this subsection, because it is important to resist the temptation to make inferences prior to specification of one's database. The therapist's hypotheses and inferences are listed in the second subsection. The labeling of this subsection (interpretations and hypotheses) stresses both the speculative nature of such inferences as well as the desirability of further testing of hypotheses.

III. **Therapist.** This section encourages the clinician to examine his or her own behavior, retaining the distinction between database and inferences. Such information is frequently not a part of traditional case notes. The use of this category appears likely to increase the therapist's awareness of his or her own behavior and to alter the therapist's perspective so that he or she is both subject and object. The underlying assumption that the behavior of both parties can be observed and interpreted in a similar manner discourages the clinician from making attributions regarding his or her own behavior differently from attributions regarding the client's behavior (e.g., situational vs. dispositional). Information in this section also provides a basis for an evaluation of the internal consistency of a therapist's behavior, correspondence to a theoretical stance, and the evolution of a therapist's own style. Data regarding the therapist's reaction to the client can also provide diagnostic information; with experience, the therapist learns to recognize his or her typical responses to persons who display various kinds of behavior.

IV. **Therapist-Client Interaction.** This section marks a shift in focus from intrapersonal to interpersonal dynamics. The assumption of reciprocal influence that underlies this section encourages an interactional point of view. Because of the process orientation, this section can be extremely valuable in its illumination of dynamics. It is especially helpful in assisting the therapist to conceptualize both parties' behavior patterns and the degree to which these are specific or nonspecific to this relationship. The novice therapist may tend to underutilize this section of the form, a manifestation of the tendency at that stage to focus on persons (especially the client) rather than on the interaction between the

INDIVIDUAL PSYCHOTHERAPY SESSION NOTES (IPSN)

I. Brief Summary of Session

Recent argument with her parents regarding lack of progress in finding another job led into discussion of pervasive feelings of inadequacy and hopelessness. She feels incapable of attaining the standards which her parents have set for her, but still she refuses to acknowledge any anger toward them. She appears more depressed and reports increased incidence of self-destructive behaviors. Does not appear to be suicidal at this time.

Therapists Observation of:	Therapist's Interpretations and Hypothesis:
II. Client: At the beginning of session, pt. talked softly with infrequent pauses; slumped in chair; rarely made eye contact. Later, many self-deprecating statements as she discussed parents' expectations. Raised voice when discussing those but denied anger. Reported drinking and contact with ex-boyfriend. Hinted re suicide, but denied intent.	Appears moderately depressed: Turning anger inward? May be exacerbated by drinking. Seems threatened by suggestion that she might feel anger toward parents. Overidealization of them is impediment. Presents self as victim and seems stuck in this role; assumes it with ex-boyfriend and parents. Could hints about suicide and drinking be to elicit rescuing by therapist?
III. Therapist Early in session felt tired, looked at watch frequently. Interventions primarily reflective and clarifying. Tone of voice gentle, soothing.	Initially impatient and bored. Am I becoming tired of her helplessness? Approach is relatively client centered, with only mild confrontations. Is this avoidance of confrontation my issue (helpless behavior annoys me) or is it due to wanting to avoid recapitualization of victimization?
IV. Therapist-Client Interaction: When pt. appears helpless or distressed, therapist is still responding supportively rather than confronting. Pt. Asked if therapist was disappointed in her lack of progress and reported surprise at the negative reply; this was discussed vis-a-vis her father	Does pt. typically elicit rescuing, or at times the opposite (frustration and alienating others with her helplessness)? Relationship with therapist is beginning to parallel relationship with father, particularly re projection of negative evaluation onto therapist and expectation of criticism.
V. Problems Addressed 1. Pt.'s feelings of unworthiness and despair re attaining the standards which she has injected. 2. Relationship with parents 3. Expectations of negative evaluations	VI. Progress Made Displays more insight into the connection between internalized standards and her depression. Beginning to express some of the anger that she has heretofore turned inward. Her expectation that therapist would also judge her negatively was examined. Therapeutic alliance solidified by discussion of her reaction to therapist.

VII. Plans

In supervision, bring up my reaction to her helplessness and consider reacting differently (first explore if this is my issue and, if not, how best to respond to her).

Look for more signs of anger and point these out as they occur.

Explore idealization of parents.

Continue to monitor suicidal ideation.

VIII. Other

Will soon need to discuss my absence due to vacation.

FIGURE 3.1. Sample notes using a replication of the Individual Psychotherapy Session Notes form. (For the sake of clarity, these notes, which are usually handwritten, have been typeset.)

client and the therapist. This section also tends to be used more as the therapeutic relationship develops and as behaviors that were formerly noted in the first or second section as independent come to be viewed in the context of an interaction.

V. **Problems Addressed.** Some clinicians, especially those who work in medical settings, are accustomed to the problem orientation exemplified in the POMR. This section differs from the POMR in that it refers specifically to problems that were addressed within the session. This is consistent with the form's focus on the analysis of events with a single session, but it links these events within the subsequent section.

VI. **Progress Made.** The assumption behind this section is a rather apparent one: that the client's progress is the ultimate criterion by which therapy must be assessed. The focus on progress highlights the need for movement within therapy and is also consistent with the APA's (1977), which mandate that the basis for continuation of a therapeutic relationship must be its beneficial impact on the client.

VII. **Plans.** At this point, the attention shifts from a present to a future focus in order to provide continuity from one session to subsequent ones. This section encourages the clinician to plan therapeutic alternatives and conceptualize issues with which the client will most likely need to deal in future sessions. Practical strategies may also be noted here.

VIII. **Other.** This is a category for the information that needs to be recorded but that does not logically belong in any of the previous sections (e.g., test data, relevant correspondence). This section could also be termed an "overflow" section.

The IPSN's Use in Supervision

We have found the IPSN format to be useful in helping fledgling therapists learn concepts and skills requisite for effective therapy. It is rarely possible or desirable to describe everything that occurred in a session. The IPSN assists the novice in learning the necessary discrimination skills by prompting him or her to consider and examine those events and observations that are important and why they are important.

Another skill the trainee needs to develop is that of regularly forming hypotheses about a client's behavior, the clinician's own behavior, and the interactions between these two parties. Simply noting or observing the client will not lead to effective treatment unless the therapist can put these observations into a theoretical perspective that can eventuate in interventions with potential for producing changes in the client. The IPSN assists the student in forming the habit of relating observations to conceptualizations, conceptualizations to treatment plans, and treatment plans to progress.

This form also can help the trainee to develop higher order observational skills. A trainee needs to learn not only to observe the client's verbal and nonverbal behavior but also the therapeutic process while he or she participates in it. Thus, one learns to become simultaneously a participant and an observer during a session in order to ensure control of the session, to understand the therapeutic process on an ongoing basis, and to develop the ability to select appropriate interventions rather than to respond unsystematically. In this respect, the therapist learns to function much like a supervisor who does not participate in a session but observes the client, the therapist, and their interaction.

It has been our experience that the developmental stage of the trainee is reflected in how the individual completes the IPSN form. Early in training, therapists typically are able to complete only sections I, V, VI, and VII comfortably and/or in-depth. The novice tends to focus attention primarily on the client, perhaps as a way of understanding the ambiguity and complexity of psychotherapeutic situations. It is not until later that most trainees seem able to observe and interpret their own behavior in therapy sessions. The ability to perceive, comprehend, and use interactional patterns is an even higher order therapeutic skill. For supervisors, the IPSN may therefore provide a means of assessing their trainees' level of skills and monitoring progress in the trainees' development as therapists.

CASE SUMMARY OUTLINE*

Joseph W. Hollis

Case summaries are essential to synthesize information and to provide baseline data for the counseling process. Summaries enable one to analyze whether or not all essential data regarding the planning and treatment of the client have been considered. In addition, summaries cause one to identify potential problems, directions for action with the client, and possible guidelines for determining whether or not satisfactory progress is being made during the series of therapy sessions.

A case summary may also be written prior to the initial interview. As such, the summary serves as a base for integrating what is known, as a baseline for comparison of future information, and as a springboard for what might be done when the individual is seen in therapy.

In addition, a case summary may be written at various times during the interval over which several therapy sessions were held. The summary may be for the counselor's benefit and may be used as a benchmark for comparisons at a later date. Similarly, a summary may be needed to send to a referral person or to someone the client identified as needing information about his or her status and/or progress. With those clients being seen within legal conditions (court cases, detention homes, penal institutions), periodic case summaries may be required. The length of the case summary is dependent upon its purpose and the amount and type of information available. A report that is one to three pages in length, single spaced, typewritten or computer generated, is generally sufficient. When appropriate, copies of test data can be incorporated into or attached to the case summary.

A typical time for writing a case summary is after termination with the client. The summary will be a vehicle for the review of pertinent information if and when it is needed. The summary is placed in the client's folder and maintained along with other pertinent information gathered during the course of therapy.

Items to include in the case summary will be determined by such factors as the purpose of the summary, the individuals who will use it, and the professional expertise of those using the information. Even though items to be included in the case summary will vary from report to report, an outline of topics to be considered is beneficial. A sample Case Summary Topical Outline is provided in Figure 3.2.

REPORTING THERAPEUTIC PROGRESS†

Joseph W. Hollis and Patsy A. Donn

The practicum student or intern frequently may receive requests from others to provide diagnostic information and reports of therapeutic progress, and to make recommendations regarding a client.

The format for reporting data will vary according to the specific requests that are made. Each progress report needs to be prepared in keeping with the request, the client, and the person to whom the report is sent. Qualitative and quantitative differences will be based upon the pro-

---

* This material appeared in a chapter entitled "Counseling Techniques and Processes," pp. 77–174, in K. Dimick and F. Krause, *Practicum Manual for Counseling and Psychotherapy,* 1980. Muncie, IN: Accelerated Development. Reprinted with permission. (Wording has been modified for consistency with this volume.)

†This material appeared in a chapter entitled "Developing Reports in Response to Requests from Others," pp. 201–208, in J. W. Hollis and P. A. Donn, Psychological Report Writing: Theory and Practice, 1979. Muncie, IN: Accelerated Development.

CASE SUMMARY
(Topical Outline)

1. **Identifying Data**
   The name, date, address, and telephone number of the client. Includes agency or school coding (client number, client file, social security number). The background (highest level attained).

2. **Reason for the Report**
   A statement as to the purpose of the current report. Examples include: interim progress reports of therapy, background information gathered prior to the initial session with the client, referral report to another agency or school, and report of termination with client.

3. **Source of Information**
   The source and the manner in which data were obtained in the preparation of this report.

4. **Statement of the Problem**
   A succinct statement of the presenting problem in therapy. May include a statement reflecting the chronicity and acuteness of the symptomology.

5. **Family and Home Background**
   Identifying information about parents and siblings (names, ages, occupations, etc.). Client's perceptions of the home environment and relationships within the family. Critical family incidents may be included.

6. **Educational History**
   Description of pertinent information in relation to educational background, including academic achievement, school instances that were significant for the understanding of the individual, and the client's attitude toward education.

7. **Physical Health History**
   A statement of the client's significant health history, current treatments and medications, familial medical history that may impact upon the client, and current treatments.

8. **Social Interactions**
   Client's perception of the quality of his or her social interactions and interpersonal relationships.

9. **Psychological Development**
   A statement of critical benchmarks in the client's psychological development, initial and current clinical impressions.

10. **Testing Assessment**
    Inclusion of the name, form, and other identifying information about each test administered to the client, about the tests administered previously by others, and the results utilized during the therapy session. Scores obtained and identification of norms used in reporting percentiles or other test scores. Interpretation of results.

11. **Occupational History**
    Chronology of the client's work history, when pertinent, jobs held, and reasons for changes. Quality of work satisfaction and interest.

12. **Hobbies, Recreational Activities**
    Interests and self-expressive uses of time.

13. **Sexual Adjustment**
    Current status, significant problems or disturbances in functioning, alternative lifestyles.

14. **Summary Statement**
    Summative statement concerning client's current disposition and status.

15. **Diagnosis/Prognosis**
    Statement of client's DSM-IV diagnosis and clinical prognosis.

16. **Treatment**
    Description of current treatment and/or recommendations for follow-up treatment.

17. **Recommendations**

FIGURE 3.2. Sample case summary topical outline.

fessional preparation of the person requesting the data, and the orientation and training of the individual preparing the report.

Requests for diagnostic information oftentimes are used by the agency or institution for the purpose of assisting in the development of treatment plans for placement of clients into appropriate programs and for providing information for the final disposition of a therapy case. Knowledge of the purpose for which the request is made is invaluable in assisting in the writing of a progress report that specifically addresses the request.

A request for treatment recommendations is a vital part of most progress reports. In some instances, the total report consists basically of treatment recommendations. The specific purpose of this report may be simply to communicate recommendations to someone else who must make a disposition of the case.

Requests for reports on the client's therapeutic progress are often made by the referring professional. In addition, other professionals who have made previous referrals of any kind for the client are appreciative of reports on progress even if reports are not requested formally. In addition, others who are working concurrently with the client find progress reports invaluable in fulfilling their professional roles. Teachers, administrators, parents, and physicians can find an appropriately prepared progress report from a fellow professional an important source of assistance.

A Therapeutic Progress Report (Form 3.9; see the "Forms" section at the end of the book), therefore, needs to include pertinent data about the method of treatment employed as well as the client's current status. Treatment recommendations are especially helpful to those who must make a final disposition of the case.

In summary, we have presented a number of instruments that can be used to monitor the progress of the client in counseling. Many students have been exposed to similar monitoring aids in their training programs. It is important to remember that the instruments chosen to monitor clients' progress are significant, but the students' skills in assessing the clients' progress are critical.

Summary

Practicum content issues are fundamental ingredients in the student's preparation for working with clients. Effective initial interactions with the client, along with the employment of assessment and monitoring activities, are essential for setting the expectations and tone of the counseling experience. The proper recording and processing of interview notes contribute to the counselor's general impression of the client and the client's progress throughout the therapy session, and as such are important skills for the beginning counselor to master. We have provided sample formats for use in making therapy notes, as well as other forms that can be used in the recording of pertinent client data.

Suggested Readings

Hansen, N. E., & Freimuth, M. (1997). Piecing the puzzle together: A model for understanding the theory practice relationship. *Counseling Psychology, 25*(4), 654–674.

Hasen, D. S. (1991). Diagnostic interviews for assessment. *Alcohol and Research World, 15*(4), 293–294.

Hohenshil, T. H. (1996). Editorial: Role of assessment and diagnosis in counseling. *Journal of Counseling and Development, 75*(1), 64–68.

Howatt, W. A. (2000). *The human services counseling toolbox.* Pacific Grove, CA: Brooks Cole.

Juhnke, G. A. (1995). Mental health counseling assessment; Broadening one's understanding of the clients presenting concerns. *ERIC Digest, 70*(4), 527–870.

Lambert, M. J., & Ogles, B. M. (1992). Choosing outcome assessment devices: An organizational and conceptual scheme. *Journal of Counseling and Development, 70*(4), 527–563.

Meier, S. T. (1999). Training the practitioner-scientist; bridging case conceptualization, assessment and intervention. *Counseling Psychologist, 27*(6), 846–870.

Morrison, J. (1995). *DSM IV made easy: The clinician's guide to diagnosis.* New York: Guilford Press.

Patterson, L. E., & Well, E. (2000). *The counseling process,* 5th ed. Pacific Grove, CA: Brooks Cole.

Prieito, L. R. (1998). Practicum class supervision in CACREP accredited programs: A national study. *Counselor Education and Supervision, 38*(2), 113–124.

Schweitzer, A. M. (1996). Using the inverted pyramid heuristic. *Counselor Education and Supervision, 35*(4), 258–268.

Seligman, L. (1993). Teaching treatment planning. *Counselor Education and Supervision, 32*(4), 287–298.

Seligman, L. (1996). *Diagnosis and treatment planning in counseling.* New York: Plenum Press.

Stevens, M. J., & Morris, S. J. (1995). A format for case conceptualization. *Counselor Education and Supervision, 35*(1), 82–95.

Van Denberg, T. F., & Schmidt, J. A. (1992) Interpersonal assessment in counseling and pyschotherapy. *Journal of Counseling and Development, 71*(1), 84–91.

References

American Psychological Association. (1977). *Standards for providers of psychological services.* Washington, DC: Author.

Cormier, S., & Cormier, B. (1998). *Interviewing strategies for helpers: Fundamental skills and cognitive behavioral interventions.* Pacific Grove, CA: Brooks Cole.

Hollis, J. W., & Donn, P. A. (1979). *Psychological report writing: Theory and practice.* Muncie, IN: Accelerated Development.

Hutchins, D. E., & Cole, C. G. (1992). *Helping relationships and strategies.* Monterey, CA: Brooks Cole.

Ivey, A. E. (1999). *Intentional interviewing and counseling.* Pacific Grove, CA: Brooks Cole.

Kanfer, F. H., & Schefft, B. K. (1988). *Guiding the process of therapeutic change.* Champaign, IL: Research Press.

Weed, L. (1968). Medical records that guide and teach. *New England Journal of Medicine, 278,* 595–600, 652–657.

Weinrach, S. G. (1989). Guidelines for clients of private practitioners: committing the structure to print. *Journal of Counseling and Development, 67,* 299–300.

John C. Boylan

Practicum Process Issues

This chapter has been designed to help beginning practicum students to think about, conceptualize, and plan their initial counseling experience. The topics to be presented are not new to the student but are included here for the purpose of reviewing, in a systematized manner, a step-by-step process in preparation for counseling. The previous chapter dealt largely with the mechanics of counseling (getting permissions, building client folders, note taking, etc.). This chapter focuses upon the therapist and his or her personal approach to counseling and psychotherapy.

The completion of on-campus course work signals the beginning of the counselor's venture into the counseling profession. This initial step in counseling often brings with it a variety of concerns for the student. Facing the task of applying their knowledge base to actual work with clients can cause considerable anxiety for beginning counselors. This chapter has been organized for the purpose of presenting and reviewing the major steps in the process of preparing for that first client.

■ Philosophy-Theory-Practice Continuum

The beginning counselor is confronted with the struggle to integrate the knowledge base of their training program into a coherent method of counseling. From the very beginning of the training programs, students are encouraged to examine their own values and beliefs as they become exposed to the various philosophical and theoretical approaches to counseling. The necessity for students to develop their own "theoretical approach" to working with clients is stressed for the purpose of sensitizing students to the need for a consistent, well-thought-out approach to counseling. The first step in this process is an examination of the variety of ways in which theories determine the methods and procedures that will be implemented in the therapeutic process.

Hansen and Freimuth (1997) discuss a seven-step model that delineates the different pathways through which theories of personality and psychotherapy affect case conceptualization and intervention. The following is an adaptation of their seven-step mode:

1. **Assumptive World.** This is basically the counselor's beliefs or "personal philosophy" about the world and how it works. One's assumptive world is shaped long before exposure to "theories of counseling," and it represents the "lens" through which we view, understand, and selectively attend to data. Courses on the foundations of counseling often challenge students to get in touch with the particular way in which they see humankind and its development. An understanding of

our own view of humankind is essential in the process of developing our own approach to counseling. A philosophical base provides the student with an essential understanding of their views of humankind, from which they can then view the variety of theorists, theories, and interventions.

2. **School.** The school represents the premises of a worldview as applied to a given topic in psychology. For example, if a student's belief system stresses the subjective view of the individual rather than an objective view of the individual, it is likely that the student would follow a humanistic approach to therapy. Similarly, if a student viewed the individual from an objective perspective, then objective approaches such as those put forth by Freud and Skinner would seem to be the preferred approach. Furthermore, schools are distinguished from one another on the basis of their assumptions. However, it is important to recognize that no school is validated by empirical means; rather, one believes a certain set of assumptions about human behavior and then adopts the change process that best fits with those assumptions (Freimuth, 1992).

3. **Theory.** The purpose of a theory is to give content and a sharper focus to the assumptions of a school. For example, Maloney (1991) divided the cognitive school into the rational cognitivists and the cognitive structivists; both give priority to cognition, but only the latter emphasizes affect.

4. **Theorist.** Theorists differ in their understanding of a theory's tenets. As an existentialist, does the work of May, Frankl, or Binswanger seem most valid? According to Maloney (1991) many therapists, especially novices, feel relief when they first identify a particular theorist whose ideas most closely parallel their own. The most complete understanding of the theory's tenets is accomplished by reading the original works of the theorist.

5. **Working Hypothesis.** The interpretation of a particular client's problem and needs, as understood through the lens of the therapist's preferred theory, is referred to as the *working hypothesis*. Implicit in the working hypothesis is the theory derived outcomes (self-actualization, decision making, "choosing," etc.). It should also be noted that the manner in which the therapist conceptualizes an intake interview will often differ in emphasis based on the theoretical grounding of the therapist. For example, a therapist grounded in Freudian theory will likely place an emphasis on developmental history.

6. **Strategy.** The method or steps taken in the therapy process to achieve the desired treatment outcomes. According to Hansen and Freimuth (1997) a therapist's assumptive world, school, theory, and theorists influence the therapist's thinking about theories and psychotherapy. However, the working hypothesis is the bridge between theory and psychotherapy and strategy and technique. Strategies represent what the therapist wants to accomplish through chosen interventions. Therapists choose and emphasize certain strategies based on their theoretical orientation and diagnostically specific working hypothesis (Messer, 1986).

7. **Techniques.** Techniques are defined as the actions therapists take to implement a given strategy. This area refers closely to what the therapist actually does with the client in session, actions such as listening, interpreting, mirroring, and questioning. The techniques chosen by the therapist are shaped by his or her chosen theory.

The therapist who organizes his or her thoughts about therapy, beginning with their assumptions about the individual and culminating in the choosing of appropriate therapeutic techniques, is well on the way to gaining confidence about his or her own approach to the therapy session. The translation of the therapist's knowledge base into workable therapeutic interventions is an essential part of the practice of counseling and psychotherapy.

Initial Client Contact

The initial client contact is a crucial point in the process of counseling and psychotherapy. The initial interview or intake interview is an information gathering process rather than a therapeutic process. Frequently, someone other than the counselor or therapist conducts the interview and passes critical information on to the counselor. Regardless of who does the interview, however, it is essential that certain data be collected to provide the counselor with the information necessary to understand the client's presenting problem(s) and current life issues. According to Cormier and Cormier (1998), the most important areas of focus are:

- identifying information about the client;
- general appearance and demeanor of the client;
- history related to the presenting problem(s);
- past counseling or psychiatric history;
- educational and job history;
- health and medical history;
- social and developmental history;
- family, marital, and sexual history;
- assessment of client communication patterns;
- results of mental status or diagnostic history.

It is through this initial contact and data gathering process that the counselor is challenged to use his or her personal talents through the application of appropriate interpersonal skills. The interviewer must demonstrate skills that promote the understanding of self and others in an attempt to gather relevant data about the client and his or her concerns. The following skills are extremely helpful in gathering background history and relevant intake data and in promoting understanding of the client.

Basic Helping Skills

The following is a list of some of the basic helping skills used in the gathering of background history and relevant intake data, as well as in the promoting of client self-understanding.

Attending. Attending involves the therapist's becoming aware of the client's communication through undistracted attentiveness to the client. Attending helps the client feel listened to and understood.

Listening. Listening implies a passive act of taking in the content of the helper's communication, but it actually involves a very active process of responding to total messages. Listening skills are basic to all interviewing, whether the purpose be gaining information, conducting structured in-depth interviews, or informal helping (Brammer & MacDonald, 1996). The following are four areas of listening responses: clarification, paraphrasing, reflecting, and summarization. These listening responses are described in further detail below.

Clarification. Clarification is the method of bringing vague material into sharper focus. Clarification is used when the therapist cannot make sense out of the client's responses. Clarification requests should result in the therapist obtaining clearer statements from the client.

Paraphrasing. Paraphrasing is the method of restating the client's basic message in a similar manner, but usually with fewer words. The main purpose of paraphrasing is for therapists to test their own understanding of what the client has said (Brammer & MacDonald, 1996).

Reflecting. Reflecting is a method of expressing to a client that the therapist is located within the client's frame of reference, and that he or she understands the client's deep concerns. There are three areas of reflection: reflection of feeling, reflection of experience, and reflection of content (Brammer & MacDonald, 1996).

Summarization. Summarization is a skill that helps to indicate the therapist's understanding of the client's statements. Summarization indicates that attention has been paid to what the client says (content), how those statements are said (feeling), and the purpose, timing, and effect of those statements (process). Summarization gives the client a feeling of movement in exploring ideas and feelings, as well as an awareness of progress in learning and problem solving (Brammer & MacDonald, 1996).

These areas of listening responses are further illustrated in Figure 4.1. In addition to a summary of their definitions and goals, the figure provides examples of effective behavior and phrasing used by the therapist to employ these skills.

BASIC LISTENING RESPONSES

Skill	Definition	Example	Goal
Clarification	A question often used after an ambiguous client message	A question beginning with: "Do you mean that? Are you saying that?" Plus a rephrasing of the client's message (Cormier & Cormier, 1998)	To help the client elaborate and to check out the accuracy of what you heard
Paraphrasing	A method of expressing the client's essential feelings, experience, and content	Cl: I really enjoy his company; he is intelligent, witty and kind Co: You like him a lot. Cl: I really do.	To help the client feel understood and to clarify perceptions of what he or she said.
Reflecting	A method of expressing the client's essential feelings, experience, and content	*Reflection of Feeling* Co: You feel angry that he avoids you. *Reflection of Experience* Co: You say you are relaxed but every time we talk about school, you clinch your fists. *Reflection of Content* Cl: Mom's constant criticism upsets me. Co: It really hurts.	To bring vaguely expressed feeling into focus. Descriptive feedback implying nonverbal body language. To clarify client's ideas, which he/she is expressing with difficulty
Summarization	The process of attending to what the helper says (*content*), how it is said (*feeling*), and the purpose timing, and effect of the statements (*process*) (Brammer & McDonald, 1996, p. 105)	Co: From your talk about your wife and your relationship with your kids, you appear to have experienced feelings of having let them down.	To help the client see a common theme, which helps the client review progress. To put together key ideas and feelings

FIGURE 4.1. Examples of the goals and effective behaviors associated with the basic listening responses.

Asking Appropriate Questions

In addition to these basic helping skills, questioning is one of the most useful ways of understanding and helping the client, particularly when used in conjunction with the basic helping skills. Like all other counseling skills, effective questioning requires the counselor to be sensitive to the client's emotional state, to demonstrate proper timing of questions, and to contain the questioning in an attempt to control the flow of information from the client. Questioning enables the counselor to gather information and to deepen the level of discussion with the client or to broaden its focus.

Two types of appropriate questions are the *open question* and the *closed question*. The two methods are designed to elicit different data. Open questions encourage clients to share information and to talk freely. They serve to help clients describe how they think, feel, and act. Open questions are questions that cannot be answered with a "yes" or "no" response. Many open questions begin with words such as *who, what, when, where, how,* and *why.* For example:

- How did you get our number?
- When did you first start feeling depressed?
- What motivated you to make an appointment?
- Where are you currently working?
- How long have you been having family problems?

Closed questions are questions that can be answered with a simple "yes" or "no" response. Closed questions are generally easier to ask and can serve to help pinpoint information and bring closure. For example:

- Do you have a home phone?
- Are you currently going to school?
- Have you ever been to counseling before?
- Does anyone know about your concern?
- Is there a history of depression in your family?

A note of caution regarding the use of closed questions: The use of closed questions exclusively creates a notion in the client that you will ask questions and the client can merely respond in a yes or no fashion. Generally, the use of both open and closed questions is helpful. Combining open and closed questions can be used to gather data in one area before moving on to another topic.

Assessment in Counseling

The process of assessment centers on gathering information from the client for the purpose of identifying the problem or problems that the client brings to the counseling session. The results of assessment activities enable the counselor to integrate the information they have gathered into the treatment planning process. It should be noted that assessment activities are primarily for the benefit of the client, enabling him or her to come to an understanding of his or her problems and to cope with real-life concerns.

Assessment activities in counseling can take many forms. Regardless of the approach taken by the counselor, assessment needs to be viewed as an ongoing, continuous process that begins with the initial intake and culminates with the termination of counseling. All too often, the counselor learns that the presenting problem is only the tip of the iceberg and that new or more urgent needs arise during the therapy process. Viewing assessment as a continuous process enables the counselor to modify and adjust treatment plans, therapeutic goals, and intervention strategies as needed.

According to Juhnke (1995) continuous assessment includes qualitative, behavioral, and client record-reviewing activities. Qualitative assessment activities can include role playing, simulations, and games. These methods are employed for the purpose of gathering additional data from the client. The use of qualitative methods in session provides for the processing of information and feedback to the client. Behavioral assessment examines the overt behavior of the client. According to Galassi and Perot (1992), behavioral assessment emphasizes the identification of antecedents to problem behaviors and consequences that reduce their frequency or eliminate them. Indirect methods of behavior assessment might include talking to significant others about the client's issues and problems. Direct behavioral methods involve observing the client, administering behavioral checklists, and having the client self-monitor his or her behavior. A review of the client's records affords the counselor the opportunity to examine possible patterns of behavior. Likewise, it can provide the counselor with a history of past therapy experiences of the client, as well as an understanding of the client's history in light of the client's presenting concerns.

Assessment is not restricted to the use of objective, standardized, quantifiable procedures; rather, it includes interviewing, behavioral observation, and other qualitative methods. A helpful resource in understanding assessment and assessment interviewing is provided by Howatt (2000), who suggested that a number of goals need to be kept in mind when conducting an assessment interview. These goals include:

1. to gather consistent and comprehensive information;
2. to identify and define a person's major strengths;
3. to identify the problem(s) that bring the client to counseling;
4. to introduce a degree of order by prioritizing problems;
5. to teach the inadequacy of a quick fix to problems;
6. to clarify diagnostic uncertainty;
7. to measure cognitive functioning;
8. to differentiate treatment assignments;
9. to develop rapport and create a healthy working environment; and
10. to focus on the therapeutic interventions.

In a similar fashion, Patterson and Welfel (2000) discussed five components to the data-gathering and hypothesis-testing process of assessment. The following is a summary of those components (Patterson & Welfel, pp. 121–123):

1. **Understanding of the boundaries of the problem.** Both the counselor and the client need to recognize the scope and limits of the difficulty the client is experiencing. It is important to know the problem boundaries in current functioning as well as the history and duration of the problem.

2. **Mutual understanding of the patterns and intensity of the problem.** Recognition on the part of the counselor and client that problems are not expressed at a uniform level all the time helps the client realize that understanding the pattern of the problem makes its causation clearer. Understanding the intensity of the problem helps the client to get a clearer sense of the dimensions of feelings and associated behavior.

3. **Understanding of the degree to which the presenting problem influences functioning in other parts of the client's life.** The aim is to learn how circumscribed or diffuse the difficulty is and to clarify the degree to which it is compromising other unrelated parts of the client's experience.

4. **Examination of the ways of solving the client's problem that he or she has already tried before entering counseling.** This process aids understanding of the impact of the problem's history on the current status of the problem. It is also helpful in the selection of strategies for change.

5. **Understanding of the strengths and coping skills of the client.** This process helps in keeping a balanced perspective of the problem and aids in the client's realization that he or she has the resources to bring about the resolution of problems.

Thorough assessment of the problem or problems that the client brings to therapy helps both the counselor and client to understand the boundaries, patterns, and intensity of those problems in the client's life.

■ Diagnosis in Counseling

The use of diagnosis by counselors has been a controversial issue in the training of counselors (Denton, 1990; Gladding, 1992). The controversy stems from the belief that in the counseling profession, counselors should follow the developmental model of treating clients with developmental concerns and should leave more severe cases to other trained professionals. In addition, it is felt that the use of diagnosis contradicts some of the more accepted models of counseling (i.e., client-centered, humanistic, etc.). However, it remains a fact that practicing counselors in schools, agencies, and mental health facilities are routinely asked to diagnose and treat clients who have severe mental health issues. This is especially true for counselors in private practice, who are routinely confronted with a managed care environment that requires the use of diagnosis for treatment consideration as well as for insurance coverage. In reality, this is nothing new. Every time a counselor treats a client, he or she is making a diagnosis when choosing and implementing therapeutic interventions. Whether it is through the use of the *Diagnostic and Statistical Manual IV* (DSM-IV; American Psychiatric Association, 1994), the highly formulized diagnostic system, or some other system, diagnosis is a reality for trained counselors.

In a similar fashion, counselors are frequently asked to participate in collaborative mental health service teams that work together in planning, coordinating, evaluating, and providing direct service to clients. Geroski and Rodgers (1997) suggested that because school counselors interact with a large number of children and adolescents on a daily basis, they are uniquely able to identify students who manifest particularly worrisome behaviors possibly consistent with significant mental health issues. The counselor is able to provide direct interventions and support services for some of these students (Geroski & Rodgers, 1997, p. 231).

However, many school counselors lack training in the formal use of the DSM-IV. Hohenshil (1996) observed that it is rapidly becoming a necessity for all counselors to be skilled in the language of the DSM-IV, regardless of their employment setting. Thus, in order to become a viable member of a collaborative mental health system, the counselor must at the very least become familiar with the language of the DSM-IV. Familiarity with the language of the DSM-IV is not, in any sense, a substitute for formal training in its use. However, a rudimentary knowledge of the DSM-IV can assist the counselor in student referral and collaborative mental health services.

Hohenshil (1996), in an editorial entitled "Role of Assessment and Diagnosis in Counseling," discussed the usefulness of diagnostic information and the reasons why counselors should diagnose. Hohenshil suggested that diagnosis is not a static process that occurs at a fixed point in time, but that testing, assessment and diagnosis are intertwined throughout the stages of the counseling process. The following is a summary of Hohenshil stages:

1. **Referral:** The collection of data begins at this stage and counselors begin to hypothesize about possible diagnosis. Referral information often consists of self-reports and reports from educational, medical, and social records.

2. **Symptom Identification:** Symptom information is obtained through the use of diagnostic interviews, problem checklists, mental status examinations, and behavioral observations and testing.

3. **Diagnosis:** The process of comparing the client's symptoms to the diagnostic criteria of some classification system. The DSM-IV classification system is the most widely used system of classification for counselors in agency and mental health systems.

4. **Treatment Planning:** This process requires accurate diagnosis because intervention techniques correspond to particular developmental problems or mental disorders. Treatment planning normally includes the description of the behavior, treatment objectives and interventions, and the client's prognosis.

5. **Treatment:** The treatment of the client follows the outline in the overall treatment plan. The use of assessment data is important in determining when treatment termination is in order.

6. **Follow-Up:** Follow-up of the client is essential to determine if symptoms are in remission or if additional counseling is necessary for the client.

Diagnostic Classification System

Information on the DSM-IV is included here to provide an overview of this classification and coding system. We believe that school, agency, and mental health counselors must become familiar with the DSM-IV. Obviously, knowledge of the classification and coding is *not* a substitute for formal training in the use of the DSM-IV. Rather, the information is included in this text as a resource and reference to the classification system.

The DSM-IV employs five axes to record biological, social, and psychological assessment of the client. The first three axes are for the recording of mental and physical diagnoses; the others enable the counselor to note environmental problems and to provide an assessment of the client's functioning over the course of the previous year. Following are descriptions of the five axes employed in the DSM-IV:

Axis I	Includes every mental diagnosis with the exception of personality disorders and mental illness
Axis II	Personality disorders and mental retardation
Axis III	General medical conditions
Axis IV	Psychosocial and environmental problems
Axis V	Global assessment of functioning BF (a 100-point scale reflecting the patient's current overall occupational, social, and psychological functioning)

Severity and Course Modifiers

Following is a list of the severity and course modifiers employed in the DSM-IV:

Mild	The patient has few symptoms other than those that meet the minimum criteria for diagnosis.
Moderate	The patient experiences intermediate symptomatology between mild and severe.
Severe	The patient has many more symptoms than the minimum criteria for diagnosis or some symptoms are especially severe.
In partial remission	The patient previously met the full criteria for diagnosis but now the symptoms are too few to fulfill the criteria.
In full remission	The patient is considered symptom free.

The use of the multiaxial system facilitates comprehensive and systematic evaluation with attention to the various mental disorders and general medical conditions, psychosocial and environmental problems, and level of functioning that might be overlooked if the focus were on assessing a single presenting problem. The use of a multiaxial system provides a convenient format for organizing and communicating clinical information, for capturing the complexity of the clinical situations, and for describing the heterogeneity of individuals presenting with the same diagnosis (American Psychiatric Association, 1999).

DSM-IV Codes and Classification

The following codes are intended to be used in conjunction with the text descriptions for each disorder found in the DSM-IV of the American Psychiatric Association:

- NOS = Not Otherwise Specified.
- An "X" appearing in a diagnostic code indicates that a specific code number is required.
- An ellipsis (. . .) is used in the names of certain disorders to indicate that the name of a specific mental disorder or general medical condition should be inserted when recording the name (e.g., 293.0 Delirium Due to Hypothyroidism).
- Numbers in parentheses are page numbers.
- If criteria are currently met, one of the following severity specifiers may be noted after the diagnosis: mild, moderate, or severe.
- If criteria are no longer met, one of the following specifiers may be noted: in partial remission, in full remission, or prior history.

Disorders Usually First Diagnosed in Infancy, Childhood, or Adolescence (37)

MENTAL RETARDATION (39)
Note: These disorders are coded on Axis II.
317   Mild Mental Retardation (41)
318.0   Moderate Mental Retardation (41)
318.1   Severe Mental Retardation (41)
318.2   Profound Mental Retardation (41)
319   Mental Retardation, Severity Unspecified (42)

LEARNING DISORDERS (46)
315.00   Reading Disorder (48)
315.1   Mathematics Disorder (50)
315.2   Disorder of Written Expression (51)
315.9   Learning Disorder NOS (53)

MOTOR SKILLS DISORDER
315.4   Developmental Coordination Disorder (53)

COMMUNICATION DISORDERS (55)
315.31   Expressive Language Disorder (55)
315.32   Mixed Receptive-Expressive Language Disorder (58)
315.39   Phonological Disorder (61)
307.0   Stuttering (63)
307.9   Communication Disorder NOS (65)

PERVASIVE DEVELOPMENTAL DISORDERS (65)
299.00   Autistic Disorder (66)
299.80   Rett's Disorder (71)
299.10   Childhood Disintegrative Disorder (73)
299.80   Asperger's Disorder (75)
299.80   Pervasive Developmental Disorder NOS (77)

ATTENTION-DEFICIT AND DISRUPTIVE BEHAVIOR DISORDERS (78)
314.xx   Attention-Deficit/Hyperactivity Disorder (78)
   .01   Combined Type
   .00   Predominantly Inattentive Type
   .01   Predominantly Hyperactive-Impulsive Type
314.9   Attention-Deficit/Hyperactivity Disorder NOS (85)
312.xx   Conduct Disorder (85)
   .81   Childhood-Onset Type
   .82   Adolescent-Onset Type
   .89   Unspecified Onset
313.81   Oppositional Defiant Disorder (91)
312.9   Disruptive Behavior Disorder NOS (94)

FEEDING AND EATING DISORDERS OF INFANCY OR EARLY CHILDHOOD (94)
307.52   Pica (95)
307.53   Rumination Disorder (96)
307.59   Feeding Disorder of Infancy or Early Childhood (98)

TIC DISORDERS (100)
307.23   Tourette's Disorder (101)
307.22   Chronic Motor or Vocal Tic Disorder (103)
307.21   Transient Tic Disorder (104)
            Specify if: Single Episode/Recurrent
307.20   Tic Disorder NOS (105)

ELIMINATION DISORDERS (106)
_____   Encopresis (106)
787.6   With Constipation and Overflow Incontinence
307.7   Without Constipation and Overflow Incontinence
307.6   Enuresis (Not Due to a General Medical Condition) (108)
            Specify type: Nocturnal Only/Diurnal Only/Nocturnal and Diurnal

OTHER DISORDERS OF INFANCY, CHILDHOOD, OR ADOLESCENCE
309.21   Separation Anxiety Disorder (110)
            Specify if: Early Onset
313.23   Selective Mutism (114)
313.89   Reactive Attachment Disorder of Infancy or Early Childhood (116)
            Specify type: Inhibited Type/Disinhibited Type
307.3   Stereotypic Movement Disorder (118)
            Specify if: With Self-Injurious Behavior
313.9   Disorder of Infancy, Childhood or Adolescence NOS (121)

Delirium, Dementia, and Amnestic and Other Cognitive Disorders (123)

DELIRIUM (124)
293.0   Delirium Due to . . . [Indicate the General Medical Condition] (127)
_____   Substance Intoxication Delirium (*refer to Substance-Related Disorders for substance-specific codes*) (129)
_____   Substance Withdrawal Delirium (*refer to Substance-Related Disorders for substance-specific codes*) (129)
_____   Delirium Due to Multiple Biologies (*code each of the specific etiologies*) (132)
780.09   Delirium NOS (133)

DEMENTIA (133)
290.xx   Dementia of the Alzheimer's Type, With Early Onset (*also code 331.0 Alzheimer's disease on Axis III*) (139)
   .10   Uncomplicated
   .11   With Delirium
   .12   With Delusions
   .13   With Depressed Mood
            Specify if: With Behavioral Disturbance
290.xx   Dementia of the Alzheimer's Type, With Late Onset (*also code 331.0 Alzheimer's disease on Axis III*) (139)

.0   Uncomplicated
.3   With Delirium
.20   With Delusions
.21   With Depressed Mood
     Specify if: With Behavioral Disturbance
290.xx   Vascular Dementia (143)
.40   Uncomplicated
.41   With Delirium
.42   With Delusions
.43   With Depressed Mood
     Specify if: With Behavior Disturbance
294.9   Dementia Due to HIV Disease (*also code 043.1 HIV infection affecting central nervous system on Axis III*) (148)
294.1   Dementia Due to Head Trauma (*also code 854.00 head injury on Axis III*) (148)
294.1   Dementia Due to Parkinson's Disease (*also code 332.0 Parkinson's on Axis III*) (148)
294.1   Dementia Due to Huntington's Disease (*also code 333.4 Huntington's disease on Axis III*) (149)
290.10   Dementia Due to Pick's Disease (*also code 331.1 Pick's disease on Axis III*) (149)
290.10   Dementia Due to Greutzfeldt-Jakob Disease (*also code 046.1 Greutzfeldt-Jakob disease on Axis III*) (150)
294.1   Dementia Due to . . . *[Indicate the General Medical Condition not listed above (also code the general medical condition on Axis III)]* (151)
_____   Substance-Induced Persisting Dementia (*refer to Substance-Related Disorders for substance-specific codes*) (152)
_____   Dementia Due to Multiple Etiologies (*code each of the specific etiologies*) (154)
294.8   Dementia NOS (155)

AMNESTIC DISORDERS (156)
294.0   Amnestic Disorder Due to . . . *[Indicate the General Medical Condition]* (158)
     Specify if: Transient/Chronic
_____   Substance-Induced Persisting Amnestic Disorder (*refer to Substance-Related Disorders for substance-specific codes*) (161)
294.8   Amnestic Disorder NOS (163)

OTHER COGNITIVE DISORDERS (163)
294.9   Cognitive Disorder NOS (163)

Mental Disorders Due to a General Medical Condition Not Elsewhere Classified (165)

293.89   Catatonic Disorder Due to . . . *[Indicate the General Medical Condition]* (169)
310.1   Personality Change Due to . . . *[Indicate the General Medical Condition]* (171)
     Specify type: Labile Type/Disinhibited Type/Aggressive Type/Apathetic Type/Paranoid Type/Other Type/Combined Type/Unspecified Type

293.9   Mental Disorder NOS Due to . . . *[Indicate the General Medical Condition]* (174)

Substance-Related Disorders (175)

[a]*The following specifiers may be applied to Substance Dependence:*
   With Physiological Dependence/Without Physiological Dependence
   Early Full Remission/Early Partial Remission
   Sustained Full Remission/Sustained Partial Remission
   On Agonist Therapy/In a Controlled Environment

The following specifiers apply to Substance-Induced Disorders as noted:
   [I]With Onset During Intoxication/[W]With Onset During Withdrawal

ALCOHOL-RELATED DISORDERS (194)
Alcohol Use Disorders
303.90   Alcohol Dependence[a] (195)
305.0   Alcohol Abuse (196)
Alcohol-Induced Disorders
303.0   Alcohol Intoxication (196)
291.81   Alcohol Withdrawal (197)
     Specify if: With Perceptual Disturbances
291.0   Alcohol Intoxication Delirium (129)
291.0   Alcohol Withdrawal Delirium (129)
291.2   Alcohol-Induced Persisting Dementia (152)
291.1   Alcohol-Induced Persisting Amnestic Disorder (161)
291.x   Alcohol-Induced Psychotic Disorder (310)
.5   With Delusions[I,W]
.3   With Hallucinations[I,W]
291.89   Alcohol-Induced Mood Disorder[I,W] (370)
291.89   Alcohol-Induced Anxiety Disorder[I,W] (439)
291.89   Alcohol-Induced Sexual Dysfunction[I] (519)
291.89   Alcohol-Induced Sleep Disorder[I,W] (601)
291.9   Alcohol-Related Disorder NOS (204)

AMPHETAMINE- (OR AMPHETAMINE-LIKE) RELATED DISORDERS (204)
Amphetamine Use Disorders
304.40   Amphetamine Dependence[a] (206)
305.70   Amphetamine Abuse (206)
Amphetamine-Induced Disorders
292.89   Amphetamine Intoxication (207)
     Specify if: With Perceptual Disturbances
292.0   Amphetamine Withdrawal (208)
292.81   Amphetamine Intoxication Delirium (129)
292.xx   Amphetamine-Induced Psychotic Disorder (310)
.11   With Delusions[I]
.12   With Hallucinations[I]
292.84   Amphetamine-Induced Mood Disorder[I,W] (370)
292.89   Amphetamine-Induced Anxiety Disorder[I] (439)
292.89   Amphetamine-Induced Sexual Dysfunction[I] (519)
292.89   Amphetamine-Induced Sleep Disorder[I,W] (601)
292.9   Amphetamine-Related Disorder NOS (211)

CAFFEINE-RELATED DISORDERS (212)

Caffeine-Induced Disorders

305.90   Caffeine Intoxication (212)
292.89   Caffeine-Induced Anxiety Disorder[I] (439)
292.89   Caffeine-Induced Sleep Disorder[I] (601)
292.9   Caffeine-Related Disorder NOS (215)

CANNABIS-RELATED DISORDERS (215)

Cannabis Use Disorders

304.30   Cannabis Dependence[a] (216)
305.20   Cannabis Abuse (217)

Cannabis-Induced Disorders

292.89   Cannabis Intoxication (217)
         Specify if: With Perceptual Disturbances
292.81   Cannabis Intoxication Delirium (129)
292.xx   Cannabis-Induced Psychotic Disorder (310)
   .11   With Delusions[I]
   .12   With Hallucinations[I]
292.89   Cannabis-Induced Anxiety Disorder[I] (439)
292.9   Cannabis-Related Disorder NOS (221)

COCAINE-RELATED DISORDERS (221)

Cocaine Use Disorders

304.20   Cocaine Dependence[a] (222)
305.60   Cocaine Abuse (223)

Cocaine-Induced Disorders

292.89   Cocaine Intoxication (223)
         Specify if: With Perceptual Disturbances
292.0   Cocaine Withdrawal (225)
292.81   Cocaine Intoxication Delirium (129)
292.xx   Cocaine-Induced Psychotic Disorder (310)
   .11   With Delusions[I]
   .12   With Hallucinations[I]
292.84   Cocaine-Induced Mood Disorder[I,W] (370)
292.89   Cocaine-Induced Sexual Dysfunction[I] (519)
292.89   Cocaine-Induced Sleep Disorder[I,W] (601)
292.9   Cocaine-Related Disorder NOS (229)

HALLUCINOGEN-RELATED DISORDERS (229)

Hallucinogen Use Disorders

304.50   Hallucinogen Dependence[a] (230)
305.30   Hallucinogen Abuse (231)

Hallucinogen-Induced Disorders

292.89   Hallucinogen Intoxication (232)
292.89   Hallucinogen Persisting Perception
         Disorder (Flashbacks) (233)
292.81   Hallucinogen Intoxication Delirium (129)
292.xx   Hallucinogen-Induced Psychotic Disorder (310)
   .11   With Delusions[I]
   .12   With Hallucinations[I]
292.84   Hallucinogen-Induced Mood Disorder[I] (370)
292.89   Hallucinogen-Induced Anxiety Disorder[I] (439)
292.9   Hallucinogen-Related Disorder NOS (236)

INHALANT-RELATED DISORDERS (236)

Inhalant Use Disorders

304.60   Inhalant Dependence[a] (238)
305.90   Inhalant Abuse (238)

Inhalant-Induced Disorders

292.89   Inhalant Intoxication (239)

292.81   Inhalant Intoxication Delirium (129)
292.82   Inhalant-Induced Persisting Dementia (152)
292.xx   Inhalant-Induced Psychotic Disorder (310)
   .11   With Delusions[I]
   .12   With Hallucinations[I]
292.84   Inhalant-Induced Mood Disorder[I] (370)
292.89   Inhalant-Induced Anxiety Disorder[I] (439)
292.9   Inhalant-Related Disorder NOS (242)

NICOTINE-RELATED DISORDERS (242)

Nicotine Use Disorder

305.10   Nicotine Dependence[a] (243)

Nicotine-Induced Disorder

292.0   Nicotine Withdrawal (244)
292.9   Nicotine-Related Disorder NOS (247)

OPIOID-RELATED DISORDERS (247)

Opioid Use Disorders

304.00   Opioid Dependence[a](248)
305.50   Opioid Abuse (249)

Opioid-Induced Disorders

292.89   Opioid Intoxication (249)
         Specify if: With Perceptual Disturbances
292.0   Opioid Withdrawal (250)
292.81   Opioid Intoxication Delirium (129)
292.xx   Opioid-Induced Psychotic Disorder (310)
   .11   With Delusions[I]
   .12   With Hallucinations[I]
292.84   Opioid-Induced Mood Disorder[I] (370)
292.89   Opioid-Induced Sexual Dysfunction[I] (519)
292.89   Opioid-Induced Sleep Disorder[I,W] (601)
292.9   Opioid-Related Disorder NOS (255)

PHENCYCLIDINE-
(OR PHENCYCLIDINE-LIKE)
RELATED DISORDERS (255)

Phencyclidine Use Disorders

304.60   Phencyclidine Dependence[a]
305.90   Phencyclidine Abuse (257)

Phencyclidine-Induced Disorders

292.89   Phencyclidine Intoxication (257)
         Specify if: With Perceptual
         Disturbances
292.81   Phencyclidine Intoxication Delirium (129)
292.xx   Phencyclidine-Induced Psychotic Disorder (310)
   .11   With Delusions[I]
   .12   With Hallucinations[I]
292.89   Phencyclidine-Induced Mood Disorder[I] (370)
292.89   Phencyclidine-Induced Anxiety Disorder[I]
         (439)
292.9   Phencyclidine-Related Disorder NOS (261)

SEDATIVE-, HYPNOTIC-, OR ANXIOLYTIC-
RELATED DISORDERS (261)

Sedative-, Hypnotic-, or Anxiolytic-Use Disorders

304.10   Sedative, Hypnotic, or Anxiolytic Depen-
         dence[a] (262)
305.40   Sedative, Hypnotic, or Anxiolytic Abuse
         (263)

Sedative-, Hypnotic-, or Anxiolytic-Induced Disorders

292.89 Sedative, Hypnotic, or Anxiolytic Intoxication (263)

292.0 Sedative, Hypnotic, or Anxiolytic Withdrawal (264)
  Specify if: With Perceptual Disturbances

292.81 Sedative, Hypnotic, or Anxiolytic Intoxication Delirium (129)

292.81 Sedative, Hypnotic, or Anxiolytic Withdrawal Delirium (129)

292.82 Sedative-, Hypnotic-, or Anxiolytic-Induced Persisting Dementia (152)

292.83 Sedative-, Hypnotic-, or Anxiolytic-Induced Persisting Amnestic Disorder (161)

292.xx Sedative-, Hypnotic-, or Anxiolytic-Induced Psychotic Disorder (310)
  .11 With Delusions[I,W]
  .12 With Hallucinations[I,W]

292.84 Sedative-, Hypnotic-, or Anxiolytic-Induced Mood Disorder[I,W] (370)

292.89 Sedative-, Hypnotic-, or Anxiolytic-Induced Anxiety Disorder[W] (439)

292.89 Sedative-, Hypnotic-, or Anxiolytic-Induced Sexual Dysfunction[I] (519)

292.89 Sedative-, Hypnotic-, or Anxiolytic-Induced Sleep Disorder[I,W] (601)

292.9 Sedative-, Hypnotic-, or Anxiolytic-Related Disorder NOS (269)

POLYSUBSTANCE-RELATED DISORDER

304.80 Polysubstance Dependence[a] (270)

OTHER (OR UNKNOWN) SUBSTANCE-RELATED DISORDERS (270)

Other (or Unknown) Substance Use Disorders

304.90 Other (or Unknown) Substance Dependence[a] (176)

305.90 Other (or Unknown) Substance Abuse (182)

Other (or Unknown) Substance-Induced Disorders

292.89 Other (or Unknown) Substance Intoxication (183)
  Specify if: With Perceptual Disturbances

292.0 Other (or Unknown) Substance Witdrawal (184)
  Specify if: With Perceptual Disturbances

292.81 Other (or Unknown) Substance-Induced Delirium (129)

292.82 Other (or Unknown) Substance-Induced Persisting Dementia (152)

292.83 Other (or Unknown) Substance-Induced Persisting Amnestic Disorder (161)

292.xx Other (or Unknown) Substance-Induced Psychotic Disorder (310)
  .11 With Delusions[I,W]
  .12 With Hallucinations[I,W]

292.84 Other (or Unknown) Substance-Induced Mood Disorder[I,W] (370)

292.89 Other (or Unknown) Substance-Induced Anxiety Disorder[I,W] (439)

292.89 Other (or Unknown) Substance-Induced Sexual Dysfunction[I] (519)

292.89 Other (or Unknown) Substance-Induced Sleep Disorder[I,W] (601)

292.9 Other (or Unknown) Substance-Related Disorder NOS (272)

Schizophrenia and Other Psychotic Disorders (273)

295.xx Schizophrenia (274)
The following Classification of Longitudinal Course applies to all subtypes of Schizophrenia:
  Episodic with Interepisode Residual Symptoms
    Specify if: Episodic with Prominent Negative Symptoms/Episodic with No Interepisode Residual Symptoms
  Continuous
    Specify if: With Prominent Negative Symptoms
  Single Episode in Partial Remission
    Specify if: With Prominent Negative Symptoms/Single Episode in Full Remission
  Other or Unspecified Pattern
  .30 Paranoid Type (287)
  .10 Disorganized Type (287)
  .20 Catatonic Type (288)
  .90 Undifferentiated Type (289)
  .60 Residual Type (289)

295.40 Schizophreniform Disorder (290)
  Specify if: Without Good Prognostic Features/With Good Prognostic Features

295.70 Schizoaffective Disorder (292)
  Specify type: Bipolar Type/DepressiveType

297.1 Delusional Disorder (296)
  Specify type: Erotomanic Type/Grandiose Type/Jealous Type/Persecutory Type/Somatic Type/Mixed Type/Unspecified Type

298.8 Brief Psychotic Disorder (302)
  Specify if: With Marked Stressor(s)/ Without Marked Stressor(s)/With Postpartum Onset

297.3 Shared Psychotic Disorder (305)

293.xx Psychotic Disorder Due to [*Indicate the General Medical Condition*] (306)
  .81 With Delusions
  .82 With Hallucinations
  ____ Substance-Induced Psychotic Disorder (*refer to Substance-Related Disorders for substance-specific codes*) (310)
    Specify if: With Onset During Intoxication/With Onset During Withdrawal

298.9 Psychotic Disorder NOS (315)

Mood Disorders (317)

Code current state of Major Depressive Disorder or Bipolar 1 Disorder in fifth digit:
  1 = Mild
  2 = Moderate
  3 = Severe Without Psychotic Features

4 = Severe With Psychotic Features
    Specify: Mood-Congruent Psychotic Features/Mood-Incongruent Psychotic Features
5 = In Partial Remission
6 = In Full Remission
0 = Unspecified

The following specifiers apply (for current or most recent episode) to Mood Disorders as noted:
    [a]Severity/Psychotic/Remission Specifiers/[b]Chronic/[c]With Catatonic Features/[d]With Melancholic Features/[e]With Atypical Features/[f]With Postpartum Onset

The following specifiers apply to Mood Disorders as noted:
    [g]With or Without Full Interepisode Recovery/[h]With Seasonal Pattern/[i]With Rapid Cycling

DEPRESSIVE DISORDERS

296.xx	Major Depressive Disorder (339)	
.2x	Single Episode[a,b,c,d,e]	
.3x	Recurrent[a,b,c,d,e,f,g,h]	
300.4	Dysthymic Disorder (345)	

    Specify if: Early Onset/Late Onset
    Specify: With Atypical Features
311   Depressive Disorder NOS (350)

BIPOLAR DISORDERS

296.xx   Bipolar I Disorder
  .0x   Single Manic Episode[a,e,f]
    Specify if: Mixed
  .40   Most Recent Episode Hypomanic[g,h,i]
  .4x   Most Recent Episode Manic[a,c,f,g,h,i]
  .6x   Most Recent Episode Mixed[a,c,f,g,h,i]
  .5x   Most Recent Episode Depressed[a,b,c,d,e,f,g,h,i]
  .7   Most Recent Episode Unspecified[g,h,i]
296.89   Bipolar II Disorder[a,b,c,d,e,f,g,h,i]
    Specify (current or most recent episode): Hypomanic/Depressed
301.13   Cyclothymic Disorder (363)
296.80   Bipolar Disorder NOS (366)

293.83   Mood Disorder Due to . . . *[Indicate the General Medical Condition]* (366)
    Specify type: With Depressive Features/With Major Depressive-Like Episode/With Manic Features/With Mixed Features
_____   Substance-Induced Mood Disorder *(refer to Substance-Related Disorders for substance-specific codes)* (370)
    Specify type: With Depressive Features/With Manic Features/With Mixed Features
    Specify if: With Onset During Intoxication/With Onset During Withdrawal
296.90   Mood Disorder NOS (375)

Anxiety Disorders (393)

300.01   Panic Disorder Without Agoraphobia (397)
300.21   Panic Disorder With Agoraphobia (397)
300.22   Agoraphobia Without History of Panic Disorder (403)
300.29   Specific Phobia (405)
    Specify type: Animal Type/Natural Environment Type/Blood-Injection-Injury Type/Situational Type/Other Type
300.23   Social Phobia (411)
    Specify if: Generalized
300.3   Obsessive-Compulsive Disorder (417)
    Specify if: With Poor Insight
309.81   Posttraumatic Stress Disorder (424)
    Specify if: Acute/Chronic
    Specify if: With Delayed Onset
308.3   Acute Stress Disorder (429)
300.02   Generalized Anxiety Disorder (432)
293.84   Anxiety Disorder Due to . . . *[Indicate the General Medical Condition]* (436)
    Specify if: With Generalized Anxiety/With Panic Attacks/With Obsessive-Compulsive Symptoms
_____   Substance-Induced Anxiety Disorder *(refer to Substance Related Disorders for substance-specific codes)* (439)
    Specify if: With Generalized Anxiety/With Panic Attacks/With Obsessive-Compulsive Symptoms/With Phobic Symptoms
    Specify if: With Onset During Intoxication/With Onset During Withdrawal
300.0   Anxiety Disorder NOS (444)

Somatoform Disorders (445)

300.81   Somatization Disorder (446)
300.82   Undifferentiated Somatoform Disorder (450)
300.11   Conversion Disorder (452)
    Specify type: With Motor Symptom or Deficit/With Sensory Symptom or Deficit/With Seizures or Convulsions/With Mixed Presentation
307.xx   Pain Disorder (458)
  .80   Associated With Psychological Factors
  .89   Associated With Both Psychological Factors and a General Medical Condition.
    Specify if: Acute/Chronic
300.7   Hypochrondriasis (462)
    Specify if: With Poor Insight
300.7   Body Dysmorphic Disorder (466)
300.82   Somatoform Disorder NOS (468)

Factitious Disorders (471)

300.xx   Factitious Disorder (471)
  .16   With Predominantly Psychological Signs and Symptoms
  .19   With Predominantly Physical Signs and Symptoms

.19   With Combined Psychological and
        Physical Signs and Symptoms
300.19 Factitious Disorder NOS (475)

Dissociative Disorders (477)

300.12 Dissociative Amnesia (478)
300.13 Dissociative Fugue (481)
300.14 Dissociative Identity Disorder (484)
300.6   Depersonalization Disorder (488)
300.15 Dissociative Disorder NOS (490)

Sexual and Gender Identity Disorders (493)

SEXUAL DYSFUNCTIONS (493)
The following specifiers apply to all primary Sexual Dysfunctions:
    Lifelong Type/Acquired Type
    Generalized Type/Situational Type
    Due to Psychological Factors/Due to Combined Factors

Sexual Desire Disorders
302.71 Hypoactive Sexual Desire Disorder (496)
302.79 Sexual Aversion Disorder (499)

Sexual Arousal Disorders
302.72 Female Sexual Arousal Disorder (500)
302.72 Male Erectile Disorder (502)

Orgasmic Disorders
302.73 Female Orgasmic Disorder (505)
302.74 Male Orgasmic Disorder (507)
302.75 Premature Ejaculation (509)

Sexual Pain Disorders
302.76 Dyspareunia (Not Due to a General
        Medical Condition) (511)
306.51 Vaginismus (Not Due to a General Medical
        Condition) (513)

Sexual Dysfunction Due to a General Medical Condition (515)

625.8   Female Hypoactive Sexual Desire Disorder Due
        to . . . *[Indicate the General Medical Condition]*
        (515)
608.89 Male Hypoactive Sexual Desire Disorder Due
        to . . . *[Indicate the General Medical Condition]*
        (515)
607.84 Male Erectile Disorder Due to . . . *[Indicate
        the General Medical Condition]* (515)
625.0   Female Dyspareunia Due to . . . *[Indicate
        the General Medical Condition]* (515)
608.89 Male Dyspareunia Due to . . . *[Indicate the
        General Medical Condition]* (515)
625.8   Other Female Sexual Dysfunction Due
        to . . . *[Indicate the General Medical Condition]* (515)
608.89 Other Male Sexual Dysfunction Due
        to . . . *[Indicate the General Medical Condition]* (515)

_____ Substance-Induced Sexual Dysfunction
        *(refer to Substance-Related Disorders for
        substance-specific codes)* (519)
            Specify if: With Impaired Desire/With
            Impaired Arousal/With Impaired
            Orgasm/With Sexual Pain
            Specify if: With Onset During Intoxication
302.70 Sexual Dysfunction NOS (522)

PARAPHILIAS (522)
302.4   Exhibitionism (525)
302.80 Fetishism (526)
302.89 Frotteurism (527)
302.2   Pedophilia (527)
            Specify if: Sexually Attracted to Males/
            Sexually Attracted to Females/Sexually
            Attracted to Both
            Specify if: Limited to Incest
            Specify Type: Exclusive Type/Nonexclusive
            Type
302.83 Sexual Masochism (529)
302.84 Sexual Sadism (530)
302.3   Transvestic Fetishism (530)
            Specify if: With Gender Dysphoria
302.81 Voyeurism (532)
300.7   Paraphilia NOS (532)

GENDER IDENTITY DISORDERS (532)
302.xx Gender Identity Disorder (532)
    .6   in Children
    .85   in Adolescents or Adults
            Specify if: Sexually Attracted to Males/
            Sexually Attracted to Females/Sexually
            Attracted to Both/Sexually attracted to
            Neither
302.6   Gender Identity Disorder NOS (538)
302.9   Sexual Disorder NOS (538)

Eating Disorders (551)

307.1   Anorexia Nervosa (539)
            Specify type: Restricting Type/ Binge
            Eating-Purging Type
307.51 Bulimia Nervosa (545)
            Specify type: Purging Type/ Nonpurging
            Type
307.50 Eating Disorder NOS (550)

Sleep Disorders (551)

PRIMARY SLEEP DISORDERS (553)
Dyssomnias (553)
307.42 Primary Insomnia (553)
307.44 Primary Hypersomnia (557)
            Specify if: Recurrent
347   Narcolepsy (562)
780.59 Breathing-Related Sleep Disorder (567)
307.45 Circadian Rhythm Sleep Disorder (573)
            Specify type: Delayed Sleep Phase Type/
            Jet Lag Type/Shift Work Type/Unspecified
            Type

307.47   Dyssomnia NOS (579)

Parasomnias (579)
307.47   Nightmare Disorder (580)
307.46   Sleep Terror Disorder (583)
307.46   Sleepwalking Disorder (587)
307.47   Parasomnia NOS (592)

SLEEP DISORDERS RELATED TO ANOTHER
MENTAL DISORDER (592)
307.42   Insomnia Related to . . . *[Indicate the Axis I
         or Axis II Disorder] (592)*
307.44   Hypersomnia Related to . . . *[Indicate the
         General Medical Condition] (592)*

OTHER SLEEP DISORDERS
780.xx   Sleep Disorder Due to . . . *[Indicate the
         General Medical Condition] (597)*
   .52   Insomnia Type
   .54   Hypersomnia Type
   .59   Parasomnia Type
   .59   Mixed Type
_____   Substance-Induced Sleep Disorder *(refer to
         Substance-Related Disorders for substance-
         specific codes) (601)*
            Specify type: Insomnia Type/Hypersom-
            nia Type/Parasomnia Type/Mixed Type
            Specify if: With Onset During With-
            drawal

Impulse-Control Disorders Not Elsewhere Classified (609)

312.34   Intermittent Explosive Disorder (609)
312.32   Kleptomania (612)
312.33   Pyromania (614)
312.31   Pathological Gambling (615)
312.39   Trichotillomania (618)
312.30   Impulse-Control Disorder NOS (621)

Adjustment Disorders (623)

309.xx   Adjustment Disorder (623)
   .0   With Depressed Mood
   .24   With Anxiety

   .28   With Mixed Anxiety and Depressed Mood
   .3   With Disturbance of Conduct
   .4   With Mixed Disturbance of Emotions
          and Conduct
   .9   Unspecified
             Specify if: Acute/Chronic

Personality Disorders (629)

Note: These disorders are coded on Axis II
301.0   Paranoid Personality Disorder (634)
301.20   Schizoid Personality Disorder (638)
301.22   Schizotypal Personality Disorder (641)
301.7   Antisocial Personality Disorder (645)
301.83   Borderline Personality Disorder (650)
301.50   Histrionic Personality Disorder (655)
301.81   Narcissistic Personality Disorder (658)
301.82   Avoidant Personality Disorder (662)
301.6   Dependent Personality Disorder (665)
301.4   Obsessive-Compulsive Personality
         Disorder (669)
301.9   Personality Disorder NOS (673)

Other Conditions That May Be a Focus of Clinical Attention (675)

PSYCHOLOGICAL FACTORS AFFECTING
MEDICAL CONDITION (675)
316   . . . *[Specified Psychological Factor]*
         Affecting . . . *[Indicate the General Medical
         Condition] (675) Choose name based on
         nature of factors:*
         Mental Disorder Affecting Medical Condition
         Psychological Symptoms Affecting
         Medical Condition
         Personality Traits or Coping Style Affect-
         ing Medical Condition Maladaptive Health
         Behaviors Affecting Medical Condition
         Maladaptive Health Behaviors Affecting
         Medical Condition
         Stress-Related Physiological Response
         Affecting Medical Condition
         Other or Unspecified Psychological Factors
         Affecting Medical Condition

■ Case Conceptualization and Treatment Planning

The process of case conceptualization and treatment planning can be a daunting task for beginning counselors. Determining how to best conceptualize a case and following through with an appropriate treatment plan requires the counselor to thoughtfully consider the development of his or her own strategy. To assist in that process, we now provide a variety of methods and models of case conceptualization and treatment planning for your consideration.

Models of Case Conceptualization: The Analytical Thinking Model

One of the first models of case conceptualization is found in the literature of social work. Wilson, in a textbook entitled *Recording Guidelines for Social Workers* (1980), discusses the Analytical Thinking Model (ATM) for use by students in analyzing case situations. The following is a summary of the steps and procedures of the ATM model.

1. Mentally review everything that is known about the client up to the point of case conceptualization (i.e., intake interview, mental status, developmental history).

2. List, in outline form, 10 or 15 key factors known about the case. Sort out relevant from irrelevant data.

3. Review your list. Ask: "What feelings might my client be experiencing, knowing what I know about him or her?" For each feeling, try to determine at whom or what that feeling might be directed, why you think the client might have that feeling, and how the feeling might be manifested behaviorally.

4. Consider who the significant others are in the client's life. Choose one or two people and follow step 3 for each of them. Examine interactional patterns between these people and your client.

5. Develop a treatment plan by listing any possible case outcomes or treatment goals, regardless of whether they are realistic or unrealistic. Label each plan or outcome as either realistic or unrealistic. For each realistic goal:
   (a) State the goal.
   (b) Break the goal down into subgoals that must be achieved before the overall goal can be achieved.
   (c) State exactly what treatment techniques or interventions will be used to accomplish the goal or subgoal. Rank the treatment goals in order of priority and give an estimated time for completion of each.
   (d) Finally, write a diagnostic statement that summarizes your thoughts in steps 2 through 4. Make a heading "Treatment plan" and summarize what you came up with in step 5 (Wilson, 1980, pp 144–146).

Models of Case Conceptualization: The Stevens and Morris Model

Stevens and Morris (1995) developed a format for case conceptualization to foster the systematic collection and integration of clinical data. Their 14-step format is adapted here to provide counselors-in-training with a framework from which they can develop their own approach to case conceptualization. Each step provides the therapist with an opportunity to focus on a specific area of client behavior or history; together, these steps allow the therapist to examine the client and his or her presenting problems as a whole, thus giving a more complete conceptualization of the client's case.

1. **Background Data:** This step includes the gathering of information typically asked for in a clinical intake, including the client's age, sex, race, ethnicity, physical appearance, and marital status.

Family background, educational and employment history, medical and mental health history, drug usage, and prior treatments are areas of focus in gathering this information.

2. **Presenting Concern:** This focus area enables the therapist to consider the client's own account of each of the client's concerns as he or she views them. Such an exploration allows the therapist to help the client identify the affective, behavioral, cognitive, and interpersonal features of the problems. Examination of the parameters of the presenting concerns (prior occurrence, onset, duration, frequency, and severity) and a view of the client's expectations, stressors, and support systems also takes place during this step.

3. **Verbal Content:** In this step, the therapist focuses on identified theme(s) that have emerged. A main goal at this step is discrimination between central and peripheral data.

4. **Verbal Style:** This area of focus involves the recognition of how something is said by the client, rather than what is said. Tone of voice, volume, fluency, and so on are important indicators.

5. **Nonverbal Behavior:** Here, the counselor focuses on and recognizes the relevant nonverbal behavior of the client, such as eye contact, facial expression, and postures.

6. **Client's Emotional Experience:** In this step, the counselor makes inferences about what and how the client felt in the session, based upon the counselor's own observation.

7. **Counselors Experience of the Client:** Here, the counselor explores his or her own personal reaction to the client, such as boredom, interest, or confusion. (Source: Counselor Education and Supervision, September 95, Volume 35, Issue I, p 82, 13p)

8. **Client-Counselor Interaction:** This step allows the summarization of patterns in the exchange between the counselor and client. Particularly relevant here is consideration of what the counselor and client do in relation to each other during the session; for example, Do they ask questions? Answer questions? Give advice? Receive advice?

9. **Test Data and Supporting Materials:** Here, the therapist examines all pertinent records of the client (i.e., educational, medical, psychological). A thorough assessment of the significant data and supporting materials enables the therapist to examine how such information converges or departs from other data, thus allowing more effective diagnosis and treatment planning.

10. **Diagnosis:** At this stage, the counselor gives his or her diagnostic impression using the DSM-IV multiaxial classification system.

11. **Inferences and Assumption:** The therapist develops a working model based upon observations and clinical hypotheses. A working model enables the development of a clear understanding of the client's problems and how psychological mechanisms produce those problems.

12. **Goals of Treatment:** This step involves the negotiation of short- and long-term goals of treatment between counselor and client.

13. **Intervention:** In this step, the therapist determines the most effective techniques and strategies that can be used for the attainments of the treatment goals negotiated in the previous step.

14. **Evaluation of Outcomes:** Finally, the therapist establishes criteria for the evaluation of outcomes of treatment. Criteria can include things such as self-report, test data, grades, or reports of others.

Models of Case Conceptualization: The "Linchpin" Model

Bergner (1998) suggested that using a "linchpin" concept would ideally culminate in the construction of an empirically grounded, comprehensive formulation for case conceptualization that would (a) organize all of the key factors of a case around one causal, explanatory source; (b) frame this source in terms of factors amenable to direct intervention; and (c) lend itself to being shared with the client to his or her considerable benefit (p. 287). According to Bergner (1998), a clinical case formulation would embody the characteristics listed below:

1. **Organize Facts Around a "Linchpin":** Clients generally tend to provide a great deal of information about themselves, often above and beyond the data initially sought by the counselor. In addition to

the presenting complaint, clients provide a wealth of information about their problem, including their emotional state, personal history, goals, expectations, and history of their concerns. However, in most cases, clients have not organized this data into a theory of their problem(s). Similarly, relevant information about such factors as personal beliefs and values, which can create problems, has been left out of their discussion. Organizing around a "linchpin" helps to organize all the information obtained, but also identifies the core state of affairs from which all the client's difficulties spring. According to Bergner (1998), a linchpin, as the metaphor implies, is what holds everything together; it is what, if removed, might cause destructive consequences to fall apart.

2. **Target Factors Amenable to Intervention:** It is essential that the counselor look at factors that are currently maintaining the client's dysfunctional state and that are directly amenable to therapeutic intervention. The focus is to target the factors that currently maintain the problem and that permit translation into therapeutic factors.

3. **Share the Data With the Client:** The case formulation shared with the client results in (a) the client organizing his or her thinking about the problem; (b) the client identifying key or central maintaining factors in his or her dysfunction, making them the focal point of change efforts; and/or (c) maximizing the client's sense of control or power over what he or she is doing, sensing, feeling. As a result, case formulation becomes a collaborative effort between the therapist and client in an attempt to work through the client's problems.

Models of Case Conceptualization: The Inverted Pyramid Method

A different approach to case conceptualization was provided by Schwitzer (1996), who discussed the Inverted Pyramid Method for client conceptualization. The purpose of this method is to identify and understand client concerns and to provide a diagram that visually guides the conceptualization process.

Step I: Problem Identification. The first step involves the exploration of the client's functioning, with emphasis on the inclusion of any potentially useful descriptive information about the client's particular difficulty.

Step II: Thematic Grouping. The second step involves the process of organizing the client's problems into intuitively logical groupings or constellations. Thematic grouping entails grouping together those of the client's problems that seem to serve similar functions or that operate in similar ways.

Step III: Theoretical Inference About Client Concerns. The third step requires that the counselor make inferences by applying selective general principles to his or her reasoning about a client's situation. Previously identified symptom constellations are refined further, as the inverted pyramid implies, allowing the counselor to progress down to deeper aspects of the client's problems. This honing-down process emphasizes a smaller number of themes that are unifying, central, explanatory, causal, or underlying in nature (Schwitzer, 1996, pp. 259–260). As a result, these themes can then be made a focus of treatment.

Step IV: Narrowed Inferences About Client Difficulties. Finally, the unifying, causal, or interpretive themes inferred from the above process are honed into existential, fundamental, or underlying questions of life and death (suicidal ideation or behavior), deep-rooted shame, or rage. This step will help the beginning counselor to apply a theoretical framework to the client's most threatening or disruptive difficulties.

Finally, Murdock (1991) is an excellent source of information on case conceptualization. Murdock presented a model that focuses on a thorough understanding of the student's counseling theory. As a first step in the process of case conceptualization, this process should be followed by integrating knowledge of the client into a clear conceptualization of the client and his/her concerns.

CASE CONCEPTUALIZATION: APPLYING THEORY TO INDIVIDUALS*

Nancy L. Murdock

A model of case conceptualization is presented that can be used with any theoretical approach to counseling. Issues surrounding the use of this model are discussed.

Over the course of training, counseling students are taught numerous counseling theories, yet little systematic attention is directed toward using these theories to understand and help individual clients. In many counseling texts students are directed to construct their own perspective in working with clients (Corsini & Wedding, 1989; Gilliland, James & Bowman, 1989; Ive & Simek-Downing, 1980; Pietofesa, Hoffman & Splete, 1984), a stance that seems to encourage a flexible eclecticism. Other writers argue for the adoption of a single theoretical perspective in counseling practice (Patterson, 1985; Russell, 1986). Regardless of which path the student takes (it is not my intent to enter this debate), it seems that the learning process prior to this choice could be enhanced by increased emphasis on applying the various theories students are taught in the course of their training.

Theoretical case conceptualization is a different process, but it also may be one of the most effective routes to complete understanding of a theoretical perspective. The process of conceptualization fosters a more thorough understanding of a theory because it requires complex types of learning (Bloom, Madaus, & Hastings, 1981). Bloom et al. identified six levels of learning. The first two, knowledge and comprehension, are routinely achieved in teaching theories of counseling. However, the higher levels of learning—application, analysis, synthesis, and evaluation—are involved in applying theory if the application process involves critical evaluation of the approach in question. Case conceptualization should engage all of these learning processes. Conceptualization also should result in an awareness of the strengths and weaknesses of a particular approach. Some clients may present problems or issues that require extension of the theory beyond the convenient examples provided in textbooks. For example, a client displaying a great deal of emotion presents a conceptual challenge for person-centered theory (Raskin & Rogers, 1989), because this theory has traditionally focused on helping clients who repress affect. Understanding the emotive client from this perspective requires more conceptual work and therefore a more complete understanding of person-centered theory.

Numerous calls have been made for counselor educators to teach the skills and processes of case conceptualization (Bernier, 1980; Borders & Leddick, 1987; Fuqua, Johnson, Anderson, & Newman, 1984; Holloway, 1988). Although various models of case conceptualization have been proposed (e.g., Biggs, 1988; Halgin, 1985; Held, 1984; Hulse & Jennings, 1984; Loganbill & Stoltenberg, 1983; Swensen, 1968), most of these do not emphasize the integrated application of a single theoretical perspective. Most efforts seem to specify categories of information that are essential to the counseling process (e.g., specific demographic information, interpersonal style, and personality dynamics; Hulse & Jennings, 1984; Loganbill & Stoltenberg, 1983), or they construct an integrative eclectic approach useful in conceptualizing cases (Halgin, 1985; Held, 1984; Swensen, 1968). Biggs (1988) discussed briefly how theory contributes to case conceptualization and detailed factors that influence the conceptualization process. Models that guide the systemic application of one theory that can be used with a wide range of theoretical approaches, however, seem scarce. This article presents a model that I find useful in teaching case conceptualization, in the supervision of practicum students, and in my own counseling practice. My primary purpose

*Reprinted from *Counselor Education and Supervision*, Vol. 30, pp. 355–365. Copyright 1991 by the American Counseling Association. Reprinted with permission. No further reproduction authorized without written permission of the American Counseling Association.

was to provide a structure that can be used with almost any well-developed theory of counseling and that will help the student through this most difficult and complex process.

Theoretical Structure

Before applying a theory, the counselor must have a solid understanding of the theory in question. The counselor needs to have some idea of where the client "should" be going and why the client has come to counseling. Linked to this theoretically based construction are the specific areas of the client's presentation that are considered most important. To give a rather simplistic example, a counselor adopting a behavioral approach that emphasizes operant learning (e.g., Kazdin, 1980) assumes that the client presents for help because of faulty learning (or the failure to learn a desired behavior). This therapist is then interested in a number of aspects of the client's life, including (a) the specific behavior to be modified, (b) the history of the behavior, (c) the type of learning that first produced the behavior, and (d) the stimuli that evoke the behavior. In contrast, psychoanalytic therapists (e.g., Arlow, 1989) would be interested in very different information because, from their theoretical base, the origins of dysfunction are found in conflicts that reside in the unconscious. Thus, psychoanalysts would be interested in issues such as (a) what the client remembers of early childhood, (b) past and current relationships with siblings and other significant persons, and (d) the client's character style as indicated by current interactions. The preceding types of issues are considered preliminary to the actual process of conceptualizing a client; they represent information that ensures the needed understanding of the theory before it is applied. Following are some questions that can be used to help counselors obtain a sufficient level of understanding prior to application:

1. **What is the core motivation of human existence?** Whether explicit or implicity, theories of counseling tend to emphasize one major theme that directs or governs individuals' lives. For example, classic psychoanalytic theory emphasizes the conflict between the various mental structures. In contrast, Gestalt theorists (Perls, Hefferline & Goodman, 1951) postulated that humans tend toward homeostasis.

2. **How is the core motivation expressed in healthy ways? What are the characteristics of a healthy personality?** Too often counselors find themselves focused on definitions of pathology. At least as important (and possibly more so) are definitions of health. Definitions of psychological health are theory linked. Cognitive theorists (e.g., Beck & Weishaar, 1989) are interested in helping the client become healthy through the elimination of faulty thought processes. According to multigenerational family theorists, (e.g., Kerr & Bowen 1988), health is defined as relatively clear differentiation from the family of origin. Thus, the counselor seeking to remain theory-consistent must recognize that the approach chosen specifies the most important characteristics that define psychological health.

   Cross-cultural and gender-role issues are important factors to consider at this point. Because many theories were developed in a restricted cultural context (i.e., Western, White, male, middle to upper socioeconomic status), definitions of health and dysfunction are products of these cultures. The degree to which these definitions apply across cultures and to women is certainly not established, although the idea that human universals exist has not been entirely disconfirmed (Draguns, 1981). Therefore, the practitioner must take great care in applying these definitions, and the degree to which the theory's definitions of health are inconsistent with the client's cultural definitions must be carefully addressed. For example, theories that advocate autonomy from one's family of origin may be in conflict with the cultural norms learned by a Japanese client (Sue & Zane, 1987). If confronted with this type of situation, the counselor must assess the impact of helping the client individuate. Deciding that individuation might do more harm than good, the counselor may simply attempt to help the client understand the effect of his or her family system. In this case, understanding of cultural norms may help the client devise ways to individuate that do not seriously conflict with important cultural rules. At times, however, the counselor may find that extension of a theory in an attempt to incorporate cultural concerns is impossible and may at this point consider adopting a theoretical structure more compatible with the client's cultural background.

3. **How does the process of development get derailed or stuck? What are the factors that contribute to psychological dysfunction?** The complement of the question of psychological health is the issue of how

individuals get "unhealthy." Theories are often better at specifying factors that lead to dysfunction than they are at describing psychological health. In considering these definitions, attention to cultural and gender-role issues is again critical. Classic psychoanalytic theory has been criticized, for example, because its definition of health for women is stereotypic, tending to support traditional roles and values. Therefore, a nontraditional female client may be judged to be dysfunctional under this system. A counselor aware of this bias could revise this definition but still remain theory-consistent by acknowledging the influence of sexual conflicts while avoiding interpretations that promote stereotypes.

4. **What stages of the client's life are considered key in the developmental process?** Theorists clearly differ on developmental factors. Some theories incorporate almost no developmental theory (e.g., rational emotive therapy, Ellis, 1989), while others stipulate that development is crucial to the presenting problem (e.g., psychoanalytic theory).

5. **Who are the critical individuals in the client's presentation? Does the theory restrict the focus to the individual, or does it extend to interactions with family and acquaintances or to multigenerational issues?** Most theories deal with social interaction in some form. Some theories conclude that internal processes are primary (e.g., cognitive theories), although they may affect relationship events. Other approaches postulate that relationships are the key to psychological functioning (i.e., interpersonal theory; Kiesler, 1983; Strong & Claiborn, 1982) and, therefore, place great emphasis on these factors in determining psychological health. Past relationships are significant for some approaches, even relationships generations removed (Kerr & Bowen, 1988).

6. **What are the relative importance of affect, cognition, and behavior in this theory?** Theories place different emphases on the roles of affect, cognition, and behavior in determining psychological life. Some approaches identify emotional factors as primary (e.g., person centered, Gestalt, and psychoanalytic), others emphasize cognitive factors (cognitive therapy and rational emotive therapy), and still others target behavior (Behavioral approaches). Regardless of the focus, the other two components are usually considered, so this postulate does not direct the counselor to ignore any of these domains. Neglect of any of these factors probably indicate a misunderstanding of the theory; rather, the point of this discussion is to understand the theoretical relationships of these components.

Gathering Information

Armed with a theoretical framework, the counselor attempting to apply theory must next understand the client as fully as possible. Two types of information are important in this process. First, the counselor will probably want general information that is not strongly linked to theory, such as demographics (age, sex, and ethnic origin), current living situation, and physical health. Although different theories might place different emphasis on this type of information, or ignore it altogether, a counselor needs to avoid misunderstandings due to cultural bias.

Second, the counselor seeks information that is theory specific as determined by his or her understanding the basic issues emphasized by the theory. The six questions that help build theoretical understanding (listed in the previous section) can guide this information search.

Integration

Perhaps the most difficult aspect of case conceptualization is the process of tatting together in a coherent way the pieces of the puzzle presented by the client. The counselor must translate the specific presentation of the client into theoretical terms. This process requires the counselor to carefully compare the client's presentation to the theoretical structure to be used. The following are some questions to be considered:

1. **Do the details of the presenting problem fit the theory's postulates concerning psychological dysfunction?** If the elements of the client's presenting problem fit easily, the counselor can proceed to treatment planning, keeping in mind that further information gained from the client may alter this conceptualization. Because clients rarely speak in theoretical terms, however, it is more likely that some, or many, elements seem to be outside of the theory's structure to at least some degree. In fact, the first difficulty in the process of conceptualization is that the counselor is often tempted to focus narrowly on

the "presenting problem." For instance, clients often present with interpersonal problems that can be labeled as lack of assertiveness. Although this label might be useful at times, the counselor attempting to use theoretical conceptualization may get distracted by the label. At this point, the counselor usually reports that a particular theory says nothing about assertiveness and hence decides to use another theory instead. Instead of prematurely abandoning the theoretical approach, the counselor should consider why (in a theoretical sense) the client is nonassertive. To answer this question, the counselor must return to the core principles of the theoretical structure to focus on the underlying mechanisms that lead to the appearance of the "symptom." A cognitive counselor would therefore translate lack of assertion into behavior that is the result of distorted thinking and proceed to determine what irrational thoughts or beliefs the client holds. The process of going beyond "symptoms" therefore involves translating them into theoretical terms that emphasize the links between client presentation and theoretical definitions of health and dysfunction.

The example of the person-centered therapist confronted with a highly emotional client also can illustrate this process. According to the procedures outlined previously, the therapist would consider how emotional outbursts could be understood through the construct of incongruence. For example, the counselor might see the affect as resulting from aspects of experience that are distorted and then denied, but which are then overtly expressed, because repressive processes are depleted by unusual levels of stress. Again, the general method is to first detach from the symptom to a more general understanding and then transfer back to the anomaly.

In rare cases, discrepancies between client presentation and theory may call for a change of perspective. I have not encountered this situation, except in cases where the client is of a different culture from that in which the theory originated. As previously noted in the case of the Japanese client (Sue & Zane, 1987), at times the core postulates may be in direct opposition to the norms of the client's culture. Therefore, the counselor must make a careful study of the multicultural counseling situation and may decide that modification to deal with cultural issues does not destroy the usefulness of the theory. Alternatively, the counselor may elect to shift perspectives to one that is more consistent with client's culture. In instances in which hypothetical cases are in use (e.g., in practicing case conceptualization in theory classes), abandoning the original perspective should be considered a last resort as it may lead to a superficial understanding of the theory. In practicums, in which students are conceptualizing the clients they are counseling, consideration of alternative theoretical structures might be introduced more quickly than when hypothetical cases are in use because the risk of harm to the client is real.

Issues regarding gender bias seem more subtle. Most theoretical definitions of health do not seem blatantly biased (except perhaps for classic psychoanalytic theory, which in some interpretations emphasizes the acceptance of traditional aspects of the female role). Some of the major theories of counseling could be criticized for relying on a male-biased model of health in their emphasis on rational thoughts and consequent relative neglect of affective processes (e.g., rational emotive therapy, cognitive therapy, and cognitive-behavior modification). Likewise, the experiential theories (person-centered, Gestalt, and other existential approaches) could be criticized for being female-biased in their reliance on what is a stereotypically feminine process (affect). This bias, however, seems somehow less clear than cultural bias, and in many cases it seems likely that gender bias often resides in the application of the theory, not in its basic assumptions. For behavior regardless of what theory he or she is applying (an analogous situation may occur in multicultural counseling). If the counselor determines that the source of gender bias lies in the central postulates of the theory, the counselor has the same option as those outlined for the situation in which cultural bias appears.

2. **How do other aspects of the client's presentation fit with the postulates of the theory and the presenting problems?** Once the counselor has gained a theoretical understanding of the presenting problem, the counselor must integrate this knowledge with the rest of the client's presentation to obtain a coherent picture of the client. In the person-centered example, the therapist would look for other aspects of experience that are repressed, plus examine the conditions of worth held by the client and how they were learned. Also, the therapist would look for evidence of the client's self-actualizing tendencies that are sure to be at least faintly evident.

3. **Based on this theory, where does the client need to go (i.e., what changes does the theory specify)?** Because the beginnings of intervention start with the understanding of the theory's definition of the healthy person, the therapist should establish how this client would appear as a healthy

person. In the case of the emotive client, the person-centered therapist would want the client to be able to experience the volatile emotions in a meaningful, accepting way. Similarly, the Gestalt counselor would want the client to increase his or her awareness in all areas of experience.

4. **How can I help the client get where he or she needs to go?** Interventions designed for the client should follow directly from the definitions of health developed for this individual. Some theorists are specific about productive interventions, whereas others are less so. Rather than confining the therapist to theory-specified interventions, I agree with other authors (e.g., Lazarus, 1974) that many interventions could be employed to help a given client. An important point to add, however, is that these interventions should be undertaken with a theoretical goal in mind. The critical question becomes why this intervention now? I cannot count the times students have offered empty-chair interventions but have had no specific theoretical goal in mind. Another common problem is that students often equate intervention with technique. Techniques are easily understood because they are generally concrete, circumscribed actions taken by the counselor. Interventions (at least in my understanding) can be more general in nature (such as when psychoanalytic counselor provides an ambiguous situation on which the client can project) and are often overlooked by students even though they are powerful change tools. Continuing the person-centered example, a major intervention is allowing the client to disclose to an accepting, empathic therapist. Instead, the student who must choose an intervention may identify a more concrete technique (such as having the client keep a self-talk log). Although such a specific technique may be helpful in the case, the student may bypass the simpler, broader interventions specified by person-centered theory.

5. **How will I know when the client is better?** Although implicit in the specification of health as defined by theory, it should be emphasized that the specific criteria for health for the client be defined by the counselor through applying the basic concepts of the theory.

This consideration brings up yet another important question: What about the client's input in this process? When conceptualizing from a theoretical base, are we ignoring the client's stated goals and wishes? Misguided use of theory could result in this rigid stance. Careful consideration, however, of the client's goals in light of the theory can integrate this aspect of the client's presentation into the theoretical structure. In my example, the client's stated wish to deal with her affective outbursts can be construed as the client's self-actualizing tendencies, encouraging her toward more authentic experiencing of her existence.

Uses of this Model

The case conceptualization model presented in this article can be used in several ways. Because this approach was only recently developed, I have no empirical outcome data to present, simply my impressions that are based on the comments of students who have used the model. As noted by previous writers in the area of case conceptualization (Bernier, 1980; Borders & Leddick, 1987; Funqua et al., 1984; Holloway, 1988), cognitive style and developmental issues need to be recognized in the training process. Therefore, the following suggestions for using this model are loosely guided by such concerns.

In beginning-level (master's) theories courses, I have presented the model as a general outline to teach case conceptualization. Students at this stage are struggling to learn the various theories presented, and the six questions about theoretical structure seem to help them organize information. Application of theory seems to be most difficult at this level of learning, and these students have had little or no supervised counseling experience. Laboratory sections of several classes are devoted to case conceptualization, using the steps of the integration portion of the model as a guide. One case is assigned across small groups of students, and groups present and compare their conceptualization.

In practicums, I ask students to present their theoretical perspectives by answering the six questions outlined under theoretical structure. This process helps them to clarify the basic assumptions of their perspectives. Often, students find this process quite difficult, because they have devoted little systematic thought to organizing their perspectives. They are then asked to conceptualize cases based on the guidelines in the model. Students report that the structure gives direction to what is normally a rather ambiguous assignment. My observation is that their conceptualizations seem clearer and more organized than those when they do not have guidelines for follow.

I am currently using this model in my advanced (doctoral) Theories of Counseling course. In this class, students spend the majority of class time presenting theoretical conceptualizations of clients they have previously counseled. Class members supply written case studies for class use. Each student is responsible for supplying readings on a major theoretical approach, and all students complete reaction papers on each theory studied. Students are also required to develop a research proposal that tests a well-developed theory relevant to counseling. The first portion of each class meeting (approximately 45 minutes of a 2-hour and 40-minute total class time) is devoted to outlining each theory according to the six questions relevant to theoretical structure. For the remainder of the class, two class members present case conceptualization (of different clients) developed according to the model as if they were proponents of the theory under discussion. The presenters attempt to integrate aspects of the client's presentation, set theory-based goals, and design theoretically consistent interventions. These presentations can be organized around the five integration questions specified by the model. The rest of the class challenges these conceptualizations, with particular attention paid to theoretical anomalies in the cases or in the presenters' theoretical explanations. Presenters are required to use only explanations that are consistent with the approach they are advocating and are therefore not able to avoid aspects of the cases that are theoretically inconvenient by shifting to other perspectives. This case-intensive approach leads to active discussions that include cross-cultural and gender-role issues. Often, different theoretical approaches are pitted against one another and compared for their utilities in understanding the case in question. The case conceptualization model, therefore, guides students in all steps of the application process, and students report that this approach is quite helpful to them.

Conclusion

Given the lack of systematic guides for the process of case conceptualization, the model presented seems to be a step toward improved teaching in this area. As mentioned previously, however, the model is relatively untested, because it has been evolving over the last several years. Further use of the model will demonstrate whether it achieves its purpose of leading to a clearer understanding of the counseling process, improved training of students and thus, better services to our clients.

■ Treatment Planning

The variety of case conceptualization models just presented should enable counselors to choose a model that best "fits" their view of counseling. In addition, the models presented can be adapted to serve as a starting point for the development of the counselor's own way of viewing clients and their problems, and then for determining the best course of treatment. Following the completion of the case conceptualization process, the counselor must decide how to plan effectively for the treatment of his or her client.

Treatment planning is an essential part of the overall process of developing a coherent approach to counseling an individual. According to Seligman (1993) treatment planning in counseling is a method of plotting out the counseling process so that both counselor and client have a road map that delineates how they will proceed from the point of origin (client's presenting problem) to resolution, thus alleviating troubling and dysfunctional symptoms and patterns and establishing improved coping mechanisms and self-esteem. Seligman further explained how treatment planning plays many important roles in the counseling process:

- A carefully developed treatment plan, fully grounded in research on treatment effectiveness, provides assurance that treatment with a high likelihood of success is being provided.
- Written treatment plans allow counselors to demonstrate accountability without difficulty.
- Treatment plans can substantiate the value of the work being done by a single counselor or by an agency and can assist in obtaining funding as well as providing a sound defense in the event of a malpractice suit.
- Use of treatment plans that specify goals and procedures can help counselors and clients to track their progress; they can determine if goals are being met as planned and, if they are not, can reassess the treatment plan.
- Treatment plans also provide a sense of structure and direction to the counseling process and can help counselors and clients to develop shared and realistic expectations for the process.

Earlier in 1990, Seligman developed a 12-step model for treatment planning. This process, called "DO A CLIENT MAP," (Seligman, 1996, pp. 187–188) includes:

D: Diagnosis. Diagnosis of the problem, employing the use of the DSM-IV as an essential instrument that provides the counselor with a knowledge of the mental problems, conditions, stressors, and coping capacities of the client.

O: Objectives of Treatment. Determination of the objectives and goals of the client. This planning takes place early in the treatment process. It is essential that counselors and clients work together to establish objectives and goals.

A: Assessment. The counselor can employ the use of inventories of personality, abilities, interests, and values. Furthermore, the counselor can use other health professionals to assist in the process.

C: Clinical. This area includes the counselor qualities that are associated with positive outcomes in therapy.

L: Location. Determination of the type of agency or practice (outpatient, inpatient, day treatment, etc.) most suited to the client.

I: Interventions. This area includes the theoretical orientation of the counselor and the specific techniques or interventions employed.

E: Emphasis. This area includes the level of directiveness and structure, the level of support and confrontation, and the level of exploration.

N: Number of People. Who are the people involved in counseling? Is the client involved in individual, group, or family therapy?

T: Timing. Determination of the length of the counseling sessions. When will the counseling occur?

M: Medication. Determination of the reasons for use of medication with the client, as well as acknowledgment of any precautions that must be considered. Why does this client need medication?

A: Adjunctive Services. Services that can help the client between sessions. Such adjunctive services can include skill development, focused counseling, personal growth, peer support groups, and alternative care.

P: Prognosis. Determined by the natural course of the mental disorder, the presence of coexisting disorders, the highest level of functioning duration and the severity of the disorder, the pattern of onset, the client's age at onset, the availability of support services, the experience of the therapist, the client's expectations and compliance with treatment.

In a similar fashion, Jongsma and Peterson in the *Complete Psychotherapy Treatment Planner* (1995), discussed the utility of treatment planning and its benefits to the client, therapist, treatment team, and treatment agency. A summary of their points suggests the following.

- The client benefits from a written treatment plan because it delineates issues to be covered in treatment.
- Both client and therapist benefit because they are forced to think about therapy outcomes. Measurable and clear objectives allow the client to channel efforts into specific changes that lead to the long-term goal of problem resolution.
- Providers are aided by treatment plans because they are forced to think analytically about interventions that are best suited to the objective attainment of the client.
- Clinicians benefit from a treatment plan because it is a measure of protection from litigation.
- Agencies benefit from treatment planning by increasing the quality and uniformity of the documentation in a clinical record.

In addition to the utility of treatment plans, Jongsma and Peterson (1995, pp. 2–6) have identified 6 specific steps for developing a treatment plan. A summary of their steps include the following.

1. **Problem Selection:** During assessment procedures, a primary problem will usually emerge. Secondary problems may also become evident. When the problem selection becomes clear to the clinician, it is essential that the opinion of the client (his or her prioritization of issues) be carefully considered. Client motivation to participate in treatment can depend, to some extent, on the degree to which treatment addresses his or her need.

2. **Problem Definition:** Each problem selected for treatment focus requires a specific definition about how it is evidenced in the client. The DSM-IV and International Classification of Diseases (ICD-9) offer specific definitions and statements to choose from or to serve as a example for the counselor to develop his or her own personally developed statements.

3. **Goal Development:** These goal statements need not be crafted in measurable terms but can be global, long-term goals that indicate a desired positive outcome to the treatment procedures.

4. **Objective Construction:** Objectives must be stated in behaviorally measurable terms. Each objective should be developed as a step toward attaining the broad treatment goal. There should be two objectives for each problem, but the clinician can construct them as needed for goal attainment. Target attainment dates should be listed for each objective.

5. **Intervention Creation:** Interventions are designed to help the client complete the objectives. There should be one intervention for every objective. Interventions are selected on the basis of client needs and the treatment provider's full repertoire.

6. **Diagnosis Determination:** Determination of an appropriate diagnosis is based on an evaluation of the client's complete clinical presentation. The clinician must compare the behavioral, emotional, cognitive, and interpersonal symptoms that the client presents to the criteria for diagnosis of mental illness conditions as described in the DSM-IV. The clinician's knowledge of DSM-IV criteria and his or her complete understanding of the client's assessment data contribute to the most reliable and valid diagnosis.

Finally, Sperry, L., Gudeman, J. E., Blackwell, B., and Faulkner, L. R. (1992) offers another treatment plan format that is quite elaborate. Sperry cited the "Seven P's of Treatment Planning," or seven dimensions for articulating and explaining the nature and origins of the patient's presentation. The Seven P's are presentation, predisposition, precipitants, pattern, perpetuates, plan and prognosis. For our purposes, step 6, called treatment planning, is most relevant. It includes:

1. Patient expectations for current treatment, both outcome and method. Take note of the patient's formulation or explanation for his or her symptoms or disorder.

2. Treatment outcome goals (short and long term), in biological, psychological, and social areas.

3. Rationale for the treatment plan: setting, format, duration, frequency, and treatment strategy.

Summary

This chapter presented a review of some of the major components of effective planning for therapy. Students should add to this review the additional methods and approaches learned in their training programs in an effort to develop an overview of their own approach to counseling the individual.

Similarly, we believe that this chapter can be adapted for use by students in school counseling, agencies, and mental health counseling programs. Remember that assessment of the client and his or her problems and the manner in which the counselor conceptualizes and treats the problem are key aspects of any approach to counseling the individual. Finally, we hope that a review of the materials will enable counselors-in-training to choose for their use those materials that are in keeping with their understanding of the philosophy-theory-practice continuum.

Suggested Readings

Bergner, R. (1993). Victims into perpetrators. *Psychotherapy, 30,* 452–462.
Brammar, L. M. (1996). *The helping relationship: Process and skills* (6th ed.). Boston: Allyn and Bacon Publishers.

Hasen, D. S. (1991). Diagnostic interviews for assessment. *Alcohol and Research World, 15*(4), 293–294.

Lambert, M. J., & Ogles, B. M. (1992). Choosing outcome assessment devices: An organizational and conceptual scheme. *Journal of Counseling and Development, 70*(4), 537–563.

Meier, S. T. (1999). Training the practitioner-scientist: Bridging case conceptualization, assessment and intervention. *Counseling Psychologist, 27*(6), 846–870.

Morrison, J. (1995). *DSM-IV made easy: The clinician's guide to diagnosis.* New York: Guilford Press.

Murdock, N. (1991). Case conceptualization: Applying theory to individuals. *Counselor Education and Supervision, 30,* 355–365.

Prieito, L. R. (1998). Practium class supervision in CACREP accredited programs: A national study. *Counselor Education and Supervision, 38*(2), 113–124.

Seligman, L. (1990). *Selecting effective treatments.* San Francisco: Jossey-Bass.

Van Denburg, T. F., & Schmidt, J. A. (1992). Interpersonal assessment in counseling and psychotherapy. *Journal of Counseling and Development, 71*(1), 84–91.

References

American Psychiatric Association. (1994). *Diagnostic and statistical manual of mental disorders* (4th ed.). Washington, DC: Author.

Bergner, R. (1998). Characteristics of optimal clinical case formulations. *American Journal of Psychotherapy, 52*(3), 287–301.

Cormier, S., & Cormier, B. (1998). *Interview strategies for helpers.* Pacific Grove, CA: Brooks Cole.

Denton, W. (1990). A family systems analysis of DSM III-R. *Journal of Marital and Family Therapy, 16,* 113–125.

Freimuth, N. (1992). Is the best always preferred? *American Psychologist, 47,* 673–674.

Galassi, J. P., & Perot, A. P. (1992). What should we know about behavioral assessment: An approach for counselors. *Journal of Counseling and Development, 75*(5), 634–631.

Geroski, A. M., & Rogers, K. A. (1997). Using the DSM IV to enhance collaboration among school counselors, clinical counselors and primary care physicians. *Journal of Counseling and Development, 75*(3), 231.

Gladding, S. T. (1992). *Counseling: A comprehensive profession.* New York: Maxwell MacMillan International.

Hansen, N. E., & Freimuth, M. (1997). Piecing the puzzle together: A model for understanding the theory-practice relationship. *Counseling Psychology, 25*(4), 654–674.

Hohenshill, T. H. (1996). Editorial: Role of assessment and diagnosis in counseling. *Journal of Counseling and Development, 75*(1), 64–68.

Howatt, W. A. (2000). *The human services counseling toolbox.* Pacific Grove, CA: Brooks Cole.

Jongsma, A. E. & Peterson, M. (1995). *The complete psychotherapy treatment planner.* New York: Wiley.

Juhnke, G. A. (1995). *Mental health counseling assessment: Broadening one's understanding of the client and the client's presenting concerns.* ERIC Digest. Greensboro, NC: ERIC Clearing House on Counseling and Student Services.

Maloney, M. J. (1991). *Human change processes: The scientific foundations of psychotherapy.* New York: Basic Books.

Messer, S. B. (1986). Behavioral and psychoanalytic perspectives at therapeutic choice points. *American Psychologist, 41,* 1261–1272.

Patterson, L. E., & Welfel, E. (2000). *The counseling process* (5th ed.). Pacific Grove, CA: Brooks Cole.

Schwetzer, A. M. (1996). *Using the Inverted Pyramid Heuristic.* Counselor Education and Supervision, 35(4), 258–268.

Seligman, L. (1993). Teaching treatment planning. *Counselor Education and Supervision, 32*(4), 287–298.

Seligman, L. (1966). *Diagnosis and treatment planning in counseling.* New York: Plenum Press.

Sperry, L., Gudeman, J. E., Blackwell, B., & Faulkner, L. R. (1992). *Psychiatric case formulations.* Washington, DC: American Psychiatric Press.

Stevens, M. J., & Morris, S. J. (1995). A format for case conceptualization. *Counselor Education and Supervision, 35*(1), 82–95.

Wilson, S. J. (1980). *Recording guidelines for social workers.* New York: Free Press.

Judith Scott
Eileen Petty Reilly

CHAPTER

5

Monitoring the Professional Development of Practicum Students

◼ Role and Function of the Supervisor in Practicum

According to the ACES, the role and function of the supervisor in practicum is threefold:

1. to observe ethical and legal protection of clients' and supervisees' rights;

2. to meet the training and professional development needs of supervisees in ways consistent with the client's welfare and programmatic requirements; and

3. to establish policies, procedures, and standards for implementing programs (Counselor Education and Supervision, 1995).

Supervisors are considered to be master practitioners who, because of their special clinical skills and experience, have been identified by the field site to monitor and oversee the professional activities of the counseling student.

University supervisors share a similar role in promoting applied skills but have an indirect, or liaison, relationship to the field site (Ronnestaad & Skovholt, 1993). The function of the supervisor has been variously described in the literature. Dye (1994) suggested that supervision should provide high levels of encouragement, support, feedback, and structure. Psychotherapy supervisors undertake multiple levels of responsibility as teachers, mentors, and evaluators (Whitman & Jacobs, 1998). Bernard and Goodyear (1992) suggested that supervisors take on the role of teacher when they directly lecture, instruct, and inform the supervisee. Supervisors act as counselors when they assist supervisees in noticing their own "blindspots" as consultants when relating as colleagues during cotherapy.

The most controversial area of supervision lies in the contrast between clinical functions and administrative supervision functions. Clinical supervision functions emphasize counseling, consultation, and training related to the direct service provided to the client by the counselor trainee. Administrative functions emphasize work assignments, evaluation, and institutional and professional accountability in services and programs. For example, when clinical supervision is the emphasis, the counselor trainee's development of clinical skills is the focus of the supervisor-supervisee interaction. Feedback is related to professional and ethical standards and the clinical literature. In contrast, when administrative supervision is the focus, issues such as keeping certain hours, meeting deadlines, following policy and procedures, and making judgments about whether work is to be accomplished at a minimally acceptable level are emphasized. Feedback is related to institutional standards. Ideally, it is recommended that the same person should not provide both clinical supervision and administrative supervision. Realistically, this is not always the case. Therefore, separate meetings should be scheduled for clinical and administrative supervision.

The counselor trainee can expect to receive both clinical and administrative feedback. However, the emphasis of this chapter is directed toward clinical supervision and the intervention, assessment, and evaluative techniques related to a clinical supervisory situation. The student may want to reflect on the proportion of clinical to administrative supervision that he or she is receiving in practicum.

In clinical supervision the importance of developing a working relationship with the supervisor cannot be understated. Similarly, students need to consider their own attitudes, biases, and expectations as they enter into the supervisory process.

Kaiser (1997), in discussing the supervisor-supervisee relationship, suggested that supervision take place in the context of the relationship between supervisor and supervisee. Kaiser sites the following three components of this relationship: the use of power and authority, creation of shared meaning, and creation of trust (p. 16). It is essential that the counselor trainee recognize that supervisors do have power over trainees, primarily because they will be evaluating the trainees' work. Thus trainees need to be open and honest with their supervisors in order to gain effective guidance and feedback. Similarly, the creation of shared meaning between supervisor and supervisee relates to understanding and agreement between the two parties. The degree to which understanding and agreement are obtained determines how the two parties can communicate. Finally, the creation of trust between the supervisor and supervisee develops out of the creation of shared meaning and by building confidence in the mutual understanding between the two parties. Scott (1976) emphasized the importance of establishing collegial relationship within the supervisor-supervisee interaction. The relationship is characterized by balance and a shared responsibility for understanding the counseling process. A disruption in this balance or an inability to establish collegiality should be open areas of discussion in order to identify learning problems. A general rule is that disruptions in the supervisor-supervisee relationship always take precedence.

Another view of the supervisor-supervisee relationship was presented by Bernard and Goodyear (1992). Their focus was directed toward three supervisee roles and three areas of concentration. Earlier the authors sited the three roles of teacher, counselor, and consultant to identify specific issues in supervision. The three areas of focus for skill building are: (a) process, (b) conceptualization, and (c) personalization. Process issues examine how communication is conveyed. For example, is the supervisee reflecting the client emotion? Did the supervisee reframe the situation? Could the use of paradox help the client to be less resistant? Conceptualization issues include how well supervisees can explain their application of a specific theory to a particular case. How well do they see the big picture? Personalization issues pertain to the counselor's use of his or her self in therapy, to determine that all involved are not defensively present in the relationship.

■ The Supervisor-Supervisee Relationship

Direct supervision of clinical work is perhaps the most important element in the training of a counselor or psychotherapist. Supervision is more than a didactic experience. It includes intensive interpersonal interaction with all of the potential complications that such relationships can include. Research has documented the importance of the supervisor-supervisee relationship. Several studies have related success in supervision to the quality of the relationship between the supervisor and supervisee (Alpher, 1991; Freeman, 1992; Kadushin, 1992). Relationship qualities of warmth, acceptance, trust, and understanding are defined as fundamental to positive supervision. Good supervision must integrate both task- and relationship-oriented behavior. In positive supervision experiences, a critical balance exists between relationship and task focus. In negative supervision experiences, the total emotional focus is on the negative relationship.

The supervisee enters into the supervisory relationship with a number of predictable anxieties. Common sources of supervisee anxiety are (a) concern over whether he or she will be successful in the internship and (b) power issues within the supervisor-supervisee relationship. Concern over performance and approval by supervisors can lead to a defensive stance on the part of the student trainee. It is not uncommon for trainees to react by criticizing their supervisors, therefore becoming resistant to supervisory feedback and evaluation.

The literature cited in the foregoing section may provide the practicum student with sufficient rationale and motivation to consider the supervisor-supervisee relationship as an important area on which to focus during supervision. Relational concerns and conflicts clearly detract from the amount of learning in supervision.

Approaches in Supervision

The practicum student often approaches clinical supervision with mixed feelings. On the positive side, supervision can be regarded as a helpful, supportive interaction that focus on validating some practices, improving others, and learning new techniques and insights about the counseling process. On the negative side, supervision can be regarded as an interaction that will expose inadequacies and leave the student with even more feelings of incompetence. Both sets of expectations coexist as the student approaches supervision. The tendency, particularly in the early stages of supervision, is for the student to work at proving himself or herself as a counselor so that the negative feelings of inadequacy will diminish. This is a natural and understandable tendency. However, giving full reign to this tendency would lead the supervision process away from ambiguous aspects of counseling requiring clarification, and could lead to avoidance or defensiveness about aspects of the student's approach to counseling that need improvement. Generally, the initial phases of supervision are spent establishing a working alliance between the supervisor and supervisee. This holds true for the various approaches to supervision that might be implemented. To reduce the practicum student's anxieties about supervision and to facilitate the creation of a working alliance, a preview of how supervision could be implemented is in order. A review of the various practices in counseling supervision has resulted in the identification and explication of five major approaches to supervision (Bradley, 1989).

The Psychotherapeutic Approach to Supervision

This approach revolves around increasing awareness, understanding, and use of interpersonal and intrapersonal dynamics. The supervisee can expect that awareness of his or her own dynamics will be a focus. Techniques associated with this approach are Interpersonal Process Recall (IPR) and unstructured and intensive therapeutic supervision. The IPR technique requires the supervisee to listen to or view an audio- or videotape of a session with a client. The recall supervisor uses inductive questioning to direct the counselor's attention to the interpersonal and intrapersonal dynamics in the interaction. The unstructured technique requires that the counselor bring something to the supervisor for discussion. This may be a tape of a session, a professional problem, or a consulting concern. If the concern involves any human interaction, the dynamics of the interaction can receive focus. The role of the supervisor is to focus on the interaction and respond so that the supervisee can give attention to the dynamics involved (Bradley, 1989, pp. 65–124).

The Behavioral Approach to Supervision

This approach focuses on the skill behaviors of the counselor. Skill behaviors include the feelings, thoughts, and acts of the counselor. The goal of behavioral supervision is to develop and refine skill behaviors appropriate to counseling. In order to set supervision goals, skill analysis and assessment must be done. Any one of several models that identify skill dimensions of counseling competency, and the supervisor's own repertoire of identified counseling competencies, may be used. Skill behavior analysis is best implemented when the purpose of the skill and the process sequence of the skill are identified and understood. After supervisory goals are set, strategies to accomplish the goals are constructed and implemented (Bradley, 1989, pp. 125–189).

The Integrative Approach to Supervision

This approach combines methods and techniques from several supervisory approaches and represents the usual practice of a large number of supervisors. The Carkhuff Training Model and the Psychobehavioral Model are two integrative approaches identified by Bradley (1989). In the Carkhuff Training Model, the practicum student can expect that the supervisor will model facilitative interpersonal skills as well as action-oriented skills. While the supervisor offers psychologically facilitative conditions, the supervisee is directed through a three-stage program of learning activities that encompasses (a) discrimination training to recognize and differentiate between high and low levels of facilitative conditions, (b) communication training to develop and demonstrate competence in responding, and (c) developing courses of action through which intervention strategies are taught and practiced.

In the Psychobehavioral model, a blend of insight counseling and action-oriented counseling is utilized. The practicum student can expect to proceed through three stages of supervision:

1. **the initial stage,** in which exploration of anxieties, expectations, and experiences focusing on interpersonal and intrapersonal dynamics are combined with skill development activities;

2. **the intermediate stage,** which involves a more confrontational approach to supervision that examines dynamic patterns and provides therapeutic feedback from the supervisor; and

3. **the terminal stage,** in which the supervisor functions more as a consultant, and training activities are minimal (Bradley, 1989, pp. 201–203).

The Systems Approach to Supervision

In this approach, systems technology is applied to the supervisory function. The trainee and his or her performance are viewed in the context of the helping services the counselor is responsible for delivering. The supervisor is a consultant who collaborates with trainees in conceptualizing the counseling activities in terms of broad goals and performance objectives within the total counseling or helping service program. The practicum student can expect to meet with the supervisor to review an activity plan to determine how realistic it may be and how likely it is to reach intended goals and objectives (Bradley, 1989, pp. 229–256).

The Person-Process Model of Supervision: A Developmental Approach to Supervision

In the Person-Process Model (PPM), developmental theory is applied to the supervisory process. Loevinger's work on ego and development provides the theory base for the first component of PPM, entitled "Understanding the Personal Meaning Making System of the Supervisee." Supervisees proceed through the preconformist level, which coincides with the impulsive and self-protective stages of Loevinger's developmental model. Persons at this level think very simply and concretely. The conformist level, in which supervisees have a genuine concern about what others think of them, follows. Supervisees at this level are receptive to criticisms and recommendations made by a supervisor or coworker. The third level of personal meaning making is a self-aware, postconformist level. Supervisees at this level demonstrate greater cognitive complexity in the way they approach their work (D'Andrea, 1989, pp. 257–296).

The five approaches to supervision that have been reviewed are those that are most likely to be experienced by the practicum student. Because the trainee will probably have more than one supervisor during the field experiences, it is likely that he or she may be working with a university supervisor who utilizes the behavioral approach to supervision while simultaneously working with a field site supervisor who utilizes a systems approach to supervision. The trainee is advised to be open to any one of the approaches to supervision by recognizing the goals and advantages inherent in each.

Assessing Professional Development

In this section we will address the need for, the categories of, and the skills necessary for professional evaluation and development. We believe that the practicum student, the intern, and the practicing professional should continually strive to increase the depth and understanding of themselves and their area of expertise. One never truly arrives at a complete understanding, however. Each client session affords not only the client but also the counselor or trainee with the opportunity for growth and development. For this to occur, the counselor or trainee must continually examine and reflect on his or her strengths and weaknesses. A comprehensive framework for such evaluation has been proposed in the *Handbook of Counseling Supervision* (Borders & Leddick, 1987). Three broad skill categories have been identified as those within which self-assessment, supervisor assessment, goal identification, and evaluation can be implemented. These skill categories are (a) counseling performance skills, (b) cognitive counseling skills, and (c) developmental level.

Counseling Performance Skills

Counseling performance skills refer to "What the counselor does during a session or his counseling behaviors" (p. 14). These skills include (a) basic helping skills, (b) theory-based techniques, and (c) procedural skills.

Basic Helping Skills

The basic helping skills are the building blocks of communication. Egan (1994) suggested that these skills are not special skills peculiar to helping, but rather "extensions of the kinds of skills all of us need in our everyday interpersonal transactions" (p. 90). Basic helping skills include, but are not limited to (a) attending, or the ability to be with a client, both physically and psychologically, and (b) active listening, or the ability to capture and understand the messages that clients communicate. The importance and significance of these skills cannot be overemphasized. It is imperative that the practicum student understand that for the client to grow, meaningful communication must take place. For meaningful communication to occur, a common humanity must be recognized. Although the relationship between student and client may be unequally weighted in power of one sort or another, the student must strive to grow beyond this. If the student identifies only with the role she plays in the counseling relationship, communication is limited, literally, to role-playing. No one grows. The student must develop trust and accept vulnerability enough to reach beyond role-to-role relating so growth can occur.

Students must remember that their clients may see the world very differently and may give significance to life events in ways that do not immediately make sense. Although we cannot have direct experience of how a client sees the world, we can try to make sense of the client's explanations (Malley & Reilly, 1999). This is the beginning of honest communication. One accomplishes this by continually working on one's attending and active listening skills

Egan (1994) suggested that there are three levels of attending to clients. The first microskill or level deals with mechanics. What does the counselor do to attend? Egan used the acronym SOLER to remind counselors and trainees to

S	Face the client **squarely**
O	Adopt an **open** posture
L	At times, **lean** toward the client
E	Maintain good **eye contact**
R	Try to be relatively **relaxed**

The second level addresses the counselors' ability to read or be attuned to the cues and messages they are sending through their bodies as they interact with clients. The third level addresses the quality of the total human presence between counselor and client. While attending behaviors help the counselor or trainee focus on what he or she brings to the counseling session, active listening skills help the counselor or trainee understand what the client brings. Egan (1994) suggested that active listening has four components. The first is the ability to read the client's nonverbal behavior; this includes facial expressions, physiological responses, physical characteristics, and bodily behavior. The second component is the ability to read and understand the client's verbal messages; this is when the counselor listens to the client's descriptions of experiences, behaviors, and affect. The third component of active listening is listening for context, trying to understand the whole person in relation to his or her world. Finally, the fourth is listening for sour notes—gaps, distortions, or dissonance—that are part of the client's experience.

Theory-Based Techniques

Theory-based techniques are performance skills that the counselor or trainee uses to help the client address those gaps and distortions uncovered during therapy. For example, how does the counselor or trainee challenge a client's irrational belief system? How does the counselor or trainee manage client reluctance and resistance?

The techniques chosen by the counselor or trainee should be based on two considerations: (a) the goals of the therapy sessions, and (b) the style or theory the therapist or trainee is implementing. The techniques used by a counselor or trainee practicing psychotherapy will be very different from those used by someone who is practicing reality therapy. The importance here is not the validity of different approaches but rather the appropriate use and understanding of varying techniques. Again, to remain a professional one must continually seek supervision and evaluation of one's skills, knowledge, and understanding in their area of expertise.

Procedural Skills

Procedural skills are counseling performance skills that give structure to the counseling session. They help maintain continuity from session to session and enable the counselor or trainee to open and close sessions smoothly. Procedural skills are many, varied, and often case specific. There is one skill of particular importance, however, that is utilized in all cases: the art of questioning. It is through questioning that the counselor or trainee guides and directs therapy sessions. Hunsaker and Alessandra (1986) suggested that there are two basic forms of questions:

open questions, which are nondirective, and closed, which are directive. By utilizing these two basic forms of questions the counselor or trainee can guide and structure the therapy session. Additionally, the counselor or trainee may use clarifying questions to seek verification of content, developmental questions to draw out a broad response on a narrow topic, or closure questions to encourage agreement and/or successful implementation of a suggested plan or solution (p. 111). What is important for the practicum student to remember is that although the art of questioning can be considered a basic helping skill, it is a technique that adds structure and form, making it a necessary procedural skill.

Cognitive Counseling Skills

While basic helping skills are an important aspect of any counseling or therapeutic process, the practicum student must concomitantly learn the cognitive skills of the counseling process. Cognitive skills address the intentionality of the practicum student's interventions with the client. In order for a practicum student's counseling intervention response to be of help to the client, the client's statements must be understood not only within the dyad that is presently taking place between the practicum student and the client, but also within the total context of the therapeutic relationship as it evolves over time.

The incipient stage of cognitive counseling skill development is the tentative formation of an understanding of the client's personality. At first, the practicum student experiences the client's dynamics in the same manner as one experiences a developing photograph. The picture is not clear at first, changing from one configuration to another in rapid sequence. The ultimate reason why the practicum student is searching for an accurate picture of the client's dynamics is so the student can utilize counseling intervention responses that are constructive and appropriate to the client's needs. In short, diagnosis must precede helpful differential treatment for the client. The information from which a tentative hypothesis develops about the client's basic personality comes from two sources. The first source of information is the client. The practicum student must become aware of the myriad ways clients communicate information to them, either when they are telling and explicating their stories, or in the fashion by which they respond to the practicum students' responses to them. Client anxiety is expressed in various ways. The client may express some anxiety directly to the practicum student, but usually people are reluctant to express these feelings until they have developed a sense of trust and relationship.

However, anxiety, by its very nature, seeks modes of expression of which the client is very often unaware. Certain aspects of dialogue may be accompanied by nonverbal expressions such as covering the mouth, crossing one's legs, total body movement away from the student, joining the hands together with the knuckles extending upward, or closing one's eyes. The speech pattern of the client may change from a slow and measurable pace to a rapid one. Voice intonation may vary, or the client may unexpectedly pause before answering.

The practicum student must learn not only to be aware of when inadvertent communication takes place, but when and in what context of dialogue the behavior was manifested. Also, the practicum student must simultaneously collect all this information in a cognitive mailbox so to speak and sort it out as the counseling sessions continue.

Clients' behavioral reactions to the experiences they encounter in life must also be noted and mentally recorded by the student. When faced with a situation that calls for assertiveness, does the client instead respond with anger or submissiveness? In regard to relationship with others, especially intimate ones, is the person dependent, dominant, or indifferent? Which experiences seem to make him or her afraid and which ones do not? Does the client deny anger when it is quite obvious to the practicum student that anger is extant?

The second source of information about the client comes from the practicum student. In a counseling session the practicum student is experiencing himself or herself simultaneously as he or she is experiencing the client. In other words the student is experiencing the total constellation of the experience as it is unfolding. Ultimately the practicum student must be able to form a cognitive configuration, taken from these various sources of data, of the client's personality structure, a synthesis, if you will, of the client's dynamics. In this way the practicum student learns to respond in a deliberate and thoughtful manner to the client rather than in some capricious fashion that is not helpful.

Developmental Level

Along with basic helping and cognitive skills, practicum students must learn the skills of their own self-development as it relates to their effectiveness with clients. As previously mentioned, not only is the practicum student experiencing the client in a counseling session, the student is also experiencing his or her own personality dynamics simultaneously.

Clients bring to the counseling sessions many varied and sundry dynamics, some of which are not in their conscious awareness. Just as the practicum student must learn to anticipate the potential presentation of just about any problem he or she could imagine, so too must the practicum student expect that he or she will have reactions to the problem, as well as to the client. The practicum student must learn the developmental skill of being separate, but not distant, from the client. Being drawn into a client's dynamics will cause the student to lose perspective on the counseling process.

Practicum students are not expected to have the wherewithal to automatically or instinctively address any cognitive or affective response they have to their clients' problems or their reactions to their clients' problems or personalities. What students are expected to do is to recognize just what reactions they might have that would be aversive to appropriate therapeutic intervention and to openly work through these reactions with their peers and supervisor.

Clients may bring problems to the practicum student such as their admitted physical and/or sexual abuse of their children or their bigotry. At times practicum students may find problems of this nature disconcerting. Student counselors should be well aware that sometimes their clients will respond to them in ways that they will find offensive or degrading. The more intimate and revealing sessions become, the more emotional intensity is generated between the practicum counselor and the client; this emotional intensity will sometimes be directly or inadvertently directed at the student counselor. It is the nature of the counseling process that clients who have unmeet needs will expect these needs to be met by the counselor. The fact of the matter is that part of the counseling process is to educate the client about the fact that each person is accountable and responsible for meeting his or her own emotional needs.

The practicum student only provides a structure that is receptive to and facilitative of a situation that allows clients to determine what choices can be made that are in their best interest and will meet their needs. The structure the practicum student provides for the client is implicitly and explicitly formed to allow and afford clients the dignity and respect indigenous to their right to make their own decisions. When, over time, a client does not find a quick fix to his or her problem, the practicum student may anticipate that the client will utilize whatever ineffective coping mechanisms he or she has used in the past to get results. Consequently, the client may arrive late to the counseling session, scream at the practicum student, or in any other way create some sabotage in the place of doing his or her work.

Practicum students must be ready for any and all forms of seductive and manipulative behavior from the client and must be prepared to stand their ground against such actions. For example, a client may say he or she is sexually attracted to the practicum student. The practicum student must learn how to help the client with this issue, rather than hiding from it or running away from the client.

Many client behaviors are geared toward testing the competency level of the practicum student. Practicum students should be well aware that one of the major issues they will face, given the complexity of the counseling process, is that of their own thoughts and feelings about their competency.

Just as a facilitative structure is provided for the client by the practicum student, so too is a facilitative structure provided for the practicum student by the program in which he or she is matriculating. Practicum students are expected, through structured sessions with their peers and supervisors, to be open to the many cognitive, affective experiences associated with the counseling process that they may find perplexing. In some ways, to become a better therapist the practicum student must pass through a similar process as the one that his or her client must pass through to become a better person, and both will need support. Both student and client must be open to the proffered support to succeed in their endeavor.

We suggest that the practicum student spend time early and often in the supervisory relationship discussing and clarifying the three skills categories of counseling performance skills, cognitive counseling skills, and developmental level. This discussion will facilitate the self-assessment process. At the early phases of practicum, it is possible that the performance skills area will be targeted for work while the areas of cognitive counseling and development level will have only a preliminary awareness level to them. As practicum advances toward internship, however, the performance skills may move to the background and cognitive counseling skills and the developmental level may be targeted (see Figure 5.1). It is because of this progression that the monitoring of counseling performance skills is included here.

Monitoring Counseling Performance Skills

Self-Assessment of Counseling Performance

Several kinds of assessment are utilized throughout the practicum experience. These include self-assessment, peer assessment, and supervisor assessment. Initially, a self-assessment is recommended so that the student can enter into supervision activities with peers and supervisors with a clearer idea of the performance skill areas that may need to be validated and reinforced as well as performance skills that need to be developed. Although beginning practicum students may shy away from such activities, afraid of their own inadequacies, they should be encouraged to practice self-assessment frequently and diligently. They should be reminded that at the heart of helping is communication, the transmitting of the thoughts, feelings, and attitudes that shape

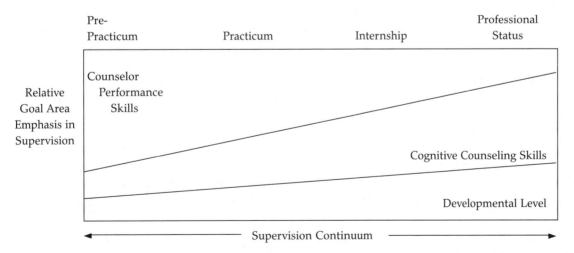

FIGURE 5.1. Schematic representation of relative goal emphasis in supervision and the shift in goal emphasis as the student progresses from prepracticum to completion of internship.

our lives. The counselor or trainee plays an active role in this process and thus is responsible for understanding the personal qualities (thoughts, feelings, attitudes, and skills) he or she brings to the relationship. Counselors speak from a context of personal experience and learning. Therefore, they must be aware of who they are as helpers, of how personal experiences influence their image, and of how that image is communicated to their clients (Malley & Reilly, 1999).

We recommend that the practicum student begin the supervisory process by reflecting on all previous experiences that he or she brings to the current field-training situation. These would include educational preparation, related work experience, volunteer activities, paraprofessional counseling activities, and supervision related to counseling. When entering into supervisory interactions, the practicum student should be prepared to provide peers and supervisors with his or her perceptions of the performance skill areas in which he or she is well grounded and also of the areas that need more development. Two self-assessment activities have been included at the end of the book to assist the practicum student in evaluating his or her counseling skills. The first activity, the Self-Assessment of Basic Helping Skills and Procedural Skills (Form 5.1), focuses on basic helping and procedural skills. The second self-assessment activity, which can be used prior to meeting with peer supervisors or a new supervisor, is completion of the Counseling Techniques List (Form 5.2), which is described in the following section, entitled "Techniques Used in Counseling and Psychotherapy," by Joseph Hollis.

After completing Forms 5.1 and 5.2, the practicum student is encouraged to write a brief statement concerning his or her needs in supervision that are related to counseling performance skills. For example, the student may decide that basic helping skills related to challenging and achieving a balance among empathy, probing, and clarification responses are in need of development. Or he or she may decide to focus on theory-based skills, such as the interpretation of transference, or procedural skills, such as how to end sessions and establish continuity from session to session.

TECHNIQUES USED IN COUNSELING AND PSYCHOTHERAPY*

Joseph W. Hollis

Major growth has occurred in the counseling and psychotherapy professions in recent years. Different philosophical positions have given rise to new theories, which in turn have produced a search for additional approaches. The number of counselors, therapists, and clinicians has increased, while also expanding the scope of individuals to whom counseling services has [sic] been made available.

Because no one counseling technique is appropriate for all clients or is flexible enough to use at the various depths required in counseling, additional counseling techniques have become a necessity. Research and experimentation have led to new techniques and to an identification of which techniques are most appropriate when using a specific theoretical base with a client in the remedial, preventive, or developmental area. Thus, the counseling profession has developed to the stage where each counselor can select techniques according to his or her own philosophical base and according to the client's needs. When the counselor recognizes his or her own limitations in using a wide range of techniques, this knowledge enables the counselor to refer certain clients, seek consultation when working with some clients, request that a co-counselor or co-

---

* This material was taken from a chapter entitled "Counseling Techniques and Process," pp. 77–174, in K. Dimick and F. Krause (Eds.), *Practicum Manual for Counseling and Psychotherapy,* 1980. Muncie, IN: Accelerated Development. Reprinted with permission.

therapist work with specific clients, or limit one's practice to clients who can be assisted with the competencies of the counselor.

The Counseling Techniques List (Form 5.2) provides a list of counseling and psychotherapy techniques, which, while not all-inclusive, does represent techniques used by a broad spectrum of philosophical bases. The number of counseling techniques used by any one counselor varies. If a counselor reviews his or her tape recordings from several sessions with different clients, ten to fifteen different techniques may be identified that were used frequently with competence. An additional ten to fifteen may be identified that were used but were used with less frequency or, in some cases, with less professional competence.

Suggestions for using the accompanying Counseling Techniques List are dependent upon one's professional development. However, students in my course used the list primarily in two ways:

1. To check out and expand their knowledge about counseling techniques, and

2. To introspect into their own counseling, philosophical bases, and treatment approaches.

For further information about using the Counseling Techniques List please read the directions at the beginning of Form 5.2. These directions should be read in their entirety before proceeding with the completion of the form.

■ Ongoing Self-Assessment

Continuing reflection upon and assessment of one's counseling practices (frequently termed self-supervision) are integral parts of the practicum and internship experiences, and indeed of any counseling experience. Professional self-assessment is a career-long process that occurs while transcribing interview notes, reviewing tapes of counseling sessions, preparing for a session, and keeping journals of personal feelings and attitudes about counseling practice. It is important that the practicum student begins early to build strong habits of self-supervision. A number of different forms and directed activities can assist the trainee with organizing and focusing these self-assessment activities. We suggest that the trainee keep a file of all self-assessment activities as a record or his or her professional development.

Several forms that have been cited in previous chapters of this manual are excellent aids for focusing self-assessment. The Tape Critique Form (Form 2.5) provides a systematic approach to reviewing and assessing sessions that have been audio- or videotaped. The Therapy Notes (Form 3.8) and the Case Summary (see Figure 3.2) provide an organization for written review of counseling sessions and can demonstrate cognitive counseling skills and the developmental level of the trainee. An additional aid for self-assessment is also included at the end of the book; the Self-Rating by the Student Counselor Form (Form 5.3) is to be used after a therapy session.

■ Peer Assessment

Peer supervision and assessment has been identified as a valuable aid in the supervision process. This modality is, however, recommended with some precautions. Peer supervision should be used only as a supplement to regular supervision and seems best utilized within the behavioral skills training areas. The peer supervisor can promote skill awareness through ratings and shared perceptions, but it is important to make sure that any peer supervision activities that are initiated occur after group supervision has provided sufficient training and practice (Boyd, 1978). After a particular counseling skill has been introduced, modeled, and practiced within the group context, peer rating of counseling tapes can be implemented. We suggest that the peer critique of tapes be structured to focus on the rating of specific skills. For instance, the target skills might be identified as one or more of the facilitative skills such as basic empathy, asking open-ended questions, or concreteness. Other targeted skills could be the recognition and handling of positive or negative affect or the effective use of probes. A Peer Rating Form (Form 5.4), used to structure the use of peer rating activities, has been included in the "Forms" section at the end of the book.

Another approach to improving the use of functional basic skills is to teach students to identify their dysfunctional counseling behaviors and then to minimize those behaviors (Collins, 1990). Instead of rating functional skills, peer reviewers can measure the incidence of dysfunctional skills such as premature problem solving or excessive questioning in their review of counseling tapes. The goal would be for the counselor to decrease or eliminate dysfunctional counseling behaviors in actual sessions. Collins (1990, p. 70), in a study of the occurrence of dysfunctional counseling behaviors in both role playing and real client interviews of social work students, identified the following as dysfunctional behaviors:

- **Poor beginning statements:** Session starts with casual talk or chitchatting instead of engagement skills.
- **Utterances:** Counselor responses consist of short utterances or one-word responses such as "uh-huh," "yeah," "okay," or "sure"; two different types of utterance responses rated were: utterances (alone) and utterances (preceding a statement).
- **Closed questions:** Counselor asks questions that require one-word answers by clients, such as yes or no, or their age or number of children.
- **Why questions:** Counselor asks statements starting with the word "why."
- **Excessive questioning:** Counselor asks three or more questions in a row without any clear reflective component to the questions. *Reflective component* refers to restating content the client has expressed in his or her statement to the counselor.
- **Premature advice or premature problem solving:** Counselor gives advice that is considered premature, i.e., advice given in the first 10 minutes of the session or after the first interview, judgmental statements, or problem solving where the counselor is doing the work for the client.
- **Minimization:** Counselor downplays the client's problem, gives glib responses, or offers inappropriate comments such as "Life can't be all that bad."

Carmichael (1992) has developed a Peer Supervision Rating Sheet, which was created for use in group supervision. Items included on the rating sheet were drawn from the work of Wittmer and Myrick (1974), Ivey and Gluckstern (1974), Egan (1986), and Cormier and Hockney (1987). Consistent with the previously mentioned precautions regarding the use of peer supervisors, this rating sheet was intended to keep the peer supervisor focused during observations and to reinforce the learning of counseling skills. Prior to using the rating sheet, each element in the rating sheet was discussed and students generated examples of what would consitute level 1, 3, and 5 ratings. Although this rating sheet was developed and used to rate student-role-played counseling sessions, it could also be used to rate real counseling session tapes.

Elements included on Carmichael's Peer Supervision Rating Sheet are rated on a continuum from 1, which is the poorest, to 5, which is the strongest. These elements are as follows:

- Establishes rapport
- Keeps focus
- Explores problem
- Reflects feeling
- Makes open-ended statements
- Communicates clearly
- Does not use questions

- Displays congruent nonverbal and verbal behavior
- Uses problem-solving model
- Attains closure
- Summarizes
- Clarifies
- Generates alternatives
- Confronts
- Uses humor appropriately (Carmichael, p. 61)

Monitoring Cognitive Skills

The case conceptualization approach is a primary modality included in individual and group supervision that addresses the skill category of cognitive counseling skills. The goals of using the case presentation approach in supervision are to help the "trainee to have a basic understanding of the client's underlying psychological dynamics and behavior" (Loganbill & Stoltenberg, 1983, p. 235); to "enhance participant's cognitive complexity" (McAuliffe, 1992, p. 164); and to "improve supervised conceptualization skills through development of complex and integrated thinking skills" (Biggs, 1988, p. 242). Case conceptualization formats have been suggested that primarily emphasize the understanding of client dynamics (Loganbill & Stoltenberg, 1983), that emphasize the relationship between the client's condition and the choice of intervention (Biggs, 1988; McAuliffe, 1992), and that emphasize the complex understanding of a theoretical perspective (Murdock, 1991). Each of these approaches can be useful in helping the trainee to move toward higher levels of understanding and effectiveness in the practice of counseling and psychotherapy.

Biggs (1988), applying Perry's (1970) framework of intellectual development, characterized the supervisee as moving from a dualistic position in cognitive development, where he or she may demand the correct answer from the supervisor, to a multiplistic position, where no particular approach to dealing with clients is more correct than any other, to a commitment-in-relativism position, where the counselor can defend particular clinical decisions while recognizing the tentativeness and uncertainty of a choice. The task for the supervisor is to promote divergent thinking and problem finding in the counselor by using skillful probes, discussing cognitive conflicts among group members, and supporting the reasoning process. Three major tasks are included in the case conceptualization format:

1. identifying how observations and inferences are used to provide evidence for clinical judgments;
2. describing and discussing major dimensions of the counseling relationship; and
3. describing assumptions regarding the client's personality, problem condition, and choice of treatment (Biggs, 1988, p. 243).

An alternate case presentation format has been proposed by McAuliffe (1992). Similar guidelines are incorporated regarding the goal of moving toward cognitive complexity and the role of the supervisor in promoting critical thinking. Supervisees are also expected to present evidence for their judgments in the case presentation format. This proposed format employs the acronym SOAP (subjective, objective, assessment, plan). The *subjective* portion asks the counselor to describe reasons for presenting the case, including a description of the client's presenting problem. The second part, *objective*, includes background information regarding test results, previous work in therapy, and summary of present work as it relates to the presenting problem. In the *assessment* segment, the counselor gives a tentative 5-axis DSM-IV diagnostic impression. The final portion, the *plan*, contains a summary of work done to date and a treatment plan. Group dialogue then follows and can include a discussion of how treatment may vary based on the theoretical perspective used.

A case conceptualization format that emphasizes a complete understanding of a theoretical perspective is presented in chapter 4 of this volume, where Boylan discuss case conceptualization as part of the philosophy-theory-practice continuum. For more information on this particular format, see Nancy L. Murdock's section entitled "Case Conceptualization: Applying Theory to Individuals" in chapter 4.

Supervisor Monitoring and Assessment Activities

Assessment is provided by the supervisor at various times throughout the practicum and internship experiences. The first assessment occurs at the onset of supervision to facilitate a working alliance between supervisor and supervisee and to establish mutually agreed upon goals. The supervisor is referred to the *Handbook of Counseling Supervision* (Borders & Leddick, 1987) for a review of standardized assessment and evaluation instruments that can be used for this purpose. The self-assessment format (see Form 5.1, the Self-Assessment of Basic Helping Skills and Procedural Skills) discussed earlier in this chapter has been presented as one approach to the goal setting process. The supervisor reviews and discusses awareness, knowledge, and practice in the categories of counseling performance skills, cognitive counseling skills, and developmental level of the trainee. Based on this dialogue and the use of standardized measures (if preferred), short-term and long-term goal statements can be formulated. We suggest that the goal statements be developed within the categories of performance skills, cognitive skills, and developmental level. These goal statements then become the context within which the professional development of the practicum student can be interpreted. Progress toward goals can be reviewed at the midpoint and completion of each term of practicum and internship. Goals can also be renegotiated at the midpoint review to adjust for any special circumstances. The Goal Statement Agreement (Form 5.5) is a useful tool for the recording and analysis of both short- and long-term goals of the practicum student; a copy of this form are provided in the "Forms" section at the end of this volume. A sample of a completed goal statement is shown in Figure 5.2.

Continuing assessment of the student's work occurs regularly during the weekly individual and/or group supervision sessions conducted at both the field site and the university setting. In internship, where the student may be working full time in a location too far away from campus for regular weekly meetings, sessions with the site supervisor will be held on a weekly basis, or more frequently if time permits. An Interviewer Rating Form (Form 5.6) provides one approach to organizing and focusing the supervisor ratings of an individual session.

Two additional rating forms have been included (see the "Forms" section) in order to provide structured rating of the trainee at the midpoint and endpoint of the practicum. The Site Supervisor's Evaluation of Student Counselor's Performance (Form 5.7) is recommended for use at the midpoint of practicum. This can be used as an adjunct to the Goal Statement Agreement (Form 5.5) and can be interpreted within the goal statement categories. The more extensive Counselor Competency Scale (Form 5.8) is recommended for use at the endpoint of practicum. This scale provides a broader array of performance and cognitive skills to be rated. We recommend using this scale in addition to the final assessment of progress toward the student's goal statement objectives.

Summary

Practicum students are not expected to have the wherewithal to automatically or instinctively address all of their clients' problems. Students are, however, expected to strive to develop a meaningful helping relationship with those clients. This kind of client relationship is achieved by focusing on the development of counseling performance skills. By strengthening their basic help-

GOAL STATEMENT AGREEMENT

Directions: The student completes the agreement in duplicate and submits once copy to the supervisor.

Student's name _____ Supervisor's name _____

Date submitted _____

Short-Term Goals

Counceling Performance Skills   Demonstrate application of facilitative and challenging skills in client interviews.

Cognitive Counseling Skills   Demonstrate awareness in important client information.

Developmental Level   Decrease anxiety concerning supervision.

Long-Term Goals

Counseling Performance Skills   Demonstrate ability to integrate and apply skills related to client self-exploration, goal setting, and action.

Cognitive Counseling Skills   Demonstrate ability to analyze client and counselor interaction from at least one theoretical frame of reference.

Developmental Level   Demonstrate ability to collaborate and discuss with supervisor regarding appropriate application of an identified counseling method.

FIGURE 5.2. Sample completed Goal Statement Agreement form (Form 5.5).

ing, theory base, and procedural skills, practicum students are building a repertoire of the skills and knowledge required of a helping professional. The forms cited in this chapter can be used by students to enhance their skills and assess their work with clients. Practicum students must remember that the essence of helping is communication between the counselor and the client. A counselor is first a person, then a counselor.

Suggested Readings

Alpher, V. (1991). Interdependence and parallell processes: A case study of structured analysis of social behavior in supervision and short term dynamic psychotherapy. *Psychotherapy, 28*(2), 218–231.

Cohen, R. J., & DeBetz, B. (1977). Responsive supervision of the psychiatric resident and clinical psychology intern. *American Journal of Psychoanalysis, 37,* 51–64.

Deck, M., & Morrow, J. (1989). Supervision: An interpersonal relationship. In L. Bradley (Ed.), *Counselor supervision: Principles, process, and practice* (2nd ed., pp. 35–62). Muncie, IN: Accelerated Development.

Eckstein, R. (1972). Supervision of psychotherapy. Is it teaching? It is therapy? Or is it administration? In D. E. Hendrickson & F. H. Krause (Eds.), *Counseling and psychotherapy: Training and supervision.* Columbus, OH: Charles E. Merrill.

Falvey, J. E. (1987). *Handbook of administrative supervision.* Alexandria, VA: Association for Counselor Education and Supervision.

Hart, G., & Falvey, E. (1987). Field supervision of counselors in training: A survey of the North Atlantic Region. *Counselor Education and Supervision, 26,* 204–212.

Hutt, C. H., Scott, J., & King, M. (1983). A phenomenological study of supervisee's positive and negative experiences in supervision. *Psychotherapy: Theory, Research, and Practice, 20,* 118–123.

Kadushin, A. (1976). *Supervision in social work.* New York: Columbia University Press.

Kadushin, A. (1992). *Supervision in social work* (3rd ed.). New York: Columbia University Press.

Moskowitz, S., & Rupert, P. (1983). Conflict resolution within the supervisory relationship. *Professional Psychology: Research and Practice, 14,* 632–641.

Nash, V. C. (1975). The clinical supervision of psychotherapy. *Dissertation Abstracts International, 36,* 2480B–2481B. (University Microfilms No. 75–24, 581)

Ricoh, M. J. (1980). The dilemmas of supervision in dynamics psychotherapy. In A. K. Hess (Ed.), Psychotherapy supervision: Theory, research, and practice (pp. 68–76). New York: Wiley.

Scott, J. (1976). Process supervision. In J. Scott (Ed.), *A monography on training supervisors in the helping professions* (pp. 1–10). Continuation of Northeastern EPDA/PPS Center/Satellite Project, Award Number GG-070-2021(725).

References

Bernard, J., & Goodyear, R. (1992). *Fundamentals of clinical supervision.* Boston: Allyn Bacon.

Biggs, D. A. (1988). The case presentation approach in clinical supervision. *Counselor Education and Supervision, 20,* 240–248.

Borders, L. D., & Leddick, G. R. (1987). *Handbook of counseling supervision.* Alexandria, VA: Association for Counselor Education and Supervision.

Boyd, J. (1978). The behavioral approach to counselor supervision. In J. Boyd (Ed.), *Counselor supervision* (pp. 89–132). Muncie, IN: Accelerated Development.

Bradley, L. (1989). *Counselor supervision: Principles, process and practice* (2nd ed.). Muncie, IN: Accelerated Development.

Carmichael, K. (1992). Peer rating form in counselor supervision. *Texas Association of Counseling and Development Journal, 20*(1), 57–61.

Collins, D. (1990). Identifying dysfunctional counseling skills behaviors. *The Clinical Supervisor, 8*(1), 67–69.

Cormier, S., & Hockney, H. (1987). *The professional counselor: A process guide to helpng.* Englewood Cliffs, NJ: Prentice-Hall.

D'Andrea, M. (1989). Person-process model of supervision: A developmental approach. In L. Bradley (Ed.), *Counselor supervision: Principles, process, practice* (2nd ed., pp. 257–296). Munice, IN: Accelerated Development.

Dye, H. W. (1987). Aces attitudes: Supervisors' competencies and a national certification program. ERIC/CAPS Resources in Education, Document Number Ed. 283098.

Egan, G. (1986). *The skilled helper: A systematic approach to effective helping.* Monterey, CA: Brooks/Cole.

Egan, G. (1994). *The skilled helper: A problem-management approach to helping.* Pacific Grove, CA: Brooks/Cole.

Hunsaker, P. L., & Alessandra, A. J. (1986). *The art of managing people.* New York: Simon & Schuster.

Ivey, A., & Gluckstern, N. (1984). *Basic attending skills.* North Amherst, MA: Microtraining Associates.

Kaiser, T. L. (1997). *Supervisory relationships.* Pacific Grove, CA: Brooks/Cole.

Loganbill, C., & Stoltenberg, C. (1983). The case conceptualization format: A training device for practicum. *Counselor Education and Supervision, 22,* 235–241.

Malley, P. B., & Reilly, E. P. (1999). *Legal and ethical dimensions for mental health professionals.* Philadelphia, PA: Accelerated Development.

McAuliffe, G. (1992). A case presentation approach to group supervision for community college counselors. *Counselor Education and Supervision, 31,* 163–174.

Murdock, N. (1991). Case conceptualization: Applying theory to individuals. *Counselor Education and Supervision, 30,* 355–365.

Perry, W. F. (1970). *Forms of intellectual and ethical development in college years.* New York: Holt, Rinehart, & Winston.

Ronnestad, W. H., & Skovholt, T. M. (1993). Supervision of beginning and advanced graduate students of counseling and psychotherapy. Journal of Counseling and Development, 71, 396–405.

Whitman, S. M., & Jacobs, E. G. (1998). Responsibility of the psychotherapy supervisor. *American Journal of Psychotherapy, 52*(2), 166–176.

Wittmer, J., & Myrick, R. (1974). *Facilitative teaching: Theory and practice.* Santa Monica, CA: Goodyear Publishing.

P A R T

II

ETHICS AND THE LAW

Part II addresses the ethical and legal issues of concern to the practicum student and the professional counselor or therapist. Chapter 6, "Ethical Issues," addresses the ethical principles and virtues encountered in the counseling profession. This chapter also provides the complete and most recent ethical codes and professional standards of both the ACA and the APA. Chapter 7, "Legal Issues," discusses preparation for and implementation of the therapeutic relationship (the "special relationship"), the meaning and implications of malpractice, and legal guidelines relating to client solicitation, informed consent, confidentiality, and dual relationships.

Patrick B. Malley
Eileen Petty Reilly

CHAPTER

6

Ethical Issues

All mental health professionals should be knowledgeable about the specific ethical codes of their profession. Copies of the codes appropriate for one's profession can be obtained through the professional organization that represents each of the various specialties of professional practice. In this chapter excerpts of ethical codes are provided to explicate the various professional positions.

As Huber and Baruth (1987) noted, "Ethics is concerned with the conduct of human beings as they make moral decisions" (p. 37). Beauchamp and Childress (1994) defined it this way: "Ethics is a generic term for various ways of understanding and examining the moral life" (p. 4).

▉ Ethical Codes

Ethical codes are the written set of ethical standards for the professional mental health provider. Each profession (psychology, social work, counseling, etc.) has a code specific to its particular client relationships. The codes are both national and regional. Mental health professionals have an obligation to behave in ways that do not violate these codes. Violations of the standards by a mental health worker can result in sanctions or loss of licensure.

The primary obligation of mental health professionals is to promote the well being of their clients, and ethical codes were developed to protect the integrity of this process. They allow mental health professionals to police their own members, thus reducing the need for government regulation of the profession. These codes are normative in nature in that they prescribe what mental health professionals ought to do. If a counselor finds himself or herself facing an ethical dilemma, he or she can refer to the codes for guidance.

▉ Ethical Principles

Should ethical codes not be specific or thorough enough to answer a question, one should employ ethical principles in evaluating the situation. Ethical principles are used to make decisions about moral issues inherent in a particular ethical dilemma. An ethical dilemma is a situation in which one must make a choice between competing and contradictory ethical mandates. The ethical codes do not and cannot always provide solutions to such dilemmas. Ethical principles establish a moral structure to solve dilemmas and guide future ethical thinking.

The ethical principles described in this section are based on the work of Beauchamp and Childress (1994) and Kitchener (1984). They have their roots in common sense morality, and they detail a structure of *prima facie* obligation; that is, they are considered adequate to solve ethical dilemmas unless they are refuted. If they prove to be inadequate, given the complexity of the dilemma, one must consult ethical theory.

Autonomy

The principle of autonomy says that individuals are free to direct the course of their lives, so long as their choices do not interfere with the autonomy of others. If people want to be treated as autonomous beings, they must also respect and treat others as autonomous beings. Autonomy also implies the freedom to make one's own judgments. The concept of autonomy assumes the ability to make rational judgments. Autonomy provides the foundation for many psychological tenets. Mental health professionals must enter practice with respect for

- the client and individual differences,
- the client's ability to make his or her own decisions,
- the client's right to privacy,
- the client's autonomous nature, and
- the client's competence.

Beneficence

Sound ethical practices require that mental health professionals work for the health and welfare of their clients. Clients who contract for professional psychological services must be able to expect positive benefits from the interactions. This assumes an expectation of competence. Thus, *mental health professionals should never contract with clients whose problems are outside their areas of expertise.* They should also be careful not to become paternalistic with their clients. Paternalism involves an assumption that one knows what is best for another and attempts to regulate behavior according to one's personal prejudices.

Justice

The meaning of justice as an ethical principle is said to have originated with Aristotle (Beauchamp & Childress, 1979), who suggested that justice means treating equals equally and unequals unequally but in proportion to their relative differences. Thus, equal people have the right to be treated equally and nonequal people have the right to be treated differently if the inequality is relevant to the issue in question. For example, politicians may be equal as persons but have different party affiliations. Should these politicians need medical care, they should be treated equally and fairly. Should they aspire to office and run for reelection, they may be treated differently by their constituents.

Nonmaleficence

The principle of nonmaleficence requires that one refrain from intentionally inflicting harm or taking actions that might harm another. Nonmaleficence, like the Hippocratic oath, requires, first, that one do no harm.

Fidelity

Issues of fidelity arise for mental health professionals when two people voluntarily enter into a client-counselor relationship. Fidelity involves keeping promises; it also involves the issue of loyalty.

■ Ethical Virtues

A virtue is a quality that is socially or morally valued. As such, virtues involve more than just actions; they are ideals and moral habits embedded in the traditions and practices of a culture. Using these ideals to guide one's life develops character. The ideals may be different in different cultures. Virtue ethics focus on the actor, not the act.

Moral virtue denotes the qualities of a person that are perceived as worthy of merit in the context of issues related to ideal conduct. For instance, integrity is a character trait that conveys a certain quality of inner strength. Public spiritedness could be described as a virtue involving doing good for the community. Some of the more salient virtues found in the professional literature are integrity, discretion, prudence, respectfulness, benevolence, hope, humility, perseverance, and courage.

Virtue and Culture

Virtues are meritorious qualities that are specific to communities and cultures. They constitute the expectations of behavior in a community that has a shared set of purposes and assumptions. For example, in certain cultures it is expected that women will defer to men. In other cultures, however, this behavior is seen as disrespectful. Edel, Flower, and O'Connor (1994) reported that those who have a Western perspective of morality often are not aware of the clear distinctions they draw between right and wrong. But the view that something is either right or wrong is not commonly held in North African and Mediterranean cultures. People in these cultures are more interested in preserving the honor of others. Virtues are not always totally relative to culture; views of courage and cowardice, for example, are shared across cultures. Mental health professionals who work with cultures different from those in which they were nurtured should be keenly aware that different cultures might have different hierarchies of values.

Virtue and Ideals

Proponents of virtue ethics believe that mental health professionals should do more than simply learn rules and regulations. They assert that counselors should also be dedicated to cultivating traits and dispositions that motivate them to excellence. The therapist who is motivated to do what is right because it is right—not simply out of fear of reprisal—is a virtuous therapist. Aspiration to the moral ideal is inextricably linked to the aspiration for ideal moral action.

According to this view, the pursuit of ideals must be important for the mental health professional. The therapist has an imperative to approximate the ideal with respect to these virtues (Jordan & Meara, 1990). Proponents of virtue ethics believe that focusing only on ethical principles has severe limitations. As Jordan and Meara (1990) noted, "Case studies risk becoming primarily abstract thought puzzles to be analyzed according to specialized rules. Other critical psychological dimensions, such as human pain, pathos and historical particularity, tend to be underestimated or forgotten" (p. 108). Perhaps the recent emphasis on the formal and abstract dimensions of ethical problem solving, to the exclusion of other dimensions, is what prompted the following criticisms of the current APA code of ethics:

> The current APA code (1995), which was the result of a massive, careful consultative effort, has been sharply criticized for a number of problems, including being "too lawyerly," . . . not being as sensitive to minority issues as codes, ...being more concerned about the profession than the public, . . . and having mediocre expectations for teaching psychologists. (Meara, Schmidt, & Day, 1996, p. 5)

Virtue and Skill

Hauerwas (1981) described virtues as "specific skills required to live faithfully to a traditional understanding of the moral product in which its adherents participate" (p. 115). Jordan and Meara (1990) demonstrated how the virtues of prudence and discretion translate into skills that help the mental health professional in his or her therapeutic endeavors:

> In the psychotherapeutic context, prudence enables the professional to hear the client's history, current life situation, and future hopes, but he or she does this with cautious attentiveness to the client's natural and subtle but self-serving distortions of memory, identity, and expectations. Discretion enables the therapist to make genuine responses to these distortions. In addition, prudence and discretion encourage an alert realization that the psychotherapeutic interaction is in part always open-ended and unpredictable. (p. 112)

Another example of virtue helping to develop demonstrative skills can be shown in a counselor's responsibility for informed consent. While much attention has been given to *what* should be disclosed to a client so as to properly obtain informed consent, little attention is paid to *how* the client should be informed. How the client is informed, and how he or she is treated, are as important as the information involved (May, 1984, cited in Jordan & Meara, 1990).

Limitations of Virtue Ethics

Bersoff (1996) questioned whether decisions actually are made by virtue ethics:

> The difference between virtue and principle is not clear to my mind. "What shall I do?" and "Who shall I be?" are not competing questions. The answers to both are inextricably woven. Who I am is determined by what I do.
>
> Character traits, although potentially malleable, are developed as a result of genetics. Not even years of professional training, in which students are sensitized to ethics, will necessarily produce a virtuous agent able to employ virtuous ideals. Intensive therapy over many years often fails to accomplish this goal. Secondly, if acting ethically depends on one's character, I wonder if the outcomes of professional training will be too individualized and idiosyncratic. An ethical code and ethical conduct, I would assert, rely on consensual decision making about the integrity of the profession, not the singular vagaries of a psychologist's character. (pp. 88–89)

Kitchener (1996) wondered how character traits differ from the more common construct of personality traits. She asserted that psychologists need a better understanding of what character traits are and how they relate to psychological constructs before they begin to develop them.

American Counseling Association Code of Ethics and Standards of Practice*

Code of Ethics

PREAMBLE

The American Counseling Association is an educational, scientific, and professional organization whose members are dedicated to the enhancement of human development throughout the life-span. Association members recognize diversity in our society and embrace a cross-cultural approach in support of the worth, dignity, potential, and uniqueness of each individual.

The specification of a code of ethics enables the association to clarify to current and future members, and to those served by members, the nature of the ethical responsibilities held in common by its members. As the code of ethics of the association, this document establishes principles that define the ethical behavior of association members. All members of the American Counseling Association are required to adhere to the Code of Ethics and the Standards of Practice. The Code of Ethics will serve as the basis for processing ethical complaints initiated against members of the association.

Section A: The Counseling Relationship

A.1. Client Welfare
 a. *Primary Responsibility.*
   The primary responsibility of counselors is to respect the dignity and to promote the welfare of clients.
 b. *Positive Growth and Development.*
   Counselors encourage client growth and development in ways that foster the clients' interest and welfare; counselors avoid fostering dependent counseling relationships.
 c. *Counseling Plans.*
   Counselors and their clients work jointly in devising integrated, individual counseling plans that offer reasonable promise of success and are consistent with abilities and circumstances of clients. Counselors and clients regularly review counseling plans to ensure their continued viability and effectiveness, respecting clients' freedom of choice. (See A.3.b.)
 d. *Family Involvement.*
   Counselors recognize that families are usually important in clients' lives and strive to enlist family understanding and involvement as a positive resource, when appropriate.
 e. *Career and Employment Needs.*
   Counselors work with their clients in considering employment in jobs and circumstances that are consistent with the clients' overall abilities, vocational limitations, physical restrictions, general tempera-

ment, interest and aptitude patterns, social skills, education, general qualifications, and other relevant characteristics and needs. Counselors neither place nor participate in placing clients in positions that will result in damaging the interest and the welfare of clients, employers, or the public.

A.2. Respecting Diversity
 a. *Nondiscrimination.*
   Counselors do not condone or engage in discrimination based on age, color, culture, disability, ethnic group, gender, race, religion, sexual orientation, marital status, or socioeconomic status. (See C.5.a., C.5.b., and D.1.i.)
 b. *Respecting Differences.*
   Counselors will actively attempt to understand the diverse cultural backgrounds of the clients with whom they work. This includes, but is not limited to, learning how the counselor's own cultural/ethnic/racial identity impacts her or his values and beliefs about the counseling process. (See E.8. and F.2.i.)

A.3. Client Rights
 a. *Disclosure to Clients.*
   When counseling is initiated, and throughout the counseling process as necessary, counselors inform clients of the purposes, goals, techniques, procedures, limitations, potential risks, and benefits of services to be performed, and other pertinent information. Counselors take steps to ensure that clients understand the implications of diagnosis, the intended use of tests and reports, fees, and billing arrangements. Clients have the right to expect confidentiality and to be provided with an explanation of its limitations, including supervision and/or treatment team professionals; to obtain clear information about their case records; to participate in the ongoing counseling plans; and to refuse any recommended services and be advised of the consequences of such refusal. (See E.5.a. and G.2.)
 b. *Freedom of Choice.*
   Counselors offer clients the freedom to choose whether to enter into a counseling relationship and to determine which professional(s) will provide counseling. Restrictions that limit choices of clients are fully explained. (See A.1.c.)
 c. *Inability to Give Consent.*
   When counseling minors or persons unable to give voluntary informed consent, counselors act in these clients' best interests. (See B.3.)

A.4. Clients Served by Others
   If a client is receiving services from another mental health professional, counselors, with client consent,

inform the professional persons already involved and develop clear agreements to avoid confusion and conflict for the client. (See C.6.c.)

A.5. Personal Needs and Values

a. *Personal Needs.*

In the counseling relationship, counselors are aware of the intimacy and responsibilities inherent in the counseling relationship, maintain respect for clients, and avoid actions that seek to meet their personal needs at the expense of clients.

b. *Personal Values.*

Counselors are aware of their own values, attitudes, beliefs, and behaviors and how these apply in a diverse society, and avoid imposing their values on clients. (See C.5.a.)

A.6. Dual Relationships

a. *Avoid When Possible.*

Counselors are aware of their influential positions with respect to clients, and they avoid exploiting the trust and dependency of clients. Counselors make every effort to avoid dual relationships with clients that could impair professional judgment or increase the risk of harm to clients. (Examples of such relationships include, but are not limited to, familial, social, financial, business, or close personal relationships with clients.) When a dual relationship cannot be avoided, counselors take appropriate professional precautions such as informed consent, consultation, supervision, and documentation to ensure that judgment is not impaired and no exploitation occurs. (See F.1.b.)

b. *Superior/Subordinate Relationships.*

Counselors do not accept as clients superiors or subordinates with whom they have administrative, supervisory, or evaluative relationships.

A.7. Sexual Intimacies With Clients

a. *Current Clients.*

Counselors do not have any type of sexual intimacies with clients and do not counsel persons with whom they have had a sexual relationship.

b. *Former Clients.*

Counselors do not engage in sexual intimacies with former clients within a minimum of 2 years after terminating the counseling relationship. Counselors who engage in such relationship after 2 years following termination have the responsibility to examine and document thoroughly that such relations did not have an exploitative nature, based on factors such as duration of counseling, amount of time since counseling, termination circumstances, client's personal history and mental status, adverse impact on the client, and actions by the counselor suggesting a plan to initiate a sexual relationship with the client after termination.

A.8. Multiple Clients

When counselors agree to provide counseling services to two or more persons who have a relationship (such as husband and wife, or parents and children), counselors clarify at the outset which person or persons are clients and the nature of the rela-

tionships they will have with each involved person. If it becomes apparent that counselors may be called upon to perform potentially conflicting roles, they clarify, adjust, or withdraw from roles appropriately. (See B.2. and B.4.d.)

A.9. Group Work

a. *Screening.*

Counselors screen prospective group counseling/therapy participants. To the extent possible, counselors select members whose needs and goals are compatible with goals of the group, who will not impede the group process, and whose well-being will not be jeopardized by the group experience.

b. *Protecting Clients.*

In a group setting, counselors take reasonable precautions to protect clients from physical or psychological trauma.

A.10. Fees and Bartering (See D.3.a. and D.3.b.)

a. *Advance Understanding.*

Counselors clearly explain to clients, prior to entering the counseling relationship, all financial arrangements related to professional services including the use of collection agencies or legal measures for nonpayment. (A.11.c.)

b. *Establishing Fees.*

In establishing fees for professional counseling services, counselors consider the financial status of clients and locality. In the event that the established fee structure is inappropriate for a client, assistance is provided in attempting to find comparable services of acceptable cost. (See A.10.d., D.3.a., and D.3.b.)

c. *Bartering Discouraged.*

Counselors ordinarily refrain from accepting goods or services from clients in return for counseling services because such arrangements create inherent potential for conflicts, exploitation, and distortion of the professional relationship. Counselors may participate in bartering only if the relationship is not exploitative, if the client requests it, if a clear written contract is established, and if such arrangements are an accepted practice among professionals in the community. (See A.6.a.)

d. *Pro Bono Service.*

Counselors contribute to society by devoting a portion of their professional activity to services for which there is little or no financial return (pro bono).

A.11. Termination and Referral

a. *Abandonment Prohibited.*

Counselors do not abandon or neglect clients in counseling. Counselors assist in making appropriate arrangements for the continuation of treatment, when necessary, during interruptions such as vacations, and following termination.

b. *Inability to Assist Clients.*

If counselors determine an inability to be of professional assistance to clients, they avoid entering or immediately terminate a counseling relationship. Counselors are knowledgeable about referral resources and suggest appropriate alternatives. If clients decline the suggested referral, counselors should discontinue the relationship.

c. *Appropriate Termination.*

Counselors terminate a counseling relationship, securing client agreement when possible, when it is reasonably clear that the client is no longer benefiting, when services are no longer required, when counseling no longer serves the client's needs or interests, when clients do not pay fees charged, or when agency or institution limits do not allow provision of further counseling services. (See A.10.b. and C.2.g.)

A.12. Computer Technology

a. *Use of Computers.*

When computer applications are used in counseling services, counselors ensure that (1) the client is intellectually, emotionally, and physically capable of using the computer application; (2) the computer application is appropriate for the needs of the client; (3) the client understands the purpose and operation of the computer applications; and (4) a follow-up of client use of a computer application is provided to correct possible misconceptions, discover inappropriate use, and assess subsequent needs.

b. *Explanation of Limitations.*

Counselors ensure that clients are provided information as a part of the counseling relationship that adequately explains the limitations of computer technology.

c. *Access to Computer Applications.*

Counselors provide for equal access to computer applications in counseling services. (See A.2.a.)

Section B: Confidentiality

B.1. Right to Privacy

a. *Respect for Privacy.*

Counselors respect their clients right to privacy and avoid illegal and unwarranted disclosures of confidential information. (See A.3.a. and B.6.a.)

b. *Client Waiver.*

The right to privacy may be waived by the client or his or her legally recognized representative.

c. *Exceptions.*

The general requirement that counselors keep information confidential does not apply when disclosure is required to prevent clear and imminent danger to the client or others or when legal requirements demand that confidential information be revealed. Counselors consult with other professionals when in doubt as to the validity of an exception.

d. *Contagious, Fatal Diseases.*

A counselor who receives information confirming that a client has a disease commonly known to be both communicable and fatal is justified in disclosing information to an identifiable third party, who by his or her relationship with the client is at a high risk of contracting the disease. Prior to making a

disclosure the counselor should ascertain that the client has not already informed the third party about his or her disease and that the client is not intending to inform the third party in the immediate future. (See B.1.c and B.1.f.)

e. *Court-Ordered Disclosure.*

When court ordered to release confidential information without a client's permission, counselors request to the court that the disclosure not be required due to potential harm to the client or counseling relationship. (See B.1.c.)

f. *Minimal Disclosure.*

When circumstances require the disclosure of confidential information, only essential information is revealed. To the extent possible, clients are informed before confidential information is disclosed.

g. *Explanation of Limitations.*

When counseling is initiated and throughout the counseling process as necessary, counselors inform clients of the limitations of confidentiality and identify foreseeable situations in which confidentiality must be breached. (See G.2.a.)

h. *Subordinates.*

Counselors make every effort to ensure that privacy and confidentiality of clients are maintained by subordinates including employees, supervisees, clerical assistants, and volunteers. (See B.1.a.)

i. *Treatment Teams.*

If client treatment will involve a continued review by a treatment team, the client will be informed of the team's existence and composition.

B.2. Groups and Families

a. *Group Work.*

In group work, counselors clearly define confidentiality and the parameters for the specific group being entered, explain its importance, and discuss the difficulties related to confidentiality involved in group work. The fact that confidentiality cannot be guaranteed is clearly communicated to group members.

b. *Family Counseling.*

In family counseling, information about one family member cannot be disclosed to another member without permission.

Counselors protect the privacy rights of each family member. (See A.8., B.3., and B.4.d.)

B.3. Minor or Incompetent Clients

When counseling clients who are minors or individuals who are unable to give voluntary, informed consent, parents or guardians may be included in the counseling process as appropriate. Counselors act in the best interests of clients and take measures to safeguard confidentiality. (See A.3.c.)

B.4. Records

a. *Requirement of Records.*

Counselors maintain records necessary for rendering professional services to their clients and as required by laws, regulations, or agency or institution procedures.

b. *Confidentiality of Records.*
Counselors are responsible for securing the safety and confidentiality of any counseling records they create, maintain, transfer, or destroy whether the records are written, taped, computerized, or stored in any other medium. (See B.1.a.)

c. *Permission to Record or Observe.*
Counselors obtain permission from clients prior to electronically recording or observing sessions. (See A.3.a.)

d. *Client Access.*
Counselors recognize that counseling records are kept for the benefit of clients, and therefore provide access to records and copies of records when requested by competent clients, unless the records contain information that may be misleading and detrimental to the client. In situations involving multiple clients, access to records is limited to those parts of records that do not include confidential information related to another client. (See A.8., B.1.a., and B.2.b.)

e. *Disclosure or Transfer.*
Counselors obtain written permission from clients to disclose or transfer records to legitimate third parties unless exceptions to confidentiality exist as listed in Section B.1. Steps are taken to ensure that receivers of counseling records are sensitive to their confidential nature.

B.5. Research and Training

a. *Data Disguise Required.*
Use of data derived from counseling relationships for purposes of training, research, or publication is confined to content that is disguised to ensure the anonymity of the individuals involved. (See B.1.g. and G.3.d.)

b. *Agreement for Identification.*
Identification of a client in a presentation or publication is permissible only when the client has reviewed the material and has agreed to its presentation or publication. (See G.3.d.)

B.6. Consultation

a. *Respect for Privacy.*
Information obtained in a consulting relationship is discussed for professional purposes only with persons clearly concerned with the case. Written and oral reports present data germane to the purposes of the consultation, and every effort is made to protect client identity and avoid undue invasion of privacy.

b. *Cooperating Agencies.*
Before sharing information, counselors make efforts to ensure that there are defined policies in other agencies serving the counselor's clients that effectively protect the confidentiality of information.

Section C: Professional Responsibility

C.1. Standards Knowledge
Counselors have a responsibility to read, understand, and follow the Code of Ethics and the Standards of Practice.

C.2. Professional Competence

a. *Boundaries of Competence.*
Counselors practice only within the boundaries of their competence, based on their education, training, supervised experience, state and national professional credentials, and appropriate professional experience. Counselors will demonstrate a commitment to gain knowledge, personal awareness, sensitivity, and skills pertinent to working with a diverse client population.

b. *New Specialty Areas of Practice.*
Counselors practice in specialty areas new to them only after appropriate education, training, and supervised experience. While developing skills in new specialty areas, counselors take steps to ensure the competence of their work and to protect others from possible harm.

c. *Qualified for Employment.*
Counselors accept employment only for positions for which they are qualified by education, training, supervised experience, state and national professional credentials, and appropriate professional experience. Counselors hire for professional counseling positions only individuals who are qualified and competent.

d. *Monitor Effectiveness.*
Counselors continually monitor their effectiveness as professionals and take steps to improve when necessary. Counselors in private practice take reasonable steps to seek out peer supervision to evaluate their efficacy as counselors.

e. *Ethical Issues Consultation.*
Counselors take reasonable steps to consult with other counselors or related professionals when they have questions regarding their ethical obligations or professional practice. (See H.1.)

f. *Continuing Education.*
Counselors recognize the need for continuing education to maintain a reasonable level of awareness of current scientific and professional information in their fields of activity. They take steps to maintain competence in the skills they use, are open to new procedures, and keep current with the diverse and/or special populations with whom they work.

g. *Impairment.*
Counselors refrain from offering or accepting professional services when their physical, mental, or emotional problems are likely to harm a client or others. They are alert to the signs of impairment, seek assistance for problems, and, if necessary, limit, suspend, or terminate their professional responsibilities. (See A.11.c.)

C.3. Advertising and Soliciting Clients

a. *Accurate Advertising.*
There are no restrictions on advertising by counselors except those that can be specifically justified to protect the public from deceptive practices. Counselors advertise or represent their services to the public by identifying their credentials in an accurate manner that is not false, misleading, deceptive,

or fraudulent. Counselors may only advertise the highest degree earned which is in counseling or a closely related field from a college or university that was accredited when the degree was awarded by one of the regional accrediting bodies recognized by the Council on Postsecondary Accreditation.

b. *Testimonials.*

Counselors who use testimonials do not solicit them from clients or other persons who, because of their particular circumstances, may be vulnerable to undue influence.

c. *Statements by Others.*

Counselors make reasonable efforts to ensure that statements made by others about them or the profession of counseling are accurate.

d. *Recruiting Through Employment.*

Counselors do not use their places of employment or institutional affiliation to recruit or gain clients, supervisees, or consultees for their private practices. (See C.5.e.)

e. *Products and Training Advertisements.*

Counselors who develop products related to their profession or conduct workshops or training events ensure that the advertisements concerning these products or events are accurate and disclose adequate information for consumers to make informed choices.

f. *Promoting to Those Served.*

Counselors do not use counseling, teaching, training, or supervisory relationships to promote their products or training events in a manner that is deceptive or would exert undue influence on individuals who may be vulnerable. Counselors may adopt textbooks they have authored for instruction purposes.

g. *Professional Association Involvement.*

Counselors actively participate in local, state, and national associations that foster the development and improvement of counseling.

C.4. Credentials

a. *Credentials Claimed.*

Counselors claim or imply only professional credentials possessed and are responsible for correcting any known misrepresentations of their credentials by others. Professional credentials include graduate degrees in counseling or closely related mental health fields, accreditation of graduate programs, national voluntary certifications, government-issued certifications or licenses, ACA professional membership, or any other credential that might indicate to the public specialized knowledge or expertise in counseling.

b. *ACA Professional Membership.*

ACA professional members may announce to the public their membership status. Regular members may not announce their ACA membership in a manner that might imply they are credentialed counselors.

c. *Credential Guidelines.*

Counselors follow the guidelines for use of credentials that have been established by the entities that issue the credentials.

d. *Misrepresentation of Credentials.*

Counselors do not attribute more to their credentials than the credentials represent, and do not imply that other counselors are not qualified because they do not possess certain credentials.

e. *Doctoral Degrees From Other Fields.*

Counselors who hold a master's degree in counseling or a closely related mental health field, but hold a doctoral degree from other than counseling or a closely related field, do not use the title "Dr." in their practices and do not announce to the public in relation to their practice or status as a counselor that they hold a doctorate.

C.5. Public Responsibility

a. *Nondiscrimination.*

Counselors do not discriminate against clients, students, or supervisees in a manner that has a negative impact based on their age, color, culture, disability, ethnic group, gender, race, religion, sexual orientation, or socioeconomic status, or for any other reason. (See A.2.a.)

b. *Sexual Harassment.*

Counselors do not engage in sexual harassment. Sexual harassment is defined as sexual solicitation, physical advances, or verbal or nonverbal conduct that is sexual in nature, that occurs in connection with professional activities or roles, and that either (1) is unwelcome, is offensive, or creates a hostile workplace environment, and counselors know or are told this; or (2) is sufficiently severe or intense to be perceived as harassment to a reasonable person in the context. Sexual harassment can consist of a single intense or severe act or multiple persistent or pervasive acts.

c. *Reports to Third Parties.*

Counselors are accurate, honest, and unbiased in reporting their professional activities and judgments to appropriate third parties including courts, health insurance companies, those who are the recipients of evaluation reports, and others. (See B.1.g.)

d. *Media Presentations.*

When counselors provide advice or comment by means of public lectures, demonstrations, radio or television programs, prerecorded tapes, printed articles, mailed material, or other media, they take reasonable precautions to ensure that (1) the statements are based on appropriate professional counseling literature and practice; (2) the statements are otherwise consistent with the Code of Ethics and the Standards of Practice; and (3) the recipients of the information are not encouraged to infer that a professional counseling relationship has been established. (See C.6.b.)

e. *Unjustified Gains.*

Counselors do not use their professional positions to seek or receive unjustified personal gains, sexual favors, unfair advantage, or unearned goods or services. (See C.3.d.)

C.6. Responsibility to Other Professionals

a. *Different Approaches.*

Counselors are respectful of approaches to professional counseling that differ from their own. Counselors know and take into account the traditions and practices of other professional groups with which they work.

b. *Personal Public Statements.*

When making personal statements in a public context, counselors clarify that they are speaking from their personal perspectives and that they are not speaking on behalf of all counselors or the profession. (See C.5.d.)

c. *Clients Served by Others.*

When counselors learn that their clients are in a professional relationship with another mental health professional, they request release from clients to inform the other professionals and strive to establish positive and collaborative professional relationships. (See A.4.)

Section D: Relationships With Other Professionals

D.1. Relationships With Employers and Employees

a. *Role Definition.*

Counselors define and describe for their employers and employees the parameters and levels of their professional roles.

b. *Agreements.*

Counselors establish working agreements with supervisors, colleagues, and subordinates regarding counseling or clinical relationships, confidentiality, adherence to professional standards, distinction between public and private material, maintenance and dissemination of recorded information, work load, and accountability. Working agreements in each instance are specified and made known to those concerned.

c. *Negative Conditions.*

Counselors alert their employers to conditions that may be potentially disruptive or damaging to the counselor's professional responsibilities or that may limit their effectiveness.

d. *Evaluation.*

Counselors submit regularly to professional review and evaluation by their supervisor or the appropriate representative of the employer.

e. *In-Service.*

Counselors are responsible for in-service development of self and staff.

f. *Goals.*

Counselors inform their staff of goals and programs.

g. *Practices.*

Counselors provide personnel and agency practices that respect and enhance the rights and welfare of each employee and recipient of agency services. Counselors strive to maintain the highest levels of professional services.

h. *Personnel Selection and Assignment.*

Counselors select competent staff and assign responsibilities compatible with their skills and experiences.

i. *Discrimination.*

Counselors, as either employers or employees, do not engage in or condone practices that are inhumane, illegal, or unjustifiable (such as considerations based on age, color, culture, disability, ethnic group, gender, race, religion, sexual orientation, or socioeconomic status) in hiring, promotion, or training. (See A.2.a. and C.5.b.)

j. *Professional Conduct.*

Counselors have a responsibility both to clients and to the agency or institution within which services are performed to maintain high standards of professional conduct.

k. *Exploitative Relationships.*

Counselors do not engage in exploitative relationships with individuals over whom they have supervisory, evaluative, or instructional control or authority.

l. Employer Policies.

The acceptance of employment in an agency or institution implies that counselors are in agreement with its general policies and principles. Counselors strive to reach agreement with employers as to acceptable standards of conduct that allow for changes in institutional policy conducive to the growth and development of clients.

D.2. Consultation (See B.6.)

a. *Consultation as an Option.*

Counselors may choose to consult with any other professionally competent persons about their clients. In choosing consultants, counselors avoid placing the consultant in a conflict of interest situation that would preclude the consultant being a proper party to the counselor's efforts to help the client. Should counselors be engaged in a work setting that compromises this consultation standard, they consult with other professionals whenever possible to consider justifiable alternatives.

b. *Consultant Competency.*

Counselors are reasonably certain that they have or the organization represented has the necessary competencies and resources for giving the kind of consulting services needed and that appropriate referral resources are available.

c. *Understanding With Clients.*

When providing consultation, counselors attempt to develop with their clients a clear understanding of problem definition, goals for change, and predicted consequences of interventions selected.

d. *Consultant Goals.*

The consulting relationship is one in which client adaptability and growth toward self-direction are consistently encouraged and cultivated. (See A.1.b.)

D.3. Fees for Referral

a. *Accepting Fees From Agency Clients.*

Counselors refuse a private fee or other remuneration for rendering services to persons who are entitled to such services through the counselor's employing agency or institution. The policies of a particular agency may make explicit provisions for agency clients to receive counseling services from members of its staff in private practice. In such instances, the clients must be informed of other options open to them should they seek private counseling services. (See A.10.a., A.11.b., and C.3.d.)

b. *Referral Fees.*

Counselors do not accept a referral fee from other professionals.

D.4. Subcontractor Arrangements

When counselors work as subcontractors for counseling services for a third party, they have a duty to inform clients of the limitations of confidentiality that the organization may place on counselors in providing counseling services to clients. The limits of such confidentiality ordinarily are discussed as part of the intake session. (See B.1.e. and B.1.f.)

Section E: Evaluation, Assessment, and Interpretation

E.1. General

a. *Appraisal Techniques.*

The primary purpose of educational and psychological assessment is to provide measures that are objective and interpretable in either comparative or absolute terms. Counselors recognize the need to interpret the statements in this section as applying to the whole range of appraisal techniques, including test and nontest data.

b. *Client Welfare.*

Counselors promote the welfare and best interests of the client in the development, publication, and utilization of educational and psychological assessment techniques. They do not misuse assessment results and interpretations and take reasonable steps to prevent others from misusing the information these techniques provide. They respect the client's right to know the results, the interpretations made, and the bases for their conclusions and recommendations.

E.2. Competence to Use and Interpret Tests

a. *Limits of Competence.*

Counselors recognize the limits of their competence and perform only those testing and assessment services for which they have been trained. They are familiar with reliability, validity, related standardization, error of measurement, and proper application of any technique utilized. Counselors using computer-based test interpretations are trained in the construct being measured and the specific instrument being used prior to using this type of computer application. Counselors take reasonable measures to ensure the proper use of psychological assessment techniques by persons under their supervision.

b. *Appropriate Use.*

Counselors are responsible for the appropriate application, scoring, interpretation, and use of assessment instruments, whether they score and interpret

such tests themselves or use computerized or other services.

c. *Decisions Based on Results.*

Counselors responsible for decisions involving individuals or policies that are based on assessment results have a thorough understanding of educational and psychological measurement, including validation criteria, test research, and guidelines for test development and use.

d. *Accurate Information.*

Counselors provide accurate information and avoid false claims or misconceptions when making statements about assessment instruments or techniques. Special efforts are made to avoid unwarranted connotations of such terms as IQ and grade equivalent scores. (See C.5.c.)

E.3. Informed Consent

a. *Explanation to Clients.*

Prior to assessment, counselors explain the nature and purposes of assessment and the specific use of results in language the client (or other legally authorized person on behalf of the client) can understand, unless an explicit exception to this right has been agreed upon in advance. Regardless of whether scoring and interpretation are completed by counselors, by assistants, or by computer or other outside services, counselors take reasonable steps to ensure that appropriate explanations are given to the client.

b. *Recipients of Results.*

The examinee's welfare, explicit understanding, and prior agreement determine the recipients of test results. Counselors include accurate and appropriate interpretations with any release of individual or group test results. (See B.1.a. and C.5.c.)

E.4. Release of Information to Competent Professionals

a. *Misuse of Results.*

Counselors do not misuse assessment results, including test results, and interpretations, and take reasonable steps to prevent the misuse of such by others. (See C.5.c.)

b. *Release of Raw Data.*

Counselors ordinarily release data (e.g., protocols, counseling or interview notes, or questionnaires) in which the client is identified only with the consent of the client or the client's legal representative. Such data are usually released only to persons recognized by counselors as competent to interpret the data. (See B.1.a.)

E.5. Proper Diagnosis of Mental Disorders

a. *Proper Diagnosis.*

Counselors take special care to provide proper diagnosis of mental disorders. Assessment techniques (including personal interview) used to determine client care (e.g., locus of treatment, type of treatment, or recommended follow-up) are carefully selected and appropriately used. (See A.3.a. and C.5.c.)

b. *Cultural Sensitivity.*

Counselors recognize that culture affects the manner in which clients' problems are defined. Clients' socioeconomic and cultural experience is considered when diagnosing mental disorders.

E.6. Test Selection

a. *Appropriateness of Instruments.*
Counselors carefully consider the validity, reliability, psychometric limitations, and appropriateness of instruments when selecting tests for use in a given situation or with a particular client.

b. *Culturally Diverse Populations.*
Counselors are cautious when selecting tests for culturally diverse populations to avoid inappropriateness of testing that may be outside of socialized behavioral or cognitive patterns.

E.7. Conditions of Test Administration

a. *Administration Conditions.*
Counselors administer tests under the same conditions that were established in their standardization. When tests are not administered under standard conditions or when unusual behavior or irregularities occur during the testing session, those conditions are noted in interpretation, and the results may be designated as invalid or of questionable validity.

b. *Computer Administration.*
Counselors are responsible for ensuring that administration programs function properly to provide clients with accurate results when a computer or other electronic methods are used for test administration. (See A.12.b.)

c. *Unsupervised Test Taking.*
Counselors do not permit unsupervised or inadequately supervised use of tests or assessments unless the tests or assessments are designed, intended, and validated for self-administration and/or scoring.

d. *Disclosure of Favorable Conditions.*
Prior to test administration, conditions that produce most favorable test results are made known to the examinee.

E.8. Diversity in Testing
Counselors are cautious in using assessment techniques, making evaluations, and interpreting the performance of populations not represented in the norm group on which an instrument was standardized. They recognize the effects of age, color, culture, disability, ethnic group, gender, race, religion, sexual orientation, and socioeconomic status on test administration and interpretation and place test results in proper perspective with other relevant factors. (See A.2.a.)

E.9. Test Scoring and Interpretation

a. *Reporting Reservations.*
In reporting assessment results, counselors indicate any reservations that exist regarding validity or reliability because of the circumstances of the assessment or the inappropriateness of the norms for the person tested.

b. *Research Instruments.*
Counselors exercise caution when interpreting the results of research instruments possessing insuffi-

cient technical data to support respondent results. The specific purposes for the use of such instruments are stated explicitly to the examinee.

c. *Testing Services.*
Counselors who provide test scoring and test interpretation services to support the assessment process confirm the validity of such interpretations. They accurately describe the purpose, norms, validity, reliability, and applications of the procedures and any special qualifications applicable to their use. The public offering of an automated test interpretations service is considered a professional-to-professional consultation. The formal responsibility of the consultant is to the consultee, but the ultimate and overriding responsibility is to the client.

E.10. Test Security
Counselors maintain the integrity and security of tests and other assessment techniques consistent with legal and contractual obligations. Counselors do not appropriate, reproduce, or modify published tests or parts thereof without acknowledgment and permission from the publisher.

E.11. Obsolete Tests and Outdated Test Results
Counselors do not use data or test results that are obsolete or outdated for the current purpose. Counselors make every effort to prevent the misuse of obsolete measures and test data by others.

E.12. Test Construction
Counselors use established scientific procedures, relevant standards, and current professional knowledge for test design in the development, publication, and utilization of educational and psychological assessment techniques.

Section F: Teaching, Training, and Supervision

F.1. Counselor Educators and Trainers

a. *Educators as Teachers and Practitioners.*
Counselors who are responsible for developing, implementing, and supervising educational programs are skilled as teachers and practitioners. They are knowledgeable regarding the ethical, legal, and regulatory aspects of the profession, are skilled in applying that knowledge, and make students and supervisees aware of their responsibilities. Counselors conduct counselor education and training programs in an ethical manner and serve as role models for professional behavior. Counselor educators should make an effort to infuse material related to human diversity into all courses and/or workshops that are designed to promote the development of professional counselors.

b. *Relationship Boundaries With Students and Supervisees.*
Counselors clearly define and maintain ethical, professional, and social relationship boundaries with their students and supervisees. They are aware of the differential in power that exists and the student's or supervisee's possible incomprehension of that power differential. Counselors explain to students and supervisees the potential for the relationship to become exploitive.

c. *Sexual Relationships.*

Counselors do not engage in sexual relationships with students or supervisees and do not subject them to sexual harassment. (See A.6. and C.5.b)

d. *Contributions to Research.*

Counselors give credit to students or supervisees for their contributions to research and scholarly projects. Credit is given through coauthorship, acknowledgment, footnote statement, or other appropriate means, in accordance with such contributions. (See G.4.b. and G.4.c.)

e. *Close Relatives.*

Counselors do not accept close relatives as students or supervisees.

f. *Supervision Preparation.*

Counselors who offer clinical supervision services are adequately prepared in supervision methods and techniques. Counselors who are doctoral students serving as practicum or internship supervisors to master's level students are adequately prepared and supervised by the training program.

g. *Responsibility for Services to Clients.*

Counselors who supervise the counseling services of others take reasonable measures to ensure that counseling services provided to clients are professional.

h. *Endorsement.*

Counselors do not endorse students or supervisees for certification, licensure, employment, or completion of an academic or training program if they believe students or supervisees are not qualified for the endorsement. Counselors take reasonable steps to assist students or supervisees who are not qualified for endorsement to become qualified.

F.2. Counselor Education and Training Programs

a. *Orientation.*

Prior to admission, counselors orient prospective students to the counselor education or training program's expectations, including but not limited to the following: (1) the type and level of skill acquisition required for successful completion of the training, (2) subject matter to be covered, (3) basis for evaluation, (4) training components that encourage self-growth or self-disclosure as part of the training process, (5) the type of supervision settings and requirements of the sites for required clinical field experiences, (6) student and supervisee evaluation and dismissal policies and procedures, and (7) up-to-date employment prospects for graduates.

b. *Integration of Study and Practice.*

Counselors establish counselor education and training programs that integrate academic study and supervised practice.

c. *Evaluation.*

Counselors clearly state to students and supervisees, in advance of training, the levels of competency expected, appraisal methods, and timing of evaluations for both didactic and experiential components. Counselors provide students and supervisees with periodic performance appraisal and evaluation feedback throughout the training program.

d. *Teaching Ethics.*

Counselors make students and supervisees aware of the ethical responsibilities and standards of the profession and the students' and supervisees' ethical responsibilities to the profession. (See C.1. and F.3.e.)

e. *Peer Relationships.*

When students or supervisees are assigned to lead counseling groups or provide clinical supervision for their peers, counselors take steps to ensure that students and supervisees placed in these roles do not have personal or adverse relationships with peers and that they understand they have the same ethical obligations as counselor educators, trainers, and supervisors. Counselors make every effort to ensure that the rights of peers are not compromised when students or supervisees are assigned to lead counseling groups or provide clinical supervision.

f. *Varied Theoretical Positions.*

Counselors present varied theoretical positions so that students and supervisees may make comparisons and have opportunities to develop their own positions. Counselors provide information concerning the scientific bases of professional practice. (See C.6.a.)

g. *Field Placements.*

Counselors develop clear policies within their training program regarding field placement and other clinical experiences. Counselors provide clearly stated roles and responsibilities for the student or supervisee, the site supervisor, and the program supervisor. They confirm that site supervisors are qualified to provide supervision and are informed of their professional and ethical responsibilities in this role.

h. *Dual Relationships as Supervisors.*

Counselors avoid dual relationships such as performing the role of site supervisor and training program supervisor in the student's or supervisee's training program. Counselors do not accept any form of professional services, fees, commissions, reimbursement, or remuneration from a site for student or supervisee placement.

i. *Diversity in Programs.*

Counselors are responsive to their institution's and program's recruitment and retention needs for training program administrators, faculty, and students with diverse backgrounds and special needs. (See A.2.a.)

F.3. Students and Supervisees

a. *Limitations.*

Counselors, through ongoing evaluation and appraisal, are aware of the academic and personal limitations of students and supervisees that might impede performance. Counselors assist students and supervisees in securing remedial assistance when needed, and dismiss from the training program supervisees who are unable to provide competent service due to academic or personal limitations. Counselors seek professional consultation and document their decision to dismiss or refer students or supervisees for assistance. Counselors ensure that students and supervisees have recourse to address decisions made to require them to seek assistance or to dismiss them.

b. *Self-Growth Experiences.*

Counselors use professional judgment when designing training experiences conducted by the counselors themselves that require student and supervisee self-growth or self-disclosure. Safeguards are provided so that students and supervisees are aware of the ramifications their self-disclosure may have on counselors whose primary role as teacher, trainer, or supervisor requires acting on ethical obligations to the profession. Evaluative components of experiential training experiences explicitly delineate predetermined academic standards that are separate and do not depend on the student's level of self-disclosure. (See A.6.)

c. *Counseling for Students and Supervisees.*

If students or supervisees request counseling, supervisors or counselor educators provide them with acceptable referrals. Supervisors or counselor educators do not serve as counselor to students or supervisees over whom they hold administrative, teaching, or evaluative roles unless this is a brief role associated with a training experience. (See A.6.b.)

d. *Clients of Students and Supervisees.*

Counselors make every effort to ensure that the clients at field placements are aware of the services rendered and the qualifications of the students and supervisees rendering those services. Clients receive professional disclosure information and are informed of the limits of confidentiality. Client permission is obtained in order for the students and supervisees to use any information concerning the counseling relationship in the training process. (See B.1.e.)

e. *Standards for Students and Supervisees.*

Students and supervisees preparing to become counselors adhere to the Code of Ethics and the Standards of Practice. Students and supervisees have the same obligations to clients as those required of counselors. (See H.1.)

Section G: Research and Publication

G.1. Research Responsibilities

a. *Use of Human Subjects.*

Counselors plan, design, conduct, and report research in a manner consistent with pertinent ethical principles, federal and state laws, host institutional regulations, and scientific standards governing research with human subjects. Counselors design and conduct research that reflects cultural sensitivity appropriateness.

b. *Deviation From Standard Practices.*

Counselors seek consultation and observe stringent safeguards to protect the rights of research participants when a research problem suggests a deviation from standard acceptable practices. (See B.6.)

c. *Precautions to Avoid Injury.*

Counselors who conduct research with human subjects are responsible for the subjects' welfare throughout the experiment and take reasonable precautions to avoid causing injurious psychological, physical, or social effects to their subjects.

d. *Principal Researcher Responsibility.*

The ultimate responsibility for ethical research practice lies with the principal researcher. All others involved in the research activities share ethical obligations and full responsibility for their own actions.

e. *Minimal Interference.*

Counselors take reasonable precautions to avoid causing disruptions in subjects' lives due to participation in research.

f. *Diversity.*

Counselors are sensitive to diversity and research issues with special populations. They seek consultation when appropriate. (See A.2.a. and B.6.)

G.2. Informed Consent

a. *Topics Disclosed.*

In obtaining informed consent for research, counselors use language that is understandable to research participants and that (1) accurately explains the purpose and procedures to be followed; (2) identifies any procedures that are experimental or relatively untried; (3) describes the attendant discomforts and risks; (4) describes the benefits or changes in individuals or organizations that might be reasonably expected; (5) discloses appropriate alternative procedures that would be advantageous for subjects; (6) offers to answer any inquiries concerning the procedures; (7) describes any limitations on confidentiality; and (8) instructs that subjects are free to withdraw their consent and to discontinue participation in the project at any time. (See B.1.f.)

b. *Deception.*

Counselors do not conduct research involving deception unless alternative procedures are not feasible and the prospective value of the research justifies the deception. When the methodological requirements of a study necessitate concealment or deception, the investigator is required to explain clearly the reasons for this action as soon as possible.

c. *Voluntary Participation.*

Participation in research is typically voluntary and without any penalty for refusal to participate. Involuntary participation is appropriate only when it can be demonstrated that participation will have no harmful effects on subjects and is essential to the investigation.

d. *Confidentiality of Information.*

Information obtained about research participants during the course of an investigation is confidential. When the possibility exists that others may obtain access to such information, ethical research practice requires that the possibility, together with the plans for protecting confidentiality, be explained to participants as a part of the procedure for obtaining informed consent. (See B.1.e.)

e. *Persons Incapable of Giving Informed Consent.*

When a person is incapable of giving informed consent, counselors provide an appropriate explanation, obtain agreement for participation, and obtain appropriate consent from a legally authorized person.

f. *Commitments to Participants.*

Counselors take reasonable measures to honor all commitments to research participants.

g. *Explanations After Data Collection.*

After data are collected, counselors provide participants with full clarification of the nature of the study to remove any misconceptions. Where scientific or human values justify delaying or withholding information, counselors take reasonable measures to avoid causing harm.

h. *Agreements to Cooperate.*

Counselors who agree to cooperate with another individual in research or publication incur an obligation to cooperate as promised in terms of punctuality of performance and with regard to the completeness and accuracy of the information required.

i. *Informed Consent for Sponsors.*

In the pursuit of research, counselors give sponsors, institutions, and publication channels the same respect and opportunity for giving informed consent that they accord to individual research participants. Counselors are aware of their obligation to future research workers and ensure that host institutions are given feedback information and proper acknowledgment.

G.3. Reporting Results

a. *Information Affecting Outcome.*

When reporting research results, counselors explicitly mention all variables and conditions known to the investigator that may have affected the outcome of a study or the interpretation of data.

b. *Accurate Results.*

Counselors plan, conduct, and report research accurately and in a manner that minimizes the possibility that results will be misleading. They provide thorough discussions of the limitations of their data and alternative hypotheses. Counselors do not engage in fraudulent research, distort data, misrepresent data, or deliberately bias their results.

c. *Obligation to Report Unfavorable Results.*

Counselors communicate to other counselors the results of any research judged to be of professional value. Results that reflect unfavorably on institutions, programs, services, prevailing opinions, or vested interests are not withheld.

d. *Identity of Subjects.*

Counselors who supply data, aid in the research of another person, report research results, or make original data available take due care to disguise the identity of respective subjects in the absence of specific authorization from the subjects to do otherwise. (See B.1.g. and B.5.a.)

e. *Replication Studies.*

Counselors are obligated to make available sufficient original research data to qualified professionals who may wish to replicate the study.

G.4. Publication

a. *Recognition of Others.*

When conducting and reporting research, counselors are familiar with and give recognition to previous work on the topic, observe copyright laws, and give full credit to those to whom credit is due. (See F.1.d. and G.4.c.)

b. *Contributors.*

Counselors give credit through joint authorship, acknowledgment, footnote statements, or other appropriate means to those who have contributed significantly to research or concept development in accordance with such contributions. The principal contributor is listed first and minor technical or professional contributions are acknowledged in notes or introductory statements.

c. *Student Research.*

For an article that is substantially based on a student's dissertation or thesis, the student is listed as the principal author. (See F.1.d. and G.4.a.)

d. *Duplicate Submission.*

Counselors submit manuscripts for consideration to only one journal at a time. Manuscripts that are published in whole or in substantial part in another journal or published work are not submitted for publication without acknowledgment and permission from the previous publication.

e. *Professional Review.*

Counselors who review material submitted for publication, research, or other scholarly purposes respect the confidentiality and proprietary rights of those who submitted it.

Section H: Resolving Ethical Issues

H.1. Knowledge of Standards

Counselors are familiar with the Code of Ethics and the Standards of Practice and other applicable ethics codes from other professional organizations of which they are member, or from certification and licensure bodies. Lack of knowledge or misunderstanding of an ethical responsibility is not a defense against a charge of unethical conduct. (See F.3.e.)

H.2. Suspected Violations

a. *Ethical Behavior Expected.*

Counselors expect professional associates to adhere to the Code of Ethics. When counselors possess reasonable cause that raises doubts as to whether a counselor is acting in an ethical manner, they take appropriate action. (See H.2.d. and H.2.e.)

b. *Consultation.*

When uncertain as to whether a particular situation or course of action may be in violation of the Code of Ethics, counselors consult with other counselors who are knowledgeable about ethics, with colleagues, or with appropriate authorities.

c. *Organization Conflicts.*
If the demands of an organization with which counselors are affiliated pose a conflict with the Code of Ethics, counselors specify the nature of such conflicts and express to their supervisors or other responsible officials their commitment to the Code of Ethics. When possible, counselors work toward change within the organization to allow full adherence to the Code of Ethics.

d. *Informal Resolution.*
When counselors have reasonable cause to believe that another counselor is violating an ethical standard, they attempt to first resolve the issue informally with the other counselor if feasible, providing that such action does not violate confidentiality rights that may be involved.

e. *Reporting Suspected Violations.*
When an informal resolution is not appropriate or feasible, counselors, upon reasonable cause, take action such as reporting the suspected ethical violation to state or national ethics committees, unless this action conflicts with confidentiality rights that cannot be resolved.

f. *Unwarranted Complaints.*
Counselors do not initiate, participate in, or encourage the filing of ethics complaints that are unwarranted or intend to harm a counselor rather than to protect clients or the public.

H.3. Cooperation With Ethics Committees
Counselors assist in the process of enforcing the Code of Ethics. Counselors cooperate with investigations, proceedings, and requirements of the ACA Ethics Committee or ethics committees of other duly constituted associations or boards having jurisdiction over those charged with a violation. Counselors are familiar with the ACA Policies and Procedures and use it as a reference in assisting the enforcement of the Code of Ethics.

Standards of Practice

All members of the American Counseling Association (ACA) are required to adhere to the Standards of Practice and the Code of Ethics. The Standards of Practice represent minimal behavioral statements of the Code of Ethics. Members should refer to the applicable section of the Code of Ethics for further interpretation and amplification of the applicable Standard of Practice.

Section A: The Counseling Relationship

Standard of Practice One (SP-1): Nondiscrimination. Counselors respect diversity and must not discriminate against clients because of age, color, culture, disability, ethnic group, gender, race, religion, sexual orientation, marital status, or socioeconomic status. (See A.2.a.)

Standard of Practice Two (SP-2): Disclosure to Clients. Counselors must adequately inform clients, preferably in writing, regarding the counseling process and counseling relationship at or before the time it begins and throughout the relationship. (See A.3.a.)

Standard of Practice Three (SP-3): Dual Relationships. Counselors must make every effort to avoid dual relationships with clients that could impair their professional judgment or increase the risk of harm to clients. When a dual relationship cannot be avoided, counselors must take appropriate steps to ensure that judgment is not impaired and that no exploitation occurs. (See A.6.a. and A.6.b.)

Standard of Practice Four (SP-4): Sexual Intimacies With Clients. Counselors must not engage in any type of sexual intimacies with current clients and must not engage in sexual intimacies with former clients within a minimum of 2 years after terminating the counseling relationship. Counselors who engage in such relationship after 2 years following termination have the responsibility to examine and document thoroughly that such relations did not have an exploitative nature.

Standard of Practice Five (SP-5): Protecting Clients During Group Work. Counselors must take steps to protect clients from physical or psychological trauma resulting from interactions during group work. (See A.9.b.)

Standard of Practice Six (SP-6): Advance Understanding of Fees. Counselors must explain to clients, prior to their entering the counseling relationship, financial arrangements related to professional services. (See A.10. a.-d. and A.11.c.)

Standard of Practice Seven (SP-7): Termination. Counselors must assist in making appropriate arrangements for the continuation of treatment of clients, when necessary, following termination of counseling relationships. (See A.11.a.)

Standard of Practice Eight (SP-8): Inability to Assist Clients. Counselors must avoid entering or immediately terminate a counseling relationship if it is determined that they are unable to be of professional assistance to a client. The counselor may assist in making an appropriate referral for the client. (See A.11.b.)

Section B: Confidentiality

Standard of Practice Nine (SP-9): Confidentiality Requirement. Counselors must keep information related to counseling services confidential unless disclosure is in the best interest of clients, is required for the welfare of others, or is required by law. When disclosure is required, only information that is essential is revealed and the client is informed of such disclosure. (See B.1. a.'f.)

Standard of Practice Ten (SP-10): Confidentiality Requirements for Subordinates. Counselors must take measures to ensure that privacy and confidentiality of clients are maintained by subordinates. (See B.1.h.)

Standard of Practice Eleven (SP-11): Confidentiality in Group Work. Counselors must clearly communicate to group members that confidentiality cannot be guaranteed in group work. (See B.2.a.)

Standard of Practice Twelve (SP-12): Confidentiality in Family Counseling. Counselors must not disclose information about one family member in counseling to another family member without prior consent. (See B.2.b.)

Standard of Practice Thirteen (SP-13): Confidentiality of Records. Counselors must maintain appropriate confidentiality in creating, storing, accessing, transferring, and disposing of counseling records. (See B.4.b.)

Standard of Practice Fourteen (SP-14): Permission to Record or Observe. Counselors must obtain prior consent from clients in order to record electronically or observe sessions. (See B.4.c.)

Standard of Practice Fifteen (SP-15): Disclosure or Transfer of Records. Counselors must obtain client consent to disclose or transfer records to third parties, unless exceptions listed in SP-9 exist. (See B.4.e.)

Standard of Practice Sixteen (SP-16): Data Disguise Required. Counselors must disguise the identity of the client when using data for training, research, or publication. (See B.5.a.)

Section C: Professional Responsibility

Standard of Practice Seventeen (SP-17): Boundaries of Competence. Counselors must practice only within the boundaries of their competence. (See C.2.a.)

Standard of Practice Eighteen (SP-18): Continuing Education. Counselors must engage in continuing education to maintain their professional competence. (See C.2.f.)

Standard of Practice Nineteen (SP-19): Impairment of Professionals. Counselors must refrain from offering professional services when their personal problems or conflicts may cause harm to a client or others. (See C.2.g.)

Standard of Practice Twenty (SP-20): Accurate Advertising. Counselors must accurately represent their credentials and services when advertising. (See C.3.a.)

Standard of Practice Twenty-One (SP-21): Recruiting Through Employment. Counselors must not use their place of employment or institutional affiliation to recruit clients for their private practices. (See C.3.d.)

Standard of Practice Twenty-Two (SP-22): Credentials Claimed. Counselors must claim or imply only professional credentials possessed and must correct any known misrepresentations of their credentials by others. (See C.4.a.)

Standard of Practice Twenty-Three (SP-23): Sexual Harassment. Counselors must not engage in sexual harassment. (See C.5.b.)

Standard of Practice Twenty-Four (SP-24): Unjustified Gains. Counselors must not use their professional positions to seek or receive unjustified personal gains, sexual favors, unfair advantage, or unearned goods or services. (See C.5.e.)

Standard of Practice Twenty-Five (SP-25): Clients Served by Others. With the consent of the client, counselors must inform other mental health professionals serving the same client that a counseling relationship between the counselor and client exists. (See C.6.c.)

Standard of Practice Twenty-Six (SP-26): Negative Employment Conditions. Counselors must alert their employers to institutional policy or conditions that may be potentially disruptive or damaging to the counselor's professional responsibilities, or that may limit their effectiveness or deny clients' rights. (See D.1.c.)

Standard of Practice Twenty-Seven (SP-27): Personnel Selection and Assignment. Counselors must select competent staff and must assign responsibilities compatible with staff skills and experiences. (See D.1.h.)

Standard of Practice Twenty-Eight (SP-28): Exploitative Relationships With Subordinates. Counselors must not engage in exploitative relationships with individuals over whom they have supervisory, evaluative, or instructional control or authority. (See D.1.k.)

Section D: Relationship With Other Professionals

Standard of Practice Twenty-Nine (SP-29): Accepting Fees From Agency Clients. Counselors must not accept fees or other remuneration for consultation with persons entitled to such services through the counselor's employing agency or institution. (See D.3.a.)

Standard of Practice Thirty (SP-30): Referral Fees. Counselors must not accept referral fees. (See D.3.b.)

Section E: Evaluation, Assesment and Interpretation

Standard of Practice Thirty-One (SP-31): Limits of Competence. Counselors must perform only testing and assessment services for which they are competent. Counselors must not allow the use of psychological assessment techniques by unqualified persons under their supervision. (See E.2.a.)

Standard of Practice Thirty-Two (SP-32): Appropriate Use of Assessment Instruments. Counselors must use assessment instruments in the manner for which they were intended. (See E.2.b.)

Standard of Practice Thirty-Three (SP-33): Assessment Explanations to Clients. Counselors must provide explanations to clients prior to assessment about the nature and purposes of assessment and the specific uses of results. (See E.3.a.)

Standard of Practice Thirty-Four (SP-34): Recipients of Test Results. Counselors must ensure that accurate and appropriate interpretations accompany any release of testing and assessment information. (See E.3.b.)

Standard of Practice Thirty-Five (SP-35): Obsolete Tests and

Outdated Test Results. Counselors must not base their assessment or intervention decisions or recommendations on data or test results that are obsolete or outdated for the current purpose. (See E.11.)

Section F: Teaching, Training, and Supervision

Standard of Practice Thirty-Six (SP-36): Sexual Relationships With Students or Supervisees. Counselors must not engage in sexual relationships with their students and supervisees. (See F.1.c.)

Standard of Practice Thirty-Seven (SP-37): Credit for Contributions to Research. Counselors must give credit to students or supervisees for their contributions to research and scholarly projects. (See F.1.d.)

Standard of Practice Thirty-Eight (SP-38): Supervision Preparation. Counselors who offer clinical supervision services must be trained and prepared in supervision methods and techniques. (See F.1.f.)

Standard of Practice Thirty-Nine (SP-39): Evaluation Information. Counselors must clearly state to students and supervisees in advance of training the levels of competency expected, appraisal methods, and timing of evaluations. Counselors must provide students and supervisees with periodic performance appraisal and evaluation feedback throughout the training program. (See F.2.c.)

Standard of Practice Forty (SP-40): Peer Relationships in Training. Counselors must make every effort to ensure that the rights of peers are not violated when students and supervisees are assigned to lead counseling groups or provide clinical supervision. (See F.2.e.)

Standard of Practice Forty-One (SP-41): Limitations of Students and Supervisees. Counselors must assist students and supervisees in securing remedial assistance, when needed, and must dismiss from the training program students and supervisees who are unable to provide competent service due to academic or personal limitations. (See F.3.a.)

Standard of Practice Forty-Two (SP-42): Self-Growth Experiences. Counselors who conduct experiences for students or supervisees that include self-growth or self-disclosure must inform participants of counselors' ethical obligations to the profession and must not grade participants based on their nonacademic performance. (See F.3.b.)

Standard of Practice Forty-Three (SP-43): Standards for Stu-

dents and Supervisees. Students and supervisees preparing to become counselors must adhere to the Code of Ethics and the Standards of Practice of counselors. (See F.3.e.)

Section G: Research and Publication

Standard of Practice Forty-Four (SP-44): Precautions to Avoid Injury in Research. Counselors must avoid causing physical, social, or psychological harm or injury to subjects in research. (See G.1.c.)

Standard of Practice Forty-Five (SP-45): Confidentiality of Research Information. Counselors must keep confidential information obtained about research participants. (See G.2.d.)

Standard of Practice Forty-Six (SP-46): Information Affecting Research Outcome. Counselors must report all variables and conditions known to the investigator that may have affected research data or outcomes. (See G.3.a.)

Standard of Practice Forty-Seven (SP-47): Accurate Research Results. Counselors must not distort or misrepresent research data, nor fabricate or intentionally bias research results. (See G.3.b.)

Standard of Practice Forty-Eight (SP-48): Publication Contributors. Counselors must give appropriate credit to those who have contributed to research. (See G.4.a. and G.4.b.)

Section H: Resolving Ethical Issues

Standard of Practice Forty-Nine (SP-49): Ethical Behavior Expected. Counselors must take appropriate action when they possess reasonable cause that raises doubts as to whether counselors or other mental health professionals are acting in an ethical manner. (See H.2.a.)

Standard of Practice Fifty (SP-50): Unwarranted Complaints. Counselors must not initiate, participate in, or encourage the filing of ethics complaints that are unwarranted or intended to harm a mental health professional rather than to protect clients or the public. (See H.2.f.)

Standard of Practice Fifty-One (SP-51): Cooperation With Ethics Committees. Counselors must cooperate with investigations, proceedings, and requirements of the ACA Ethics Committee or ethics committees of other duly constituted associations or boards having jurisdiction over those charged with a violation. (See H.3.)

American Psychological Association Ethical Principles of Psychologists and Code of Conduct*

Introduction

The American Psychological Association's (APA's) Ethical Principles of Psychologists and Code of Conduct (hereinafter referred to as the Ethics Code) consists of an Introduction, a Preamble, six General Principles (A–F), and specific Ethical Standards. The Introduction discusses the intent, organization, procedural considerations, and scope of application of the Ethics Code. The Preamble and General Principles are *aspirational* goals to guide psychologists toward the highest ideals of psychology. Although the Preamble and General Principles are not themselves enforceable rules, they should be considered by psychologists in arriving at an ethical course of action and may be considered by ethics bodies in interpreting the Ethical Standards. The Ethical Standards set forth *enforceable* rules for conduct as psychologists. Most of the Ethical Standards are written broadly, in order to apply to psychologists in varied roles, although the application of an Ethical Standard may vary depending on the context. The Ethical Standards are not exhaustive. The fact that a given conduct is not specifically addressed by the Ethics Code does not mean that it is necessarily either ethical or unethical.

Membership in the APA commits members to adhere to the APA Ethics Code and to the rules and procedures used to implement it. Psychologists and students, whether or not they are APA members, should be aware that the Ethics Code may be applied to them by state psychology boards, courts, or other public bodies.

This Ethics Code applies only to psychologists' work-related activities, that is, activities that are part of the psychologists' scientific and professional functions or that are psychological in nature. It includes the clinical or counseling practice of psychology, research, teaching, supervision of trainees, development of assessment instruments, conducting assessments, educational counseling, organizational consulting, social intervention, administration, and other activities as well. These work-related activities can be distinguished from the purely private conduct of a psychologist, which ordinarily is not within the purview of the Ethics Code.

The Ethics Code is intended to provide standards of professional conduct that can be applied by the APA and by other bodies that choose to adopt them. Whether or not a psychologist has violated the Ethics Code does not by itself determine whether he or she is legally liable in a court action, whether a contract is enforceable, or whether other legal consequences occur. These results are based on legal rather than ethical rules. However, compliance with or violation of the Ethics Code may be admissible as evidence in some legal proceedings, depending on the circumstances.

In the process of making decisions regarding their professional behavior, psychologists must consider this Ethics Code, in addition to applicable laws and psychology board regulations. If the Ethics Code establishes a higher standard of conduct than is required by law, psychologists must meet the higher ethical standard. If the Ethics Code standard appears to conflict with the requirements of law, then psychologists make known their commitment to the Ethics Code and take steps to resolve the conflict in a responsible manner. If neither law nor the Ethics Code resolves an issue, psychologists should consider other professional materials[1] and the dictates of their own conscience, as well as seek consultation with others within the field when this is practical.

The procedures for filing, investigating, and resolving complaints of unethical conduct are described in the current Rules and Procedures of the APA Ethics Committee. The actions that APA may take for violations of the Ethics Code include actions such as reprimand, censure, termination of APA membership, and referral of the matter to other bodies. Complainants who seek remedies such as monetary damages in alleging ethical violations by a psychologist must resort to private negotiation, administrative bodies, or the courts. Actions that violate the Ethics Code may lead to the imposition of sanctions on a psychologist by bodies other than APA, including state psychological associations, other professional groups, psychology boards, other state or federal agencies, and payors for health services. In addition to actions for violation of the Ethics Code, the APA Bylaws provide that APA may take action against a member after his or her conviction of a felony, expulsion or suspension from an affiliated state psychological association, or suspension or loss of licensure.

---

[1]Professional materials that are most helpful in this regard are guidelines and standards that have been adopted or endorsed by professional psychological organizations. Such guidelines and standards, whether adopted by the American Psychological Association (APA) or its Divisions, are not enforceable as such by this Ethics Code, but are of educative value to psychologists, courts, and professional bodies. Such materials include, but are not limited to, the APA's General Guidelines for Providers of Psychological Services (1987), Specialty Guidelines for the Delivery of Services by Clinical Psychologists, Counseling Psychologists, Industrial/Organizational Psychologists, and School Psychologists (1981), Guidelines for Computer Based Tests and Interpretations (1987), Standards for Educational and Psychological Testing (1985), Ethical Principles in the Conduct of Research With Human Participants (1982), Guidelines for Ethical Conduct in the Care and Use of Animals (1986), Guidelines for Providers of Psychological Services to Ethnic, Linguistic, and Culturally Diverse Populations (1990), and Publication Manual of the American Psychological Association (3rd ed., 1983). Materials not adopted by APA as a whole include the APA Division 41 (Forensic Psychology)/American Psychology-Law Society's Specialty Guidelines for Forensic Psychologists (1991).

Preamble

Psychologists work to develop a valid and reliable body of scientific knowledge based on research. They may apply that knowledge to human behavior in a variety of contexts. In doing so, they perform many roles, such as researcher, educator, diagnostician, therapist, supervisor, consultant, administrator, social interventionist, and expert witness. Their goal is to broaden knowledge of behavior and, where appropriate, to apply it pragmatically to improve the condition of both the individual and society. Psychologists respect the central importance of freedom of inquiry and expression in research, teaching, and publication. They also strive to help the public in developing informed judgments and choices concerning human behavior. This Ethics Code provides a common set of values upon which psychologists build their professional and scientific work.

This Code is intended to provide both the general principles and the decision rules to cover most situations encountered by psychologists. It has as its primary goal the welfare and protection of the individuals and groups with whom psychologists work. It is the individual responsibility of each psychologist to aspire to the highest possible standards of conduct. Psychologists respect and protect human and civil rights, and do not knowingly participate in or condone unfair discriminatory practices. The development of a dynamic set of ethical standards for a psychologist's work-related conduct requires a personal commitment to a lifelong effort to act ethically; to encourage ethical behavior by students, supervisees, employees, and colleagues, as appropriate; and to consult with others, as needed, concerning ethical problems. Each psychologist supplements, but does not violate, the Ethics Code's values and rules on the basis of guidance drawn from personal values, culture, and experience.

General Principles

Principle A: Competence

Psychologists strive to maintain high standards of competence in their work. They recognize the boundaries of their particular competencies and the limitations of their expertise. They provide only those services and use only those techniques for which they are qualified by education, training, or experience. Psychologists are cognizant of the fact that the competencies required in serving, teaching, and/or studying groups of people vary with the distinctive characteristics of those groups. In those areas in which recognized professional standards do not yet exist, psychologists exercise careful judgment and take appropriate precautions to protect the welfare of those with whom they work. They maintain knowledge of relevant scientific and professional information related to the services they render, and they recognize the need for ongoing education. Psychologists make appropriate use of scientific, professional, technical, and administrative resources.

Principle B: Integrity

Psychologists seek to promote integrity in the science, teaching, and practice of psychology. In these activities psychologists are honest, fair, and respectful of others. In describing or reporting their qualifications, services, products, fees, research, or teaching, they do not make statements that are false, misleading, or deceptive. Psychologists strive to be aware of their own belief systems, values, needs, and limitations and the effect of these on their work. To the extent feasible, they attempt to clarify for relevant parties the roles they are performing and to function appropriately in accordance with those roles. Psychologists avoid improper and potentially harmful dual relationships.

Principle C: Professional and Scientific Responsibility

Psychologists uphold professional standards of conduct, clarify their professional roles and obligations, accept appropriate responsibility for their behavior, and adapt their methods to the needs of different populations. Psychologists consult with, refer to, or cooperate with other professionals and institutions to the extent needed to serve the best interests of their patients, clients, or other recipients of their services. Psychologists' moral standards and conduct are personal matters to the same degree as is true for any other person, except as psychologists' conduct may compromise their professional responsibilities or reduce the public's trust in psychology and psychologists. Psychologists are concerned about the ethical compliance of their colleagues' scientific and professional conduct. When appropriate, they consult with colleagues in order to prevent or avoid unethical conduct.

Principle D: Respect for People's Rights and Dignity

Psychologists accord appropriate respect to the fundamental rights, dignity, and worth of all people. They respect the rights of individuals to privacy, confidentiality, self-determination, and autonomy, mindful that legal and other obligations may lead to inconsistency and conflict with the exercise of these rights. Psychologists are aware of cultural, individual, and role differences, including those due to age, gender, race, ethnicity, national origin, religion, sexual orientation, disability, language, and socioeconomic status. Psychologists try to eliminate the effect on their work of biases based on those factors, and they do not knowingly participate in or condone unfair discriminatory practices.

Principle E: Concern for Others' Welfare

Psychologists seek to contribute to the welfare of those with whom they interact professionally. In their professional actions, psychologists weigh the welfare and rights of their patients or clients, students, supervisees, human research participants, and other affected persons, and the welfare of animal subjects of research. When conflicts occur among psychologists' obligations or concerns, they attempt to resolve these conflicts and to perform their roles in a responsible fashion that avoids or minimizes harm. Psychologists are sensitive to real and ascribed differences in power between themselves and others, and they do not exploit or mislead other people during or after professional relationships.

Principle F: Social Responsibility

Psychologists are aware of their professional and scientific responsibilities to the community and the society in which they work and live. They apply and make public their knowledge of psychology in order to contribute to human welfare. Psychologists are concerned about and work to mitigate the causes of human suffering. When undertaking research, they strive to advance human welfare and the science of psychology. Psychologists try to avoid misuse of their work. Psychologists comply with the law and encourage the development of law and social policy that serve the interests of their patients and clients and the public. They are encouraged to contribute a portion of their professional time for little or no personal advantage.

Ethical Standards

1. General Standards

These General Standards are potentially applicable to the professional and scientific activities of all psychologists.

1.01 Applicability of the Ethics Code.

The activity of a psychologist subject to the Ethics Code may be reviewed under these Ethical Standards only if the activity is part of his or her work-related functions or the activity is psychological in nature. Personal activities having no connection to or effect on psychological roles are not subject to the Ethics Code.

1.02 Relationship of Ethics and Law.

If psychologists' ethical responsibilities conflict with law, psychologists make known their commitment to the Ethics Code and take steps to resolve the conflict in a responsible manner.

1.03 Professional and Scientific Relationship.

Psychologists provide diagnostic, therapeutic, teaching, research, supervisory, consultative, or other psychological services only in the context of a defined professional or scientific relationship or role. (See also Standards 2.01, Evaluation, Diagnosis, and Interventions in Professional Context, and 7.02, Forensic Assessments.)

1.04 Boundaries of Competence.

(a) Psychologists provide services, teach, and conduct research only within the boundaries of their competence, based on their education, training, supervised experience, or appropriate professional experience.

(b) Psychologists provide services, teach, or conduct research in new areas or involving new techniques only after first undertaking appropriate study, training, supervision, and/or consultation from persons who are competent in those areas or techniques.

(c) In those emerging areas in which generally recognized standards for preparatory training do not yet exist, psychologists nevertheless take reasonable steps to ensure the competence of their work and to protect patients, clients, students, research participants, and others from harm.

1.05 Maintaining Expertise.

Psychologists who engage in assessment, therapy, teaching, research, organizational consulting, or other professional activities maintain a reasonable level of awareness of current scientific and professional information in their fields of activity, and undertake ongoing efforts to maintain competence in the skills they use.

1.06 Basis for Scientific and Professional Judgments.

Psychologists rely on scientifically and professionally derived knowledge when making scientific or professional judgments or when engaging in scholarly or professional endeavors.

1.07 Describing the Nature and Results of Psychological Services.

(a) When psychologists provide assessment, evaluation, treatment, counseling, supervision, teaching, consultation, research, or other psychological services to an individual, a group, or an organization, they provide, using language that is reasonably understandable to the recipient of those services, appropriate information beforehand about the nature of such services and appropriate information later about results and conclusions. (See also Standard 2.09, Explaining Assessment Results.)

(b) If psychologists will be precluded by law or by organizational roles from providing such information to particular individuals or groups, they so inform those individuals or groups at the outset of the service.

1.08 Human Differences.

Where differences of age, gender, race, ethnicity, national origin, religion, sexual orientation, disability, language, or socioeconomic status significantly affect psychologists' work concerning particular individuals or groups, psychologists obtain the training, experience, consultation, or supervision necessary to ensure the competence of their services, or they make appropriate referrals.

1.09 Respecting Others.

In their work-related activities, psychologists respect the rights of others to hold values, attitudes, and opinions that differ from their own.

1.10 Nondiscrimination.

In their work-related activities, psychologists do not engage in unfair discrimination based on age, gender, race, ethnicity, national origin, religion, sexual orientation, disability, socioeconomic status, or any basis proscribed by law.

1.11 Sexual Harassment.

(a) Psychologists do not engage in sexual harassment. Sexual harassment is sexual solicitation, physical advances, or verbal or nonverbal conduct that is sexual in nature, that occurs in connection with the psychologist's activities or roles as a psychologist, and that either: (1) is unwelcome, is offensive, or creates a hostile workplace environment, and the psychologist knows or is told this; or (2) is sufficiently severe or intense to be abusive to a reasonable person in the context. Sexual harassment can consist of a single intense or severe act or of multiple persistent or pervasive acts.

(b) Psychologists accord sexual-harassment complainants and respondents dignity and respect. Psychologists do not participate in denying a person academic admittance or advancement, employment, tenure, or promotion, based solely upon their having made, or their being the subject of, sexual harassment charges. This does not preclude taking action based upon the outcome of such proceedings or consideration of other appropriate information.

1.12 Other Harassment.

Psychologists do not knowingly engage in behavior that is harassing or demeaning to persons with whom they interact in their work based on factors such as those persons' age, gender, race, ethnicity, national origin, religion, sexual orientation, disability, language, or socioeconomic status.

1.13 Personal Problems and Conflicts.

(a) Psychologists recognize that their personal problems and conflicts may interfere with their effectiveness. Accordingly, they refrain from undertaking an activity when they know or should know that their personal problems are likely to lead to harm to a patient, client, colleague, student, research participant, or other person to whom they may owe a professional or scientific obligation.

(b) In addition, psychologists have an obligation to be alert to signs of, and to obtain assistance for, their personal problems at an early stage, in order to prevent significantly impaired performance.

(c) When psychologists become aware of personal problems that may interfere with their performing work-related duties adequately, they take appropriate measures, such as obtaining professional consultation or assistance, and determine whether they should limit, suspend, or terminate their work-related duties.

1.14 Avoiding Harm.

Psychologists take reasonable steps to avoid harming their patients or clients, research participants, students, and others with whom they work, and to minimize harm where it is foreseeable and unavoidable.

1.15 Misuse of Psychologists' Influence.

Because psychologists' scientific and professional judgments and actions may affect the lives of others, they are alert to and guard against personal, financial, social, organizational, or political factors that might lead to misuse of their influence.

1.16 Misuse of Psychologists' Work.

(a) Psychologists do not participate in activities in which it appears likely that their skills or data will be misused by others, unless corrective mechanisms are available. (See also Standard 7.04, Truthfulness and Candor.)

(b) If psychologists learn of misuse or misrepresentation of their work, they take reasonable steps to correct or minimize the misuse or misrepresenta-

tion.

1.17 Multiple Relationships.

(a) In many communities and situations, it may not be feasible or reasonable for psychologists to avoid social or other nonprofessional contacts with persons such as patients, clients, students, supervisees, or research participants. Psychologists must always be sensitive to the potential harmful effects of other contacts on their work and on those persons with whom they deal. A psychologist refrains from entering into or promising another personal, scientific, professional, financial, or other relationship with such persons if it appears likely that such a relationship reasonably might impair the psychologist's objectivity or otherwise interfere with the psychologist's effectively performing his or her functions as a psychologist, or might harm or exploit the other party.

(b) Likewise, whenever feasible, a psychologist refrains from taking on professional or scientific obligations when pre-existing relationships would create a risk of such harm.

(c) If a psychologist finds that, due to unforeseen factors, a potentially harmful multiple relationship has arisen, the psychologist attempts to resolve it with due regard for the best interests of the affected person and maximal compliance with the Ethics Code.

1.18 Barter (With Patients or Clients).

Psychologists ordinarily refrain from accepting goods, services, or other nonmonetary remuneration from patients or clients in return for psychological services because such arrangements create inherent potential for conflicts, exploitation, and distortion of the professional relationship. A psychologist may participate in bartering only if (1) it is not clinically contraindicated, and (2) the relationship is not exploitative. (See also Standards 1.17, Multiple Relationships, and 1.25, Fees and Financial Arrangements.)

1.19 Exploitative Relationships.

(a) Psychologists do not exploit persons over whom they have supervisory, evaluative, or other authority such as students, supervisees, employees, research participants, and clients or patients. (See also Standards 4.05 - 4.07 regarding sexual involvement with clients or patients.)

(b) Psychologists do not engage in sexual relationships with students or supervisees in training over whom the psychologist has evaluative or direct authority, because such relationships are so likely to impair judgment or be exploitative.

1.20 Consultations and Referrals.

(a) Psychologists arrange for appropriate consultations and referrals based principally on the best interests of their patients or clients, with appropriate consent, and subject to other relevant considerations, including applicable law and contractual obligations. (See also Standards 5.01, Discussing the Limits of Confidentiality, and 5.06, Consultations.)

(b) When indicated and professionally appropriate,

psychologists cooperate with other professionals in order to serve their patients or clients effectively and appropriately.

(c) Psychologists' referral practices are consistent with law.

1.21 Third-Party Requests for Services.

(a) When a psychologist agrees to provide services to a person or entity at the request of a third party, the psychologist clarifies to the extent feasible, at the outset of the service, the nature of the relationship with each party. This clarification includes the role of the psychologist (such as therapist, organizational consultant, diagnostician, or expert witness), the probable uses of the services provided or the information obtained, and the fact that there may be limits to confidentiality.

(b) If there is a foreseeable risk of the psychologist's being called upon to perform conflicting roles because of the involvement of a third party, the psychologist clarifies the nature and direction of his or her responsibilities, keeps all parties appropriately informed as matters develop, and resolves the situation in accordance with this Ethics Code.

1.22 Delegation to and Supervision of Subordinates.

(a) Psychologists delegate to their employees, supervisees, and research assistants only those responsibilities that such persons can reasonably be expected to perform competently, on the basis of their education, training, or experience, either independently or with the level of supervision being provided.

(b) Psychologists provide proper training and supervision to their employees or supervisees and take reasonable steps to see that such persons perform services responsibly, competently, and ethically.

(c) If institutional policies, procedures, or practices prevent fulfillment of this obligation, psychologists attempt to modify their role or to correct the situation to the extent feasible.

1.23 Documentation of Professional and Scientific Work.

(a) Psychologists appropriately document their professional and scientific work in order to facilitate provision of services later by them or by other professionals, to ensure accountability, and to meet other requirements of institutions or the law.

(b) When psychologists have reason to believe that records of their professional services will be used in legal proceedings involving recipients of or participants in their work, they have a responsibility to create and maintain documentation in the kind of detail and quality that would be consistent with reasonable scrutiny in an adjudicative forum. (See also Standard 7.01, Professionalism, under Forensic Activities.)

1.24 Records and Data.

Psychologists create, maintain, disseminate, store, retain, and dispose of records and data relating to their research, practice, and other work in accordance with law and in a manner that permits compliance with the requirements of this Ethics Code.

(See also Standard 5.04, Maintenance of Records.)

1.25 Fees and Financial Arrangements.

(a) As early as is feasible in a professional or scientific relationship, the psychologist and the patient, client, or other appropriate recipient of psychological services reach an agreement specifying the compensation and the billing arrangements.

(b) Psychologists do not exploit recipients of services or payors with respect to fees.

(c) Psychologists' fee practices are consistent with law.

(d) Psychologists do not misrepresent their fees.

(e) If limitations to services can be anticipated because of limitations in financing, this is discussed with the patient, client, or other appropriate recipient of services as early as is feasible. (See also Standard 4.08, Interruption of Services.)

(f) If the patient, client, or other recipient of services does not pay for services as agreed, and if the psychologist wishes to use collection agencies or legal measures to collect the fees, the psychologist first informs the person that such measures will be taken and provides that person an opportunity to make prompt payment. (See also Standard 5.11, Withholding Records for Nonpayment.)

1.26 Accuracy in Reports to Payors and Funding Sources. In their reports to payors for services or sources of research funding, psychologists accurately state the nature of the research or service provided, the fees or charges, and where applicable, the identity of the provider, the findings, and the diagnosis. (See also Standard 5.05, Disclosures.)

1.27 Referrals and Fees.

When a psychologist pays, receives payment from, or divides fees with another professional other than in an employer - employee relationship, the payment to each is based on the services (clinical, consultative, administrative, or other) provided and is not based on the referral itself.

2. Evaluation, Assessment, or Intervention

2.01 Evaluation, Diagnosis, and Interventions in Professional Context.

(a) Psychologists perform evaluations, diagnostic services, or interventions only within the context of a defined professional relationship. (See also Standards 1.03, Professional and Scientific Relationship.)

(b) Psychologists' assessments, recommendations, reports, and psychological diagnostic or evaluative statements are based on information and techniques (including personal interviews of the individual when appropriate) sufficient to provide appropriate substantiation for their findings. (See also Standard 7.02, Forensic Assessments.)

2.02 Competence and Appropriate Use of Assessments and Interventions.

(a) Psychologists who develop, administer, score, interpret, or use psychological assessment techniques, interviews, tests, or instruments do so in a manner and for purposes that are appropriate in light of the research on or evidence of the usefulness and proper application of the techniques.

(b) Psychologists refrain from misuse of assessment techniques, interventions, results, and interpretations and take reasonable steps to prevent others from misusing the information these techniques provide. This includes refraining from releasing raw test results or raw data to persons, other than to patients or clients as appropriate, who are not qualified to use such information. (See also Standards 1.02, Relationship of Ethics and Law, and 1.04, Boundaries of Competence.)

2.03 Test Construction.

Psychologists who develop and conduct research with tests and other assessment techniques use scientific procedures and current professional knowledge for test design, standardization, validation, reduction or elimination of bias, and recommendations for use.

2.04 Use of Assessment in General and With Special Populations.

(a) Psychologists who perform interventions or administer, score, interpret, or use assessment techniques are familiar with the reliability, validation, and related standardization or outcome studies of, and proper applications and uses of, the techniques they use.

(b) Psychologists recognize limits to the certainty with which diagnoses, judgments, or predictions can be made about individuals.

(c) Psychologists attempt to identify situations in which particular interventions or assessment techniques or norms may not be applicable or may require adjustment in administration or interpretation because of factors such as individuals' gender, age, race, ethnicity, national origin, religion, sexual orientation, disability, language, or socioeconomic status.

2.05 Interpreting Assessment Results.

When interpreting assessment results, including automated interpretations, psychologists take into account the various test factors and characteristics of the person being assessed that might affect psychologists' judgments or reduce the accuracy of their interpretations. They indicate any significant reservations they have about the accuracy or limitations of their interpretations.

2.06 Unqualified Persons.

Psychologists do not promote the use of psychological assessment techniques by unqualified persons. (See also Standard 1.22, Delegation to and Supervision of Subordinates.)

2.07 Obsolete Tests and Outdated Test Results.

(a) Psychologists do not base their assessment or intervention decisions or recommendations on data or test results that are outdated for the current purpose.

(b) Similarly, psychologists do not base such decisions or recommendations on tests and measures that are obsolete and not useful for the current purpose.

2.08 Test Scoring and Interpretation Services.

(a) Psychologists who offer assessment or scoring procedures to other professionals accurately describe the purpose, norms, validity, reliability, and applications of the procedures and any special qualifications applicable to their use.

(b) Psychologists select scoring and interpretation services (including automated services) on the basis of evidence of the validity of the program and procedures as well as on other appropriate considerations.

(c) Psychologists retain appropriate responsibility for the appropriate application, interpretation, and use of assessment instruments, whether they score and interpret such tests themselves or use automated or other services.

2.09 Explaining Assessment Results.

Unless the nature of the relationship is clearly explained to the person being assessed in advance and precludes provision of an explanation of results (such as in some organizational consulting, pre-employment or security screenings, and forensic evaluations), psychologists ensure that an explanation of the results is provided using language that is reasonably understandable to the person assessed or to another legally authorized person on behalf of the client. Regardless of whether the scoring and interpretation are done by the psychologist, by assistants, or by automated or other outside services, psychologists take reasonable steps to ensure that appropriate explanations of results are given.

2.10 Maintaining Test Security.

Psychologists make reasonable efforts to maintain the integrity and security of tests and other assessment techniques consistent with law, contractual obligations, and in a manner that permits compliance with the requirements of this Ethics Code. (See also Standard 1.02, Relationship of Ethics and Law.)

3. Advertising and Other Public Statements

3.01 Definition of Public Statements.

Psychologists comply with this Ethics Code in public statements relating to their professional services, products, or publications or to the field of psychology. Public statements include but are not limited to paid or unpaid advertising, brochures, printed matter, directory listings, personal resumes or curriculum vitae, interviews or comments for use in media, statements in legal proceedings, lectures and public oral presentations, and published materials.

3.02 Statements by Others.

(a) Psychologists who engage others to create or place public statements that promote their professional practice, products, or activities retain professional responsibility for such statements.

(b) In addition, psychologists make reasonable efforts to prevent others whom they do not control (such as employers, publishers, sponsors, organizational clients, and representatives of the print or broadcast media) from making deceptive statements concerning psychologists' practice or professional or scientific activities.

(c) If psychologists learn of deceptive statements about their work made by others, psychologists make reasonable efforts to correct such statements.

(d) Psychologists do not compensate employees of press, radio, television, or other communication media in return for publicity in a news item.

(e) A paid advertisement relating to the psychologist's activities must be identified as such, unless it is already apparent from the context.

3.03 Avoidance of False or Deceptive Statements.

(a) Psychologists do not make public statements that are false, deceptive, misleading, or fraudulent, either because of what they state, convey, or suggest or because of what they omit, concerning their research, practice, or other work activities or those of persons or organizations with which they are affiliated. As examples (and not in limitation) of this standard, psychologists do not make false or deceptive statements concerning (1) their training, experience, or competence; (2) their academic degrees; (3) their credentials; (4) their institutional or association affiliations; (5) their services; (6) the scientific or clinical basis for, or results or degree of success of, their services; (7) their fees; or (8) their publications or research findings. (See also Standards 6.15, Deception in Research, and 6.18, Providing Participants With Information About the Study.)

(b) Psychologists claim as credentials for their psychological work, only degrees that (1) were earned from a regionally accredited educational institution or (2) were the basis for psychology licensure by the state in which they practice.

3.04 Media Presentations.

When psychologists provide advice or comment by means of public lectures, demonstrations, radio or television programs, prerecorded tapes, printed articles, mailed material, or other media, they take reasonable precautions to ensure that (1) the statements are based on appropriate psychological literature and practice, (2) the statements are otherwise consistent with this Ethics Code, and (3) the recipients of the information are not encouraged to infer that a relationship has been established with them personally.

3.05 Testimonials.

Psychologists do not solicit testimonials from current psychotherapy clients or patients or other persons who because of their particular circumstances are vulnerable to undue influence.

3.06 In-Person Solicitation.

Psychologists do not engage, directly or through agents, in uninvited in-person solicitation of business from actual or potential psychotherapy patients or clients or other persons who because of their particular circumstances are vulnerable to undue influence. However, this does not preclude attempting to implement appropriate collateral contacts with significant others for the purpose of benefiting an already engaged therapy patient.

4. Therapy

4.01 Structuring the Relationship.

(a) Psychologists discuss with clients or patients as early as is feasible in the therapeutic relationship appropriate issues, such as the nature and anticipated course of therapy, fees, and confidentiality. (See also Standards 1.25, Fees and Financial Arrangements, and 5.01, Discussing the Limits of Confidentiality.)

(b) When the psychologist's work with clients or patients will be supervised, the above discussion includes that fact, and the name of the supervisor, when the supervisor has legal responsibility for the case.

(c) When the therapist is a student intern, the client or patient is informed of that fact.

(d) Psychologists make reasonable efforts to answer patients' questions and to avoid apparent misunderstandings about therapy. Whenever possible, psychologists provide oral and/or written information, using language that is reasonably understandable to the patient or client.

4.02 Informed Consent to Therapy.

(a) Psychologists obtain appropriate informed consent to therapy or related procedures, using language that is reasonably understandable to participants. The content of informed consent will vary depending on many circumstances; however, informed consent generally implies that the person (1) has the capacity to consent, (2) has been informed of significant information concerning the procedure, (3) has freely and without undue influence expressed consent, and (4) consent has been appropriately documented.

(b) When persons are legally incapable of giving informed consent, psychologists obtain informed permission from a legally authorized person, if such substitute consent is permitted by law.

(c) In addition, psychologists (1) inform those persons who are legally incapable of giving informed consent about the proposed interventions in a manner commensurate with the persons' psychological capacities, (2) seek their assent to those interventions, and (3) consider such persons' preferences and best interests.

4.03 Couple and Family Relationships.

(a) When a psychologist agrees to provide services to several persons who have a relationship (such as husband and wife or parents and children), the psychologist attempts to clarify at the outset (1) which of the individuals are patients or clients and (2) the relationship the psychologist will have with each person. This clarification includes the role of the psychologist and the probable uses of the services provided or the information obtained. (See also Standard 5.01, Discussing the Limits of Confidentiality.)

(b) As soon as it becomes apparent that the psychologist may be called on to perform potentially conflicting roles (such as marital counselor to husband and wife, and then witness for one party in a divorce proceeding), the psychologist attempts to clarify and adjust, or withdraw from, roles appropriately. (See also Standard 7.03, Clarification of Role, under Forensic Activities.)

4.04 Providing Mental Health Services to Those Served by Others.

In deciding whether to offer or provide services to those already receiving mental health services elsewhere, psychologists carefully consider the treatment issues and the potential patient's or client's welfare. The psychologist discusses these issues with the patient or client, or another legally authorized person on behalf of the client, in order to minimize the risk of confusion and conflict, consults with the other service providers when appropriate, and proceeds with caution and sensitivity to the therapeutic issues.

4.05 Sexual Intimacies With Current Patients or Clients.
Psychologists do not engage in sexual intimacies with current patients or clients.

4.06 Therapy With Former Sexual Partners.
Psychologists do not accept as therapy patients or clients persons with whom they have engaged in sexual intimacies.

4.07 Sexual Intimacies With Former Therapy Patients.

(a) Psychologists do not engage in sexual intimacies with a former therapy patient or client for at least two years after cessation or termination of professional services.

(b) Because sexual intimacies with a former therapy patient or client are so frequently harmful to the patient or client, and because such intimacies undermine public confidence in the psychology profession and thereby deter the public's use of needed services, psychologists do not engage in sexual intimacies with former therapy patients and clients even after a two-year interval except in the most unusual circumstances. The psychologist who engages in such activity after the two years following cessation or termination of treatment bears the burden of demonstrating that there has been no exploitation, in light of all relevant factors, including (1) the amount of time that has passed since therapy terminated, (2) the nature and duration of the therapy, (3) the circumstances of termination, (4) the patient's or client's personal history, (5) the patient's or client's current mental status, (6) the likelihood of adverse impact on the patient or client and others, and (7) any statements or actions made by the therapist during the course of therapy suggesting or inviting the possibility of a post-termination sexual or romantic relationship with the patient or client. (See also Standard 1.17, Multiple Relationships.)

4.08 Interruption of Services.

(a) Psychologists make reasonable efforts to plan for facilitating care in the event that psychological services are interrupted by factors such as the psychologist's illness, death, unavailability, or relocation or by the client's relocation or financial limitations. (See also Standard 5.09, Preserving Records and Data.)

(b) When entering into employment or contractual relationships, psychologists provide for orderly and appropriate resolution of responsibility for patient or client care in the event that the employment or contractual relationship ends, with paramount consideration given to the welfare of the patient or client.

4.09 Terminating the Professional Relationship.

(a) Psychologists do not abandon patients or clients. (See also Standard 1.25e, under Fees and Financial Arrangements.)

(b) Psychologists terminate a professional relationship when it becomes reasonably clear that the patient or client no longer needs the service, is not benefiting, or is being harmed by continued service.

(c) Prior to termination for whatever reason, except where precluded by the patient's or client's conduct, the psychologist discusses the patient's or client's views and needs, provides appropriate pretermination counseling, suggests alternative service providers as appropriate, and takes other reasonable steps to facilitate transfer of responsibility to another provider if the patient or client needs one immediately.

5. Privacy and Confidentiality

These Standards are potentially applicable to the professional and scientific activities of all psychologists.

5.01 Discussing the Limits of Confidentiality.

(a) Psychologists discuss with persons and organizations with whom they establish a scientific or professional relationship (including, to the extent feasible, minors and their legal representatives) (1) the relevant limitations on confidentiality, including limitations where applicable in group, marital, and family therapy or in organizational consulting, and (2) the foreseeable uses of the information generated through their services.

(b) Unless it is not feasible or is contraindicated, the discussion of confidentiality occurs at the outset of the relationship and thereafter as new circumstances may warrant.

(c) Permission for electronic recording of interviews is secured from clients and patients.

5.02 Maintaining Confidentiality.
Psychologists have a primary obligation and take reasonable precautions to respect the confidentiality rights of those with whom they work or consult, recognizing that confidentiality may be established by law, institutional rules, or professional or scientific relationships. (See also Standard 6.26, Professional Reviewers.)

5.03 Minimizing Intrusions on Privacy.

(a) In order to minimize intrusions on privacy, psychologists include in written and oral reports, consultations, and the like, only information germane to the purpose for which the communication is made.

(b) Psychologists discuss confidential information obtained in clinical or consulting relationships, or evaluative data concerning patients, individual or organizational clients, students, research participants, supervisees, and employees, only for appropriate scientific or professional purposes and only with persons clearly concerned with such matters.

5.04 Maintenance of Records.

Psychologists maintain appropriate confidentiality in creating, storing, accessing, transferring, and disposing of records under their control, whether these are written, automated, or in any other medium. Psychologists maintain and dispose of records in accordance with law and in a manner that permits compliance with the requirements of this Ethics Code.

5.05 Disclosures.

(a) Psychologists disclose confidential information without the consent of the individual only as mandated by law, or where permitted by law for a valid purpose, such as (1) to provide needed professional services to the patient or the individual or organizational client, (2) to obtain appropriate professional consultations, (3) to protect the patient or client or others from harm, or (4) to obtain payment for services, in which instance disclosure is limited to the minimum that is necessary to achieve the purpose.

(b) Psychologists also may disclose confidential information with the appropriate consent of the patient or the individual or organizational client (or of another legally authorized person on behalf of the patient or client), unless prohibited by law.

5.06 Consultations.

When consulting with colleagues, (1) psychologists do not share confidential information that reasonably could lead to the identification of a patient, client, research participant, or other person or organization with whom they have a confidential relationship unless they have obtained the prior consent of the person or organization or the disclosure cannot be avoided, and (2) they share information only to the extent necessary to achieve the purposes of the consultation. (See also Standard 5.02, Maintaining Confidentiality.)

5.07 Confidential Information in Databases.

(a) If confidential information concerning recipients of psychological services is to be entered into databases or systems of records available to persons whose access has not been consented to by the recipient, then psychologists use coding or other techniques to avoid the inclusion of personal identifiers.

(b) If a research protocol approved by an institutional review board or similar body requires the inclusion of personal identifiers, such identifiers are deleted before the information is made accessible to persons other than those of whom the subject was advised.

(c) If such deletion is not feasible, then before psychologists transfer such data to others or review such data collected by others, they take reasonable steps to determine that appropriate consent of personally identifiable individuals has been obtained.

5.08 Use of Confidential Information for Didactic or Other Purposes.

(a) Psychologists do not disclose in their writings, lectures, or other public media, confidential, personally identifiable information concerning their patients, individual or organizational clients, students, research participants, or other recipients of their services that they obtained during the course of their work, unless the person or organization has consented in writing or unless there is other ethical or legal authorization for doing so.

(b) Ordinarily, in such scientific and professional presentations, psychologists disguise confidential information concerning such persons or organizations so that they are not individually identifiable to others and so that discussions do not cause harm to subjects who might identify themselves.

5.09 Preserving Records and Data.

A psychologist makes plans in advance so that confidentiality of records and data is protected in the event of the psychologist's death, incapacity, or withdrawal from the position or practice.

5.10 Ownership of Records and Data.

Recognizing that ownership of records and data is governed by legal principles, psychologists take reasonable and lawful steps so that records and data remain available to the extent needed to serve the best interests of patients, individual or organizational clients, research participants, or appropriate others.

5.11 Withholding Records for Nonpayment.

Psychologists may not withhold records under their control that are requested and imminently needed for a patient's or client's treatment solely because payment has not been received, except as otherwise provided by law.

6. Teaching, Training Supervision, Research, and Publishing

6.01 Design of Education and Training Programs.

Psychologists who are responsible for education and training programs seek to ensure that the programs are competently designed, provide the proper experiences, and meet the requirements for licensure, certification, or other goals for which claims are made by the program.

6.02 Descriptions of Education and Training Programs.

(a) Psychologists responsible for education and training programs seek to ensure that there is a current and accurate description of the program content, training goals and objectives, and requirements that must be met for satisfactory completion of the program. This information must be made readily available to all interested parties.

(b) Psychologists seek to ensure that statements concerning their course outlines are accurate and not misleading, particularly regarding the subject matter to be covered, bases for evaluating progress, and the nature of course experiences. (See also Standard 3.03, Avoidance of False or Deceptive Statements.)

(c) To the degree to which they exercise control, psychologists responsible for announcements, catalogs, brochures, or advertisements describing workshops, seminars, or other non-degree granting educational programs ensure that they accurately describe the audience for which the program is intended, the educational objectives, the presenters, and the fees involved.

6.03 Accuracy and Objectivity in Teaching.

(a) When engaged in teaching or training, psychologists present psychological information accurately and with a reasonable degree of objectivity.

(b) When engaged in teaching or training, psychologists recognize the power they hold over students or supervisees and therefore make reasonable efforts to avoid engaging in conduct that is personally demeaning to students or supervisees. (See also Standards 1.09, Respecting Others, and 1.12, Other Harassment.)

6.04 Limitation on Teaching.

Psychologists do not teach the use of techniques or procedures that require specialized training, licensure, or expertise, including but not limited to hypnosis, biofeedback, and projective techniques, to individuals who lack the prerequisite training, legal scope of practice, or expertise.

6.05 Assessing Student and Supervisee Performance.

(a) In academic and supervisory relationships, psychologists establish an appropriate process for providing feedback to students and supervisees.

(b) Psychologists evaluate students and supervisees on the basis of their actual performance on relevant and established program requirements.

6.06 Planning Research.

(a) Psychologists design, conduct, and report research in accordance with recognized standards of scientific competence and ethical research.

(b) Psychologists plan their research so as to minimize the possibility that results will be misleading.

(c) In planning research, psychologists consider its ethical acceptability under the Ethics Code. If an ethical issue is unclear, psychologists seek to resolve the issue through consultation with institutional review boards, animal care and use committees, peer consultations, or other proper mechanisms.

(d) Psychologists take reasonable steps to implement appropriate protections for the rights and welfare of human participants, other persons affected by the research, and the welfare of animal subjects.

6.07 Responsibility.

(a) Psychologists conduct research competently and with due concern for the dignity and welfare of the participants.

(b) Psychologists are responsible for the ethical conduct of research conducted by them or by others under their supervision or control.

(c) Researchers and assistants are permitted to perform only those tasks for which they are appropriately trained and prepared.

(d) As part of the process of development and implementation of research projects, psychologists consult those with expertise concerning any special population under investigation or most likely to be affected.

6.08 Compliance With Law and Standards.

Psychologists plan and conduct research in a manner consistent with federal and state law and regulations, as well as professional standards governing the conduct of research, and particularly those standards governing research with human participants and animal subjects.

6.09 Institutional Approval.

Psychologists obtain from host institutions or organizations appropriate approval prior to conducting research, and they provide accurate information about their research proposals. They conduct the research in accordance with the approved research protocol.

6.10 Research Responsibilities.

Prior to conducting research (except research involving only anonymous surveys, naturalistic observations, or similar research), psychologists enter into an agreement with participants that clarifies the nature of the research and the responsibilities of each party.

6.11 Informed Consent to Research.

(a) Psychologists use language that is reasonably understandable to research participants in obtaining their appropriate informed consent (except as provided in Standard 6.12, Dispensing with Informed Consent). Such informed consent is appropriately documented.

(b) Using language that is reasonably understandable to participants, psychologists inform participants of the nature of the research; they inform participants that they are free to participate or to decline to participate or to withdraw from the research; they explain the foreseeable consequences of declining or withdrawing; they inform participants of significant factors that may be expected to influence their willingness to participate (such as risks, discomfort, adverse effects, or limitations on confidentiality, except as provided in Standard 6.15, Deception in Research); and they explain other aspects about which the prospective participants inquire.

(c) When psychologists conduct research with individuals such as students or subordinates, psychologists take special care to protect the prospective participants from adverse consequences of declining or withdrawing from participation.

(d) When research participation is a course requirement or opportunity for extra credit, the prospective participant is given the choice of equitable alternative activities.

(e) For persons who are legally incapable of giving informed consent, psychologists nevertheless (1) provide an appropriate explanation, (2) obtain the participant's assent, and (3) obtain appropriate permission from a legally authorized person, if such substitute consent is permitted by law.

6.12 Dispensing With Informed Consent.

Before determining that planned research (such as research involving only anonymous questionnaires, naturalistic observations, or certain kinds of archival research) does not require the informed consent of research participants, psychologists consider applicable regulations and institutional review board requirements, and they consult with colleagues as appropriate.

6.13 Informed Consent in Research Filming or Recording.

Psychologists obtain informed consent from research participants prior to filming or recording them in any form, unless the research involves simply naturalistic observations in public places and it is not anticipated that the recording will be used in a manner that could cause personal identification or harm.

6.14 Offering Inducements for Research Participants.

(a) In offering professional services as an inducement to obtain research participants, psychologists make clear the nature of the services, as well as the risks, obligations, and limitations. (See also Standard 1.18, Barter [With Patients or Clients].)

(b) Psychologists do not offer excessive or inappropriate financial or other inducements to obtain research participants, particularly when it might tend to coerce participation.

6.15 Deception in Research.

(a) Psychologists do not conduct a study involving deception unless they have determined that the use of deceptive techniques is justified by the study's prospective scientific, educational, or applied value and that equally effective alternative procedures that do not use deception are not feasible.

(b) Psychologists never deceive research participants about significant aspects that would affect their willingness to participate, such as physical risks, discomfort, or unpleasant emotional experiences.

(c) Any other deception that is an integral feature of the design and conduct of an experiment must be explained to participants as early as is feasible, preferably at the conclusion of their participation, but no later than at the conclusion of the research. (See also Standard 6.18, Providing Participants With Information About the Study.)

6.16 Sharing and Utilizing Data.

Psychologists inform research participants of their anticipated sharing or further use of personally identifiable research data and of the possibility of unanticipated future uses.

6.17 Minimizing Invasiveness.

In conducting research, psychologists interfere with the participants or milieu from which data are collected only in a manner that is warranted by an appropriate research design and that is consistent with psychologists' roles as scientific investigators.

6.18 Providing Participants With Information About the Study.

(a) Psychologists provide a prompt opportunity for participants to obtain appropriate information about the nature, results, and conclusions of the research, and psychologists attempt to correct any misconceptions that participants may have.

(b) If scientific or humane values justify delaying or withholding this information, psychologists take reasonable measures to reduce the risk of harm.

6.19 Honoring Commitments.

Psychologists take reasonable measures to honor all commitments they have made to research participants.

6.20 Care and Use of Animals in Research.

(a) Psychologists who conduct research involving animals treat them humanely.

(b) Psychologists acquire, care for, use, and dispose of animals in compliance with current federal, state, and local laws and regulations, and with professional standards.

(c) Psychologists trained in research methods and experienced in the care of laboratory animals supervise all procedures involving animals and are responsible for ensuring appropriate consideration of their comfort, health, and humane treatment.

(d) Psychologists ensure that all individuals using animals under their supervision have received instruction in research methods and in the care, maintenance, and handling of the species being used, to the extent appropriate to their role.

(e) Responsibilities and activities of individuals assisting in a research project are consistent with their respective competencies.

(f) Psychologists make reasonable efforts to minimize the discomfort, infection, illness, and pain of animal subjects.

(g) A procedure subjecting animals to pain, stress, or privation is used only when an alternative procedure is unavailable and the goal is justified by its prospective scientific, educational, or applied value.

(h) Surgical procedures are performed under appropriate anesthesia; techniques to avoid infection and minimize pain are followed during and after surgery.

(i) When it is appropriate that the animal's life be terminated, it is done rapidly, with an effort to minimize pain, and in accordance with accepted procedures.

6.21 Reporting of Results.

(a) Psychologists do not fabricate data or falsify results in their publications.

(b) If psychologists discover significant errors in their published data, they take reasonable steps to correct such errors in a correction, retraction, erratum, or other appropriate publication means.

6.22 Plagiarism.

Psychologists do not present substantial portions or elements of another's work or data as their own, even if the other work or data source is cited occasionally.

6.23 Publication Credit.

(a) Psychologists take responsibility and credit, including authorship credit, only for work they have actually performed or to which they have contributed.

(b) Principal authorship and other publication credits accurately reflect the relative scientific or professional contributions of the individuals involved, regardless of their relative status. Mere possession of an institutional position, such as Department Chair, does not justify authorship credit. Minor contributions to the research or to the writing for publications are appropriately acknowledged, such as in footnotes or in an introductory statement.

(c) A student is usually listed as principal author on any multiple-authored article that is substantially based on the student's dissertation or thesis.

6.24 Duplicate Publication of Data.

Psychologists do not publish, as original data, data that have been previously published. This does not preclude republishing data when they are accompanied by proper acknowledgment.

6.25 Sharing Data.

After research results are published, psychologists do not withhold the data on which their conclusions are based from other competent professionals who seek to verify the substantive claims through re-analysis and who intend to use such data only for that purpose, provided that the confidentiality of the participants can be protected and unless legal rights concerning proprietary data preclude their release.

6.26 Professional Reviewers.

Psychologists who review material submitted for publication, grant, or other research proposal review respect the confidentiality of and the proprietary rights in such information of those who submitted it.

7. Forensic Activities

7.01 Professionalism.

Psychologists who perform forensic functions, such as assessments, interviews, consultations, reports, or expert testimony, must comply with all other provisions of this Ethics Code to the extent that they apply to such activities. In addition, psychologists base their forensic work on appropriate knowledge of and competence in the areas underlying such work, including specialized knowledge concerning special populations. (See also Standards 1.06, Basis for Scientific and Professional Judgments; 1.08, Human Differences; 1.15, Misuse of Psychologists' Influence; and 1.23, Documentation of Professional and Scientific Work.)

7.02 Forensic Assessments.

(a) Psychologists' forensic assessments, recommenda-

tions, and reports are based on information and techniques (including personal interviews of the individual, when appropriate) sufficient to provide appropriate substantiation for their findings. (See also Standards 1.03, Professional and Scientific Relationship; 1.23, Documentation of Professional and Scientific Work; 2.01, Evaluation, Diagnosis, and Interventions in Professional Context; and 2.05, Interpreting Assessment Results.)

(b) Except as noted in (c), below, psychologists provide written or oral forensic reports or testimony of the psychological characteristics of an individual only after they have conducted an examination of the individual adequate to support their statements or conclusions.

(c) When, despite reasonable efforts, such an examination is not feasible, psychologists clarify the impact of their limited information on the reliability and validity of their reports and testimony, and they appropriately limit the nature and extent of their conclusions or recommendations.

7.03 Clarification of Role.

In most circumstances, psychologists avoid performing multiple and potentially conflicting roles in forensic matters. When psychologists may be called on to serve in more than one role in a legal proceeding - for example, as consultant or expert for one party or for the court and as a fact witness - they clarify role expectations and the extent of confidentiality in advance to the extent feasible, and thereafter as changes occur, in order to avoid compromising their professional judgment and objectivity and in order to avoid misleading others regarding their role.

7.04 Truthfulness and Candor.

(a) In forensic testimony and reports, psychologists testify truthfully, honestly, and candidly and, consistent with applicable legal procedures, describe fairly the bases for their testimony and conclusions.

(b) Whenever necessary to avoid misleading, psychologists acknowledge the limits of their data or conclusions.

7.05 Prior Relationships.

A prior professional relationship with a party does not preclude psychologists from testifying as fact witnesses or from testifying to their services to the extent permitted by applicable law. Psychologists appropriately take into account ways in which the prior relationship might affect their professional objectivity or opinions and disclose the potential conflict to the relevant parties.

7.06 Compliance With Law and Rules.

In performing forensic roles, psychologists are reasonably familiar with the rules governing their roles. Psychologists are aware of the occasionally competing demands placed upon them by these principles and the requirements of the court system, and attempt to resolve these conflicts by making known their commitment to this Ethics Code and taking steps to resolve the conflict in a responsible manner. (See also Standard 1.02, Relationship of Ethics and Law.)

8. Resolving Ethical Issues

8.01 Familiarity With Ethics Code.

Psychologists have an obligation to be familiar with this Ethics Code, other applicable ethics codes, and their application to psychologists' work. Lack of awareness or misunderstanding of an ethical standard is not itself a defense to a charge of unethical conduct.

8.02 Confronting Ethical Issues.

When a psychologist is uncertain whether a particular situation or course of action would violate this Ethics Code, the psychologist ordinarily consults with other psychologists knowledgeable about ethical issues, with state or national psychology ethics committees, or with other appropriate authorities in order to choose a proper response.

8.03 Conflicts Between Ethics and Organizational Demands.

If the demands of an organization with which psychologists are affiliated conflict with this Ethics Code, psychologists clarify the nature of the conflict, make known their commitment to the Ethics Code, and to the extent feasible, seek to resolve the conflict in a way that permits the fullest adherence to the Ethics Code.

8.04 Informal Resolution of Ethical Violations.

When psychologists believe that there may have been an ethical violation by another psychologist, they attempt to resolve the issue by bringing it to the attention of that individual if an informal resolution appears appropriate and the intervention does not violate any confidentiality rights that may be involved.

8.05 Reporting Ethical Violations.

If an apparent ethical violation is not appropriate for informal resolution under Standard 8.04 or is not resolved properly in that fashion, psychologists take further action appropriate to the situation, unless such action conflicts with confidentiality rights in ways that cannot be resolved. Such action might include referral to state or national committees on professional ethics or to state licensing boards.

8.06 Cooperating With Ethics Committees.

Psychologists cooperate in ethics investigations, proceedings, and resulting requirements of the APA or any affiliated state psychological association to which they belong. In doing so, they make reasonable efforts to resolve any issues as to confidentiality. Failure to cooperate is itself an ethics violation.

8.07 Improper Complaints.

Psychologists do not file or encourage the filing of ethics complaints that are frivolous and are intended to harm the respondent rather than to protect the public.

History and Effective Date

This version of the APA Ethics Code was adopted by the American Psychological Association's Council of Representatives during its meeting, August 13 and 16, 1992, and is effective beginning December 1, 1992. Inquiries concerning the substance or interpretation of the APA Ethics Code should be addressed to the Director, Office of Ethics, American Psychological Association, 750 First Street, NE, Washington, DC 20002-4242.

This Code will be used to adjudicate complaints brought concerning alleged conduct occurring after the effective date. Complaints regarding conduct occurring prior to the effective date will be adjudicated on the basis of the version of the Code that was in effect at the time the conduct occurred, except that no provisions repealed in June 1989, will be enforced even if an earlier version contains the provision. The Ethics Code will undergo continuing review and study for future revisions; comments on the Code may be sent to the above address.

The APA has previously published its Ethical Standards as follows:

American Psychological Association. (1953). *Ethical standards of psychologists.* Washington, DC: Author.
American Psychological Association. (1958). Standards of ethical behavior for psychologists. American Psychologist, 13, 268–271.
American Psychological Association. (1963). Ethical standards of psychologists. *American Psychologist, 18,* 56–60.
American Psychological Association. (1968). Ethical standards of psychologists. *American Psychologist, 23,* 357–361.
American Psychological Association. (1977, March). Ethical standards of psychologists. *APA Monitor,* 22–23.
American Psychological Association. (1979). *Ethical standards of psychologists.* Washington, DC: Author.
American Psychological Association. (1981). Ethical principles of psychologists. *American Psychologist, 36,* 633–638.
American Psychological Association. (1990). Ethical principles of psychologists (Amended June 2, 1989). *American Psychologist, 45,* 390–395.

Request copies of the APA's Ethical Principles of Psychologists and Code of Conduct from the APA Order Department, 750 First Street, NE, Washington, DC 20002-4242, or phone (202) 336-5510.

124 / PRACTICUM AND INTERNSHIP

Summary

The ethical issues presented by the authors in this chapter are critical for the establishment and maintenance of the counseling relationship. Knowledge of the ethical codes for counselors and psychologists assures that the practitioner is well aware of the standards for conducting proper therapeutic activities. To this end, the codes of ethics and professional standards of the ACA and the APA have been presented in full. It is our hope that students will take time to become familiar with the terms of these codes in order to ensure that their services will comply with the appropriate professional standards.

Suggested Readings

Alexander, P. C., & Lupfer, S. L. (1987). Family characteristics and long-term consequences associated with sexual abuse. *Archives of Sexual Behavior, 16,* 235–245.

Allsopp, A., & Prosen, S. (1988). Teacher reactions to a child sexual abuse training program. *Elementary School Guidance Counseling, 22,* 299–305.

American Association for Marriage and Family Therapy. (1991). *Code of ethical principles for marriage and family therapists.* Washington DC: Author.

American Medical Association. (1988). *LLL progress on the prevention and control of AIDS* (Reference Committee E, pp. 204–222, 473). Washington DC: Author.

American Psychiatric Association. (1987). *Diagnostic and statistical manual of mental disorders* (3rd ed.). Washington, DC: Author.

American Psychological Association. (1981). Ethical principals of psychologists. *American Psychologist, 36,* 633–638.

American Psychological Association. (1991). APA Council of Representatives adopts new AIDS policies. *Psychology and AIDS Exchange, 7,* 1.

American School Counselor Association. (1992). *Ethical standards for school counselors.* Alexandria, VA: Author.

Annell, Al. L. (Ed.). (1971). *Depressive states in childhood and adolescence.* New York: Halstead.

Applebaum, P. S. (1985). Tarasoff and the clinician: Problems in fulfilling the duty to protect. *American Journal of Psychiatry, 142*(4), 425–429.

Applebaum, P. S., & Meisel, M. A. (1986). Therapists' obligations to report their patients' criminal acts. *Bulletin of the American Academy of Psychiatry and the Law, 14*(3), 221–229.

Atcherson, E. (1993, Fall). Ethics and information: How vulnerable is your campus to computer crime? *CUPA Journal, 4,* 35–38.

Banning, A. (1989). Mother-son incest: Confronting as prejudice. *Child Abuse and Neglect, 13,* 563–570.

Baxter, A. (1986). *Techniques for dealing with child sexual abuse.* Springfield, IL: Charles C. Thomas.

Beauchamp, T. L. (1985). Suicide: Matters of life and death. *Suicide and Life-Threatening Behavior, 24*(2), 190–195.

Beauchamp, T. L., & Childress, J. F. (1979) *Principles of biomedical ethics.* New York: Oxford University Press.

Bednar, R. L., Bednar, S. C., Lambert, M. J., & Waite, D. R. (1991). *Psychology with high-risk clients: Legal and professional standards.* Pacific Grove, CA: Brooks/Cole.

Besharov, D. J. (1988). Child abuse and neglect reporting and investigation: Policy guidelines for decision making. *Family Law Quarterly, 22*(1), 1–16.

Borys, D. S., & Pope, K. S. (1989). Dual relationships between therapist and client: A national study of psychologists, psychiatrists, and social workers. *Professional Psychology: Research and Practice, 20*(5), 283–293.

Boynton v. Burglass, No. 89-1409, Fla. Ct. App., 3d Dist. (September 24, 1991).

Brainer, C. J., Reyna, C. F., & Brandse, E. (1996). Are children's false memories more persistent than their true memories? *Psychological Science, 6*(6), 359–364.

Brassard, M. R., Germain, R., & Hart, S. N. (1987). *Psychological maltreatment of children and youth.* New York: Pergamon.

Briere, J. (1989). *Therapy for adults molested as children: Beyond survival.* New York: Springer-Verlag.

Bross, A. (1991, July 7). A touch of evil. *The Boston Globe Magazine,* 12–25.

Bross, D. C. (1984). When children are battered by the law. *Barrister, 11*(4), 8–11.

Buckley, J. (1988). Legal proceedings, reforms, and emergency issues in child sexual abuse cases. *Behavioral Science and the Law, 6*(2), 153–180.

Butler, S. (1978). *Conspiracy of silence.* San Francisco: New Glide.

Capuzzi, D., & Golden, L. (1988). *Preventing adolescent suicide.* Muncie, IN: Accelerated Development.

Carlino v. State, 294 N.Y.S. 2d 30 (1968).

Caudill, B. (1995, February). *The repressed memory war.* Presentation at the Annual Convention of the California Psychological Association, La Jolla, CA.

Celotta, B., Golden, J., Keys, S. S., & Cannon, G. (1988). A model prevention program. In D. Capuzzi & L. Golden (Eds.), *Preventing adolescent suicide* (pp. 269–296). Muncie, IN: Accelerated Development.

Chaffin, M., & Milner, J. (1993). Psychometric issues for practitioners in child maltreatment. *APSAC Advisor, 6*(1), 9–13.

Closen, M. L., & Isaacman, S. H. (1988). The duty to notify private third parties of the risks of HIV infection. *Journal of Health and Hospital Law, 21,* 295–298.

Cohen, E. D. (1990). Confidentiality, counseling, and clients who have AIDS: Ethical foundations of a model rule. *Journal of Counseling and Development, 68*(3), 282–286.

Cole, S. S. (1984–1986). Facing the challenges of sexual abuse in persons with disabilities. *Sexuality and Disability, 7,* 71–88.

Comiskey v. State of New York, 418 N.Y.S. 2d 233 (1979).

Connell, H. M. (1972). Depression in childhood. *Child Psychiatry and Human Development, 4,* 71–85.

Dalton v. State, 308 N.Y.S. 2d 441 (Sup, CF. N.Y. App. 1970).

Darton, N., Springer, K., Wright, L., & Keene-Osborn, S. (1991, October 7). The pain of the last taboo. *Newsweek,* 70–72.

Davis, J. M. (1985). Suicidal crisis in schools. *School Psychology Review, 14*(3), 117–123.

Delarosa, R. (1987). Viability of negligence actions for sexual transmission of the acquired immune deficiency syndrome virus. *Capital University Law Review, 17,* 101–195.

Deutsch, P. M., & Parker, E. C. (1985). *Rehabilitation testimony: Maintaining a professional perspective.* New York: Matthew Bender.

Dickens, B. M. (1990). Confidentiality and the duty to warn. In L. O. Gostin (Ed.) *AIDS and the health care system* (pp. 98–112). New Haven, CT: Yale University Press.

Dixon, W. A., Heppner, P. P., & Rudd, H. D. (1994). Problem-solving appraisal, hopelessness, and suicide ideation: Evidence for a mediational model. *Journal of Counseling Psychology, 41*(1), 91-98.

Dorland, D. (1974). *Dorland's medical dictionary.* New York: Macmillan.

Erickson, E. L., McEnvoy, A., & Colucci, N. D. (1984) *Child abuse and neglect: A guidebook for educators and community leaders* (2nd ed.). Holmes Beach, FL: Learning Publications.

Etherington, K. (1995). Adult male survivors of childhood sexual abuse. *Counseling Psychology Quarterly, 8*(3), 233–241

Evans, S., & Schaefer, S. (1987). Incest and chemically dependent women: Treatment implications. *Journal of Chemical Dependency Treatment, I,* 141–173.

Farrow v. Health Service Corp., 604 p 2d 474 (Utah Supreme Ct., 1979).

Finkelhor, D. (1979). *Sexually victimized children.* New York: Free Press

Finkelhor, D. (1984, September). The prevention of child sexual abuse: An overview of needs and problems. *Seicus Report,* 1–5.

Forge, J. L., & Henderson, P. (1990). Counselor competency in the courtroom. *Journal of Counseling and Development, 68,* 456–459.

Freeman, L., & Roy, J. (1976). *Betrayal.* New York: Stein & Day.

Fremouw, W., Callahan, T., & Kashden, J. (1993). Adolescent suicidal risk: Psychological, problem solving, and environmental factors. *Suicide and Life-Threatening Behavior, 23*(1).

Fromuth, M. E. (1986). The relationship of childhood sexual abuse with later psychological and sexual adjustment in a sample of college women. *Child Abuse and Neglect, 10,* 5–15.

Fujimura, L. E., Weis, D. M., & Cochran, F. R. (1985). Suicide: Dynamics and implications for counseling. *Journal of Counseling and Development, 63,* 612–615.

Fulero, S. M. (1998). Tarasoff: Ten years later. *Professional Psychology: Research and Practice, 19*(2), 184–190.

Garbarino, J., & Vondra, J. (1987). Psychological maltreatment: Issues and perspectives. In M. R. Brassard, R. Germain, & S. N. Hart (Eds.), *Psychological maltreatment of children and youth* (pp. 224–244). New York: Pergamon.

Gargiulo, R. (1990). Child abuse and neglect: An overview. In R. Goldman & R. Gargiulo (Eds.), *Children at risk: An interdisciplinary approach to child abuse and neglect* (pp. 1–36). Austin, TX: Pro-Ed.

Glantz, T. M., & Hunt, B. (1996). What rehabilitation counselors need to know about adult survivors of child sexual abuse. *Journal of Applied Rehabilitation Counseling, 27*(3), 17–22.

Goldman, R. (1993). Sexual abuse of children with special needs: Are they safe in day care? *Day Care and Early Education, 20*(4), 37–38.

Gray, E. A., & Harding, A. K. (1988). Confidentiality limits with clients who have the AIDS virus. *Journal of Counseling and Development, 66*(5), 219–223.

Grob, M. C., Klein, A. A., & Eisen, S. V. (1982). The role of the high school professional in identifying and managing adolescent suicide behavior. *Journal of Youth Suicide, 12,* 163–173.

Groth, A. N. (1979). Sexual trauma in the life histories of rapists and child molesters. *Victimology, 4,* 10–16.

Handelsman, M. M., & Galvin, M. D. (1988). Facilitation informed consent for outpatient psychotherapy: A suggested written format. *Professional Psychology: Research and Practice, 19*(2), 223–225.

Harding, A. K., Gray, L. A., & Neal, M. (1993). Confidentiality limits with clients who have HIV: A review of ethical and legal guidelines and professional policies. *Journal of Counseling and Development, 71*, 297–305.

Hass, L. J., & Malouf, J. L. (1989) *Keeping up the good work: A practitioner's guide to mental health ethics*. Sarasota, FL: Professional Resource Exchange.

Haugaard, J. J., & Emery, R. E. (1989) Methodological issues in child sexual abuse research. *Child Abuse and Neglect, 13,* 89–100.

Hedlund v. Superior Court of Orange County, 669 P.2d 41, 191 Cal. Rptr.805 (1983).

Hillman, D., & Solek-Tefft, J. (1988). Spiders and flies: *Help for parents and teachers of sexually abused children*. Lexington, MA: Lexington Books.

Hirsch, H., & White, E. (1982). The pathological anatomy of medical malpractice claims: Legal aspects of medical malpractice. *Journal of Legal Medicine, 6*(1), 25–26.

Hoffman, M. A. (1991). Counseling the HIV-infected client: A psychosocial model for assessment and intervention. *Counseling Psychologist, 19*(4), 167–542.

Hood, G. (1994). The statute of limitation barrier in civil suits brought against adult survivors of child sexual abuse: A simple solution. *University of Illinois Law Review, 2,* 417–442.

Horowitz, I. A., & Willgigng, T. E. (1984). *The psychology of law: Applications*. Boston: Little, Brown.

Hrabowy, I. (1987). *Self-reported correlates of adult-child sexual relations*. Unpublished master's thesis, Bowling Green State University, Bowling Green, OH.

Jablonski v. United States, 712 E.2d 391 (9th cir. 1983).

Josephson, G. S., & Fong-Beyette, M. L. (1987). Factors assisting female clients' disclosure of incest during counseling. *Journal of Counseling and Development, 65,* 475–478.

Kane, S., & Keeton, R. (1985, October/November). Informed consent. *Campus Voice,* 52–54.

Kaufman, J., & Zigler, E. (1987). Do abused children become abusive parents? *American Journal of Orthopsychiatry, 57,* 186–192.

Kelly, K. (1987). AIDS and ethics: An overview. *General Hospital Psychiatry, 9,* 331–340.

Kempe, R. S., & Kempe, C. H. (1978). *Child abuse*. Cambridge, MA: Harvard University Press.

Kermani, E. J., & Weiss, B. A. (1989). AIDS and confidentiality: Legal concept and its application in psychotherapy. *American Journal of Psychotherapy, 43*(1), 25–31.

Kilpatrick, A. C. (1986). Some correlates of women's childhood sexual experiences: A retrospective study. *Journal of Sex Research, 22,* 221–242.

Knapp, S., & Tepper, A. (1995, May). Risk management issues in the false memory debate. *Pennsylvania Psychologist, 55*(3), 26–27.

Knapp, S., & VandeCreek, L. (1993). What psychologists need to know about AIDS. *Journal of Training and Practice in Professional Psychology, 3*(2), 3–16.

Knapp, S., & VandeCreek, L. (1995). *Risk management for psychologists treating patients who recover lost memories of childhood abuse*. Manuscript in preparation.

Kohn, A. (1987). Shattered innocence. *Psychology Today, 21*(2), 54–58.

Krug, R. S. (1989). Adult male reports of childhood sexual abuse by mothers: Case descriptions, motivations, and long-term consequences. *Child Abuse and Neglect, 13,* 111–119.

Kush, F. R. (1990). *A descriptive study of school-based adolescent suicide prevention/intervention programs: Program components and the role of the school counselor*. Unpublished doctoral dissertation, University of Pittsburgh.

Landesman, S. H. (1987). AIDS and a duty to protect: Commentary. *Hastings Center Report, 17,* 23.

Lasko, C. A. (1986). Childhood depression questions and answers. *Journal of School Guidance and Counseling, 4,* 283–287.

Lawson, C. (1991). Mother-son sexual abuse: Rare or under-reported? A critique of the research. *Child Abuse and Neglect, 17,* 261–269.

Lipari v. Sears Roebuck, 497 F. Supp. 185 (D. Neb. 1980).

Loftus, E. F. (1994). The repressed memory controversy. *American Psychologist, 49,* 409–420.

Mathiasen, R. (1988). Evaluating suicidal risk in the college student. *NASPA Journal, 25,* 257–261.

McCormick, R. A (1989). *The critical calling: Reflections on moral dilemmas since Vatican II*. Washington, DC: Georgetown University Press.

Melton, G. B. (1991). Ethical judgments amid uncertainty: Dilemmas in the AIDS epidemic. *Counseling Psychologist, 19*(4), 561–565.

Milkovich v. Loraine Journal Inc., 497 U.S. 1 (1990).

Mitchell, J., & Morse, J. (1997). *From victim to survivor: Women survivors of female perpetrators*. Muncie, IN: Accelerated Development.

Monahan, J. (1993, March). Limiting therapist exposure to Tarasoff liability: Guidelines for risk containment. *American Psychologist, 48,* 242–250.

Morrison, C. F. (1989). AIDS: Ethical implications for psychological intervention. *Professional Psychology: Research and Practice, 20*(3), 166–171.

Murphy, W., Rau, T., & Worley, P. (1994). Offender treatment: The perils and pitfalls of profiling child sex abusers. *APSAC Advisor, 7*(1)3–4, 28–29.

National Association of Social Workers. (1990). *Policy statement on HIV and AIDS clients.* East Lansing, MI: Author.

National Association of Social Workers. 1997). *Code of ethics.* East Lansing, MI: Author.

Ney, P. G. (1987). Does verbal abuse leave deeper scars? A study of children and parents. *Canadian Journal of Psychiatry, 32,* 371–378.

Norris, T. L. (1986, October). *Victim therapy with adult survivors of child sexual abuse* (Report No. CG020400). Paper presented at the annual conference of the American Association for Marriage and Family Therapy, Orlando, FL. (ERIC Document Reproduction Service No. ED 289 133)

Paridies v. Benedictine Hospital, 431 N.Y.S.2d 175 (APP. Div. 1980).

Pate, R. H. (1992, Summer). Are you liable? *American Counselor, 10,* 23.

Peach, L., & Reddick, T. L. (1991). Counselors can make a difference in preventing adolescent suicide. *The School Counselor, 39,* 207–217.

Pearson, Q. M. (1994). Treatment techniques for adult survivors of childhood sexual abuse. *Journal of Counseling and Development, 73,* 32–37.

Peck v. The Counseling Service of Addison County, 499 A.2d 422 (1985).

Philips, I. (1983). Childhood depression: Interpersonal interactions and depressive phenomena. *American Journal of Psychiatry, 136,* 511–515.

Poland, S. (1990). *Suicide intervention in the schools.* New York: Guilford.

Pope, K. S. (1985). Dual relationships: A violation of ethical, legal, and clinical standards. *California State Psychologist, 20*(3), 1–4.

Rencken, R. H. (1989). *Intervention strategies for sexual abuse* (Report No. CG022806). Alexandria, VA: American Association for Counseling and Development. (ERIC Document Reproduction Service No. ED 323 483)

Repressed memory claims expected to soar. (1995, May). *National Psychologist, 4*(3), 3.

Rosenberg, M. L., Smith, J. C., Davidson, L. E., & Conn, J. M. (1987). The emergence of youth suicide: An epidemiological analysis and public health perspective. *Annual Review of Public Health, 8,* 417–440.

Roy, A. (1982). Risk factors for suicide in psychiatric patients. *Archives of General Psychiatry, 39,* 1089–1095.

Rutter, P. (1989). Sex in the forbidden zone. *Psychology Today, 23*(10), 34–38.

Sandoval, J. (1985). Crisis counseling: Conceptualization and general principles. *School Psychology Review, 14,* 257–265.

Sanford, L. T. (1980). *The silent children: A parent's guide to the prevention of child sexual abuse.* Garden City, NY: Doubleday.

Schlossberger, E., & Heckler, L. (1996). HIV and the family therapist's duty to warn: A legal and ethical analysis. *Journal of Marital and Family Therapy, 22*(1), 27–40.

Schroeder, L. O. (1979). Legal liability: A professional concern. *Clinical Social Work Journal, 7*(3), 194–199.

Schwitzgebel, R. L., & Schwitzgebel, R. K. (1980). *Law and psychological practice,* New York: Wiley.

Seppa, N. (1996, April). Fear of malpractice curbs some psychologists' practice. *American Psychological Monitor, 2,* 129–137.

Sheeley, V. L., & Herlihy, B. (1989). Counseling suicidal teens: A duty to warn and protect. *The School Counselor, 37,* 89–101.

Sloan, I. J. (1983). *Child abuse: Governing law and legislation.* Dobbs Ferry, NY: Oceana.

Strother, D. B. (1986). Suicide among the very young. *Phi Delta Kappan, 67,* 756–759.

Swenson, L. C. (1997). *Psychology and law for the helping professions.* Pacific Grove, CA: Brooks/Cole.

Tarasoff v. Regents of the University of California, 113 Cal. Rptr. 14, 551 P.2d. 334 (Cal. 1976).

Thompson v. County of Alameda, 614 P.2d 728 (1980).

Tueting, P., Koslow, S. H., & Hirschfield, R.M.A. (1983). *National Institute of Mental Health: Special report on depression research* (DHHS Publication No. ADM 83-1085). Washington, DC: U.S. Government Printing Office.

VandeCreek, L., & Knapp, S. (1993). *Tarasoff and beyond: Legal considerations in the treatment of life-endangering patients* (revised ed.). Sarasota, FL: Professional Resource Press.

Waldo, S., & Malley, P. B. (1992). *Tarasoff* and its progeny: Implications for school counselors. *The School Counselor, 40,* 56–63.

Weinstock, R., & Weinstock, D. (1989). Clinical flexibility and confidentiality: Effects of reporting laws. *Psychiatric Quarterly, 60*(3), 195–214.

Weisman v. Blue Shield of California, 163 CAL. App. 3d61, 209 CAL. Rptr. 169 (CAL., ct. app., 1985).

Weissman, N. H. (1984). Psychological assessment and psycho-legal formulations in psychiatric traumatology. *Psychiatric Annals, 14*(7), 517–529.

Westefeld, J. S., Whitchard, K. A., & Range, L. M. (1990). College and university student suicide: Trends and implications. *Counseling Psychologist, 18*(3), 464–476.

Wise, P. S., Smead, V. S., & Huebner, E. S. (1987). Crisis intervention: Involvement and training needs of school psychology personnel. *Journal of School Psychology, 25,* 185–187.

Wood, G. J., Marks, R., & Dilley, J. (1990). *AIDS law for mental health professionals*. San Francisco: University of California AIDS Health Project.

Yarmey, A. D., & Jones, H.P.T. (1983). Is the psychology of eye witness testimony a matter of common sense? In S. M. Lloyd-Bostock & B. R. Clifford (Eds.), *Evaluating witness evidence* (pp. 323–339). New York: Wiley.

Zerbe Enns, C. (1996). Counselors and the backlash: "Rape hype" and "false memory syndrome." *Journal of Counseling and Development, 74*, 358–366.

References

American Counseling Association. (1995). *Code of ethics and standards of practice*. Alexandria, VA: Author.

American Psychological Association. (1995). *Ethical principles of psychologists and code of conduct*. Washington, DC: Author.

Beauchamp, T. L., & Childress, J. F. (1994). *Principles of biomedical ethics* (4th ed.). New York: Oxford University Press.

Bersoff, D. H. (1996). The virtue of principle ethics. *Counseling Psychologists, 24*(1), 86–91.

Edel, A., Flower, E., & O'Connor, F. W. (1994). *Critique of applied ethics: Reflections and recommendations*. Philadelphia: Temple University Press.

Hauerwas, S. (1981*). A community of character*. South Bend, IN: University of Notre Dame Press.

Huber, C. H., & Baruth, L. G. (1987). *Ethical, legal, and professional issues in the practice of marriage and family therapy*. Columbus, OH: Merrill.

Jordan, A. E., & Meara, M. (1990). Ethics and the professional practice of psychologists: The role of virtues and principles. *Professional Psychology: Practice and Research, 21*(2), 107–115.

Kitchener, K. S. (1984). Intuition, critical evaluation, and ethical principles. The foundation for ethical decisions in counseling psychology. *Counseling Psychologist, 24*(1), 92–97.

Kitchener, K. S. (1996). There is more to ethics than principles. *Counseling Psychologist, 24*(1), 92–97.

Meara, N. M., Schmidt, L. D., & Day, J. D. (1996). Principles and virtues: A foundation for ethical decisions, policies, and character. *Counseling Psychologist, 24*(l), 4–77.

CHAPTER

7

Patrick B. Malley
Eileen Petty Reilly

Legal Issues

American cinema offers a classic depiction of the advent of justice from the American frontier. Two gunfighters square off in the street. Before they draw, the bad guy snarls, "Your days are over," to which the good guy responds, "The difference between you and me is, I know it." In short, the good guy knows that the days for settling disputes by violence are coming to an end—he knows that disputes can only be settled by law. Through the years, societies have learned that consistency, predictability, and fairness are harbingers of "life, liberty, and the pursuit of happiness"; without them, life is chaotic.

The law, as arbitrated through the court system, is society's attempt to ensure predictability, consistency, and fairness. Its purpose is to offer an alternative to private action in settling disputes. As Swenson (1997) noted, "The question is not whether mental health professionals will interact with laws and legal professionals; it is *how* they will interact both now and in the future in which intercessions by legal professionals into mental health practice become even more intrusive" (p. 32). Therefore, it is imperative that mental health professionals understand the legal system.

■ The Law

The law should be viewed as dynamic, not as static. It is not an entity that rigidly adheres to historically derived rules, but neither does it deny their relevance to current disputes. Legal principles derive from social interactions. At the same time, the law places a great deal of importance on precedence. Many laws are based on *natural law,* that is, law promulgated by prominent philosophers as an expression of man's innate moral sense. Natural law is considered absolute and unconditional. Courts usually accept prior judicial decisions as truths when they fit or appear to fit natural law (Horowitz & Willging, 1984).

As enforced through the legal system, the law can be seen as an instrument of concern by the state for the social well-being of the people. Its primary concerns are predictability, stability, and fairness; at the same time, the system must be sensitive to expansion and readaptation. Laws are a consensus of rules to be followed in a civilized society.

Classifications of the Law

Laws are classified as constitutional, statues passed by legislatures, regulations, or case laws. The distinctions between these four classifications are explained in the following descriptions:

- **Constitutional laws** are those found in state constitutions and in the United States Constitution.
- **Statutory laws** are those written by legislatures.
- Statutory laws may have enabling clauses that permit administrators to write **regulations** to clarify them. Once written, these regulations become laws.
- Finally, decisions by appeals courts create **case laws** for the people who reside in their jurisdictions. If a legal problem manifests itself and parties differ on how to solve it, they may go to a trial court. The decision made in the trial court is not published and does not become law. However, if lawyers do not believe the trial court (the lower court) interpreted the law correctly, they may bring their case to an appeals court (a higher court). The function of the appeals court is to determine whether the trial court applied the law correctly. The members of the appeals court publish the decision, and the majority decision becomes the law for that jurisdiction. The appeals court is then said to have set a precedent for that jurisdiction.

Types of Laws

Laws are enacted to settle disputes that occur in society. They arise out of social interactions as members of society develop values that are necessary to the maintenance of order and justice. They come into being based on the common thoughts and experiences of people. They are antecedents to judgments regarding right and wrong. The person who claims to have been wronged is called the *plaintiff*; the person accused of committing the wrong is the *defendant*. The dispute is known as a *lawsuit*.

Functionally, we can define three types of law: civil law, criminal law, and mental health law (Swenson, 1997), as described in the following:

- **Civil law** is applicable, for the most part, to disputes between or among people. Losing the lawsuit usually means losing money. If a person fails to obey the stipulations made as an analogue to a civil lawsuit, he or she may be subject to a criminal charge called *contempt of court*. An example would be a mother or father who does not pay child support.
- **Criminal law** is applicable to disputes between the state and people. Losing defendants often face a loss of liberty. The standard of proof is higher in a criminal case than in a civil case.
- **Mental health law** regulates how the state may act regarding people with mental illnesses. These laws enact a permission from the state to protect people from serious harm to themselves or others. They allow the state to act as a guardian for those with mental disorders, and to institutionalize them if necessary. Most experts believe mental health law is part of civil law.

The Steps in a Lawsuit

A lawsuit proceeds through standard steps. Each step has serious legal consequences and rules that must be followed. It is important to remember that most lawsuits do not go to trial; instead, they are settled at an earlier stage.

First, the plaintiff files a complaint through a lawyer to a court in the appropriate jurisdiction. *Jurisdiction* is determined by geographical and substantive factors. Filing this complaint initiates the legal proceeding.

Once the complaint is filed, the plaintiff must make a judicial effort to inform the defendant of his or her intentions (legal notice). This proceeding is called *due process.* The reason for this procedure is to allow the defendant to rebut the accusation.

Once valid due process is accomplished, a *discovery process* is in order. At this point the lawyers involved investigate the facts of the case.

In order to obtain the facts, the lawyers may use a subpoena. The *subpoena* demands access to the facts and to the presence of witnesses at court hearings. Based on this information, the two sides may settle the dispute, or they may proceed to litigation.

If the attorneys and clients decide to proceed with the lawsuit, the next step is to have *pretrial hearings*. At this step the judge determines how the laws apply to the facts. The lawsuit may be settled at this point; "The general policy of most courts is to promote settlements and, in fact, disputants settle about 90% of all cases" (Swenson, 1997, p. 46).

In the *trial phase*, each side presents evidence and attempts to discredit the evidence of the opponent.

Ultimately, the lawsuit is decided by a judge or jury. If either party is dissatisfied with the verdict, he or she may claim that the law was not correctly applied and appeal to a higher court (Swenson, 1997).

The Special Relationship

In this section we will outline the rationales that define the legal responsibilities of professional mental health workers.

Initially, in Anglo-American law, injuries were considered to have occurred when someone inflicted harm on another. This situation is call *misfeasance*. Injuries occurring from nonaction (*nonfeasance*) did not entertain legal remedy. Eventually the concept of no penalties for nonfeasance eroded, and those who were in public callings could be held liable for nonfeasance. The courts now hold that anyone who voluntarily assumes responsibility for another is in a *special relationship* with that person.

Furthermore, people in special relationships have a *duty to care* for those for whom they have assumed some responsibility. Innocent people often get hurt when a certain duty to care is not maintained. Typically, this duty is described as the care that an ordinary or average person would exercise under similar circumstances. Consequently, if one who has a duty to care does something he or she should not do, or does not do something he or she should do, as it pertains to the relationship, that person has breached the duty to care. In short, such persons have been negligent in their responsibilities.

Mental health professions are, of course, like other members of society in many ways. However, because they are professionals and have received more training and education than the average person, and because they typically are governed by licensure or certification laws, they must act under terms of a more demanding social contract. Those who deliver psychological services owe a duty to care that is defined more stringently than it is for the average member of society. For mental health professionals who offer their skills and talent to the general public, the legal test for negligence compares their behavior with the behavior of their peers.

Negligence and the Special Relationship

Most malpractice suits brought against mental health professionals are related to issues of negligence. The plaintiff must prove that the defendant behaved in a way that did not meet the standard of care for the profession. If a therapist is deemed to have violated that standard of care, he or she may be held to be negligent. The standard of care can also be negligent. The standard of care can be defined as what the average or prudent mental health professional would have done (or not done) under the same circumstances.

Mental health professionals usually use a standard that is universal to their profession. Thus, because their training is more comprehensive, psychiatrists generally are held to a different (higher) standard of care than that of counselors. Psychiatrists should know more about physical symptoms than, for example, school counselors, who may not be trained in biology. It is not expected that mental health professionals be compared to the most erudite and esoteric members of their profession; rather, they are compared to the average member of their field.

Mental health professionals may also be evaluated by comparison to the standards of their community. The standard of care may be evidenced by reference to germane literature in journals, ethical codes, ethical guidelines, ethical standards, case law (within the appropriate jurisdiction), general statues, licensing boards, and certifications boards, as well as by reference to supervisors and peers.

Elements of Malpractice

As a legal term, *malpractice* describes complaints in which a professional is accused of negligence within a special relationship. The law of malpractice refers to *torts*. A tort is a wrongful act, injury, or damage (not including a breach of contract) for which a civil action can be brought.

To win a malpractice or tort law claim, the plaintiff must prove the following:

1. A legal duty to care was owed by the defendant to the plaintiff. A professional (special) relationship was formed between the mental health professional and the client.
2. There is a standard of care, and the mental health professional breached that duty.
3. The client suffered harm or injury (demonstrated and established).
4. The mental health professional's breach of duty was the proximate cause of the harm or injury. Thus, the harm or injury was a reasonably foreseeable consequence of the breach.

When does the special relationship begin? A formal contract is not always a necessary component of the special relationship. The legal theory to establish duty comes from the *theory of contracts*. In the eyes of the law, an implicit act can create a contract (a special relationship). Payment is not necessary to determine the relationship. Rather, the simple act of ministering to clients admitted to a hospital (voluntarily or involuntarily), making notes on charts, or giving treatment in emergency rooms can be construed as behavioral manifestations of contract creations. For example, in a Utah case in which a mental health professional provided therapy to a postsurgery patient, the state supreme court said that 1 hour of therapy was enough to create a special relationship (*Farrow v. Health Services Corp.*, 1979, cited in Swenson, 1997).

Why Clients Sue

We live in a litigious society. Mental health professionals do therapy with clients who are emotionally distraught. Clinical expertise is needed on the part of the mental health professional (Bednar, Bednar, Lambert, & Waite, 1991). Good relationships with clients reduce the likelihood of lawsuits. Counselors should, thus, use their skills to create positive feelings between themselves and the clients they serve. People do not want to sue someone they like or someone who is acting in their best interests.

Suicide is a factor in 50% of psychiatric malpractice actions (Hirsch & White, 1982). Because blaming and anger are nearly universal reactions by family survivors, the mental health professional is particularly vulnerable. Swenson (1997) noted, "about 1 malpractice claim [is filed] for every 200 mental health professionals" (p. 167). The parties settled most of these claims out of court, or the courts dismissed them (Schwitzgebel & Schwitzgebel, 1980). Psychiatric litigation accounts for only 3% of medical malpractice suits (Hirsch & White, 1982).

Other Reasons to Sue

Breaking a contract is essentially the same as breaking a promise. If the breach causes damage or injury, the law may provide a monetary remedy. A client who is angry does not have to show negligence on the part of the mental health professional, only that the therapy did not achieve the purpose it was intended to achieve (Schwitzgebel & Schwitzgebel, 1980). Damages typically involve at least the cost of the therapy.

Injury to a person's reputation may occur when derogatory words or written statements are made to a third party about the person. Such injurious statements are called *defamation of character; slander* is spoken defamation, while *libel* is written defamation. In a recent unpublished case, a trade school counselor made a public remark to the effect that a student had missed classes because she had a venereal disease contracted while working as a prostitute. In fact, the disease was the result of a rape. Because of stress related to gossip, the girl quit school, went into therapy, and sued the school district. The school settled the case, paying $50,000 in damages for the injury. The school also fired the counselor (Swenson, 1997).

Mental health professionals should be extremely careful about information given in letters of recommendation, notes on educational records, or any other oral comments to students. Communication of an opinion, when it can be said to imply a false and damaging statement, could be judged as slanderous or libelous (*Milkovich v. Lorain*, 1990).

Preparing for the Special Relationship

Policy Development

Before a mental health professional begins to see clients, he or she should think through and articulate a policy toward various situations that may manifest themselves in counseling relationships. One's attitudes and values concerning advertising, client referral, termination, billing, and record keeping, for example, should be clearly articulated. Naturally, these policies must conform to the accepted ethical and legal standards. Therefore, if one is not familiar with these standards, one must make the effort to become so. For those employed in an agency or school, these policies should already be extant. However, the potential for conflict between one's own ethical standards and institutionalized standards is always present.

Advertising and Soliciting Clients

Mental health providers are permitted to market their services. They must, however, be familiar with ethical guidelines, state laws, and Federal Trade Commission regulations. Not long ago it was considered unethical and unprofessional to advertise. Advertising today is accepted as long as it meets legal and ethical guidelines. Claims of therapy effectiveness and misrepresentation of professional status or qualifications should not be made in advertising (Schwitzgebel & Schwitzgebel, 1980). Statements made to the public about services must not mislead or give the wrong impression (Hass & Malouf, 1989). The following are examples of statements regarding advertising as manifested in ethical codes:

Psychologists do not make public statements that are false, deceptive, misleading, or fraudulent, either because of what they state, convey, or suggest or because of what they omit, concerning their research practice, or other work activities or those of persons or organizations with which they are affiliated. As examples (and not in limitation) of this standard, psychologists do not make false or deceptive statements concerning (1) their training, experience, or competence; (2) their academic degrees; (3) their credentials; (4) their institutional or association affiliations; (5) their services; (6) the scientific or clinical basis for, or results or degree of success of, their services; (7) their fees; or (8) their publication or research findings. (APA, 1995, 3, 303)

There are no restrictions on advertising by counselors except those that can be specifically justified to protect the public from deceptive practices. Counselors advertise or represent their services to the public by identifying their credentials in an accurate manner that is not false, misleading, deceptive, or fraudulent. Counselors may only advertise the highest degree earned which is in counseling or a closely related field from a college or university that was accredited by one of the recognized accrediting bodies. (ACA, 1995, C, 3,a)

Marriage and family therapists assure that advertisements and publications in any media (such as directories, announcements, business cards, newspapers, radio, television, and facsimiles) convey information that is necessary for the public to make an appropriate selection of professional services. Information could include (a) office information, such as name, address, telephone number, credit card acceptability, fees, languages spoken, and office hours; (b) appropriate degrees, state licensure and/or certification, and AAMFT Clinical Member status; and (c) description of practice. (American Association for Marriage and Family Therapy, 1991, 2)

Social workers should ensure that their representations to clients, agencies, and the public of professional qualifications, credentials, educations, competence, affiliations, services provided, or results to be achieved are accurate. Social workers should claim only those relevant professional credentials they actually possess and take steps to correct any inaccuracies or misrepresentations of their credentials by others. (National Association of Social Workers, 1997, 4.06, c)

Figure 7.1 illustrates examples of both acceptable (ethical) and unacceptable (unethical) modes of advertising for mental health professionals.

Being sued is a traumatic experience and can have serious professional and financial consequences. In one case, a therapist's conscious disregard for an insurance company's rules about

An Unethical Advertisement

> Overweight, depressed, not satisfied with your job? Come down for therapy. Guaranteed results in 10 weeks. Call 412-555-1212. Ask for Tracey.

An Ethical Advertisement

> Psychological Services, Ph.D. in counseling psychology from Butler University. Specializing in Cognitive Therapy, fluent in Spanish. Call 412-555-1212.

FIGURE 7.1. Examples of unethical and ethical forms of professional advertising.

copayments gave the company relief from making any copayments and awarded it punitive damages as well (*Weisman v. Blue Shield of California,* 1985). A counselor cannot legally waive the collection of copayments in order to keep a client in therapy. Also, mental health professionals who see clients on a pro bono basis should realize that the same practice guidelines apply to the treatment of paying and nonpaying clients. Complete and accurate records should be maintained for both. Below are some examples of fee guidelines for mental health professionals:

> Counselors clearly explain to clients, prior to entering the counseling relationship, all financial arrangements related to professional services, including the use of collection agencies or legal measures for nonpayment. In establishing fees for professional counseling services, counselors consider the financial status of clients and locality. In the event that the established fee structure is inappropriate for a client, assistance is provided in attempting to find comparable services of acceptable cost. (American Counseling Association, 1995, A1.O, a, b)
>
> As early as is feasible in a professional or scientific relationship, the psychologist and the patient, client, or other appropriate recipient of psychological services reach an agreement specifying the compensation and the billing arrangements.
>
> Psychologists do not exploit recipients of services or payers with respect to fees.
>
> Psychologists' fee practices are consistent with the law.
>
> Psychologists do not misrepresent their fees. (APA, 1995, *l.25. a, b, c, d*)

Dual Relationships

Mental health professionals play many roles in society, including therapist, friend, neighbor, and business associate. It is improbable that a mental health professional could matriculate through psychological practice without forming some dual relationships. Overlapping relationships are nearly inevitable in small communities. A dual relationship occurs whenever a therapist interacts with a client in more than one capacity, for example, as a therapist *and* business partner, or as a teacher *and* investor. Any dual relationships that could interfere with the autonomy of the client or the objectivity of the counselor should be avoided. Therapists are considered to be in a professional service by the very structure of their relationship with their clients (Pope, 1985). Therapy is a contractual relationship, and the exploitation of the client's trust is unethical and perhaps illegal. Consider the following example:

> Cohen (plaintiff's attorney) asked, "Is it a commonly acceptable practice for a psychiatrist to employ a patient after therapy sessions for the purpose of typing letters or doing stenographic work?" "No, it is not," said Dr. Gaylin. "Can you tell us why?" "That would go back to the heart of transference. You have to lean over backward not to take advantage of the patient when you have a feeling that he is clearly not as free in his judgments as he would be if he weren't a patient of yours. So you don't make contracts with them." (Freeman & Roy, 1976, pp. 162-163)

Following is an example of a problem that revolved around a dual relationship, taken from a phone call reported to the APA ethics committee and as described by Pope. The case is fictionalized and names have been changed:

> Ian Shaky, a doctoral student in a clinical psychology program, was experiencing serious depression. He asked one of his professors to see him privately. The professor agreed. Several weeks later, Shaky made a serious suicidal gesture. The professor told the program director about it. Shaky was then asked to leave the program until he could resolve his problems. Shaky brought ethics charges against the professor for violating the confidentiality provisions of the therapy relationship. The

professor claimed he was not acting unethically because the student/client was a "clear danger" to himself. (Pope, 1985, p. 277)

Sexual intimacy with clients is a dual relationship that is potentially destructive to both parties, yet statistics show that 90% of mental health professionals have been tempted by the possibility at least once (Rutter, 1989). Ethical standards prohibiting sexual activity with clients date as far back as the Hippocratic Oath, which contains this passage: "In every house where I come, I will enter only for the good of my patients, keeping myself far from all intentional ill-doing and all seduction, and especially from the pleasures of love with women and men" (Dorland, 1974, p. 715).

Sweeney (1991) (cited in Swenson, 1997) estimated that 70% of clients who have had sex with a therapist were harmed. Many are depressed and feel powerless to seek a new therapist. In a survey by Borys and Pope (1989) in which professionals from several mental health fields were questioned, 0.2% of the women and 0.9% of the men admitted to sexual contact with clients. There is an ongoing discussion in the field as to whether having a sexual relationship with a client is proper after therapy has been terminated. In the survey by Borys and Pope (1989), 68% of respondents rated sex with former clients unethical. California law requires a 24-month break between therapy and a sexual relationship.

Interrupted Therapy

Mental health professionals can no more control every aspect of their lives than can a nonprofessional. Emergencies occur, batteries go dead, and it may be necessary to change appointments. The mental health professional who is absent from a session may be seen by patients as having abandoned them. Consequently, staff should be trained in appropriate procedures should an emergency arise, and clients should be informed of one's policies relevant to emergencies and other reasons for absence.

Client Records

Naturally, mental health professionals should keep records for each client. Records provide an excellent inventory of information for assisting the mental health professional in managing client cases. They also serve as documentation of a therapist's judgments, type of treatment, recommendations, and treatment outcomes.

Therapists must also keep financial records. Financial records are necessary in order to obtain third-party reimbursement for the counselor or the client. The content of records may be defined by agency policy, state licensing laws, statutory laws, or regulation laws. Records may be read in open court, and, as a result, derogatory comments about clients should never be included.

In most jurisdictions, the paper belongs to the agency, but the information on the paper belongs to the client. Clients can request copies of their records. Some jurisdictions limit access to records if such access would be harmful to a client's mental health.

The evolving standard of practice is to keep records for 7 years, although some suggest they should be kept forever. The appropriate regulatory agencies in one's jurisdiction should be consulted regarding record retention and disposition. Below are some types of information that should be kept in client records:

1. basic identifying information, such as the client's name, address, telephone number; also, if the client is a minor, the names of parents or legal guardians should be recorded;

2. signed informed consent for treatment;

3. history of the client, both medical and psychiatric, if relevant;

4. dates and types of services offered;

5. signature and title of the person who rendered the therapy;

6. a description of the presenting problem;

7. a description of assessment techniques and results;

8. progress notes for each date of service documenting the implementation of the treatment plan and changes in the treatment plan;

9. documentation of sensitive or dangerous issues, alternatives considered, and actions taken;

10. a treatment plan with explicit goals;

11. consultations with other professionals, consultations with people in the client's life, clinical supervision received, and peer consultation;

12. release of confidential information forms signed by the client;

13. fees assessed and collected.

The Use of Computers

Data on clients can be stored in word processors and database program files. In addition, the computer can be used to store information on grants, payroll accounts, fiscal planning, payments, and preparation of research. With macros and style sheets, computer programs can reduce the need for reentry of information and can make updating a client's files much faster and easier. Computer technology provides increased convenience for mental health professionals but also commands new responsibilities, knowledge, and accountability.

The use of computers also allows the mental health professional to access diagnostic categories and to offer computerized versions of various personality tests. Professionals who use these new electronic programs must be careful not to violate federal or state copyright laws that police the use of software. "A conviction for violating a computer crime statute may result in a fine, imprisonment, or both" (Atcherson, 1993, p. 36). Atcherson listed the following behaviors that may be considered illegal:

1. unauthorized access to or alterations of electronic communication;

2. unauthorized use of or access to computer resources or information;

3. unauthorized disclosure of computer-based information obtained by wiretapping, eavesdropping, or browsing through personnel data;

4. unauthorized modification or destruction of computer resources (hardware, software, or data);

5. theft of storage media or printouts;

6. user misuse, such as unauthorized copying of software or use of computer resources in committing a misdemeanor or felony;

7. misuse of local communication links or other communication links;

8. intentional spread of computer viruses.

Mental health professionals who use computers are held ethically responsible for making sure the information their clients are given is accurate. Psychological tests administered by computer programs must be treated like any other tests. They should not be used by untrained personnel. Also, data entries must be made carefully so inaccurate results do not arise. Ethical codes also stress the responsibility of mental health professionals in their use of computers:

Counselors are responsible for the appropriate application, scoring, interpretation, and use of assessment instruments, whether they score and interpret such tests themselves or use computerized or other services. (American Counseling Association, 1995, E,2,b)

Psychologists select scoring and interpretation services (including automated services) on the basis of evidence of the validity of the program and procedures as well as on other appropriate consideration (American Counseling Association, 1995, E,2,b).

Psychologists retain appropriate responsibility for the appropriate application, interpretation, and use of assessment instrument, whether they score and interpret such tests themselves or use automated or other services (American Counseling Association, 1995, E,2).

Certified counselors must ensure that computer-generated test administration and scoring programs function properly, thereby providing clients with accurate test results. (National Board for Certified Counselors, 1997, C, 12)

Liability Insurance

All mental health professionals should purchase liability insurance before they begin practice. An *occurrence-based policy* covers incidents no matter when the claim is made, as long as the policy was in force during the year of the alleged incident. Thus, if a therapist is accused today of an infraction alleged to have occurred 2 years ago (when the policy was in effect) he or she is covered even if the policy is not in force at present. A *claims-made policy* covers only claims made while the policy is in force. However, if a counselor previously had a claims-made policy, he or she may purchase *tail-coverage insurance,* which covers him or her if an alleged incident occurring during the period the policy was in effect is reported after the policy has expired.

◼ Implementing the Special Relationship

Contracting for Therapy

Not long ago, most contracts between mental health professionals and clients were oral. More formalized contracts were seen as alienating to the client. Also, common law principles, under which those agreements were governed, did not require written forms (Bednar et al., 1991). In 1985, only 29% of therapists in private practice reported using written contracts (Handelsman & Galvin, 1988). Numerous lawsuits, based on the absence of informed consent, have since changed that (Bednar et al., 1991). Counselors are now required to inform their clients in writing of the relevant facts about therapy. The clients must understand the information and sign any forms voluntarily.

Informed Consent

A written informed consent form is a contract and a promise made by the mental health professional to perform the therapy competently. There are three basic legal elements of informed consent:

1. The client must be competent. Competence refers to the legal capacity to give consent. If, because of age or mental ability, a client does not have the capacity to give consent, the therapist should consult another person or a judicial body who can legally assume responsibility for the client.

2. Both the substance of the information regarding therapy and the manner in which it is given are important. The substance of the information should include the relevant facts about therapy. This information should be presented to the client in a manner that is easily understood.

3. The client must volunteer for therapy and must not be coerced or forced to participate.

Some common themes in consent forms that should be explicated prior to therapy include the following:

1. The client should be given a description of the services to be provided, including their goals and procedures. This should be done in simple language to inform the client exactly what the mental health professional will attempt to do in the therapy sessions. The client should be appraised as to what, if any, behavior or action will be required of the client, such as homework. Clients also should know how interruptions in therapy will be handled.

2. Any anticipated results—beneficial *and* negative—should be explained. The therapist should state that there is no guarantee of success, but that specific behaviors will be targeted and goals will be set. If more than one type of therapy seems appropriate, the therapist should describe the various types.

3. The therapist should estimate the duration of the therapy and the frequency of appointments.

4. A timetable for review of client progress should be established. The client should be informed that he or she has the right to withdraw from therapy at any time and that no additional costs will result, unless such costs have been previously explicated.

5. The basis for services should be explained to the client. A timely system for collecting fees should be established.

6. The therapist should give a statement regarding confidentiality and privileged communication (these issues are dealt with in more detail below).

7. A statement acknowledging the client's informed consent should be signed by the client or by his or her parent or legal guardian.

Release of Information

The essence of a counseling relationship is trust. Mental health professionals must protect the information they receive from clients. They must keep confidential communications secret unless a well-defined exception applies.

Confidential information may be disclosed if the client (or the client's parent or legal representative) agrees and signs a consent form for such a disclosure. A *consent to waiver* does not always have to be in writing, but it is best if it is. The client should be informed of any and all implications of the wavier.

▉ Confidentiality

Therapists should provide an environment in which their clients feel they can communicate honestly about their thoughts, feelings, and behaviors. In order to feel safe in this process, most people want assurance that information about their private lives will be kept confidential. Confidentiality is the foundation of effective therapy. Should there be no prior consent or legal mandate, the only disclosure of confidential information that is ethical is that which promotes the welfare of the client. Hass and Malouf (1989, p. 30) listed some of the situations in which a decision to breach confidentiality may be made:

- court subpoena;
- duty to warn, protect, or report;

- requests for information from family members;
- seeing clients in groups;
- when there are problems defining the "client";
- sharing information with other staff members within one's agency;
- personal or professional needs of practicality (consultation, teaching, support).

Privileged Communication

When a competent client presents for therapy, any disclosure he or she makes may be protected from legal disclosure. Such communication is considered privileged. The issue at hand is the conflict between the individual's right to privacy and the need of the public to know certain information. The client is considered the holder of the privilege, and he or she is the only one who can waive that right.

Privileged communication is established by statutory law enacted by legislators. Client communication with a specified group of mental health professionals may be privileged in some states but not in others. Also, statutes may specify a wide range of exceptions to privileged communication. For instance, privileged communication laws are abrogated, in all states, by an initial report of child abuse.

Mental health professionals generally do not have legal grounds for maintaining confidentiality if they are called upon to testify in court, unless they are asked to provide communication protected by privileged communication statutes. Clients should be told whether any information they reveal will be protected by privileged communication laws before therapy begins. In the following example, the therapist (an intern) implies that the information the client is about to reveal is privileged. The court later ruled it was not. Had the client been informed that his communications were not privileged, he may not have revealed what he did.

> "Can I ask for this to be strictly confidential?" he said. The graduate student replied, "Okay, I can say this much, Reid . . . whatever you say here is confidential; and we're real selective about what the courts have access to." [The client then said,] "It's just not [like] myself to be thinking like this, to ah . . . I think a lot about, ah, rape. I think a lot about killing somebody." He then added that the impulse to kill someone with a knife was "so strong I wonder sometimes if I wouldn't actually do it, you know, if the situation was ever right. . . . and then later on I'll feel terrible about it [these feelings]." (Kane & Keeton, 1985, pp. 52–53)

Ten months later Donna Lyn Allen was killed. Reid Hall's fantasies, acquired from the graduate student's tape recording of the session, were read in open court and were described by his lawyer as the most damaging evidence leading to his conviction for murder. The judge ruled that, because the counselor was a graduate student and not a licensed professional, Hall's communications were not covered by privileged communication law. Informed consent forms at the University of Georgia now state that client-therapist privileged communication may not apply to students-in-training (Kane & Keeton).

Being a Courtroom Witness

Increasingly, mental health professionals are called upon to testify in court or at depositions. Typical cases involve personal injury, child custody, and child abuse. This exposure provides an opportunity for mental health professionals to expand their social effectiveness and to educate the public (Forge & Henderson, 1990). The role of therapists in the courtroom is to educate (Deutsch & Parker, 1985). Their obligation is to present information that is accurate and objective and to share with the judge or jury the basis of their opinions.

Being Named in a Lawsuit

Counselors named in lawsuits should immediately notify their insurance companies in writing. The notification should include all the factual information about the incident for which the counselor is being sued. If the counselor is contacted by the person who has initiated the suit or that person's lawyer, he or she should respond that an appropriate person will soon address their inquiry. Client information should *never* be revealed except to the appointed attorney. In fact, the counselor should avoid discussing anything about the case with anyone except his or her appointed attorney. The mental health professional should never admit negligence.

Summary

The legal issues addressed in this chapter were aimed at the major considerations necessary to ensure that counselors are able to protect both themselves and their clients from legal liability. It is important that all counselors and therapists have a complete understanding of the meaning of the special relationship, dual relationships, confidentiality and privileged communication, and the rights and responsibilities of helping professionals in legal situations. In addition, mental health professionals should be familiar with the steps in a lawsuit, the issue of negligence, and the elements of malpractice in an effort to avoid the liability that results from such claims. Important considerations that relate to the special relationship, including contracting for therapy with the client and the handling of sensitive data, are also presented. Before beginning the practicum and internship experience, students will want to familiarize themselves with the critical issues presented in this chapter.

References

American Association for Marriage and Family Therapy. (1991). *Code of ethical principles for marriage and family therapists*. Washington DC: Author.

American Counseling Association. (1995). *Code of ethics and standards of practice*. Alexandria, VA: Author.

American Psychological Association. (1995). *Ethical principles of psychologists and code of conduct*. Washington, DC: Author.

Atcherson, E. (1993, Fall). Ethics and information: How vulnerable is your campus to computer crime? *CUPA Journal, 4,* 35–38.

Bednar, R. L., Bednar, S. C., Lambert, M. J., & Waite, D. R. (1991). *Psychology with high-risk clients: Legal and professional standards*. Pacific Grove, CA: Brooks/Cole.

Borys, D. S., & Pope, K. S. (1989). Dual relationships between therapist and client: A national study of psychologists, psychiatrists, and social workers. *Professional Psychology: Research and Practice, 20*(5), 283–293.

Deutsch, P. M., & Parker, E. C. (1985). *Rehabilitation testimony: Maintaining a professional perspective*. New York: Matthew Bender.

Dorland, D. (1974). *Dorland's medical dictionary*. New York: Macmillan.

Forge, J. L., & Henderson, P. (1990). Counselor competency in the courtroom. *Journal of Counseling and Development, 68,* 456–459.

Freeman, L., & Roy, J. (1976). *Betrayal*. New York: Stein & Day.

Handelsman, M. M., & Galvin, M. D. (1988). Facilitation informed consent for outpatient psychotherapy: A suggested written format. *Professional Psychology: Research and Practice, 19*(2), 223–225.

Hass, L. J., & Malouf, J. L. (1989) *Keeping up the good work: A practitioner's guide to mental health ethics*. Sarasota, FL: Professional Resource Exchange.

Hirsch, H., & White, E. (1982). The pathological anatomy of medical malpractice claims: Legal aspects of medical malpractice. *Journal of Legal Medicine, 6*(1), 25–26.

Horowitz, I. A., & Willging, T. E. (1984). *The psychology of law: Applications*. Boston: Little, Brown.

Kane, S., & Keeton, R. (1985, October/November). Informed consent. *Campus Voice,* 52–54.

Milkovich v. Loraine Journal Inc., 497 U.S. 1 (1990).

National Board of Certified Counselors. (1997). *Code of ethics*. Alexandria, VA: Author.

Pope, K. S. (1985). Dual relationships: A violation of ethical, legal, and clinical standards. *California State Psychologist, 20*(3), 1–4.

Rutter, P. (1989). Sex in the forbidden zone. *Psychology Today, 23*(10), 34–38.

Schwitzgebel, R. L., & Schwitzgebel, R. K. (1980). *Law and psychological practice.* New York: Wiley.

Swenson, L. C. (1997). *Psychology and law for the helping professions.* Pacific Grove, CA: Brooks/Cole.

Weisman v. Blue Shield of California, 163 CAL. App. 3d61, 209 CAL. Rptr. 169 (CAL., ct. app., 1985).

Weissman, N. H. (1984). Psychological assessment and psycho-legal formulations in psychiatric traumatology. *Psychiatric Annals, 14*(7), 517–529.

PART

III

THE INTERNSHIP EXPERIENCE

Part III of this textbook is designed to provide the student with information critical to the internship experience. Chapter 8, "Guidelines for Interns Working With Special Populations," provides interns with strategies for dealing with the special populations they will deal with most frequently in their work. Populations discussed include clients who are harmful to themselves, clients who are a threat to others, abused children, adult survivors of sexual abuse, clients with HIV and AIDS, and substance-abusing clients. Forms for use with these client populations are included for the student's reference and use. Chapter 9, "Consultation in the Schools and Mental Health Agencies," discusses the various models and methods of consultation in these two settings and provides a form for use in rating the consultation process. Chapter 10 "Internship Preparation," addresses the selection, evaluation, and process of choosing an internship. This chapter also includes forms that the student can use in selecting an appropriate internship site. Chapter 11, "The Internship Experience," is designed to provide the intern with a variety of interventions and strategies commonly employed in agency and school settings. Crisis intervention strategies, psychopharmacological treatments, and brief therapy approaches are presented. Chapter 12, "Final Evaluation," Discusses essential forms that the student may use in assessing the internship experience as a whole, as well as a form that can be used by interns to evaluate their experience with individual clients.

CHAPTER

8

Patrick B. Malley
Eileen Petty Reilly

Guidelines for Interns Working With Special Populations

The Client Who is Potentially Harmful to Self

Definition of Suicide

Beauchamp (1985) defined suicide this way:

- the person intentionally brings about his or her own death;
- the person is not coerced by others to take the action; and,
- death is caused by conditions arranged by the person for the specific purpose of bringing about his or her own death.

Training Regarding Suicide

When working with suicidal patients, the mental health professional is held to a standard of care that says he or she has acquired the appropriate clinical and legal education to perform such a function. Mental health professionals cannot claim lack of training as a defense for negligent actions because a court may claim they "should have known." The appropriate education implies competence (Baron, 1987). Many clinicians rank working with suicidal patients as the most stressful aspect of their work (Deutsch, 1984):

> Losing a patient to suicide is so personally and professionally impactful, that almost half of the psychologists who lost a patient reported intrusive symptoms of stress in the weeks to follow the suicide . . . stress comparable to individuals who have suffered the death of a close family member. . . . Patient suicide should be acknowledged as an occupational hazard for psychologists, not only because of its frequency but also because of its impact on psychologists' professional and personal lives. . . . Training programs do not currently have established protocols for helping trainees to deal with the aftermath of a patient's suicide; therefore, trainees and their supervisors are left to their own devices. (pp. 419–420)

Bongar and Harmatz (1989) reported that the number of formal training curriculums in member departments of the Council of University Directors of Clinical Psychology is just slightly more than one third, demonstrating that little formal training in suicide prevention is conducted in psychiatric residencies, social work schools, or nursing programs (Berman, 1986). Apparently, suicide training is lacking in continuing education as well; fewer than 1 in 4 psychologists and psychiatrists in the Washington, DC area have postinternship training in suicide assessment (Berman & Cohen-Sandler, 1982).

By contrast, 77% of school counselors indicated that they have special training in suicide, but only 32% reported that this training took place in counselor education programs. Most received their training in professional workshops (59%) or school service programs (Nelson & Crawford, 1990).

A survey of school health educators nationwide examined perceived self-efficacy in identifying adolescents at risk for suicide. Most teachers in the study considered it their role to recognize students at risk for suicide. However, only 9% reported that they could recognize such a student (King, Price, Telljohann, & Wahl, 1999).

Legal, ethical, and moral tenets impose on mental health professionals the obligation to seek the best treatment for their clients. Concern for the client's welfare is always the primary priority. Therefore, all mental health professionals should make sure they understand:

1. their ethical responsibilities regarding suicidal clients,

2. their legal mandates regarding potentially suicidal clients,

3. the presenting characteristics of danger to self, and

4. the skills used to counsel clients who are a danger to themselves.

Ethical Mandates and Danger to Self

The ethical codes from several professional organizations clearly address the welfare of clients as paramount, as shown in the statements that follow:

[The school counselor] informs the appropriate authorities when the counselee's condition indicates a clear and imminent danger to the counselee or others. This is to be done after careful deliberation and, where possible, after consultation with other professionals. The counselor informs the counselee of actions to be taken so as to minimize confusion and clarify expectations. (American School Counselor Association, 1992, p. 10)

Marriage and family therapists may not disclose client confidences except (a) as mandated by law; (b) to prevent a clear and immediate danger to a person or persons; (c) where the therapist is a defendant in a civil, criminal, or disciplinary action arising from the therapy (in which case client confidences may be disclosed only in the course of that action); or (d) if there is a waiver previously obtained in writing, and then such information may be revealed only in accordance with the terms of the waiver. In circumstances where more than one person in a family receives therapy, each such family member who is legally competent to execute a waiver must agree to the waiver required by subparagraph (d). Without such a waiver from each family member legally competent to execute a waiver, a therapist cannot disclose information received from any family member. (American Association for Marriage and Family Therapy, 1991, 2.1)

Psychologists disclose confidential information without the consent of the individual only as mandated by law, or where permitted by law for a valid purpose, such as (1) to provide needed professional services to the patient or the individual or organizational client, (2) to obtain appropriate professional consultations, (3) to protect the patient or client or others from harm, or (4) to obtain payment for services, in which instance disclosure is limited to the minimum that is necessary to achieve the purpose. (APA, 1995, 5, 501)

Social workers should protect the confidentiality of all information obtained in the course of professional service, except for compelling professional reasons. The general expectation that social workers will keep information confidential does not apply when disclosure is necessary to prevent serious, foreseeable, and imminent harm to a client or other identifiable person or when laws or regulations require disclosure without a client's consent. In all instances, social workers should disclose the least amount of confidential information necessary to achieve the desired purpose; only information that is directly relevant to the purpose for which the disclosure is made should be revealed. (National Association of Social Workers, 1997, 1, 105)

Exceptions. The general requirement that counselors keep information confidential does not apply when disclosure is required to prevent clear and imminent danger to the client or others or when legal requirements demand that confidential information be revealed. Counselors consult with other professionals when in doubt as to the validity of an exception. (American Counseling Association, 1995, B.1.d.)

Legal Mandates and Danger to Self

Again, the mental health professional's special relationship with the client creates the context for the legal accountability for negligent malpractice with potentially suicidal patients. A therapist is assumed to possess superior knowledge and skills beyond those of the average person and may be considered by the courts to be responsible for the suicide of his or her patient. The client's dependence on the counselor alone is enough to shift some of the weight of the responsibility for the client's actions to the mental health professional.

This was not always the case. In England, for example, toward the latter part of the 19th century, suicide was considered self-murder, and authorities buried the bodies of those who committed suicide at the side of the road with a stake through the heart (Bednar, Bednar, Lambert, & Waite, 1991). In contrast, today a mental health professional who does not take appropriate action to prevent a suicide can be sued. The most important consideration for the courts is this: Was the suicide foreseeable? Consider the following case as an example:

> A medical patient experienced hallucinations after surgery. The patient requested psychiatric help, and a therapist conducted an hour of therapy and made no recommendations to the hospital staff. Sometime later, the patient jumped from a sixth-floor window. Injuries from the fall left him a quadriplegic. The Utah Supreme Court concluded that after an hour of therapy, a special relationship was formed. It held the therapist liable for negligently failing to accurately diagnose the patient's condition and for failing to take appropriate protective steps. (*Farrow v. Health Services Corp.*, 1979)

On the other hand, liability has not been found when apparently cooperative patients suddenly attempt suicide (*Carlino v. State*, 1968; *Dalton v. State*, 1970), or when an aggressive patient does not reveal any suicidal symptoms (*Paridies v. Benedictine Hospital*, 1980). In determining liability, courts also must decide whether the recommendations of a mental health professional were followed. In one case, a hospital was found liable when the staff did not follow the psychiatrist's recommendations (*Comiskey v. State of New York*, 1979).

Liability may be imposed if a therapist is determined to be negligent in his or her treatment of a patient. Negligence is found when the mental health professional does not perform his or her duties according to the standard of care for that particular profession. Consequently, mental health professionals should adhere to the following model, similar to the one presented later in this chapter, in the section on the *Tarasoff* case (see "The Potentially Dangerous Client" section below):

1. **Make an assessment of the danger.** This assessment is based on the client interview.
2. **Determine what action is reasonable.** The therapist may need to intensify treatment, change medication, advise voluntary commitment, or authorize involuntary commitment.
3. **Make sure the recommendation is followed.**

Characteristics of Potential Harm to Self

Because suicidal behavior is such a pressing issue for therapists, it is important that they be able to identify common characteristics of clients who may potentially cause harm to themselves. As the following excerpt indicates, there are myriad risk factors that could indicate a client's lethality:

> Studies of persons in the general population who commit suicide have shown both social and psychiatric risk factors . . . national statistical evidence shows increased suicide risk in the elderly, unmarried, unemployed, and those living alone . . . [Researchers] collected a consecutive series of 134 suicide cases in St. Louis and systematically interviewed relatives and others who had had contact with the person before the suicide. Ninety-four percent were judged to have been psychiatrically ill at the time of suicide. They found that 60 of the suicides (45%) were suffering from an affective disorder and 31 (23%) from alcoholism, and that the known prevalence of notable physical disease was 51%. . . . 114 consecutive suicide cases in Seattle found comparable figures. In England, . . . 64% had an affective disorder at the time of suicide. . . . A significantly larger proportion of the suicides with affective disorder and alcoholism were living alone compared with the US population aged 23 years and over. (Roy, 1982, p. 1089)

In a review of the literature, Fujimura, Weis, and Cochran (1985, p. 613) listed characteristics of potentially suicidal clients, including:

1. **Previous suicide attempts.** A previous suicide attempt is the single best predictor of lethality. Suicide attempts by family member or close friends exert an influence as well.
2. **Sleeping disruption.** Sleeping disruptions may increase the intensity of depression. The person may be hallucinating, possibly from an excess of drugs such as stimulants and depressants.
3. **Definitiveness of plan.** The suicidal individual must be asked to talk about this, and he or she almost always will if asked. The more definitive the plan, the more serious the intent.
4. **Reversibility of plan.** Time span is an important consideration. Using a gun or jumping from a high place are irreversible methods most of the time. Taking pills is less lethal because there is a better chance for reversibility.
5. **Proximity of others.** A person who really does not want to die will rely on intervention from other people. A person truly intent on committing suicide will ensure that no one can intervene.
6. **Giving possessions away.** The suicidal individual is likely to give away prized possessions, finalize business affairs, or revise a will.
7. **A history of severe alcohol or drug abuse.** An individual who is dependent on drugs or alcohol is at greater suicide risk.
8. **A history of psychiatric treatment or hospitalization.** The suicidal individual is likely to have received previous psychiatric treatment or to have been hospitalized.

9. **Availability of resource and support systems.** The suicidal person may not recognize the existence of support systems available.
10. **Willingness to use resource and support systems.** A suicidal person not using these systems signifies a cutting off of communication and makes the intent more serious.

Interventions

Listed below are some techniques generally recognized by therapists to facilitate the counseling process for suicidal clients:

- Listen intelligently, sensitively, and carefully to the client.
- Accept and understand the client's suicidal thoughts.
- Don't give false assurances such as, "Everything is going to be all right."
- Be supportive.
- Assure the client of your availability.
- Be firm and caring at the same time.
- Don't use euphemisms. Ask direct questions like, "Would you like to kill yourself?" rather than using vague expressions.
- Bring out any ambivalence the client has. Try to increase his or her choices.
- If the client is in crisis, don't leave him or her alone.
- Intervene to dispose of any weapons the client has.
- Tell others, especially those who would be concerned and can help. (You already have informed the client of the limits of confidentiality.)
- Help the client develop support systems.
- Trust your own judgment.
- Know the suicide hotline numbers.
- Be aware of commitment procedures in your area.
- Have the client sign a nonsuicide contract.

If you determine that the client is potentially suicidal and he or she will not consent to hospitalization, the case may be serious enough to warrant attempting an involuntary commitment to a treatment center. The procedures for commitment, whether voluntary or involuntary, vary a great deal from area to area. Laws on commitment procedures are different from state to state. Mental health professionals should be familiar with the legal aspects of commitment in their areas. Copies of a Suicide Consultation Form (Form 8.1) and a Suicide Contract (Form 8.2) are included in the "Forms" section at the end of this book; students may use these forms, in consultation with their supervisors, to facilitate their counseling of clients who are potentially harmful to themselves.

Childhood Depression

Stress, once identified primarily with adolescents, is becoming more prevalent in elementary school children. Today, the literature on suicide and children reveals a more prevalent sense of suicidal behaviors and ideation in children. As stress in the lives of children increases, symptoms such as anxiety, depression, helplessness, and hopelessness increase as well. Research has revealed that, while suicide in very young children is rare, suicidal thoughts, threats, and attempts are not. Clinicians are beginning to believe that depression in very young children is a real and often unrecognized problem (Connell, 1972; Philips, 1983). Estimates of the prevalence of childhood depression are erratic, ranging from less than 2% to as much as 30% of elementary school children affected (Annell, 1971; Tueting, Koslow, & Hirschfield, 1983). Presently, anxiety in children is being studied as indicative of childhood depression (Allan, Koushani, Dahlmeier, Beck, & Reid, 1998).

Lasko (1986) discussed the prevalence of childhood depression in this way:

> Through research, a strong familial component of depression has been uncovered. Investigators have found that a large percentage of depressed children have a close relative, often a parent, who is depressed. Conversely, many depressed parents have children who are impaired. . . .
>
> School counselors and other educators play significant roles in the lives of children. Therefore, it is imperative that counselors be aware of the existence and features of the disorder. Counselors, with their training and skills, and with the consultative functions they serve in schools, can assume roles of child advocates. This can be accomplished by bringing the phenomenon of childhood depression to the attention of school personnel and parents and by bringing depressed children to the attention of those individuals who can aid them. To fight the battle against childhood depression, counselors must be armed with knowledge and keep on-hand a vast storehouse of compassion and concern. (pp. 285–287)

In situations in which childhood depression exists, school counselors need to take an active role in providing comfort and support to those in need. It is particularly important to provide this type of support to those whose feelings of depression may, in time, lead to suicidal behavior.

School-Based Suicide Prevention Programs

As stated above, suicide among American youth is growing at an alarming rate. Currently, it is the fastest growing cause of death among adolescents in the United States (Sheeley & Herlihy, 1989). Suicide is the third leading—in some states the second leading—cause of death among young people (Rosenberg, Smith, Davidson, & Conn, 1987; Strother, 1986). Although the number of adolescent suicides has increased 300% in the past 30 years (Peach & Reddick, 1991), actual cases are considered underreported because of the tendency to disguise these cases as accidents (Capuzzi & Golden, 1988). Some researchers believe suicides to be underreported by a ratio of 4 to 1 (Davis, 1985).

The tragedy of suicide is further complicated by the strong possibility that it can be prevented (Eisenberg, 1984). Professionals concur that most potential suicide victims want to be saved and often send out signals for help. Considering the magnitude of this problem, schools have a moral imperative to develop suicide prevention programs (Celotta, Golden, Keys, & Cannon, 1988). These are most effective when they are comprehensive and systematic—in short, when they are *proactive* (Kush, 1990).

The literature suggests that, to be effective, school-based programs must be comprehensive and systematic and include strategies for suicide prevention, intervention during, and postintervention following a completed suicide. Comprehensive and systematic programs also must be ongoing, intact, and continuously updated. Many researchers who have developed models of school-based programs share this position. A review of recent literature reveals the following components as those most often recommended for school-based adolescent suicide prevention and intervention programs:

- A written, formal policy statement for reacting to suicide and suicidal ideation
- Staff in-service training and orientation for the program
- Mental health professionals on site
- A mental health team
- Prevention materials for distribution to parents
- Prevention materials for distribution to students
- Psychological screening programs to identify at-risk students
- Prevention-focused classroom discussions

- Mental health counseling for at-risk students
- Suicide prevention and intervention training for school counselors
- Faculty training for detection of suicide warning signs
- Postintervention component in the event of an actual suicide
- Written statement describing specific criteria for counselors to assess the lethality of a potential suicide
- Written policy describing how the program will be evaluated

Suicide Intervention in the School

More and more, the courts have been called upon to decide liability issues in relation to suicidal clients and the responsibility of school counselors. The Maryland Court of Appeals ruled that school counselors have a legal duty to prevent the suicide of a student client if the counselor foresees a danger of suicide (Pate, 1992). Appropriate intervention steps cannot be implemented, however, until lethality is determined. The following process should be followed as soon as a student is suspected of being suicidal:

1. **Ask directly during a session.** Ask the student, without hesitation, if he or she is thinking about killing himself or herself. If the student claims to have had suicidal ideation, the strength of the intent should be determined. Continue with the questioning.

2. **Ask if he or she has attempted suicide before.** If so, how many times were attempts made and when were they made? The more attempts and the more recent the attempts, the more serious the situation becomes.

3. **Ask how the previous attempts were made.** If the student took aspirin, for example, ask how many. One? Six? Twenty? Then ask about the consequences of the attempts. For example, was there medical intervention?

4. **Ask why.** Why did the student attempt suicide before? Why the suicidal thoughts now?

5. **Does the student have a plan?** Ask about the details. The more detailed the plan is, the more lethal it is. Does the student know when and how the attempt will be made? Assess the lethality of the method. This assessment is critical. Does the student have a weapon? Using a gun or hanging oneself leaves little time for medical help.

6. **Ask about the student's** *preoccupation with suicide.* Does he or she think about it only at home or during a particular incident—or does it go beyond all other activities?

7. **Ask about drug use.** Drug use complicates the seriousness of the situation because people tend to be less inhibited when under the influence of drugs. Although the student may deny drug use, try to get as much information as possible.

8. **Observe nonverbal actions.** Is the student agitated, tense, or sad? Is he or she inebriated? Use caution if the student seems to be at peace. This peaceful state may be the result of having organized a suicide plan, with completion being the next step.

9. **Try to gauge the level of depression.** A student may not be depressed because he or she is anxious about completing the plan.

This process will help you determine the level of suicide risk for a student. A low-risk student may have thoughts about suicide but has never attempted suicide in the past, does not have a plan, is not taking drugs, and is not preoccupied with the ideation. Most students at low risk will agree to the therapist's contacting their parents, which should be done. The statements must be monitored closely, however, as a low-risk student can quickly become a high-risk student.

A typical high-risk student has a plan but may or may not have attempted suicide in the past. Of course, a previous attempt is an important factor in assessing lethality, especially if the attempt was recent. But counselors should remember that many first-time attempts are successful. The current situation must never be minimized. The plan of a high-risk student usually is detailed and the ideation frequent. At this point, other people need to become involved, including the counselor's supervisor, principal, and school nurse.

Ideally, the school will have some type of suicide intervention policy. The goal in a high-risk situation is to have the student undergo a psychiatric evaluation as soon as possible, whether by voluntary or by involuntary commitment. The student's parents must be notified; confidentiality is not an issue if the limits of confidentiality were explained previously via informed consent. Although confidentiality laws vary from state to state, a counselor usually is not bound if the client intends to harm himself or herself or someone else (Kane & Keeton, 1985). It is absolutely imperative, however, that school counselors discuss confidentiality limits at the beginning of every client intake session.

Mental health professionals may encounter crisis situations in three different ways, and each requires some specific guidelines.

1. First, the student may attempt suicide on school premises. The counselor should refer to the school's policy regarding this intervention.

2. Second, the student may disclose suicidal ideation directly to the therapist. In this case, the counselor should assess lethality using the process outlined above.

3. Third, peers may inform the counselor of a suicidal student. Seven out of ten students will tell a peer about suicidal ideation before telling anyone else. It is especially important to take this information seriously. The decision by the Maryland Court of Appeals mentioned above involved a peer's informing a counselor of another student's intention to kill herself. The counselor confronted the teen, but she denied any problems, so the counselor did not notify her parents. The failure to inform the parents was deemed to be negligence (Pate, 1992).

Below are some guidelines for each of the situations listed above:

1. **If a suicide attempt occurs on the premises.** Involve appropriate school personnel, then notify the police and an ambulance service. Also notify the parents (or guardian). Let them know where their child is being taken. If the parents (or guardian) are not available, notify the next closest relative. See to it that the student receives proper medical and psychiatric care. Often, the hospital will send the student back to the school after the crisis without a psychiatric evaluation. Counselors should guard against this occurance.

2. **If the student discloses suicidal ideation to you.** First, consult your supervisor or another mental health professional. Go over the assessment of lethality with the student. This process will help you establish the standard of care. Call the parents (or guardian) and tell them to go to the appropriate psychiatric facility. Explain to the parents and the student that an evaluation or diagnosis does not necessarily mean commitment. If the parents resist this process, you may need to contact your local Children and Youth Services for assistance. Be sure to contact the parents in the presence of the child, to eliminate the "he said/she said" phenomenon.

3. **If a peer tells you about another student's suicidal intent.** Confront the student. If the student admits the suicidal ideation, follow the procedure outlined above. If the student denies the ideation, notify the parents (or guardian). Of course, you must inform the student about this disclosure.

Suicide Intervention in the College and University

Obtaining accurate data on suicide rates of college students is difficult. Most colleges and universities employ ineffective record-keeping systems, and the data that exist tend to be inconsistent.

Because of concern about negative publicity, colleges may underreport or mislabel suicides (Westfeld, Whitchard, & Range, 1990).

College students face certain issues that are unique to this setting. Striving for academic success, having unclear vocational goals, and being away from home, possibly for the first time, may cause students to become depressed (Mathiasen, 1988). Also, research has shown poor problem solving skills under high stress to influence suicidal college students (Fremouw, Callahan, & Kashden, 1993).

Middle and secondary schools today are taking more responsibility for preventing student suicides. Colleges and universities also have an obligation to respond to and prevent suicides. Campus seminars on suicide prevention and programming efforts can be beneficial. Workshops on dealing with stress, academic concerns, career planning, and problem solving can help students deal with the major life stresses of college. Educating faculty, staff, students, and administrators about the signs of depression and suicide should be a component in any prevention program. Residence hall staff, especially, should be educated in this area, as their exposure to students is extensive (Philips, 1983).

Mental health professionals who deal with the college population face some special considerations. The main difference between college-aged students and those who are younger is the requirement for parental notification. Some college students are minors, but the majority are over 18 years old. Legally, a mental health professional is not obligated to contact the parents of a potentially suicidal client if the student is not a minor.

Residence complicates this matter further. Out-of-state and international students are sometimes turned away from psychiatric hospitals because they have out-of-state insurance policies. This can put responsibility back on the university, even if students are of legal age. In this circumstance, the counseling center must take a more active role in helping the student receive proper psychiatric attention. Contacting the parents or guardian is necessary in this situation.

The Potentially Dangerous Client

The *Tarasoff* Case

The Events

Prosenjit Poddar was a graduate student at the University of California, Berkeley. In 1968, Poddar attended dancing classes at the International House in Berkeley, where he met a woman named Tatiana (Tanya) Tarasoff. This meeting quickly led to an obsessive, one-sided love affair. After a friendly New Year's Eve kiss under the mistletoe, Poddar began harassing Ms. Tarasoff, calling and pestering her continually. He was consistently and repeatedly rebuffed by the young woman.

In the summer of 1969, Tanya Tarasoff went to Brazil. When she returned, Poddar went to her home and again was rebuffed. Tanya Tarasoff became emotional and screamed at him. Poddar drew a pellet gun and shot at her. Desperate, the young woman ran from the house, only to be chased down and caught by Poddar, who fatally stabbed her with a kitchen knife. This tragic chain of events unleashed some unforeseen and shocking consequences for mental health professionals.

While Tanya Tarasoff was in Brazil, Poddar sought help for depression at Cowell Memorial Hospital, an affiliate of the University of California, Berkeley. His intake interview was conducted by Dr. Stuart Gold, a psychiatrist, and his therapy was conducted by a psychologist, Dr. Lawrence Moore.

In August 1969, Poddar told Dr. Moore he was going to kill Tanya Tarasoff when she returned from Brazil. Moore immediately consulted his supervisor, and they agreed that Poddar should be involuntarily committed. Dr. Moore called the police, who detained Poddar; but after questioning the man, police officials decided he was rational and released him. His freedom led directly to Tanya Tarasoff's death.

Implications of the Case

In late 1974, the California Supreme Court ruled there was cause for action for negligence against the therapist, the university, and the police for the failure to warn (*Tarasoff v. Regents of the University of California*, 1974). This case is commonly known as Tarasoff I. The court, apparently under pressure from various professional groups, agreed to a rehearing in 1976 (*Tarasoff v. Regents of the University of California*, 1976). This case is commonly known as Tarasoff II.

Whenever we mention the *Tarasoff* case throughout this book, we are citing *Tarasoff II*. In the court's final decision, presented in *Tarasoff II* on July 1, 1976, it set a new standard for therapists. The mandate was clear: *"Therapists who know or should know of patients' dangerousness to identifiable third persons have an obligation to take all reasonable steps necessary to protect the potential victims"* (Appelbaum, 1985, p. 425: emphasis ours).

Various writers on the subject of *Tarasoff* have defined the term *therapist* to include psychologists; counselors; child, marriage, and family therapists; and community mental health counselors. As Stone (cited in Waldo & Malley, 1992) noted:

> Many mental health professionals and paraprofessionals, including social workers, psychiatric social workers, psychiatric nurses, occupational therapists, pastoral counselors, and guidance counselors, provide some form of therapy. ... How many of these millions of therapist-patient contacts each year are intended to be covered by the court's decision is unclear. (p. 539)

What Tarasoff Did Not Require

Researchers have looked extensively at what the *Tarasoff* ruling requires of mental health professionals, and what it does not. VandeCreek and Knapp (1993) addressed this issue head on:

> Because the Tarasoff decision has been subject to so many misinterpretations, it is important to know what the *Tarasoff* court did *not* say. The court did not require psychotherapists to issue a warning every time a patient talks about an urge or fantasy to harm someone. On the contrary, the court stated that "a therapist should not be encouraged routinely to reveal such threats . . . unless such disclosure is necessary to avert danger to others" (*Tarasoff*, p. 347). Finally, the court did not specify that warning the intended victim was the only required response when danger arises; on the contrary, the court stated that the discharge of such duty may require the therapist to take one or more of various steps. (p. 6)

Post Tarasoff

Since the *Tarasoff* trial, other courts have ruled that liability should not be imposed on the therapist if a victim was not identified (*Thompson v. County of Alemeda*, 1980). However, other courts have ruled that the potential victim need only be foreseeably identifiable (*Jablonski v. United States*, 1983) or that the danger need only be foreseeable (*Hedlund v. Superior Court of Orange County*, 1983; *Lipari v. Sears Roebuck*, 1980). Mental health professionals have been found liable for not using prior patient records to predict violence (*Jablonski v. United States*, 1983) and for keeping inadequate records (*Peck v. The Counseling Service of Addison County*, 1985). A Florida appellate court ruled that *Tarasoff* should not be imposed because the relationship of trust and confidence, necessary for the therapeutic process, would be harmed if mental health professionals were required to warn potential victims (*Boynton v. Burglass*, 1991).

It is the special relationship between mental health professionals and clients that sets the stage for therapist liability. The *Tarasoff* case is binding only in California, and it is impossible to predict what courts in other states will do. Some states have expanded the *Tarasoff* reasoning, while others have rejected it. However, as Appelbaum and Rosenbaum (cited in Monahan, 1993, p. 243) stated:

> In jurisdictions in which appellate courts have not yet ruled on the question, the prudent clinician is well advised to proceed under the assumption that some version of *Tarasoff* liability will be imposed. The duty to protect, in short, is now a fact of professional life for nearly all American clinicians and potentially for clinical researchers as well.

Assessing Danger to Others

Appelbaum (1985) presented a model for fulfilling the *Tarasoff* obligation, urging that clinicians treating potentially dangerous patients undertake a 3-stage process of assessment, selection of a course of action, and implementation.

1. The first stage, **assessment** of the patient, has two components:
   a. First, the therapist must gather the data to evaluate the level of danger.
   b. Second, he or she must make a determination of dangerousness on the basis of that data.
2. In the second stage, the clinician who has determined that a patient is likely to be dangerous must **choose a course of action** to protect potential victims.
3. In the third stage, the therapist must **implement** his or her decisions appropriately. This requirement has two components:
   a. First, the therapist must take action to protect potential victims.
   b. Second, he or she must monitor the situation on a continuing basis to assess the success or failure of the initial response, the likelihood that the patient will be violent, and the need for further measures (Applebaum, 1985, p. 426).

The First Stage: Assessment

Information needed to assess the level of anger can be found in the client's past and current records or gathered in the counseling interview. The following questions and guidelines can be used to help determine the potential for violent behavior:

1. Does the client have a history of violent behavior? Past violence is the best predictor of future violence.
2. Does the client have a history of violent conduct with a previous assessment or diagnosis of mental illness?
3. Does the client have a history of arrests for violent conduct?
4. Does the client have a history of threats associated with violent conflict?
5. Has the client ever been diagnosed with a mental disorder for which violence is a common symptom?
6. Has the client had at least one inpatient hospitalization associated with dangerous conduct, whether voluntary or involuntary?

7. Does the client have any history of dangerous conduct, apparently unprovoked and not stress related?

8. If the client has a history of dangerous conduct, how long ago was the incident? The more recent the dangerous behavior, the more likely it is that the behavior will be repeated.

9. If you consider the client dangerous to someone else, note any threats and your observations and notify the person you think might be harmed. Those acts that have a high degree of intent or intensity are most likely to recur.

10. Determine if any serious threats, attempts, or acts harmful to others have been related to drug or alcohol intoxication.

11. Ask the client direct and focused questions, such as, "What is the most violent thing you have ever done?" and "How close have you come to becoming violent?" (Monahan, 1993, p. 244).

12. Use the reports of significant others. Often, family members can provide valuable information about a client's potential for violence. Again, ask direct questions, such as, "Are you worried that your loved one is going to hurt someone?"(Monahan, 1993, p. 244).

13. Has the client threatened others?

14. Does the client have access to weapons?

15. What is the client's relationship to the intended victim(s)?

16. Does the client belong to a social support group that condones violence?

The Second Stage: Selecting a Course of Action

Once the mental health professional has assessed the danger a client poses to others, he or she must decide what to do. Use the guidelines below to help form an action plan:

1. **If you don't consider the danger to be imminent, keep the client in intensified therapy.** Deal with the client's aggression as part of the treatment. However, if the client does not adhere to the treatment plan—that is, if he or she discontinues therapy—the danger level should be considered higher.

2. **Invite the client to participate in the disclosure decision.** This process often makes the client feel more in control. It also is prudent to contact the third party in the presence of the client. This may vitiate problems of paranoia over what has been communicated.

3. **Attempt environmental manipulations.** Medication may be initiated, changed, or increased. Have the client get rid of any lethal weapons.

4. **Keep careful records.** When recording information relevant to risk, note the source of the information (e.g., the name of the spouse), the content (e.g., the character of the threat and the circumstances under which it was disclosed), and the date on which the information was disclosed. Finally, include your rationale for any decisions you make.

5. **If warning a third party is unavoidable, disclose only the minimum amount necessary to protect the victim or the public.** State the specific threat, but reserve any opinions or predictions.

6. **Consult with your supervisor.** Your agency or school should have a contingency plan for such problems that is derived in consultation with an informed attorney, an area psychiatric facility, and local police.

The Third Stage: Monitoring the Situation

You should constantly monitor any course of action to ensure that the objectives of the initial implementation are satisfied. Follow-up procedures should be scrupulously adhered to and well documented. A Harm to Others form (Form 8.3), which can be used in the facilitation of the monitoring process, is included in the "Forms" section at the end of the book.

Patient's Past Criminal Acts

Applebaum and Meisel (1986) reported that therapists' legal obligations to report past criminal acts differ under state and federal laws. Under federal law, therapist obligations fall under a statue of "misprision of a felony." Applebaum and Meisel noted these conditions as necessary to establish guilt for a misprision of a felony:

1. The principle committed and completed the felony alleged.
2. The defendant had full knowledge of the fact.
3. The defendant failed to notify authorities.
4. The defendant took an affirmative step to conceal the crime.

The mere failure to report the crime does not appear to meet the criteria of affirmative concealment. If the mental health professional is questioned by law enforcement officials, he or she must respond truthfully but is not obligated to break confidentiality; it does not appear that the mental health professional has an obligation to say anything at all. Few states have statutes addressing misprision of a felony. Most do require the reporting of gunshot wounds, child abuse, or other specified evidence of certain crimes. The strong trend is for courts to reject the crime of misprision (Applebaum & Meisel, 1986).

The Abused Child

Child Abuse

Child abuse occurs at an alarmingly high rate. An estimated 2 million children are abused or neglected annually in the United States (General Accounting Office, 1991). The actual number of cases is not known (Gargiulo, 1990), as most professionals believe the crime is significantly underreported. (Goldman, 1993). Children with special needs are particularly vulnerable to abuse (Gargiulo, 1990; Goldman, 1993).

Presently all states have laws prohibiting child abuse (Besharov, 1988). The instrument for enforcing those laws is an administrative structure commonly known as *child protective services*. In most states anyone can report suspected child abuse if they do so in good faith. Most states also have *mandated* reporters; professionals who, in the course of their work with children, come upon evidence of abuse. Commonly mandated reporters include doctors, nurses, mental health professionals, social workers, and teachers. The malicious reporting of child abuse is against the law in all states (Besharov, 1988). The national hotline number for child abuse is 1-800-4-A-CHILD.

Definition of Child Abuse

Definitions of child abuse vary from state to state, but most states have laws addressing four different kinds of abuse:

1. **Physical abuse** is nonaccidental injury received by anybody under the age of 18. It is characterized by unexplained bruises, burns, welts, lacerations, abrasions, skeletal injuries, internal injuries, human bite marks, head injuries, and missing or loosened teeth.
2. **Sexual abuse** includes any act of rape, incest, sodomy, sexual intercourse, oral copulation, penetration of genital or anal openings by a foreign object, or child molestation. Closely related to sexual abuse is *sexual exploitation*. Sexual exploitation is using a child to produce pornographic films, magazines, or books.

3. **Emotional abuse** is blaming, belittling, or rejecting a child. It includes any persistent lack of concern by the parent for the child's welfare (Sloan, 1983).

4. **Neglect** is acting negligently toward a child by a person who is responsible for the child's well-being. The acts can be those of commission or omission. Neglect includes failure to provide for basic needs such as food, shelter, medical care, and appropriate clothing. Placing the child in an unsafe environment also can be considered neglect.

Reporting Child Abuse

Mandated reporters usually are professionals who interact with children in the course of their work. The Federal Child Abuse Prevention and Treatment Act requires that sexual, physical, and mental exploitation of children be reported. *Any circumstance that indicates serious harm or threat to a child's welfare must be reported.* Suspicion alone may not be obligatory. The existence of a *reasonable cause* to believe or suspect triggers the mandate (Besharov, 1988). "Reasonable" is what any prudent professional would do in the situation.

Confidentiality and privileged communication are not legal reasons for failing to report abuse. The laws against child abuse supersede the laws of privilege and the ethical mandates of confidentiality. If the abuse is reported in good faith, most states do not allow retribution; that is, the mental health professional cannot be sued for defamation of character even if the abuse is unfounded.

Child abuse must be reported even if the child does not want it reported and even if the mental health professional does not feel it is in the best interest of the child to do so (Weinstock & Weinstock, 1989). Most states do not have a statute of limitations on child abuse cases, unless the abuse was reported before and the charges were dismissed. "This seems to mean that the mental health professional must report abuse that occurred many years ago" (Swenson, 1997, p. 414). Liability has been imposed on mental health professionals for damages caused by not reporting child abuse (Schroeder, 1979).

Therapists who decide to file a child abuse report typically do so by calling the appropriate social service agency. They must file a written report subsequent to the call. A caseworker will be assigned to the case by the child protective services agency. If the caseworker finds probable evidence that neglect or abuse has occurred, he or she refers the case to a law enforcement agency. At that point, the state either begins a criminal prosecution or takes a civil action. If someone other than a parent or caretaker accuses a parent of sexually abusing a child, authorities may initiate both criminal and civil proceedings simultaneously (Buckley, 1988).

A Child Abuse Reporting Form (Form 8.4) is included at the end of this chapter. This asks the therapist to record basic information required to make an initial call to the authorities and to file a formal written report. The Child Abuse Reporting Form shows the required information a counselor needs to have prior to filing a report of child abuse.

Characteristics of Child Abusers

There is no such thing as a "psychological profile of a typical molester" (Chaffin & Milner, 1993; Murphy, Rau, & Worley, 1994). However, reflecting on her 19 years of psychological practice, Lamson (1995) reported seeing the following characteristics in varying degrees:

1. immaturity, emotional dependency, and narcissism with an overly strong need for attention and affection;
2. feelings of social or sexual inadequacy with adults;
3. turning to a child for emotional fulfillment that is lacking in adult relationships;

4. impaired empathy;

5. anger toward an adult partner;

6. antisocial personality traits;

7. history of childhood emotional, physical, and/or sexual abuse;

8. preoccupation with sex;

9. membership in an extremely strict, sexually repressive religion;

10. substance abuse at the time of the molestation.

Erickson, McEnvoy, and Colucci (1984) also referred to some general characteristics of child abuse perpetrators. The most widely accepted characteristics of abusing and neglectful parents are these:

1. were abused as children,

2. are socially and emotionally immature,

3. have low self-esteem,

4. expect children to act as adults,

5. cannot express frustration or anger via acceptable behaviors,

6. have expectations of their children that are not age appropriate,

7. have a history of violent marital discord,

8. abuse drugs or alcohol,

9. cannot tolerate stress,

10. lack adequate parenting skills,

11. ignore the child's needs,

12. are guarded in discussing family relationships,

13. lack appropriate role models.

The problem of psychological abuse has been studied by Garbarino and Vondra (1987), but we do not yet understand its full implications. For example, Brassard, Germain, and Hart (1987) reported that psychological abuse may last longer and have a greater impact than physical abuse. Physically abusive parents also are more likely to inflict verbal abuse (Ney, 1987). Parents who abuse both physically and verbally maximize the trauma the child experiences.

Being abused as a child generally is accepted as a risk factor for being abusive as an adult (Kaufman & Zigler, 1987). Kohn (1987) reported that abused boys, particularly, tend to be adult abusers. Another report pointing to abused children's potential for future violence was published by D. C. Bross (1984), who found that abused adolescents in a New York hospital were two to four times more violent than adolescents with no history of abuse.

Characteristics of Abused Children

The most widely accepted characteristics of the abused or neglected child are these:

1. displays inappropriate hostility, especially toward authority figures;

2. is disruptive and destructive;

3. is passive and withdrawn, cries easily;

4. is fearful at times, displays fear of going home (or to the place where abuse occurs);

5. is habitually absent from or late to school;

6. dresses inappropriately for the weather;

7. shows symptoms of "failure to thrive";

8. has bruises, bumps, or other unexplainable marks;

9. has chronically untreated medical needs;

10. is constantly hungry;

11. makes sexually oriented remarks;

12. displays sexually suggestive behavior;

13. shows discomfort of the genital areas;

14. is fearful of physical contact;

15. is fearful of certain places, people, or activities;

16. displays eating or sleeping problems;

17. acts out inappropriate sexual behaviors;

18. is aggressive or rebellious;

19. has extreme mood swings, withdraws, cries excessively;

20. lacks a positive self-image.

One must exercise caution in evaluating these general characteristics. The counselor should be concerned when several of the characteristics of the abusive parent and/or the abused child are present. The presence of only a few characteristics may be indicative only of a dysfunctional family. In observing these characteristics, the counselor should keep documented records specifically addressing these issues. This information can be added to the Child Abuse Reporting Form (Form 8.4) discussed previously.

Child Sexual Abuse

Estimated rates of the prevalence of child sexual abuse differ, depending on the definition used. If the definition is broad, the rate of occurrence is higher. If the definition is narrow, the rate is lower (Haugaard & Emery, 1989). For example, using a broad definition, Kilpatrick (1986) found that 55% of females reported they had experienced sexual interactions as children. However, only 2% experienced intercourse. Finkelhor (1979) detailed unwanted sexual experiences in childhood for 19.2% of his study respondents; Fromuth (1986) found a frequency rate of 22%; Alexander and Lupfer's (1987) research showed a rate of 25%. Hrabowy (1987) reported rates of 27.9% and 49.1% when he defined abuse differently for two groups, the first more conservatively than the second.

Despite the discrepancy in estimated rates, however, most researchers agree that child abuse is a serious and seriously underreported problem (Butler 1978; Finkelhor, 1984; Hillman & Solek-Tefft, 1988). Baxter (1986) claimed that a child is sexually abused approximately every 2 minutes in the United States. In 80% to 90% of cases reported to the authorities, the perpetrator is known to the child; often, the abuser is a member of the child's family (Baxter, 1986). Sanford (1980) noted that the perpetrator rarely is the stereotypical "dirty old man." Usually he (or, less frequently, she) is an average-looking person with no particular distinguishing characteristics and is known and trusted by the victim (Allsopp & Prosen, 1988). And, as Kempe and Kempe (1978) noted, incidents of sexual abuse cross all socioeconomic and cultural conditions.

Most of the literature on sexual abuse has focused on the abuse of female children. However, Etherington (1995) believed that male sexual abuse is not as rare as reported in the literature. In her study, 25 men who identified themselves as adult male survivors of childhood sexual abuse responded to an advertisement to be interviewed. None reported telling anybody of the abuse at the time it happened; a few disclosed later, but were given little positive psychological help. In fact, one respondent claimed that when he did report the abuse, he was told by a social worker that females didn't do that sort of thing.

Over half of the men in Etherington's study reported that they had been abused by women. Twenty-three (92%) reported sexual dissatisfaction in their adult lives, five (29%) had been convicted of sexual offenses, and seven (29%) were convicted of other offenses; in all, twelve of the respondents (48%) had been convicted of crimes. These statistics are higher than the norm. Looking at these statistics, Etherington (1995) recommended that society widen its perspective on the possible causes of male antisocial behavior.

Elliot (cited in Etherington, 1995) cited a television program that discussed issues of sexual abuse and offered a hotline so viewers could respond. The hotline was inundated with male callers, 90% of whom had never told anyone about the abuse. In all, 33% of those who called the hotline were men.

Banning (1989) claimed that there is a cultural bias today against recognizing mother-son sexual abuse that is similar to the backlash in Freud's time against his claims of father-daughter incest among his female patients. In fact, most cases of mother-son sexual abuse are revealed in long-term therapy. Such cases rarely are reported to authorities, treated seriously, or included in public statistics. Consequently, abuse surveys do not accurately reflect the prevalence of mother-son sexual abuse (Lawson, 1991).

According to Lawson (1991) there is a dearth of studies that have explored a nonclinical population of males relative to incest. Also, case studies in the literature suggest that male victims and maternal perpetrators may not consider certain types of sexual abuse as abusive at the time of occurrence (Krug, 1989). According to A. Bross (1991), many young men would rather be executed than admit that they were sexually abused. In a study of the life histories of rapists and child molesters, Groth (1979) found that one-third had experienced some type of sexual trauma in early childhood.

Lawson (1991) defined maternal sexual abuse to include the following:

- **Subtle abuse,** which includes behaviors that do not involve coercing, may or may not involve genital contact, and are not intended to harm the child. Examples of subtle maternal abuse are allowing the son to sleep in the mother's bed, massaging the child or allowing the child to massage the mother, and the mother bathing with the child.
- **Seductive abuse** is sexual stimulation that is inappropriate for the child's age and is motivated by parental need. Seductive abuse implies conscious awareness on the part of the mother. It is confusing to the child and may be experienced as overstimulating or pleasurable by the child.
- **Emasculation and humiliation** of the child's sexuality may include forcing the boy to wear female clothing. Criticizing one's rate of sexual development and threatening the child with fears of homosexuality would also be included in this category.
- **Overt sexual abuse** is defined as overtly sexualized contact between mother and son. Behaviors include attempted intercourse, fellatio, genital fondling, and clothed or unclothed touching of the genitals (pp. 265, 266).

Mitchell and Morse (1998) reported a study of women who were sexually abused by female perpetrators, mainly mothers and grandmothers. Although research is unclear on the prevalence of this phenomenon, the authors asserted that it is more common than has previously been reported. Some report that group process is the most effective way to treat adult survivors of incest if the group is made up of a heterogeneous population. In this manner witnessing to nonabuse survivors allows the abuse victim to make the transition from an internal world of trauma to a world of self object, trust, and safety (Sagalla, 2000).

Interviewing Children Who May Have Been Sexually Abused

The counselor who interviews the suspected sexually abused child must be highly skilled because it is such an intricate and delicate matter. The interviewer must not pressure the child; on the other hand, not interviewing at the appropriate time can leave the abuse unattended. The child most often will want to please the therapist. If the therapist is not highly skilled and suggests in any way what answer he or she wants, the child may feel pressure to provide that answer. Yarmey and Jones (1983) reported that 91% of psychologists and 69% of jurors believe a child responds according to the wishes of a questioner. In his review of the literature on suggestibility of children, Baxter (1986) found that most situations that involved strong suggestions were correlated with intense social pressure. Baxter also found, however, that when suggestibility is minimized and steps are taken to maximize accuracy, a child's memory is as accurate as an adult's is.

Child Development

Therapists working with young children on possible sexual abuse must be aware that the language, cognition, and logic systems of children are different than those of adults; in other words, children are not miniature adults. A child's vocabulary is much more limited, which means that children understand much more than they can say. Counselors must learn specific interviewing techniques and clinical skills to work with young children. For instance, the use of pronouns, double negatives, and compound sentences should not be employed in the interview. Instead, the counselor should focus on familiar events; for example, "Did this take place after your birthday or before your birthday?"

Children remember what happened, but their causal connections are not the same as those of adults. If they have been sexually abused, they may think (indeed, they most often do) that they caused the abuse. In addition, children often are afraid they will no longer be loved, are guilty, ashamed, and afraid they will get into trouble, and may even fear harm or death (their own or others') if the sexual abuse is disclosed.

Before the Interview

It is not possible to predetermine how long the interview should be. The ideal time is one that allows the truth of the matter to purge itself. The therapist should have information pertinent to the history of the case before starting the interview. Information such as the child's name, nicknames, family members' names, and when and where the disclosure was made will contribute to the counselor's efficacy before and during the interview.

Interviewing the Child

The main ingredient for veracity in an interview is the introduction of support and rapport. Casual clothes are appropriate most of the time. Anatomically correct dolls, hand puppets with mouths that open, and coloring paper and crayons should be immediately accessible. It is important that the therapist appear to be on the same level as the child. This requires an atmosphere that is comfortable. The counselor should be able to get down on the floor or on a pillow and make eye contact with the child. Eye contact is essential when communicating to a child that he or she is not at fault and that what happened was an injustice of the worst type. It is important to remember that the effects of sexual abuse are pervasive and emotionally difficult for the rest of the child's life.

The interviewer must not overreact to any statements the child makes. Some interviews may include interested third parties. The third party may even be the perpetrator or someone from whom the child is keeping a secret. Third parties should be directed to go to the side of the room, where they are not directly part of the interview. The therapist should arrange the parties so that eye contact is not possible between the child and adult. Above all, third parties must be instructed that they are not to be part of the interview.

Therapists must be careful not to ask leading questions. Brainer, Reyna, and Brandse (1996) reported how easy it was to implant memories of events that never happened in 5- to 8-year-old children by suggestion alone. What is more, the implanted false memories often were remembered in more detail than real memories. The biggest danger in examinations of potential sexual abuse is the interviewer who asks leading questions. Questions should be specific; most importantly, they should not suggest an answer. Questions like, "Is it true your Uncle John did this to you?" are leading and may put pressure on the child to answer affirmatively.

If the child says, "Uncle John touched me," a more appropriate response would be: "Where did Uncle John touch you?" Asking, "Did he touch you on your private parts?" is leading the child. Interviewing children is a clinical art form; mental health professionals who conduct such interviews should receive considerable supervised training in this area.

Adult Survivors of Childhood Sexual Abuse

> Sexual abuse is any sexual contact between an adult and a child 16 years of age and under. This includes exploitation (using the child for one's own sexual excitement through taking pictures, showing pictures), incest, rape, fondling, oral sex, anal sex, penetration with objects, exposure, forcing a child to commit sexual acts on other adults and/or children, forcing a child to masturbate themselves [sic] or others (adults/children), and satanic sexual rituals including sexual mutilation and torture. (Baladerian, cited in Glantz & Hunt, 1996, p. 327)

Incest may be the most damaging form of child abuse. The abused child may experience ambivalence between hate and love directed at the perpetrator. Incest usually creates emotional scarring that affects the survivor's feelings of safety and well-being throughout life (Cole, 1984–1986). Adults who were sexually abused as children typically need long-term treatment in a trusting and safe environment.

The therapist treating adult survivors of sexual abuse should encourage disclosure and allow clients to access and vent their feelings (Glantz & Hunt, 1996), always keeping in mind that patience is essential. Norris (1986) suggested challenging the survivor's low self-esteem and noted that clients should learn from the beginning that empathy from the therapist does not necessarily mean agreement. Some adult survivors of incest remember the events but have little or no affect regarding the trauma they endured. Dissociation is one primary defense mechanism of the sexually abused client:

> According to the theory [of dissociation], something happens that is so shocking that the mind grabs hold of the memory and pushes it underground, into some inaccessible corner of the unconscious. There it sleeps for years, or even decades, or even forever—isolated from the rest of mental life. Then, one day, it may rise up and emerge into consciousness. (Loftus, 1994, p. 518)

Other clients may not remember the abuse at all and deny it ever happened. Techniques such as confrontation should be avoided, because they may remind the survivor of the abuse.

Counseling Adult Survivors of Incest

One critical factor in counseling adult survivors of incest is the relationship between therapist and client. Briere (1989) noted that a therapeutic environment that fosters self-acceptance and a therapist who is accepting are especially effective. Norris (1986) also noted the importance of emphasizing the client's strengths and positive qualities, while Rencken (1989) urged therapists to support clients in their efforts to explore the abuse, confront the abuse, and recognize both their uniqueness and any commonality with other survivors. Josephson and Fong-Beyette (1987, p. 478) concluded that mental health professionals "behaving in ways that clients perceive as accepting, validating, encouraging, and knowledgeable" may help clients in their disclosure of incest.

Some researchers advocate writing letters as a safe way for clients to confront their abusers (e.g., Evans & Schaefer, 1987; Rencken, 1989). Other techniques mentioned in the literature include gestalt therapy, transactional analysis and inner child work, hypnotherapy and guided imagery, behavioral techniques, and cognitive education techniques (Pearson, 1994). However, therapists should be aware that the techniques for counseling sexual abuse survivors are increasingly being called into question. Therapists should be advised of the legal issues discussed in the latter part of this section.

False Memory Syndrome

The increased attention given to child abuse and incest is monumental. Between 1986 and 1990, the number of cases reported to child protective agencies increased from 83,000 to 375,000 (Darton, Springer, Wright, & Keene-Osborn, 1991). Estimates of the prevalence of incest range from 15% to 38% of all females (Hood, 1994).

This phenomenal increase has lead critics to pronounce that mental health professionals are creating false memories of abuse. In fact, some have asserted that therapists have created a virtual epidemic of these false memories:

> Recently, a new miracle cure has been promoted by some mental health professionals—recovered memory therapy. In less than 10 years' time this therapy, in its various forms, has devastated thousands of lives. Parents have to witness their adult children turn into monsters trying to destroy their reputations and their lives. (Ofshe & Watters, cited in Zerbe Enns, 1996, p. 4)

So bitter is this controversy that, in 1992, the False Memory Syndrome Foundation (FMSF) was founded. Its objective is to work toward the prevention of "false memory syndrome" and to combat the mental health crisis of the 1990s. Generally speaking, there is strong clinical evidence that traumatic memories can be repressed or denied, but the experimental evidence is weak. This controversy will not be resolved easily, as creating experimental conditions that introduce traumatizing events would be unethical. True memories may be distorted by new information.

A therapist who suggests or uses aggressive memory techniques may distort the original memory base. Fabricated or false memories all feel the same. "But it is also the case that imagination, like its cousin, 'guessing,' can lead people to believe that their false memories are real" (Loftus, 1994, p. 443). For example, in a research study Loftus was able to create false memories in adult participants of being lost in a shopping mall during childhood.

The controversy has been felt in courtrooms, licensing boards, and even insurance agencies. Seppa (1996) reported that complaints to licensing boards increased dramatically between 1992 and 1994. According to one insurance company, over 59% of these complaints were initiated by families of clients who maintained that, because of therapist methodology, the family was falsely accused of child abuse.

Falsely accused families are not the only ones who have been hurt by the issue. Mental health professionals have been stalked, threatened, and had demonstrations performed outside their offices. Many therapists now carefully choose their words, and some may be compromising the quality of care their clients receive out of fear of lawsuits. Others will not deal with any situation that smacks of family violence, referring such cases to other mental health professionals.

On the other side of the coin, angry alleged abuse victims have filed grievances because their therapists did not make them feel better. One group called Victims of Child Abuse Laws (VOCAL) actually encourages lawsuits against mental health professionals. Other groups have proposed legislative changes to restrict the substance of what psychologists can talk about with their clients.

Legal cases arising from the negligent retrieval of false memories were unheard of until 1992, but now they are common. The increase in "repressed memory" lawsuits may well bankrupt the professional liability insurance programs for mental health professionals (Caudill, 1995). Repressed memory claims accounted for 16% of all claims filed in 1994 against mental health professionals insured by the American Professional Agency ("Repressed Memory Claims Expected to Soar," 1995).

Techniques commonly associated with implanted memory complaints include high-pressure support groups, "body work," trance writing, age regression, "reparenting," and the inappropriate use of bibliotherapy and hypnosis (Knapp & Tepper, 1995). Many patients who have sued therapists for implanting false memories also have accused their counselors of various boundary violations (Knapp & VandeCreek, 1995). There is evidence that child abuse, like all other forms of abuse, can be forgotten for days, weeks, and many years before being recalled. However, the reconstruction of these memories is complex and, at times, a somewhat fallible process (DelMonte, 2000).

The Client With AIDS

HIV and AIDS

> As of 1992 about 250,000 Americans have had AIDS, including 100,000 who have already died of AIDS. In addition, about 2 to 2.5 million Americans have the HIV infection. . . . It is believed that by the [year 2000] at least 1% of the American population will carry HIV or have AIDS. (Knapp & VandeCreek, 1993, p. 5)

AIDS was first diagnosed in the United States in 1981. The disease spreads when someone with HIV or AIDS directly transfers body fluids to another person. People who get AIDS usually do so within 10 years of being infected with HIV; 75% die within 2 years of developing AIDS, usually of Kaposi's sarcoma, pneumocystic pneumonia, or another opportunistic infection (Kelly, 1987).

Public health laws require health professionals to report specified communicable diseases. Such reporting allows the gathering of epidemiological data on the incidence of diseases (American Medical Association, 1988). Laws in all 50 states and the District of Columbia mandate reporting diagnosed cases of AIDS to state health officials. This information is reported to the Centers for Disease Control (CDC) in Atlanta. More than 20 states have laws saying that positive HIV status is reportable in itself (Dickens, 1990). Current medical knowledge reveals that all HIV seropositive individuals, even those exhibiting no symptoms, are potentially infectious to others. All persons infected with HIV—from those who are asymptomatic seropositive to those with full-blown AIDS—are capable of transmitting the disease to third parties (Harding, Gray, & Neal, 1993).

Guidelines for Working With Clients With HIV or AIDS

A client says in therapy that he has a gun in his pocket and the gun is loaded. He also says that when he leaves the therapist's office, he is going to drive to his former place of employment, hold the gun to his boss's head, and "blow his brains out." The therapist knows the client has a history of violent conduct and has been involuntarily committed twice before for violent actions.

If the therapist does not take some reasonable action to protect the intended victim, and if the former employer dies as a result of the client's actions, the therapist almost assuredly will be guilty of an ethical and legal violation. In most jurisdictions, the therapist will be found in violation of the law.

Clients with the human immunodeficiency virus (HIV) or acquired immune deficiency syndrome (AIDS) may present mental health professionals with difficult ethical, legal, and moral problems. Unlike the case above, the ethical and legal guidelines regarding AIDS patients infecting third parties are not clear. Those who anticipate definitive ethical and legal guidelines should reflect on the instructions given physicians regarding the tube feeding of an 84-year-old hospital patient:

> I insisted that there are no rules that would replace their prudence and exempt them from the anguishing task of wrestling with the untidy and unpredictable clinical realities of individual cases. Anyone who claims to have a rule that will cut through all of the agonies of ambiguity and uncertainty is involved in deception. (McCormick, 1989, p. 358)

Ethical Positions

Generally the literature on HIV and AIDS is divided into ethical and legal discussions. We will look at the ethical considerations first. Following are statements issued by various professional organizations regarding the ethical issues surrounding the treatment of patients diagnosed with HIV or AIDS:

> A counselor who receives information confirming that a client has a disease commonly known to be both communicable and fatal is justified in disclosing information to an identifiable third party, who by his or her relationship with the client is at a high risk of contracting the disease. Prior to making a disclosure the counselor should ascertain that the client has not already informed the third party about his or her disease and that the client is not intending to inform the third party in the immediate future. (American Counseling Association, 1995, B.l.d)

> If a patient refuses to agree to change his or her behavior or to notify the person(s) at risk, or the physician has good reason to believe that the patient has failed to or is unable to comply with this agreement, it is ethically permissible for the physician to notify an identifiable person who the physician believes is in danger of contracting the virus. (American Psychiatric Association, Ad Hoc Committee on AIDS Policy, 1988, p. 541)

1. A legal duty to protect third parties from HIV infection should not be imposed.
2. If, however, specific legislation is considered, then it should permit disclosure only when (a) the provider knows of an identifiable third party who the provider has compelling reason to believe is at significant risk; and (b) the client/patient has been urged to inform the third party and has either refused or is considered unreliable in his/her willingness to notify the third party.

3. If such legislation is adopted, it should include immunity from civil and criminal liability for providers who, in good faith, make decisions to disclose or not to disclose information about HIV infection to third parties. (American Psychological Association, 1991, p. 1)

Social workers should first use the strength of their client-worker relationship to encourage clients with HIV infection to inform their sexual or needle-sharing partners of their antibody status. Clients should be counseled regarding existing partner-notification programs that can be used. If the client cannot or will not inform their sexual or needle-sharing partners, the social workers must inform the clients of the avenues, if any, they are mandated to follow. Social workers have a responsibility to consult with other practitioners and to consider legal counsel if they feel they have a duty to warn. (National Association of Social Workers, 1990, p. 5)

Ethical principles may be applied to the issue of confidentiality with the seropositive client. All clients have the right to have their private business kept confidential. However, the autonomy of a potential sexual partner also must be considered; the principles of beneficence, nonmaleficence, and justice are obviously relevant to parties outside the counseling relationship who may become infected.

Cohen (1990) noted that therapists who keep their clients' HIV status confidential "only permit the clients' grotesque violation of those very same principles" (p. 283). Gray and Harding (1988) agreed:

> Given the virulence and fatality of the disease, the increasing rate of prevalence, and the absence of conclusive scientific data regarding transmission, the right of an endangered person to know may overcome any right to privacy regarding individual identification or disclosure to a third party. (p. 221)

However, Harding et al. (1993) recommended that disclosure should occur as last resort, to use only if no other viable alternatives exist" (p. 303). Melton (1991) agreed, noting that it is better to use clinical interventions designed either to modify client behavior or to help the client warn third parties.

Others have asserted that client confidentiality should not be broken (e.g., Kermani & Weiss, 1989; Wood, Marks, & Dilley, 1990). Breaching confidentiality may have serious consequences, as Kain (1991; cited in Harding et al., 1993, p. 302) noted:

> There are, for example, possibilities that (a) permissible disclosure may instill mistrust in the counseling process, (b) some counselor disclosures may be based on fear of civil liability or moral judgment, and (c) reporting of sensitive information to public officials may generate repercussions (e.g., housing discrimination, employment limitation, denial of insurance opportunities, invasion of privacy).

Kelly (1987) argued that confidentiality is important "for the sake of all potential victims in the future, who will need to believe they can rely on the principle before they disclose information" (p. 336). And Landesman (1987) argued that disclosing confidential information could influence clients not to get the help they need again. Morrison (1989) agreed, noting that the therapist who breaks confidentiality may put the therapeutic relationship at risk.

Legal Positions

Most of a therapist's potential legal duty in breaching confidentiality with an HIV- or AIDS-positive client revolves around the *Tarasoff* case and is laid down in that verdict. The arguments in the literature are mostly syllogistic.

The first position is that a mental health professional may be liable for not warning a third party of serious and foreseeable danger, based on the *Tarasoff* case decision. The person who has HIV and is sexually active may be a serious and foreseeable danger to his or her partner(s). Therefore, a therapist should disclose the danger to the party(s) at risk.

The second position is that the therapist should not be held liable for not warning a third party based on the *Tarasoff* case. The person who is HIV- or AIDS-positive and is sexually active may be a serious and foreseeable danger to his or her partner(s). Although there are similarities between the *Tarasoff* case and sexually active clients who are seropositive, there also are many differences. Therefore, one cannot say that the therapist should disclose the positive danger to a third party at risk.

To date, no case involving confidentiality and an AIDS client has been litigated (Yu & O'Neal, cited in Schlossberger & Heckler, 1996).

Support for reporting communicable sexual diseases is based on historic legal principles. In some states, not warning family members or others in close proximity to a patient of a communicable disease may render physicians negligent in their behavior (Delarosa, 1987). Courts refer to the physician's duty to protect others from communicable diseases, and they define the mental health professional's duty in the same way (Delarosa, 1987; Fulero, 1988).

A case can be made that the physician's responsibility for notifying third parties absolves the mental health professional from responsibility to do so. However, laws requiring the reporting of HIV infection are state-specific. Some jurisdictions do not require reporting of HIV-positive status until patients have a diagnosis of AIDS.

Schlossberger and Heckler (1996) noted that the danger posed to Tanya Tarasoff violated her legal rights. In many states people do not have a legal right to know if their sexual partners are HIV-positive. Consequently, when HIV-positive clients have sexual relationships with others, they have committed no legal wrong. It follows, then, that therapists have no legal responsibility to warn in those states. In fact, Schlossberger and Heckler (1996) continued, any rule that requires the counselor to warn third parties about behaviors that are legal

> would constitute discrimination against clients of therapists and violate equality under the law: in effect, people in therapy would be held to a different legal standard than everyone else . . . we conclude that, unless state law (criminal or tort), directly or indirectly, generally requires seropositive clients to inform their partners, therapists have no legal duty to warn. Although the therapist has a legal duty to warn others subject to an illegal danger, the therapist has no duty to intervene when clients pose dangers that society, through law, grants them the right to pose. (Schlossberger & Heckler, 1996, pp. 27–40)

Some have argued that, since everyone knows about the AIDS epidemic today, the caveat of prudence on the part of sexual partners is in order, comparable to the legal doctrine of assumption of risk (Closen & Isaacman, 1988). However, the caveat may not apply to an unwitting spouse who is married to a sexually active bisexual client (Hoffman, 1991).

Others have argued that third parties should be warned only under certain conditions. Wood et al. (1990), for example, listed the following conditions that must be met before a mental health professional could be held liable for failing to warn a third party:

1. The counselor knows the patient is HIV-infected.

2. The client engages in unsafe behavior on a regular basis.

3. The client intends to continue such behavior even after counseling by the therapist.

4. HIV transmission will be the likely result.

■ The Substance-Abusing Client

Substance Abuse

Clients with psychoactive substance use disorders are among the most complex and difficult to treat. Addictive disorders constitute a serious national health threat, with the lifetime incidence of psychoactive substance abuse approaching 20% of the population. Fewer than 10% of individuals with addictive disorders receive professional treatment or belong to self-help groups (Frances & Miller, 1991).

Considerable controversy exists over the etiology of psychoactive substance use disorders. Biologically based models emphasize genetic predisposition (Goodwin & Warnock, 1991), while psychoanalytic and psychodynamic perspectives suggest that chemical dependency is symptomatic of underlying psychopathology or personality dysfunction (Cox, 1987; Forrest, 1985). Leigh (1985) suggested that substance abuse and dependence are the products of a combination of variables, including personality traits, environmental factors, and the immediate self-reinforcing properties of the desired substance.

Marlatt, Baer, and Larimer (1995) suggested that substance abuse may be an impulse/behavioral (acquired habit pattern) disorder that results in disease states (e.g., cirrhosis). Beck and Emery (1977) and Ellis, McInerney, DiGiuseppe, and Yeager (1988) identified substance-dependent cognitions (belief systems and thinking styles) as critical factors precipitating substance dependence. Wallace (1991) described the biopsychosocial model in discussing crack cocaine dependence. This model considers genetic predisposition, the pharmacological reinforcing properties of substances, psychological/personality factors, and the social-environmental component (learning and reinforcement).

Psychoactive substance-disordered individuals are a heterogeneous and highly complex population. Because of the high frequency of coexisting additional forms of psychopathology, including significant characterologic features, addictive-disordered populations are extremely challenging to work with, and success rates with particular clinical subtypes may be modest at best.

Trends and approaches in the treatment of psychoactive substance disorders are changing, partly out of necessity because of shifting reimbursement patterns of third-party providers and also because of continuing advances in biological, psychological, and psychiatric research. In addition, as more researchers come to view psychoactive substance use disorders as biopsychosocial in nature, greater emphasis is being placed on combining multiple interventions, including detoxification, intense individual and group psychotherapy, social skills training and psychoeducation, psychopharmacological trials, and community-based self-help networks.

Assessment Instruments

Mental health professionals who counsel clients for psychoactive substance pathology may find it useful to acquaint themselves with standardized assessment instruments as an adjunct to clinical interviews and observation. Two instruments that have good reliability and validity and that can be scored and interpreted quickly are the *Drug Abuse Screening Test-20* (DAST-20; Skinner, 1982) and the *Addiction Severity Index* (ASI; McClellan, Luborksy, & Cacciola, 1985; Orvaschel, 1993).

The DAST-20 is a 20-item self-report inventory that provides a quantitative index of the degree of consequences and severity of drug abuse. The DAST-20 yields a total cumulative score with severity intervals (i.e., none, low, moderate, substantial, and severe).

The ASI is a structured interview instrument that provides a multidimensional assessment of degree of impairment in various areas due to substance use (medical, employment, severity of chemical use, family/social relationships, and legal and psychiatric status).

The ASI requires both administration and interviewer severity rating skills; therefore, counselors must have adequate training to use this instrument. The DAST-20, on the other hand, requires only a tabulation of item scores, and the interpretation is objective. Although neither instrument is independently adequate to provide an accurate diagnosis, both are valuable tools for gleaning additional information as well as for identifying specific areas for treatment focus.

A Substance Abuse Assessment Form (Form 8.5) is included in the "Forms" section at the end of the book. This form provides questions for the student or intern to use when working with substance abusing or dependent clients. The form also includes a confidential informed release statement, which should be signed by the client prior to the therapist disclosing any confidential information to a third party.

Counseling Recommendations

It is important for counselors who work with substance abusing or dependent clients to adopt an objective and factual approach to assessment interviews. As many clients enter treatment for substance-related problems because of external pressures (i.e., family, employers, the legal system), the counselor must convey an impression that he or she is an ally to the client in addressing his or her problems. In asking assessment questions, the counselor should use the objective criteria as a guideline and proceed in a nonjudgmental and matter-of-fact way. He or she should avoid asking leading questions such as, "You don't abuse drugs or alcohol, do you?" (Bukstein, 1990).

Initial interviewing goals include establishing a flow of information and disclosure about the client's level of motivation for treatment and obtaining the necessary information to formulate an objective impression.

The mental health professional must realize that substance-abusing clients frequently enter treatment with a strong sense of ambivalence, which affects treatment motivation. The key to working through ambivalence is to foster *engagement and trust* as early as possible, which can be done by discussing treatment ambivalence and emphasizing the client's presenting negative consequences from substance use.

The counselor should relay the results of the assessment interview to the client in the same objective fashion and emphasize that the assessment is based on the information the client provided and from data from assessment instruments. This process may help the client work though treatment resistance as well as reinforce the therapeutic alliance. Below are some general guidelines for working with substance-abusing clients:

1. **Understand the emotional role the substance of choice plays for the client.** A central challenge for the counselor is to identify the client's rationale for using a mood-altering substance. Almost invariably that rationale has an affective base (i.e., substance use to avoid or escape negative situations or to acquire a desired affective state). Once the affective motivation is established, the counselor can undertake treatment to develop adaptive coping responses. As depth-psychology-oriented treatment may be difficult with substance-dependent clients because of relapse risk, therapists should be cautious in immediately addressing traumatic issues if the client has had only a brief period of abstinence or if affect tolerance or modulation appears tenuous.

2. **Identify the internal and external triggering events for substance cravings and impulses.** Substance-using impulses often are precipitated by events that may or may not be evident to the client. The counselor needs to detect the internal (i.e., thoughts, feelings, memories, attitudes) and external (i.e., interpersonal conflicts, social isolation, interpersonal/existential losses) antecedents for the client's substance use impulses and cravings. Helping the client identify these triggers when they occur allows him or her to implement substance-avoidance behaviors. Once substance triggers are identified, specific operationalized behavior plans for coping with them can be constructed.

3. **Confront internal versus external locus of control regarding substance-using behaviors.** Many substance-abusing clients rationalize their substance use by either relinquishing responsibility for control ("I can't help it") or externalizing control over their behavior ("My boss makes me use—he's so demanding"). The counselor must confront the client by reflecting that he or she ultimately chooses to use a substance regardless of the circumstances. Once clients accept this reality, controlling the impulses to use becomes a treatment focus.

4. **Challenge substance-dependence-reinforcing cognitions** (i.e., beliefs and thinking styles). Many substance-abusing clients present belief systems that reinforce chemical dependency ("Without my crack, I can't deal with life" or "I need a drink to control myself'). The counselor should challenge such maladaptive cognitions.

5. **Help the client learn and apply abstaining behaviors.** Coping with cravings and impulses is a vital therapeutic goal. A useful resistance skill is for the client to focus on previous negative consequences of substance use when he or she experiences cravings or impulses. This technique shifts the psychological focus from the desired and expected immediate mood-altering effect to associating the substance with emotionally negative events. This technique of "thinking the craving through" can divert clients from impulsiveness and make them aware of adaptive options. Counselors should review with clients the distinctions between thinking, feeling, and physical action (doing). Clients need to realize that they can have substance-oriented cravings and impulses and not carry them out.

6. **Practice therapeutic rather than antagonistic confrontation.** As treatment engagement on the part of the client is critical, the counselor must be careful not to confuse confrontation with intolerance. Therapeutic confrontation occurs when the counselor presents the client with concrete examples of clinical material representative of the disorder. Therapeutic confrontation is based on objective data or behavior that the client presents, not upon a conflict of personal values. Attempts to impose guilt or shame on the client increases the potential for treatment dropout. Reflecting clinical observations back to the client in a nonthreatening and constructive way increases the probability that the client will accept and work with the intervention.

7. **Establish healthy developmental goals.** An important part of counseling substance-abusing clients is addressing the frequent developmental disturbances that accompany maladaptive patterns of substance use (dropping out of school, getting fired from jobs, family disruptions, etc.). Part of the treatment plan should include a return (perhaps gradually) to normal and productive functioning. Frustration and anxiety tolerance may be a central focus, depending on the severity and duration of psychosocial disturbances.

Preventing Relapse

Relapse prevention is defined as "a self-management program designed to enhance the maintenance stage of the habit-change process" (Marlatt, 1985a, 1985b). Behaviorally, relapse prevention can be seen as one set of operationalized target behaviors implemented and practiced consistently over time that results in another set of targeted undesired behaviors being discontinued. Below are some general framework suggestions for an operationalized psychoactive substance relapse prevention program.

1. **Help the client identify high-risk situations.** High-risk situations may include attending social events where substance use is prominent or spending time at places where substances are readily available. Being aware of high-risk situations alerts the client to consider avoidance or to apply specific behavior plans for increasing controls to maintain abstinence.

2. **Help the client make necessary lifestyle changes and relationship modifications.** The client must gain awareness of specific lifestyle behaviors (theft, prostitution, drug sales, etc.) that are specifically related to the substance-using pattern. Often the client must change those behavior patterns in order to maximize the prognosis for abstinence. Likewise, specific relationships that reinforce

substance use must be confronted, modified, or even discontinued until the client has gained sufficient behavioral and impulse controls to withstand the influence of others who advocate substance use.

3. **Reduce access to psychoactive substances.** A strategic component of relapse prevention is reducing access to psychoactive substances. This may occur by removing psychoactive substances from the client's residence, eliminating routine purchases of substances (alcohol), or identifying specific places (high-risk situations) where substances are readily available or promoted.

4. **Address any underlying psychopathology.** Untreated psychiatric disorders (or psychopathology) constitute one of the most common reasons for psychoactive substance relapse (McClellan, 1986). Mood, anxiety, or personality disorders or other forms of psychopathology that persist into the abstinence period should be formally evaluated and treated. Using simultaneous combination treatments (psychotherapy, pharmacotherapy, family therapy, and self-help groups) may be most advantageous.

5. **Help the client rebound from a relapse.** Relapses happen; in specific patient subtypes (i.e., severe personality disorders, untreated mood or anxiety disorders), they may be common. The counselor must be clinically prepared for relapse and assure the client that a relapse should not be viewed fatalistically but rather as a mistake with the current treatment focus. The client should be encouraged to resume abstinence and to gain an understanding of the dynamics of the relapse. Relapses can be used as restarting points in treatment if therapeutic engagement is maintained.

Conclusion

The etiology of psychoactive substance abuse disorders is not clear. Genetic disposition, underlying pathology, personality and environmental factors, impulse or behavior disorders, and other biopsychosocial factors are some of the reasons given for substance abuse. Mental health professionals should strive to understand the emotional role the substance of choice plays for the client, identify internal and external triggering events, and help the client learn and apply abstaining behaviors.

Summary

This chapter addressed the key issues in dealing with special populations such as clients who are harmful to themselves or others, abused clients, survivors of sexual abuse, clients infected with HIV/AIDS, and substance abusing clients. These are the populations that are most commonly encountered in standard therapeutic settings and that the student will likely work with most often through the duration of the internship. Because these populations are encountered with relative frequency, it is important that interns familiarize themselves with the issues that can arise in therapy and the special considerations that must be made when determining appropriate interventions. The intervention strategies and clinical forms that are provided were designed to assist the counselor or therapist in the treatment and reporting of critical client data.

References

Alexander, P. C., & Lupfer, S. L. (1987). Family characteristics and long-term consequences associated with sexual abuse. *Archives of Sexual Behavior, 16,* 235–245.

Allan, W. D. Kashani, J. H., Dahlmeier, J. M., Beck. N., & Reid, J. C. (1998). Anxious suicidality: A new type of threatening behavior. *Suicide and Life Threatening Behavior, 28,* 251–260.

Allsopp, A., & Prosen, S. (1988). Teacher reactions to a child sexual abuse training program. *Elementary School Guidance Counseling, 22,* 299–305.

American Association for Marriage and Family Therapy. (1991). *Code of ethical principles for marriage and family therapists.* Washington, DC: Author.

American Counseling Association. (1995). *Code of ethics and standards of practice.* Alexandria, VA: Author.

American Medical Association. (1988). *LLL progress on the prevention and control of AIDS* (Reference Committee E, pp. 204–222, 473). Washington DC: Author.

American Psychiatric Association. (1987). *Diagnostic and statistical manual of mental disorders* (3rd ed.). Washington, DC: Author.

American Psychiatric Association. (1988). AIDS policy: Confidentiality and disclosure. *American Journal of Psychiatry, 145,* 541–542.

American Psychological Association. (1991). APA Council of Representatives adopts new AIDS policies. *Psychology and AIDS Exchange, 7,* 1.

American Psychological Association. (1995). *Ethical principals of psychologists.* Washington, DC: Author.

American School Counselor Association. (1992). *Ethical standards for school counselors.* Alexandria, VA: Author.

American Psychological Association. (1995). *Ethical principles of psychologists and code of conduct.* Washington, DC: Author.

Annell, Al. L. (Ed.). 1971. *Depressive states in childhood and adolescence.* New York: Halstead.

Applebaum, P. S. (1985). Tarasoff and the clinician: Problems in fulfilling the duty to protect. *American Journal of Psychiatry, 142*(4), 425–429.

Applebaum, P. S., & Meisel, M. A. (1986). Therapists' obligations to report their patients' criminal acts. *Bulletin of the American Academy of Psychiatry and the Law, 14*(3), 221–229.

Banning, A. (1989). Mother-son incest: Confronting as prejudice. *Child Abuse and Neglect, 13,* 563–570.

Baron, F. (1987). Clinical Psychology: Racing into the future with old dreams and visions. *Clinical Psychologist, 40*(4), 93–96.

Barrett, T. (1985). Does suicide prevention in the school have to be such a "terrifying" concept? *Newslink, 11*(1), 3.

Baxter, A. (1986). *Techniques for dealing with child sexual abuse.* Springfield, IL: Charles C. Thomas.

Beauchamp, T. L. (1985). Suicide: Matters of life and death. *Suicide and Life-Threatening Behavior, 24*(2), 190–195.

Beck, A., & Emery, G. D. (1977). *Cognitive therapy of substance abuse.* Philadelphia: Center for Cognitive Therapy.

Bednar, R. L., Bednar, S. C., Lambert, M. J., & Waite, D. R. (1991). *Psychology with high-risk clients: Legal and professional standards.* Pacific Grove, CA: Brooks/Cole.

Berman, A. L., & Cohen-Sandler, R. (1982). Suicide and the standard care: Optimal vs. acceptance. *Suicide and Life Threatening Behavior, 12*(2), 114–117.

Besharov, D. J. (1988). Child abuse and neglect reporting and investigation: Policy guidelines for decision making. *Family Law Quarterly, 22*(1), 1–16.

Bongar, B., & Harmatz, M. (1989). Graduate training in clinical psychology and the study of suicide. *Professional Psychology Research and Practice, 20*(4), 209–213.

Boynton v. Burglass, No. 89-1409, Fla. Ct. App., 3d Dist. (September 24, 1991).

Brainer, C. J., Reyna, C. F., & Brandse, E. (1996). Are children's false memories more persistent than their true memories? *Psychological Science, 6*(6), 359–364.

Brassard, M. R., Germain, R., & Hart, S. N. (1987). *Psychological maltreatment of children and youth.* New York: Pergamon.

Briere, J. (1989). *Therapy for adults molested as children: Beyond survival.* New York: Springer-Verlag.

Bross, A. (1991, July 7). A touch of evil. *The Boston Globe Magazine,* 12–25.

Bross, D. C. (1984). When children are battered by the law. *Barrister, 11*(4), 8–11.

Buckley, J. (1988). Legal proceedings, reforms, and emergency issues in child sexual abuse cases. *Behavioral Science and the Law, 6*(2), 153–180.

Bukstein, O. G. (1990). *A primer on psychoactive substance use disorders in DSM-I-R.* Unpublished paper, Western Psychiatric Institute and Client, Pittsburgh, PA.

Butler, S. (1978). *Conspiracy of silence.* San Francisco: New Glide.

Capuzzi, D., & Golden, L. (1988). *Preventing adolescent suicide.* Muncie, IN: Accelerated Development.

Carlino v. State, 294 N.Y.S. 2d 30 (1968).

Caudill, B. (1995, February). *The repressed memory war.* Presentation at the Annual Convention of the California Psychological Association, La Jolla.

Celotta, B., Golden, J., Keys, S. S., & Cannon, G. (1988). A model prevention program. In D. Capuzzi & L. Golden (Eds.), *Preventing adolescent suicide* (pp. 269–296). Muncie, IN: Accelerated Development.

Chaffin, M., & Milner, J. (1993). Psychometric issues for practitioners in child maltreatment. *APSAC Advisor, 6*(1), 9–13.

Chemtob, C. M., Hamada, L. S., Bauer, G. B., Kinney, B., & Torigle, R.Y. (1988). Patient suicide: Frequency and impact on psychiatrist. *American Journal of Psychiatry, 145,* 224–228.

Closen, M. L., & Isaacman, S. H. (1988). The duty to notify private third parties of the risks of HIV infection. *Journal of Health and Hospital Law, 21,* 295–299.

Cohen, E. D. (1990). Confidentiality, counseling, and clients who have AIDS: Ethical foundations of a model rule. *Journal of Counseling and Development, 68*(3), 282–286.

Cole, S. S. (1984–1986). Facing the challenges of sexual abuse in persons with disabilities. *Sexuality and Disability, 7,* 71–88.

Comiskey v. State of New York, 418 N.Y.S. 2d 233 (1979).

Connell, H. M. (1972). Depression in childhood. *Child Psychiatry and Human Development, 4,* 71–85.

Cox, M. (1987). Personality theory and research. In H. T. Blane & K. E. Leonard (Eds.), *Psychological theories of drinking and alcoholism* (pp. 55–84). New York: Guilford.

Dalton v. State, 308 N.Y.S. 2d 441 (Sup, CF. N.Y. App. 1970).

Darton, N., Springer, K., Wright, L., & Keene-Osborn, S. (1991, October 7). The pain of the last taboo. *Newsweek,* 70–72.

Davis, J. M. (1985). Suicidal crisis in schools. *School Psychology Review, 14*(3), 117–123.

Delarosa, R. (1987). Viability of negligence actions for sexual transmission of the acquired immune deficiency syndrome virus. *Capital University Law Review, 17,* 101–195.

DelMonte, M. M. (2000). Retrieved memories of childhood sexual abuse. *British Journal of Medical Psychology, 73,* 1–13.

Deutsch, C. J. (1984). Self-imported stresses among psychotherapist. *Professional Psychology: Research and Practice, 15*(6), 833–845.

Dickens, B. M. (1990). Confidentiality and the duty to warn. In L. O. Gostin (Ed.), *AIDS and the health care system* (pp. 98–112). New Haven, CT: Yale University Press.

Eisenberg, L. (1984). The epidemiology of suicide in adolescents. *Pediatric Annuals, 13*(1), 47–53.

Ellis, A., McInerney, J., DiGiuseppe, R., & Yeager, R. (1988). *Rational-emotive therapy with alcoholics and substance abusers.* New York: Pergamon.

Erickson, E. L., McEnvoy, A., & Colucci, N. D. (1984). *Child abuse and neglect: A guidebook for educators and community leaders* (2nd ed.). Holmes Beach, FL: Learning Publications.

Etherington, K. (1995). Adult male survivors of childhood sexual abuse. *Counseling Psychology Quarterly, 8*(3), 233–241

Evans, S., & Schaefer, S. (1987). Incest and chemically dependent women: Treatment implications. *Journal of Chemical Dependency Treatment, I,* 141–173.

Farrow v. Health Service Corp., 604 p 2d 474 (Utah Supreme Ct., 1979).

Finkelhor, D. (1979). *Sexually victimized children.* New York: Free Press

Finkelhor, D. (1984, September). The prevention of child sexual abuse: an overview of needs and problems. *Seicus Report,* 1–5.

Forge, J. L., & Henderson, P. (1990). Counselor competency in the courtroom. *Journal of Counseling and Development, 68,* 456–459.

Forrest, C. G. (1985). Psychodynamically oriented treatment of alcoholism and substance abuse. In T. E. Bratter & G. C. Forrest (Eds.), *Alcoholism and substance abuse* (pp. 307–336). New York: Free Press.

Frances, R. J., & Miller, S. I. (Eds.). (1991). *Clinical textbook of addictive disorders.* New York: Guilford.

Fremouw, W., Callahan, T., & Kashden, J. (1993). Adolescent suicidal risk: Psychological, problem solving, and environmental factors. *Suicide and Life-Threatening Behavior, 23*(1), 323–329.

Fromuth, M. E. (1986). The relationship of childhood sexual abuse with later psychological and sexual adjustment in a sample of college women. *Child Abuse and Neglect, 10,* 5–15.

Fujimura, L. E., Weis, D. M., & Cochran, F. R. (1985). Suicide: Dynamics and implications for counseling. *Journal of Counseling and Development, 63,* 612–615.

Fulero, S. M. (1988). Tarasoff: Ten years later. *Professional Psychology: Research and Practice, 19*(2), 184–190.

Garbarino, J., & Vondra, J. (1987). Psychological maltreatment: Issues and perspectives. In M. R. Brassard, R. Germain, & S. N. Hart (Eds.), *Psychological maltreatment of children and youth* (pp. 224–244). New York: Pergamon.

Gargiulo, R. (1990). Child abuse and neglect: An overview. In R. Goldman & R. Gargiulo (Eds.), *Children at risk: An interdisciplinary approach to child abuse and neglect* (pp. 1–36). Austin, TX: Pro-Ed.

General Accounting Office. (1991). *Child abuse prevention: Status of the challenge grant program* (GAO/HRD 91-95). Washington, DC: Author.

Glantz, T. M., & Hunt, B. (1996). What rehabilitation counselors need to know about adult survivors of child sexual abuse. *Journal of Applied Rehabilitation Counseling, 27*(3), 17–22.

Goldman, R. (1993). Sexual abuse of children with special needs: Are they safe in day care? *Day Care and Early Education, 20*(4), 37–38.

Goodwin, D. W., & Warnock, J. K. (1991). Alcoholism: A family disease. In R. J. Frances & S. I. Miller (Eds.), *Clinical textbook of addictive disorders* (pp. 485–500). New York: Guilford.

Gray, E. A., & Harding, A. K. (1988). Confidentiality limits with clients who have the AIDS virus. *Journal of Counseling and Development, 66*(5), 219–223.

Grob, M. C., Klein, A. A., & Eisen, S. V. (1982). The role of the high school professional in identifying and managing adolescent suicide behavior. *Journal of Youth Suicide, 12,* 163–173.

Groth, A. N. (1979). Sexual trauma in the life histories of rapists and child molesters. *Victimology, 4,* 10–16.

Harding, A. K., Gray, L. A., & Neal, M. (1993). Confidentiality limits with clients who have HIV: A review of ethical and legal guidelines and professional policies. *Journal of Counseling and Development, 71,* 297–305.

Haugaard, J. J., & Emery, R. E. (1989). Methodological issues in child sexual abuse research. *Child Abuse and Neglect, 13,* 89–100.

Hedlund v. Superior Court of Orange County, 669 P.2d 41, 191 Cal. Rptr. 805 (1983).

Hillman, D., & Solek-Tefft, J. (1988). *Spiders and flies: Help for parents and teachers of sexually abused children.* Lexington, MA: Lexington Books.

Hoffman, M. A. (1991). Counseling the HIV-infected client: A psychosocial model for assessment and intervention. *Counseling Psychologist, 19*(4), 167–542.

Hood, G. (1994). The statute of limitation barrier in civil suits brought against adult survivors of child sexual abuse: A simple solution. *University of Illinois Law Review, 2,* 417–442.

Hrabowy, I. (1987*). Self-reported correlates of adult-child sexual relations.* Unpublished master's thesis, Bowling Green State University, Bowling Green, OH.

Jablonski v. United States, 712 E.2d 391 (9th cir. 1983).

Josephson, G. S., & Fong-Beyette, M. L. (1987). Factors assisting female clients' disclosure of incest during counseling. *Journal of Counseling and Development, 65,* 475–478.

Kaufman, J., & Zigler, E. (1987). Do abused children become abusive parents? *American Journal of Orthopsychiatry, 57,* 186–192.

Kelly, K. (1987). AIDS and ethics: An overview. *General Hospital Psychiatry, 9,* 331–340.

Kempe, R. S., & Kempe, C. H. (1978). *Child abuse.* Cambridge, MA: Harvard University Press.

Kermani, E. J., & Weiss, B. A. (1989). AIDS and confidentiality: Legal concept and its application in psychotherapy. *American Journal of Psychotherapy, 43*(1), 25–31.

Kilpatrick, A. C. (1986). Some correlates of women's childhood sexual experiences: A retrospective study. *Journal of Sex Research, 22,* 221–242.

King, K., Price, J., Telljohann, S. K., & Wahl, J. (1999). High school health teachers perceive self-efficacy in identifying students at risk for suicide. *Journal of School Health, 69,* 202–207.

Knapp, S., & Tepper, A. (1995, May). Risk management issues in the false memory debate. *Pennsylvania Psychologist, 55*(3), 26–27.

Knapp, S., & VandeCreek, L. (1993). What psychologists need to know about AIDS. *Journal of Training and Practice in Professional Psychology, 3*(2), 3–16.

Knapp, S., & VandeCreek, L. (1995). *Risk management for psychologists treating patients who recover lost memories of childhood abuse.* Manuscript in preparation.

Kohn, A. (1987). Shattered innocence. *Psychology Today, 21*(2), 54–58.

Krug, R. S. (1989). Adult male reports of childhood sexual abuse by mothers: Case descriptions, motivations, and long-term consequences. *Child Abuse and Neglect, 13,* 111–119.

Kush, F. R. (1990). *A descriptive study of school-based adolescent suicide prevention/intervention programs: Program components and the role of the school counselor.* Unpublished doctoral dissertation, University of Pittsburgh.

Lamson, A. (1995). Evaluating child sexual abuse allegations. *Research and Treatment Issues, 11*(3–4), 24–27.

Landesman, S. H. (1987). AIDS and a duty to protect: Commentary. *Hastings Center Report, 17,* 23.

Lasko, C. A. (1986). Childhood depression questions and answers. *Journal of School Guidance and Counseling, 4,* 283–287.

Lawson, C. (1991). Mother-son sexual abuse: Rare or under-reported? A critique of the research. *Child Abuse and Neglect, 17,* 261–269.

Leigh, G. (1985). Psychosocial factors in the etiology of substance abuse. In T. E. Bratter & G. C. Forrest (Eds.), *Alcoholism and substance abuse* (pp. 3–48). New York: Free Press.

Lipari v. Sears Roebuck, 497 F. Supp. 185 (D. Neb. 1980).

Loftus, E. F. (1994). The repressed memory controversy. *American Psychologist, 49,* 409–420.

Malley, P., Kush, F., & Bogo, R. (1994). School-based adolescent suicide prevention and intervention programs: A survey. *The School Counselor, 42,* 230–237.

Marlatt, A. (1985a). Cognitive factors in the relapse process. In G. A. Marlatt & J. R. Gordon (Eds.), *Relapse prevention* (pp. 128–193). New York: Guilford.

Marlatt, A. (1985b). Relapse prevention: Theoretical rationale and overview of the model. In G. A. Marlatt & J. R. Gordon (Eds.), *Relapse prevention* (pp. 3–67). New York: Guilford.

Marlatt, G. A., Baer, J. S., & Larimer, M. (1995). Preventing alcohol abuse in college students: A harm-reduction approach. In G. M. Boyd, J. Howard, & R. A. Zucker (Eds.), *Alcohol problems among adolescents: Current directions in prevention research* (pp. 147–172). Hillsdale, NJ: Erlbaum.

Mathiasen, R. (1988). Evaluating suicidal risk in the college student. *NASPA Journal, 25,* 257–261.

McClellan, A. T. (1986). "Psychiatric severity" as a predictor of outcome from substance abuse treatments. In R. E. Meyer (Ed.), *Psychopathology and addictive disorders* (pp. 97–135). New York: Guilford.

McClellan, A. T., Luborsky, L., & Cacciola, M. A. (1985). New data from the *Addiction Severity Index*: Reliability and validity in three centers. *Journal of Nervous and Mental Disease, 173*(7), 36–47.

McCormick, R. A (1989). *The critical calling: Reflections on moral dilemmas since Vatican II.* Washington, DC: Georgetown University Press.

Melton, G. B. (1991). Ethical judgments amid uncertainty: Dilemmas in the AIDS epidemic. *Counseling Psychologist, 19*(4), 561–565.

Mitchell, J., & Morse, J. (1998). *From victim to survivor: Women survivors of female perpetrators.* Muncie, IN: Accelerated Development.

Monahan, J. (1993, March). Limiting therapist exposure to Tarasoff liability: Guidelines for risk containment. *American Psychologist, 48,* 242–250.

Morrison, C. F. (1989). AIDS: Ethical implications for psychological intervention. *Professional Psychology: Research and Practice, 20*(3), 166–171.

Murphy, W., Rau, T., & Worley, P. (1994). Offender treatment: The perils and pitfalls of profiling child sex abusers. *APSAC Advisor, 7*(1), 28–29.

National Association of Social Workers. (1990). *Policy statement on HIV and AIDS clients.* East Lansing, MI: Author.

National Association of Social Workers. (1997). *Code of ethics.* East Lansing, MI: Author.

Nelson, E., & Crawford, B. L. (1990). Suicide among elementary school age children. *Elementary School Guidance and Counseling, 25,* 123–127.

Ney, P. G. (1987). Does verbal abuse leave deeper scars? A study of children and parents. *Canadian Journal of Psychiatry, 32,* 371–378.

Norris, T. L. (1986, October). *Victim therapy with adult survivors of child sexual abuse* (Report No. CG020400). Paper presented at the annual conference of the American Association for Marriage and Family Therapy, Orlando, FL. (ERIC Document Reproduction Service No. ED 289 133).

Orvaschel, H. (1993). *Social functioning and social supports: A review of measurers suitable for use with substance abusers.* Washington, DC: National Institute on Drug Abuse, U.S. Department of Health and Human Services.

Paridies v. Benedictine Hospital, 431 N.Y.S.2d 175 (APP.Div. 1980).

Pate, R. H. (1992, Summer). Are you liable? *American Counselor, 10,* 23–26.

Peach, L., & Reddick, T. L. (1991). Counselors can make a difference in preventing adolescent suicide. *The School Counselor, 39,* 207–217.

Pearson, Q. M. (1994). Treatment techniques for adult survivors of childhood sexual abuse. *Journal of Counseling and Development, 73,* 32–37.

Peck v. The Counseling Service of Addison County, 499 A.2d 422 (1985).

Philips, I. (1983). Childhood depression: Interpersonal interactions and depressive phenomena. *American Journal of Psychiatry, 136,* 511–515.

Poland, S. (1990). *Suicide intervention in the schools.* New York: Guilford.

Rencken, R. H. (1989). *Intervention strategies for sexual abuse* (Report No. CG022806). Alexandria, VA: American Association for Counseling and Development. (ERIC Document Reproduction Service No. ED 323 483).

Repressed memory claims expected to soar. (1995, May). *National Psychologist, 4*(3), 3.

Rosenberg, M. L., Smith, J. C., Davidson, L. E., & Conn, J. M. (1987). The emergence of youth suicide: An epidemiological analysis and public health perspective. *Annual Review of Public Health, 8,* 417–440.

Roy, A. (1982). Risk factors for suicide in psychiatric patients. *Archives of General Psychiatry, 39,* 1089–1095.

Sandoval, J. (1985). Crisis counseling: Conceptualization and general principles. *School Psychology Review, 14,* 257–265.

Sanford, L. T. (1980). *The silent children: A parent's guide to the prevention of child sexual abuse.* Garden City, NY: Doubleday.

Schlossberger, E., & Heckler, L. (1996). HIV and the family therapist's duty to warn: A legal and ethical analysis. *Journal of Marital and Family Therapy, 22*(1), 27–40.

Schroeder, L. O. (1979). Legal liability: A professional concern. *Clinical Social Work Journal, 7*(3), 194–199.

Segalla, R., Wine, B., & Silvers, D. (2000). Long term group psychotherapy for women who are survivors of childhood abuse. *Psychoanalytic Inquiry, 20,* 350–358.

Seppa, N. (1996, April). Fear of malpractice curbs some psychologists' practice. *American Psychological Monitor, 2,* 129–137.

Sheeley, V. L., & Herlihy, B. (1989). Counseling suicidal teens: A duty to warn and protect. *The School Counselor, 37,* 89–101.

Skinner, H. A. (1982). *The drug abuse screening test-20 (DAST-20): Guidelines for administering and scoring.* Toronto: Addiction Research Foundation.

Sloan, I. J. (1983). *Child abuse: Governing law and legislation.* Dobbs Ferry, NY: Oceana.

Strother, D. B. (1986). Suicide among the very young. *Phi Delta Kappan, 67,* 756–759.

Swenson, L.C. (1997). *Psychology and the law for the helping professions.* Pacific Grove, CA: Brooks/Cole.

Tarasoff v. Regents of the University of California, 113 Cal. Rptr. 14, 551 P.2d. 334 (Cal. 19762).

Tarasoff v. Regents of the University of California, 13 Cal. 3d 177, 529 P.2d. 533 (1974), vacated, 17 Cal. 3d 425, 551 P.2d 334 (1976).

Thompson v. County of Alameda, 614 P.2d 728 (1980).

Tueting, P., Koslow, S. H., & Hirschfield, R.M.A. (1983). *National Institute of Mental Health: Special report on depression research* (DHHS Publication No. ADM 83-1085). Washington, DC: Government Printing Office.

VandeCreek, L., & Knapp, S. (1993). *Tarasoff and beyond: Legal considerations in the treatment of life-endangering patients* (rev. ed.). Sarasota, FL: Professional Resource Press.

Waldo, S., & Malley, P. B. (1992). *Tarasoff* and its progeny: Implications for school counselors. *The School Counselor, 40,* 56–63.

Wallace, B. (1991). *Crack cocaine.* New York: Brunner/Mazel.

Weinstock, R., & Weinstock, D. (1989). Clinical flexibility and confidentiality: Effects of reporting laws. *Psychiatric Quarterly, 60*(3), 195–214.

Weisman v. Blue Shield of California, 163 CAL. App. 3d61, 209 CAL. Rptr. 169 (CAL., ct. app., 1985).

Westfield, J. S., Witchard, K. A., & Range, L. M. (1990). College and university student suicide: Trends and implications. *Counseling Psychologist, 18*(3), 464–476.

Wise, P. S., Smead, V. S., & Huebner, E. S. (1987). Crisis intervention: Involvement and training needs of school psychology personnel. *Journal of School Psychology, 25,* 185–187.

Wood, G. J., Marks, R., & Dilley, J. (1990). *AIDS law for mental health professionals.* San Francisco: University of California AIDS Health Project.

Yarmey, A. D., & Jones, H.P.T. (1983). Is the psychology of eye witness testimony a matter of common sense? In S. M. Lloyd-Bostock & B. R. Clifford (Eds.), *Evaluating witness evidence* (pp. 323–339). New York: Wiley.

Zerbe Enns, C. (1996). Counselors and the backlash: "Rape hype" and "false memory syndrome." *Journal of Counseling and Development, 74,* 358–366.

CHAPTER

9

John C. Boylan

Consultation in the Schools and Mental Health Agencies: Models and Methods

This chapter has been included in the textbook for the purpose of providing the student with a basic understanding of consultation in schools and mental health agencies. A review of the history of consultation and of the current models of consultation is presented for the students' inspection. The authors have included two articles that examine systems and integrated approaches to consultation in the schools. The seminal work of Gerald Caplan (1970) is presented as a representative sample of mental health consultation.

It has been the authors' experience that many counselor preparation programs do not have specific course(s) designed to focus on consultation. Generally, consultation methods and models find their way into a variety of counselor preparation courses. Those students who have taken coursework in consultation will find the material to be a review. For other students, the material presented will familiarize students with some of the processes and procedures common to both school and agency consultation.

Consultation is one of the most sought-after services rendered by counselors and psychologists. Consultation was born out of the Mental Health Act of 1962 and the writing of Caplan's (1970) *The Theory and Practice of Mental Health Consultation*. From these sources have emerged the models and methods of consultation.

▦ Definition

With the growth of consultation, a diversity of opinion has developed with regard to the definition of consultation. A review of the literature by Alpert and Meyers (1983) failed to provide an agreed-upon definition of consultation. Ohlsen (1983) defined consultation as an activity in which a professional helps another person in regard to a third person or party. Caplan (1970) viewed consultation as a collaborative process between two professionals who each has his or her own area of expertise. Albee (1982) defined consultation in terms of a preventive approach to service delivery in mental health. Kirby (1985, p. 9) defined consultation in terms of four relationship conditions: (a) the relationship is voluntary, (b) the focus of attention is on the problem situation as articulated by the consultee(s), (c) the consultant is not functioning as a part of the structural hierarchy, and (d) the power that resides in the consultant's expertise is sufficient to facilitate change. Dinkmeyer, Carlson, and Dinkmeyer (1994) defined consultation as follows: "Consultation is when the main focus of the relationship is a third person (often a student) and when the relationship is characterized by collaboration on ways to help this third person" (pp. 89–90). For purposes of clarity, the definition provided by Meyers, Parsons, and Martin (1979) will be used in this chapter:

> Consultation is a helping or problem solving process occurring between a professional help giver and help seeker who has responsibility for the welfare of another person. It is a voluntary relationship in which the help giver and the help seeker share in solving a current problem of the help seeker. The help seeker profits from the relationship in such a way that future problems may be handled more positively and skillfully. (p. 4)

In addition to the problem of defining consultation, early authors (Caplan, 1970; Alpert, 1977), disagree as to the focus of consultation. The disagreement centered around consultation as a direct or an indirect service. It is important to remember that counselors and psychologists traditionally were involved in direct service to clients, i.e., consultation that focused on the individual clients and interpersonal factors affecting them.

In the 1980s, attention focused on the counselor and psychologist providing preventive approaches to service delivery (Coyne, 1987). The indirect service approach stressed consultation efforts directed toward understanding the environment of the client, with interventions aimed at assisting the professional who has responsibility for a caretaker role with the individual. With the development of indirect service approaches, the counselor or psychologist must insure that role confusion does not hamper the delivery of mental health services. An important point is to assure that counseling and consultation are seen as different and complementary forms of intervention. Bloom (1977) suggested that consultation differs from counseling or therapy in that the consultant does not assume the full responsibility for the final outcome of consultation. The consultant's role is to develop and enhance the role of the consultee, in contrast to counseling, where the focus is on the personal improvement of the client. The consultant must remember that the relationship established with the consultee is not primarily therapeutic in nature. Rather, the consultant serves in the capacity of collaborator and facilitator, to assist the consultee in performing his or her duties and responsibility in a more productive and effective manner (Bloom, p. 156).

Bloom (1977) recognized the importance of distinguishing consultation from other forms of mental health activities. He stated that consultation is different from supervision on the grounds that (a) the consultant may not be of the same professional specialty as the consultee, (b) the consultant has no administrative responsibility for the work of the consultee, (c) consultation may be more irregular than continuous in character, and (d) the consultant is not in a position of power with respect to the consultee. Similarly, Bloom (1977) differentiated consultation from counseling because in the process of counseling a clear contractual relationship exists between an individual designated as client and another individual designated as counselor. Also, the goal of consultation is improved work performance, whereas in counseling the goal is personal adjustment (p. 136).

The remainder of this chapter provides an overview and discussion of mental health consultation and school consultation models that are applicable to the practicum student and intern in counseling and psychology.

Mental Health Consultation

Mental health consultation has been widely influenced by the writing of Gerald Caplan. With the writing of the book entitled *The Theory and Practice of Mental Health Consultation* in 1970, Caplan identified four consultation types that are employed in mental health settings.

The four types of consultation are summarized here to provide the practicum student and intern with an overview of the mental health models.

- **Client-Centered Case Consultation:** A consultee has difficulty in dealing with the mental health aspects of one of his or her clients and calls in a specialist to investigate and advise on the nature of the difficulties and on how the consultee's work difficulty relates to the management of a particular case or group of cases. The consultant makes an assessment of the client's problem and recommends how the consultee should proceed.
- **Program-Centered Administrative Consultation:** The consultant is invited by an administrator to help with a current problem of program development, with some predicament in the organization of an institution, or with planning and implementation of organizational policies, including personnel policies. The consultant is expected to provide feedback to the organization in the form of a written report.
- **Consultee-Centered Case Consultation:** The consultee's work problem relates to the management of a particular client, and he or she invokes the consultant's help in order to improve handling of the case. The consultant's primary focus is upon clarifying and remedying the shortcomings in the consultee's professional functioning that are responsible for the present difficulties with the case about which he or she is seeking help.
- **Consultee-Centered Administrative Consultation:** The consultant helps the administrative staff of an organization deal with current problems in organizational policies. The focus of attention is the consultee's work difficulties and attempting to help improve his or her problem solving skills. (Caplan, 1970, pp. 109–150)

Caplan further described what he considered to be the characteristics of mental health consultation. A summary of Caplan's characteristics is presented to give the student a clear understanding of the consultation model in mental health settings.

1. Mental health consultation is a method for use between two professionals in respect to a lay client or a program of such clients.
2. The consultee's work problem must be defined by him or her as being in the mental health area, i.e., relating to (a) mental disorder or personality idiosyncrasies of the client, (b) promotion of mental health in the client, or (c) interpersonal aspects of the work situation.
3. The consultant has no administrative responsibility for the consultee's work or professional responsibility for the outcome of the client's case.
4. The consultee is under no compulsion to accept the consultant's ideas or suggestions.
5. The basic relationship between the two is coordinate. No built-in hierarchical authority tension exists.
6. The coordinate relationship is fostered by the consultant's usually being a member of another profession and coming briefly into the consultee's institution from the outside.
7. Consultation is usually given as a short series of interviews, which take place intermittently in response to the consultee's awareness of current need for help with the work problem.
8. Consultation is expected to continue indefinitely.
9. A consultant has not predetermined a body of information that he or she intends to impart on a particular consultee.
10. The twin goals of consultation are to help the consultee improve his or her handling or understanding of the current work difficulty and to increase his or her capacity to master future problems of a similar type.
11. The aim is to improve the consultee's job performance, an not his or her sense of well-being.
12. Consultation does not focus overtly on personal problems and feelings of the consultee.
13. This doesn't mean that the consultant does not pay attention to the feelings of the consultee. The consultant is particularly sensitive to these and to the disturbance of task functioning produced by personal problems.

14. Consultation is usually only one of the professional functions of a specialist, even if he or she is formally entitled "consultant."

15. Finally, mental health consultation is a method of communication between a mental health specialist and other professionals (Caplan, 1970, pp. 28–30).

An understanding of the stages and types of consultation and the characteristics of mental health counseling enables the student to begin to conceptualize an approach to consultation in light of his or her own needs as well as the needs of the consultee. The necessity of understanding a wide range of theoretical perspectives in consultation is stressed by Jacobson, Ravlin, and Cooper (1983). These authors conceptualized mental health consultation as a multilinear model:

1. The first step in the model is the development and implementation of a formal intervention plan requiring the consultant to have summarized the available information into a useful systems assessment.

2. The second step is entry into the system, which denoted the first formal contact between the two systems regarding the current consultation. Entry must be seen in the context of the agency's history.

3. The third step, relationship building, is a long-term process that transcends the time constraints of a particular consultation agreement; thus it is conceptualized as an ongoing process.

4. In the fourth step, formal interventions follow the mediation of a consultation agreement.

5. In the fifth step, though the agreement often is negotiated earlier in the consultation process, the agreement generally undergoes repeated modification in the course of the intervention process based upon the ongoing system assessment and program evaluation.

6. The sixth step, conclusion of the services provided by specific consultation, is often the precursor to subsequent cycling of the consultative process. Consequently, the termination of a consultative agreement rarely is as final as it is in clinical interventions (Jacobson, Ravlin, & Cooper, 1983, pp. 58–60).

School Consultation

Historically, consultation in schools has its roots in disciplines other than education. The fields of psychiatry, group dynamics, psychology, and organizational development have all contributed to the development of models of school consultation. Likewise, authors such as Caplan (1970) and Sarason (1971) have focused attention on the need for a coordinated sharing of expertise by professionals in the schools. The writing of these individuals has changed the focus of consultation from advice giving, in the early years, to a more coordinate, expertise-sharing process. They also have augmented the consultant's knowledge of the school as a culture and as an organization. Finally, they have contributed to a variety of techniques other than in-service education and case feedback, including group dynamics exercises, applied research techniques, themes, interference reduction, organizational development techniques, and conflict resolution procedures (Meyers et al., 1979, pp. 35–36).

Similar to mental health consultation, school consultation has generated a number of models of intervention in the schools. Parsons and Meyers (1984, pp. 5–6) discussed a model of school consultation with a focus on primary and secondary prevention. In the model are defined four categories of consultation in the schools.

- **Direct Service to the Client:** Consultation seeks to modify the behavior, attitudes, or feeling of a particular client or clients who present a problem or problems. Data about the client are gathered directly by the consultant using individual testing, interviewing, and behavioral observation of the client.

- **Indirect Service to the Client:** Consultation aims to change the behavior, attitude, or feelings of the client(s). In contrast, data are not gathered directly by the consultant. Instead the constultee gathers the necessary data to be shared with the consultant.
- **Service to the Consultee:** The target for service is the consultee rather than the consultee's client. The goal is to change the behavior, attitudes, or feelings of the consultee.
- **Service to the System:** The target for service is to improve the organizational functioning of the system as a whole. This result should lead to improved mental health for both clients and individual consultees in the organization.

Lambert (1983) discussed consultation in the schools as an interaction between a teacher and a school district employee from a mental health discipline. Although this model assumes that the consultant is school-based, nevertheless the steps in the process are the same for consultants brought in from outside the system. Lambert (1983) suggested that the process of consultation is initiated (a) when a teacher requests help, (b) when a consultant offers to assist a teacher or pupil, or (c) when a principal requests help for a teacher or for himself or herself. The objectives of school-based consultation may be a change in pupil behavior or a change in teacher behavior or both (p. 31). Lambert further elaborated what are considered to be the phases involved in school consultation:

1. The first phase is identified as the relationship building and role clarification phase, in which the consultant defuses teacher anxiety about being analyzed, exposed, and evaluated and during which time the consultant interacts so as to be seen as a helpful, nonjudgmental, and knowledgeable person.

2. The second phase, which follows several weeks later, consists of problem identification and the generation of intervention strategies. During this time, teachers and consultants are actively discussing cases, successfully sharing information from each of their professional perspectives, and developing alternative interventions to be considered and tried.

3. The third, and final, phase occurs when the teacher and consultant each understand the other's role and the teacher knows how to ask questions and can use the interaction to explore, propose, and rule out solutions. The relationship becomes one in which two professional peers can use one another effectively in exploration and discussion of matters of mutual concern (pp. 32–33).

In a similar fashion, Dustin and Ehly's (1984) model for school consultation asserts that consultation is indirect helping in which the consultant works with a second person (consultee) to help a third party (the client). This five-stage model includes the following:

1. **Phasing In:** To establish trust levels and to have the consultant employ such skills as active listening, understanding, empathy, and self-disclosure to assure relationship building between consultant and teacher

2. **Problem Identification:** To clarify the main problems being experienced by the client and to employ the skills of focusing, paraphrasing, and restatement in order to determine whether the focus of consultation is the consultee or the third party (the client).

3. **Implementation:** To assist the consultee in devising alternative change strategies. This stage is marked by consultant feedback empathy to assist the consultee in dealing with possible negative feelings associated with the process of narrowing down available strategies to the one that will be implemented.

4. **Evaluation:** To involve formation evaluation and the monitoring, implementing, and evaluating of change strategies. Consultant openness and flexibility is essential.

5. **Termination:** To bring closure to consultation arrangements and review the positive as well as negative outcomes derived from the change strategies that were implemented. The model stresses the importance of using counseling skills as they apply to the consulting process (pp. 23–28).

In the 1990s school counselors were faced with ever increasing responsibilities on the job. Finding the time to acquire the skills necessary to serve a broader set of clients was the counselors' challenge. At-risk students, reintegration of special students, and coordinating school to community services became added responsibilities of the school counselor. These indirect methods of service are sure to expand in the 21st century. In all probability, the counselor, taking on the role of consultant, will be in the forefront of the school's response to dealing with these critical issues. Consultation as a vehicle of indirect service can be used to address a variety of school issues and problems.

Many of the models of consultation (mental health, behavioral, organizational, school) can report elements of success when applied to school issues and problems. These models tend to address the issues by looking at deficits in functioning, focusing on what is wrong in the system rather than what is right in the system. A refreshing approach by Copeland and Geil (1996) suggested the application of a solution-focused method of consultation aimed at focusing on strengths rather than deficits. The job of the solution-focused consultant is to help individuals, within the system, find new solutions and amplify change. The solution-focused consultant must establish an atmosphere for solutions and change. A noncoercive, coordinate, and accepting environment will increase the chances of learning creativity and buy-in solutions.

The following is an adaptation of Copeland and Geil's stages of solution-focused consultation:

1. Develop a picture of the organization and culture. This stage involves getting all motivated parties together to discuss the "way we do things around here." The purpose is for all parties to get a picture of meanings and perceptions that influence behavior and action.

2. Identify what the organization wants to (will) accomplish. Focus upon what the organization prefers rather than expects to happen. The aim is to look to a future direction with creativity and vision.

3. Identify two or more "right solutions." Once a right solution is generated, the consultant asks for another way to accomplish the goal or vision.

4. Analyze each of the solutions in step 3 by evaluating (a) ease of implementation, (b) practicality, (c) likelihood of accomplishment of step two

5. Decide upon a small step.

6. Implement the step.

7. Examine the effects of the previous step and take another step.

8. Continue the above process until goals of step 2 are in sight (Copeland & Geil, 1996, pp. 351–354).

The solution-focused consultation model allows the consultant to be directed toward solutions without being domineering. The atmosphere of trust, respect, and open communication establishes an atmosphere for solutions and change (Copeland & Geil, 1996).

A SYSTEMS APPROACH TO SCHOOL COUNSELOR CONSULTATION*

Jo Anna White and Fran Mullis

A major component of school counselor's program is consultation with parents, teachers, administrators, and outside referral sources. This article presents an overview of the school counselor's consultation, issues related to resistance and an Adlerian model for systemic consultation. This model can be a useful tool for teachers, as well, as they consult with parents.

---

*This article appeared in *Education*, 1998, Vol. 119, No. 2, 242–252.

Children and adolescents are faced with a myriad of life stressors over which they have little control. Family transitions such as divorce and stepfamily living are such common occurrences that professionals often discount the emotional impact these changes have on children and youth. Academic difficulties related to learning disabilities, attention deficit disorder, and other neurological difficulties make going to school a stressful experience for many children. Child abuse and violence toward children is at an alarming high with children under 18 accounting for 11% of all murder victims in the United States (Greenfield, 1996).

These very serious issues affect children both emotionally and academically. Younger children have fewer resources developmentally and psychologically to improve their often dismal life situations. Teachers and other school personnel are often overwhelmed by the seriousness of children's reactions to these stressful issues, and they can clearly see how these stressors affect their students' abilities to learn and grow. It is evident to most educators that in order to help children and adolescents thrive in the school environment, collaborative efforts must be made to improve the home and school environments. Significant adults in children's lives must initiate these efforts (White, Mullis, Early, & Brigman, 1995).

The role of the school counselor is to facilitate student learning and successful socialization by focusing on the affective aspects of education. School counselors, as well as teachers and other educators, have known for decades that students' emotional well-being has a decided impact on their ability to be successful learners. While other educators are concerned with and involved in formal instructional practices, school counselors provide a developmentally appropriate, preventive guidance and counseling program that will help students to feel encouraged about the learning process as well as their relationships with others. School counselors work from a holistic, systemic approach in which they attempt to understand and assist the whole child in relationship to classroom, home, and other environments.

School counseling has a history of focusing on the remedial aspect of a program, but as the profession has matured and reexamined itself there is a clear move toward the preventive and developmental aspects of a school counseling program (Gysbers & Henderson, 1994; Muro & Kottman, 1995). " . . . the profession of school counseling has moved away from the individual, position-oriented, one-to-one, small group counseling approach to a more preventive, wellness oriented, proactive one" (Wittmer, 1993, p. 5).

The American School Counselors Association (ASCA) has long been an advocate for a balanced school counseling program that includes preventive components as well as remedial services (Campbell & Dahir, 1997). Typically school counselors organize their programs to include individual counseling, small group counseling, preventive classroom guidance lessons, and consultation with the significant adults in the student's life (Campbell & Dahir, 1997; White, et al., 1995). The ASCA described the three major components to the school counselor's role as counseling, consulting, and coordinating (ASCA, 1990). Myrick (1993) described four approaches to guidance and counseling: crisis, remedial, preventive, and developmental. He argued that these four approaches can be found in all schools. No matter what the approach to school counseling, the literature is abundant with support for the inclusion of consultation in a school counseling program (Dinkmeyer, Dinkmeyer, & Sperry, 1987; Kurpius & Rozecki, 1992; Muro & Kottman, 1995; White et al., 1995).

Rationale for School Counselor Consultation

According to Merriam-Webster (1991), a system is a regularly interacting or interdependent group of items forming a unified whole. When working with a system the focus is on the interaction of each item, or element, in the system rather than on the element itself (Gladding, 1998). The interaction of students with their teachers and other adults in the school, their interaction with other family members, and the interaction of the family with the school all have a powerful effect on the student's school success. Therefore, a systems paradigm for helping students offers an effective strategy for school counselors. Consultation with parents, teachers, and others is a systemic approach in that all of the important people in the student's life are encouraged to work together to assist the child. It is often the case that changing the way adults interact with the child (or in some cases, with each other) leads to changes in the child's behavior.

West and Idol (1993) encourage a collaborative, systemic consultation model in which all parties in the child's life work as a team to deal with individual student problems and general school problems. These teams could include parents, teachers, administrators, other school professionals and community members. The school counselor serves as a facilitator for these teams. While this team approach is valuable, it is often difficult for a school counselor to have all significant adults present at one time. Even so, school counselors can approach the problem from a systemic perspective by focusing on the connections between significant others in the child's life. There are many other reasons, discussed below, for school counselors to include systemic consultation as one of the principal components of their counseling program.

Efficient Use of Time

One very compelling reason for school counselors to consult with parents, teachers, and others, is that counselors typically have large student case loads. Although the recommended counselor-student ratio in elementary schools is 1:250, most counselors are responsible for working with 500 students or more. Consulting with teachers allows the counselor to be more efficient, because the teacher can apply strategies and information with the whole class during the entire school day or period, rather than only during a typical once-a-week individual or group counseling session. Planning strategies to be used by teachers can have an impact on hundreds of students.

A similar benefit can be achieved by consulting with parents. Not only do parents spend more time with their children than do counselors, but parents are also a very powerful influence on their children's behavior. Counselors can help parents modify their relationship with their children so that it becomes more encouraging, which may forestall the occurrence of some problems. In addition, effective strategies for handling a problem with one child can often be used for other problems in the family.

Differences in Power

Adults have much more power than children. The younger the child, the fewer resources the child has to make changes in his or her life (White et al., 1995). Counselors who work only with children frequently fight an uphill battle to stimulate changes in children's lives. By consulting with significant adults in the child's life, counselors can foster interaction with children that are more effective. Expecting children to initiate changes in their interactions with adults can be frustrating for counselors and both frightening and discouraging for children.

Maintaining a Holistic View of Problems

Student's problems are often complicated and have multiple origins. For example, poor study habits contribute to academic problems, which can bring about emotional and behavioral problems, which further contribute to the deterioration of academic work. Parents may have critical information for problem resolution that is not available to school personnel. Conversely, information that teachers, counselors, or other school personnel share with parents often is needed by parents to assist their child with a difficult situation.

Consultation with school personnel and family members allows exploration, and, hopefully, remediation of all of the factors that have a bearing on the problem. A holistic approach recognizes that children's emotions, cognitions and behaviors are connected, and they must be considered in combination in order to effect lasting change.

Involving the Teacher or Parent in the Solution

Involvement in planning a strategy for change imparts to teachers and parents a feeling of ownership in the plan and encourages a commitment to working for a solution. When people have a share in decision making they are more likely to follow through with their part in the planned intervention. Omission of input from people important to the implementation of a plan can lead to failure or even sabotage of the plan. In addition, helpful information which may be known only to parents, teachers, or counselors can be shared in a collaborative effort for change. Sharing information and ideas increases the chance of finding a workable solution.

Collaboration Between School and Home

Parental involvment in their child's education is linked to school success (Educational Resources Information Center, 1996). Inviting parents to consult with teachers and counselors about their children recognizes that they have valuable contributions to make to the consultation process, and encourages their continued involvement with the school.

The reason that many parents avoid school involvement is that they feel unappreciated or even "put down" by school personnel. Asking parents for assistance in making school a positive place for their child acknowledges that they are experts when it comes to knowing their own child, and increases the likelihood of parental cooperation.

Taking a Proactive, Preventive Approach to Problems

Teacher and counselors sometimes delay contacting parents about problems because they do not want to admit a problem exists or they do not think that parents will be responsive. Parents may not believe that problems that occur at home will influence school behavior or that home concerns are the school's business. These beliefs keep them from providing important information to school personnel.

Resistance Issues in School Counselor Consultation

Parents and teachers sometimes exhibit resistance to consultation. The consultation process itself can be opposed, and/or the strategies and interventions proposed by the school counselor or others can be the target of opposition. Typically resistance, and the person(s) exhibiting resistance, is viewed negatively. It is helpful for counselors to reframe resistance so that it can be handled more effectively. Regardless of the target of the resistance, there are several points the consultant can consider which might help to reframe it.

First, resistance is a normal and predictable response to being asked to acknowledge that a problem exists (Block, as cited in Campbell, 1993). After acknowledging that there is a problem, there is also the expectation that a change in the adult-child interaction will be forthcoming. Change brings about stress and therefore is often opposed.

Second, resistance sometimes occurs because rapport has not been established between the consultant and consultee. When school counselors recognize this type of resistance, they can use the knowledge to work on establishing a good relationship (Randolph & Graun, 1988), rather than continuing to engage in futile attempts to convince the consultee of a particular plan of action.

Third, resistance can be viewed as a sign of involvement and an opportunity to establish an alliance with the consultee (Riordan, Matheny, & Harris, 1978).

Finally, resistance sometimes indicates that parents or teachers oppose the particular course of action being discussed, not the process itself (White & Riordan, 1990). Finding an intervention that is compatible with the consultee's value system often eliminates opposition of this type.

Viewing resistance as normal part of the consultation process, rather than as a personal attack on the school counselor or an indication that the parent or teacher does not care about helping the child, provides information to the counselor which can be used to strengthen the collaborative process. Counselors must also recognize that parents and teachers may have legitimate reasons to resist consultation. Several of those reasons are discussed below.

Parent Resistance

Parents often resist becoming involved in the consultation process because they fear that they will be blamed for the problem, whatever it may be. Their own school experience may have been a negative one, and they believe that anything involving the school will be disagreeable. In addition, they may feel guilty about the problems their child is experiencing. Parents often believe that if they were "good parents" their child would not have problems. This may be one reason that parents deny that their child has a problem. It is difficult for them to admit that a problem exists because it reflects negatively on them.

Parents can feel hopeless about being able to foster change in their child's behavior. They may have tried many things in the past with little or no success. Talking with school officials again may appear to be a waste of time.

Some parents, because of their youth and inexperience, may not believe that they have anything to offer in a consultation session, or they might believe that things will work out on their own. Also, parents may be used to having the school make decisions regarding their child and have no collaborative model on which to build. For example, an invitation to participate in consultation could be seen as a summons (Campbell, 1993) which the parents cannot refuse.

Parents may be experiencing personal problems which keep them from focusing on the specific difficulties their child is having in school. These problems are part of the system and, as such, are important to acknowledge. However, financial, career, health, or other parental concerns can make participation in consultation especially burdensome and can hinder follow-up by the parents.

Differences in background and beliefs can also hamper the consultation process. Racial and cultural differences can inhibit understanding, as can discrepancies in educational or economic background. Parents might avoid consultation because they are embarrassed about their lack of formal education or their lack of economic resources. Some parents value personal privacy and are loath to share what they consider "their business" with others. Whatever the reason for parent resistance, it is important for the school counselor to be sensitive to parents' initial apprehension about consultation regarding their child.

Teacher Resistance

Teachers, like parents, are often resistant to the consultation process and to intervention strategies. They may be used to referring children to "experts" and have no model of collaboration with others to solve problems. They may also fear being blamed for the problems exhibited by the child. Teachers may also be afraid that if they disclose information during the consultation session, they may be seen as being less than professional and not doing their job (Dougherty, Dougherty, & Purcell, 1991). Although the counselor's role in consultation is not a supervisory one, uncertainty regarding the counselor's role can keep teachers from being completely open about classroom management techniques.

Sometimes teachers resist the consultation process or resist trying new strategies because they want to continue behavior with which they feel comfortable (Dougherty et al., 1991). This can result from anxiety around issues of change or from rigidity on the teacher's part.

Teachers also become discouraged because they have tried many interventions with a student that have been unsuccessful, and believe, therefore, that the student cannot be helped. Their feelings of hopelessness may result in resistance (Ellis, as cited in Dougherty et al., 1991). Sometimes feelings of hopelessness ensue from stereotypical thinking about a child. For example, it may be presumed that because a student is from a particular neighborhood, parental involvement will not be forthcoming.

Ellis (as cited in Dougherty et al., 1991) also suggested that teachers sometimes resist consultation because they fear success. It is frequently the case that teachers who are successful with problem students are given more students who have difficulty in school because they are effective with them.

Working Effectively With Resistance

Resistance to the consultation process can be overcome by emphasizing to parents and teachers that their help is essential if a successful resolution is to be found to the problem. Letting consultees know that their information and expertise is wanted can encourage them to enter into a collaborative process. The following techniques can be applied by school counselors to overcome resistance shown by parents or teachers during the consultation experience:

1. **Establish a positive atmosphere:** A positive atmosphere can be established by thanking the consultees for their participation and by identifying the child's strengths. By beginning with positive comments, parents are given the message that the consultant cares about their child, and both parents and teachers receive the message that the session will not focus entirely on negative behavior.

2. **Be empathic:** The more resistant the consultee is, the more empathic the consultant needs to be. By listening and responding empathetically, the consultant can determine the reasons for resistance, and, often, feeling "heard" can lessen opposition. Empathic listening also creates a collaborative atmosphere by demonstrating that the consultant is willing to listen to ideas and input from others. When designing intervention strategies, information gained from listening to parents and teachers can be used to devise plans that fit with their beliefs and expertise.

3. **Finds areas of agreement:** It is critical to obtain agreement in at least one area, especially if many differences exist between the consultant and consultee. Agreeing that the child is experiencing problems and that all parties want to help the child is an important beginning to the consultation process.

4. **Avoid power struggles:** No one wins a power struggle. Power struggles are an indication that resistance is occurring, and the wise consultant uses this information to determine the source of the resistance, rather than trying to win the struggle. Asking parents and teachers about their suggestions for change can avert power struggles. Additionally, asking for suggestions provides information about what has been tried, and the types of intervention that are deemed appropriate by consultees. School counselors can state that they agree that the student has a problem and that they want to help the child, but at this time they "agree to disagree" about the most appropriate way to do that.

5. **Use encouragement:** Resistance frequently occurs because of discouragement on the part of teachers and parents. Find and point out something that the teacher or parent is doing that is helpful. They can be encouraged for being concerned about the child and participating in the consultation interview. Also, listening empathetically can provide ideas about things that can be encouraged. Simply stating that being a teacher or a parent is a very difficult job can be encouraging to hear.

A Consultation Model

School counselor consultation services, like the entire counseling program, can be crisis, preventive, and developmental in nature. Consultation is predicated on the belief that in order to help students, we must attempt to affect positively the significant others in their lives. Consultation is a triadic relationship including the school counselor, the consultee (i.e., parent, teacher, administrator, other professionals) and the student. In many cases, students are not present in the consultation sessions, but they are always the focus of the approach. Ideally, sessions include all significant adults in the child's life. If this is not possible, the effect of intervention on all parties should be considered. Consultation is a proactive, problem-solving approach that encourages adults in the student's life to work together to improve social and academic concerns (Keys, Bemak, Carpenter, & King-Sears, 1998).

Consultation training is an important component to any school counselor training program (CACREP, 1996), and it is often a required course or infused into school counseling courses. In order to conduct effective consultation, school counselors must have a working model of consultation that fits their philosophy of working relationships and human behavior. One popular approach of school consultation is based on the personality theory of Alfred Adler (Dinkmeyer, Carlson, & Dinkmeyer, 1994; Gladding, 1996; Sherman & Dinkmeyer, 1987). Adler believed that, "No educator or teacher should believe that he is the only educator of a child. The waves of outside influence stream into the psyches of the children and mould the children directly or indirectly . . . " (Adler, 1930, p. 190). According to Dinkmeyer et al. (1987), Adler was a man ahead of his time. He was the first to work in consultation with clients in a public forum in front of other parents, teachers, and doctors so that they could learn through observation and large group teaching experiences.

The Adlerian approach is based on the belief that all behavior has social meaning, and one's behavior can only be understood within the social context of one's life. Adler believed that our major life goal is to belong, and that, early on, children form a definite pattern of behavior that helps them move toward that goal. Individuals create their unique lifestyles, or predictable patterns. In order to help children change, counselors must have some understanding of their individual, or predictable patterns. This must be done from a holistic perspective by enlisting the input and help of significant others in the child's life. Other Adlerian principles that facilitate effective consultation are: equality between consultant and consultee, encouragement, respect, faith in the child, and faith in the consultee (parent or teacher) (White et al., 1995). The Adlerian consultation model also can be of value to teachers as they consult with parents on a regular basis. There are four stages of this model, and each stage is essential in order to move on to the next. These stages are described below:

Developing the Relationship

The relationship between the school counselor/consultant and the counsultee is essential to the success of consultation. Adler set the stage for a respectful, encouraging relationship when he wrote in 1930, "The parents should never be reproached, even when there are just grounds. We can achieve much more when we succeed in establishing a sort of pact, when we persuade the parents to change their attitude and work with us according to our methods" (p. 241). Effective school counselor/consultants approach the consultation process with the strategic goal of developing a good working relationship with the parent or teacher. The relationship is based on equality and respect, and such a relationship can only evolve from an encouraging environment created by the consultant.

The term encouragement, used quite freely in educational language, is often misunderstood and mistaken for praise. Encouragement has a focus on the effort that one makes rather than the result of one's actions. "It is the most effective way to stimulate movement in others and to increase their feelings of worth and self acceptance" (Dinkmeyer & Losoncy, 1980, p. ix).

Problem Identification

After the consultant/school counselor has put parents or teachers at ease, it is important to get an idea of the problem from their perspective. Even though the school counselor has specific concerns, it is important to hear from the perspective of those who are extremely significant in the child's daily life. Often, parents' ideas of the problem are quite different from the school's perspective, and they often feel responsible. It is important to focus on positives and not blame. Problem identification and an agreement to work together to solve problems are essential in order to move on.

Exploration

Adlerian school counselor/consultants believe that in order to understand a child they must have an idea of how the child's family functions or the family atmosphere. In order to do this, they ask questions such as: "What are the names and ages of siblings?" "How is the child special in the family?" "How is discipline handled?" "How does a typical day go?" "What do the parents think about the child's lack of progress?" "What have been the parents' experiences in school?" Answers to these questions can provide information about how children view their lives at home.

In the case of teacher consultation it is useful to explore how the classroom operates. Issues such as how well the child gets along with other students, what the child's strengths and weaknesses are, how discipline is handled, and what specific behaviors are problematic are important. This information can assist the counselor/consultant in identifying strengths and areas of concern.

Formulate a Plan

Finally, the school counselor/consultant, parents and teachers work together to formulate a plan in which they all will be involved to help the child. This plan must be built on encouragement and cooperation. Additionally, the plan should not be overwhelming to the parent. A focus on one area at a time will help the parent and child to see small successes that can serve as building blocks for future cooperation.

It is important as the consultant and parent work together on this plan that the consultant teach the parents information that will help them to understand their child better, such as goal identification, ways to encourage, the use of typical consequences, and strategies for avoiding power struggles. For more information consult Dinkmeyer et al. (1987), Dinkmeyer and McKay (1989), and Albert (1990).

Conclusion

While there are many children in school who are suffering from family and social problems, most educators continue to focus on academics only (Noddings, 1995) Because school counselors deal with the child from a holistic perspective, they have a unique opportunity to help students feel happy and encouraged about their school experiences. This will, in turn, help them to become more productive learners and citizens.

Often school counselors work with the student only, but they know that if they have the cooperation of the student's parents and teachers the change will be more long-lasting. For this reason, most school counselors adopt a systemic approach to consultation that involves parents, teachers, administrators, and other significant people in the student's life. The Adlerian model presented in the article is based on a holistic approach to understanding a child. This model is encouraging, educational, democratic, and systemic in nature.

The Adlerian model also would serve teachers well as they consult with parents and other professions. In many schools, the school counselor provides inservice for teachers about consulting with parents. The authors are acquainted with schools in which the entire faculty and administration work from the Adlerian model in the classrooms and in consultation with others. The school counselor is the one responsible for training the faculty and modeling the approach. These schools are child-oriented, and parent-friendly. Noddings (1995, p. 336) encouraged educators to develop caring classrooms and schools "to produce people who can care competently for their own families and contribute effectively to their communities . . . our main educational aim should be to encourage the growth of competent, caring, loving, and lovable people." Effective systemic consultation, which includes the significant adults in children's lives, is a critical factor in developing caring environments.

AN INTEGRATIVE CONSULTATION FRAMEWORK:
A PRACTICAL TOOL FOR ELEMENTARY COUNSELORS*

Alex S. Hall and Meei-Ju Lin

Consultation is one of the primary responsibilities of the school counselor. The term consultation refers to the interactions between school counselors and significant adults (e.g., school teachers, administrators, or parents) in children's lives, with the purpose of assisting them to function more effectively (Thompson & Rudolph, 1988). Empirical counseling research shows that consultation is rated both as a high priority and as an important function not only in elementary school teachers's perceptions and expectations (Ginter, Scalise, & Presse, 1990; Wilgus & Shelley, 1988), but also in elementary counselors' self-ratings in actual and ideal roles (Morse & Russell, 1988). Consultation is an effective method of improving the educational progress and mental health of clients, as well as the professional functioning of counsultees (Medway & Updyke, 1985).

Current consultation models include the mental health, the behavioral, the organizational, the process, and the collaborative consultation models. Despite the fact that a wide number of these consultation models are already available to elementary school counselors, no one model has yet emerged that can be used as a superordinating framework in determining which model is likely to be most useful to elementary school counselors at this time. Available models demonstrating the sequence of the consultation process contain series limitations including the following: (a) the concept of consultation is not clearly defined (Ginter et al., 1990; Kurpius, 1985), (b) consultation models are scattered across a variety of approaches and fields (Gallessich, 1982; Medway, 1982), and (c) there remains a lack of formal training of counselors in consultation (Campbell, 1992; Carroll, 1993; Costenbader, Swartz, & Petrix, 1992). These limitations impede the implementation of consultation models by elementary school counselors. In addition, most elementary school counselors are too busy to learn each and every consultation model and the particular applications of each consultation approach. Therefore, the purpose of this article is to propose the use of an integrative framework that provides a theory-based, systematic, and eclectic approach to consultation in the elementary schools. The model we developed assumes no sophistication on the part of the counselor and can be used alone or in conjunction with other available models. This integrative consultation framework avoids the limitations of earlier models by (a) clearly defining consultation using a step-by-step framework with specific prescriptions for the consultant's role and functions, (b) providing a comprehensive treatment of all relevant variables in consultation at the elementary school level, and (c) serving as a training device for counselors who wish to professionalize their skills.

Parameters for an Integrative Consultation Model

Consultation variables are broadly investigated and discussed in the literature. Among these variables, certain common characteristics are identified. Examples of consultation variables include the consultation relationship (Brown, Pryzwansky, & Schulte, 1991; Gallessich, 1985; Gutkin & Curtis, 1982), the consultation stage (Dougherty, 1990; Gallessich, 1985; Kurpius, 1978), the consultation goal (Dougherty, 1990; Gallessich, 1985; West & Idol, 1987), the consultee role or responsibility (Brown et al., 1991; Dougherty, 1990; Gallessich, 1985; West & Idol, 1987), the consultee role (Dougherty, 1990; Gallessich, 1985; Gutkin & Curtis, 1982), and the consultant's knowledge and value system (Gallessich, 1985). In developing an integrative consultation model, all the aforementioned parameters are endorsed except the consultant's knowledge and value system, because they are usually determined by the consultant and are rarely explicated (Gallessich, 1985). In this article, the consultation parameters previously listed are reconfigured and integrated into the following section, with one addition: consultant communication skills. Communication skills are needed if consultation is to be effective, because problem solving is accomplished through interpersonal interaction, so are consultation outcomes. In this article, the foundational parameters for the integrative consultation framework are described. Furthermore, practical application of this framework to elementary school consultation is delineated.

Description of Parameters for Integrative Consultation

Our framework for an eclectic model of consultation includes the following six parameters, each of which is described briefly: consultation goal, consulting relationship, consultant role, consultee role, consultation process, and consultant communication skills.

Consultation Goal

The consultation goal refers to what the consultant and the consultee expect to accomplish. In general, the primary goal of consultation is not only to help solve a current problem, but also to help improve the consultees' skills so that they might deal more effectively with similar problems in the future. Goals will vary in relation to the consultant's theoretical orientation and in relation to the consultation stage itself. The theory base from which an elementary school counselor works will determine the goals set by both the consultant and the consultee. For example, an elementary school counselor working with a behavioral theory orientation will focus on the goal of reducing the frequency of an undesirable client-consultee behavior. Nevertheless, an elementary school counselor approaching a problem using an organizational theory orientation will want to increase organizational productivity and morale. Just as theory will derive the consultation goals, so will the stage of consultation. Consultation goals will also vary depending on the consultation stage. Specifically, a school counselor will focus on problem definition at the beginning stage but will focus on evaluation of consultation at the ending stage.

Consulting Relationship

The consulting relationship refers to the kind and quality of involvement between the consultant and consultee. This relationship is initiated by the consultee and in general involves a nonhierarchical or coordinate relationship for the purpose of solving a work-related problem (Caplan, 1970). This kind of relationship is voluntary (Dougherty, 1990) and tends to be collaborative in nature (Brown et al., 1991; Pryzwansky, 1974). The consulting relationship differs from counseling relationships in one important way: the consulting relationship provides indirect services to a third party, the client, by providing direct services to the consultee; whereas, the counseling relationship provides direct services to both a counselor and a client. The client in the consultation relationship is part of a client system (Dougherty, 1992). Because of the nature of this client system the consultant cannot separate the individual member from the larger unit of individuals involved with that client (Blake & Mouton, 1978). Therefore, the consultant works directly with the consultee and indirectly with both the client and the client system. In sum, a systems approach is essential to an understanding of contemporary consultation.

Consultant Role

In general, consultants can assume either the role of a content expert or of a process facilitator. In the content expert role, a consultant is expected to provide specific expertise that will result in solving a problem in a given client system. This usually involves first a diagnosis, then a treatment for the client, with the consultee role being that of a passive recipient of the intervention experience. Conversely, in the process facilitator role, a consultant is expected to funtion as either a catalyst or a facilitator, with the consultee role that of an active participant of the intervention effort in consultation (Schein, 1978). Therefore, the focus of an intervention using a process model of consultation is on helping the consultee figure out his or her solutions. Regardless of whether the consultant takes on an expert role or a process role, it seems apparent that both the consultant and the consultee need to be involved as collaborators in the consultation intervention, both to the degree that is appropriate at any given time and to the greatest extent possible.

Consultee Role

The characteristics of the consultee are a major influence in the consultation process. In successful school consultation, both knowledge and understanding of the consultation process by the consultee are key influencing variables (West & Idol, 1987). For elementary school consultation to be effective, the teachers, parents, or administrators involved must understand what is expected of them and how to proceed in consultation. A clear and mutually agreed-upon set of roles are essential for an effective consulting relationship (Knapp & Salend, 1984). The consultee must assume a collaborator role throughout the consultation process, and the consultee has no obligation to follow the consultant's suggestions (Brown et al., 1991; Gutkin & Curtis, 1982). In other words, the consultee remains both in charge of, and responsible for, the negotiation and the outcome inherent in the consultation process.

Consultation Process

The consultation process refers to the ways consultants work with the other person or persons to achieve consultation goals. Nearly all consultation models enumerate steps associated with problem identification and problem solving and have steps associated with data analysis, evaluation, and feedback (West & Idol, 1987). In a more extensive statement, Dougherty (1990) indicated that all consultation includes a relationship-building process, a time for definition of the problem, implementation of a plan, an evaluation component, and a termination phase. Dougherty provided a systematic way to examine the consultation process; this process is also related to three important stages of human helping: identifying problems, developing a plan for change, and producing the change itself (Egan, 1990).

Consultant Communication Skill

The counselor's communication skills have an effect on client behavior during and after the counseling session. Because of the central role of communication in consulting relationships, the verbal and nonverbal behaviors of consultants can be expected to exert similar influence over consultee behavior (Marten, Erchul, & Witt, 1992). Both the humanistic traditions (e.g., Carkhuff, 1983; Rogers, 1961), which emphasize the helper's facilitative characteristics, and the behavioral perspective (Bergan & Tombari, 1975; 1976) which emphasizes skill development, are basic approaches to interpersonal helping that require excellent communication skills. Research indicates that the consultant must communicate empathy, congruence, and positive regard to the consultee throughout the entire consulting process (Horton & Brown, 1990; Maitland, Fine, & Tracy, 1985; Weissenburger, Fine, & Poggio, 1982). Because of this, Carkhuff's helping model (1983) is seen as an appropriate framework for school-based consultation

An Integrative Framework of School-Based Consultation

Our integrative communicative framework for elementary school-based consultation is presented below. This framework is developed around the six parameters just defined. These parameters are discussed for each of the following consultation stages: entry, diagnosis, implementation, and disengagement. Note that in this discussion, we use the word consultant to signify the school counselor.

Entry Stage

The consultation process begins with the entry stage. In an elementary school setting the counselor is already physically located within the school structure or is available to the school. The primary goal of the entry stage is to complete an assessment process, initiate a collaborative relationship, and evaluate initial consultation efforts. Each school counselor needs to determine which service, counseling or consultation, better meets the needs of the consultees, and whether he or she is suitably prepared and trained to handle the tasks involved. If the preliminary assessment indicates that there is a need for consultation services, then the second goal of the entry stage is to initiate a consulting relationship.

A voluntary, nonhierarchical, and collaborative consulting relationship between the consultant and the consultee is the most important task a consultant can accomplish during the entry stage. To initiate a productive working relationship, a discussion regarding structuring of the role relationship needs to take place. In the elementary school setting, the school counselor and the teachers or administrators are likely to know each other already; because of this, the consulting relationship can be easily confused and misunderstood by the consultee if the role expections of the consultant and the consultee differ. Differences in role expectations can result in consultee resistance (Dougherty, Dougherty, & Purcell, 1991). To reduce potential client resistance, agreement concerning role expectations in consultation is vital. Carkhuff's (1983) response skills of empathy, genuineness, respect, and concreteness must be used by the consultant at the entry stage if client resistance is to be avoided.

During the entry stage, elementary school counselors, as consultants, must determine whether the time is appropriate to initiate a consulting relationship; in addition, expectations of consultation must be discussed with the consultee and a consensus must be reached regarding consultation goals. Hence, it is preferred that elementary school counselors functioning as consultants take the roles of process observer and facilitator and content collaborator to facilitate the consulting relationship, delineate the process, and work collaboratively with the consultee to achieve mutual expectations and goals.

The consultee in a consulting relationship makes dynamic contributions to the problem-solving process. Most often, it is the elementary school teacher, administrator, or parent who initiates the first contact with the school counselor and presents the problem or concern. Even when the consultation relationship is on a volunteer basis, the responsibility of problem solving is shared by both the consultant and consultee. The responsibility sharing is an important concept that the consultant as a content collaborator needs to address.

A formative evaluation begins at the entry stage and continues throughout the entire consultation process (Dougherty, 1990). A formative evaluation can consist of something as simple as generating a list of stage-relevant questions and then answering them. Examples of such questions would include: "To what degree was there congruence between the constant's abilities and consultee's needs?", " To what degree was there congruence between the role expectation of the consultant and consultee?", and "How effective were the consultant and the consultee in building a working consulting relationship with the consultee?"

Diagnosis Stage

Once the entry stage is completed, the consultation proceeds to the diagnosis stage. During the diagnosis stage, personal, interpersonal, and environmental forces involved in a given problem situation are identified. Diagnosis is viewed as a continual and reciprocal process involving both data gathering and intervention.

The goal of the diagnosis stage is to define both the problem and the relevant factors related to the problem situation. Dougherty (1990) addressed four steps of consultation diagnosis. The first step in the diagnosis stage is *data gathering*. Choosing which information domains are to be accessed depends almost entirely on the theoretical orientation of the consultant. For example, an elementary school counselor working within a behavioral model may focus on the environmental domain, whereas a counselor working within a Caplanian (Caplan, 1970) model may focus on the affective domain of the consultee. Regardless of the consultation model used in the early stage, information needs to be collected in all appropriate domains. Such domains may include client and client system. For example, when client characteristics are assessed, the information collected is related to the student's feelings, cognition, lifestyle, and developmental issues. When the client system is evaluated, the limitations that contribute to the client's problem in the environment need to be addressed.

The second step in the diagnosis stage is *problem definition*. In this stage, the client's problem is conceptualized by both the consultant and the consultee in a concrete way. From the behavioral perspective, the client's problems can be analyzed relative to the relevant domain and conceptualized in terms of how long the client's problem has taken to develop and how both past events and future expectations are related. Mutual agreement about problem definition between the consultant and the teacher or administrator is needed if consultation is to succeed.

The third step in the diagnosis stage is *goal setting*. This involves designating what is to be achieved during consultation. If goals are written down in concrete and specific terms, consultation is more likely to be successful. After the consultant and the consultee determine their mutual goals, the fourth step, *generating possible interventions*, can be used to address those goals. Possible interventions generated may reflect a collection of strategies from various models and may include interventions at the individual, group, and organizational level. Examples of these interventions have been described by Kurpius (1985).

It is essential to form a collaborative relationship between the elementary school consultant and the consultee during the diagnosis stage. The school teacher, administrator, or parent joins with the school counselor in gathering problem-related information, defining the problem, setting goals, and generating interventions. Hence, the working relationship is collaborative. If great differences exist between the consultant's and consultee's views of a problem, then the consulting relationship may become dysfunctional.

During the diagnosis stage the consultant may take the role of process or content collaborator. The particular diagnosis model a consultant adapts is influenced by the theoretical preferences held and the extent of the consultant's knowledge relevant to the consultation relationship. If the consultee is knowledgeable and can present the client's problem, the counselor as consultant may assume a process collaborator role. In this role, the consultant focuses on the process, thereby enabling the consultee to diagnose the client's problem effectively. The consultee role in the diagnosis stage requires that the school teacher, administrator, or parent works collaboratively with the counselor to define problems, set goals, and generate intervention.

Research on the behavioral perspective of consultation indicates that the consultant's verbal skills have a significant influence on the problem identification phase of consultation (Bergan & Tombari, 1976). Effective elementary school consultants are more likely to direct the consultee to topics immediately relevant to the consultation focus, and to move consultees toward an understanding of their responsibility in consultation and toward achieving a more objective view of the problem. In dealing with diagnosis issues, response skills are continually applied at the diagnosis stage. In addition, it is helpful to use advanced accurate empathy, self-disclosure, confrontation, and immediacy (Carkhuff, 1983) to establish the working alliance between the elementary school consultant and the consultee involved in the behavioral change plan.

Evaluation must occur at the diagnosis stage of consultation. Evaluation questions will relate to the comprehensiveness and meaningfulness of data gathering, clarity of problem conceptualization, adequacy of goal setting, and effectiveness of intervention.

Implementation Stage

The implementation stage is the action stage of consultation. Of course, evaluation at the implementation stage must occur. A major goal of the implementation stage is to put into effect the plan that was developed as a result of earlier consultation stages. To implement the chosen plan, at least four steps should be taken: intervention selection, plan formation, plan implementation, and plan evaluation (Dougherty, 1990). To complete these four steps, the consultant must ask the consultee the following questions: (a) What are we going to do? (b) How are we going to do it? (c) When and where are we going to do it? and (d) How well did we do it? To answer the first question, the consultee must work with the consultant to generate several possible interventions and to choose an intervention that has a high probability of success. To answer the second question, a plan must be formulated that includes objectives and procedures for implementation. To answer the third questions, the consultant and the consultee must put their plan into action and must maintain flexibility in adjusting the plan when unforeseen events occur. Finally, to answer the fourth questions, the consultant and the consultee must evaluate the outcomes of the plan.

The previous stages of consultation involved only the consultant and the consultee. In the implementation stage, the client and the client system are now contacted. In the elementary school setting, the counselor as consultant provides support to the consultee and maintains frequent contact. The consultant, however, should prevent the consultee's over reliance on the consultant's expertise. At this stage, the objective should be for consultees to learn to use the skills they have developed to solve similar problems without assistance.

During the implementation stage, the school counselor takes the role of process collaborator or content expert in working with the consultee's formulation of a plan and its enactment. When the necessary knowledge and skills in implementing the problem-solving plan are lacking in the consultee, the consultant may need to train the teacher, parents, or administrator to use the intervention, then give support in the process of implementation. The consultee should be encouraged to take ownership of the plan and its implementation. Evaluation at the implementation stage is crucial in determining the degree to which the implementation plan has been effective in reaching target goals. Both the consultant and the consultee take on the role of evaluator at this time. This evaluation can be accomplished by asking and satisfying the following questions: "What are the costs and benefits of each intervention choice?", "What is the feasibility of this plan?", " How will we implement this plan?", and "How will we evaluate the effectiveness of this plan?"

In the action stage, the elementary school counselor as consultant continues to use response and facilitation skills to maintain the consultee's involvement in and understanding of the problem situation. The skill of questioning can be used in assisting the consultee to define goals and to develop the implementation plan in objective terms, through the use of open-ended target questions, beginning with who, what, why, when, where, and how (Carkhuff, 1983).

Disengagement Stage

In the disengagement stage, the consultant prepares and begins to terminate the consultation relationship with the teacher, administrator, or parent.

Two major goals are addressed during the disengagement stage. First, the elementary school consultant and the consultee must evaluate the overall effects of the consultation process. This is referred to as "summative evaluation." Summative evaluation methods are available in the literature (e.g., Brown et al., 1991; Dougherty, 1990). The elementary school counselor does not need to be an evaluation expert, however, because several simple methods that most counselors can perform without further education or training are useful; these methods include pre-post, time-series, and self-report methods. Basically, pre-post methods assess change before and after the consultation process; time-series methods assess the trend of change during the consultation process; and, self-report methods assess information organized through rating scales, questionnaires, or checklists. All of these methods are familiar to the elementary school counselor, so the consultant can complete the evaluation process with confidence and competence.

Second, the consultant and the consultee must reduce involvement and eventually cease the consulting relationship altogether. The consultant's contact with the consultee is gradually reduced to that of periodic follow-up and, finally, termination. The plan, however, is continued even after termination and a collaborative consulting relationship is maintained in an "on call" basis. The difference between this stage and the previous consultation stages is that the triadic working relationship is first reduced gradually, and then ended.

At the disengagement stage, both the elementary school consultant and the consultee take the role of consultation observer and evaluator. They join in observing and evaluating the degree to which the plan has been implemented and the degree to which the consultation goals have been met. The consultant may intervene in the process when needed and may keep the consultation process going smoothly. Near the end of the disengagement stage, the consultant role gradually fades. At this time, the consultee becomes fully independent. When the consulting relationship is terminated, the elementary school counselor goes back to routine counseling services until the need once again arises for consultation.

Although the consulting relationship ends during the disengagement stage, the elementary school counselor should continue effective communication with the consultee. Responsive and facilitative communication skills may not occur as frequently as they did earlier in the consultation relationship due to the reduced consultation contact. At this stage, the elementary school counselor's delivery of genuine and warm messages is important in assuring the consultee that even though their consulting relationship is terminated, current and future contact is welcome.

Conclusion

A current emerging role for the school counselor is that of consultant to teacher, parents, and school administrators. For purposes of theoretical development, research, practice, and consultant training, and integrative framework for elementary school-based consultation is needed. The model presented here postulates a consultation framework that integrates five important consultation parameters: consultation goal, consulting relationship, consultant role, consultee role, and consultant communication skill. These five parameters were discussed in relations to four consultation stages: entry, diagnosis, implementation, and disengagement. This model of integrative consultation describes what can happen in the school consultation process. This framework of school consultation has three practical advantages. First, it is built on a series of higher-order, cogent, and concise concepts that are easy to understand, thus proving accessibility for elementary school counselors to deliver their consultation services more effectively. Second, the framework defines the consultant and the consultee role in consultation, a consideration that is usually neglected by school counselors. Third, the framework presents a series of parameters that uses an eclectic perspective that can be used to stimulate future research, theory building, and program evaluation in school consultation. In addition, through the use of this framework, the applied researcher and consultation trainer can proceed with their work in a more organized manner. It is our hope that future implementation and research on this framework will result in greater consultation effectiveness by elementary school counselors in the service of their consultees.

■ Guidelines for School and Mental Health Consultation

The stages of consultation outlined by Meyers et al. (1979) and Kurpius, Fuqua, and Rozecki (1993) have been adapted here and serve as guidelines for the development of the consultation plan.

Pre-entry is considered part of the consultation process because it enables the consultant to assess the degree to which he or she is the proper "fit" for the consultation situation. According to Kurpius et al. (1993), pre-entry is the preliminary stage when the consultant forms a conceptual foundation to work from and through the process of self-assessment and is able to articulate to self and others who he or she is and what services he or she can provide. Kurpius et al. (1993, p. 601) suggested that throughout this self-assessment and reflective process, consultants should understand their beliefs and values, understanding how individuals, families, programs, organizations, or systems cause, solve, or avoid problems.

Further, Kurpius et al. (1993) maintained that the pre-entry stage is essential for consultants to conceptualize the meaning and operation of consultation to themselves and be ready to do the same with their consultees or consultee system. To this end, the following questions are often helpful:

- What models, processes, theories, and paradigms do you draw on to conceptualize your model of helping?
- How do you define consultation to the consultee or consultee system?
- Do you see the process of consultation as triadic (consultant, consultee, client) or didactic (consultant and client)?
- When is vision, looking into the future, and planning a better intervention than cause-and-effect problem solving?
- What about acting as judge and evaluator of your consultees?

Entry into the System

The consultant's entry into the system is a crucial step in determining the success or failure of consultation efforts. Gallessich (1982) delineated several steps in the process of formal entry into the system. For the external consultant, entry usually begins with the exploration of the match between the organization's needs and the consultant's skill. Discussions between the consultant and members of the organization center around descriptive information about the organization, its needs, and desired outcomes. The consultant's skill, style of consultation, and a plan of how consultation efforts can be implemented in the setting are discussed and negotiated. Once the parties have agreed that consultation is indeed needed, the process proceeds to the negotiation of an informal or formal contract. The formulation of a contract follows the consultant having defined his or her function and role in the system. A clear understanding of the specific duties and functions of the consultant must be presented to personnel involved in the consultation effort. Negotiating a contract with key personnel serves to insure that the highest level of administrators as well as subordinates participate in the consultation process. Involvement of all personnel provides a smooth transition into the system and lessens the amount of resistance that can be encountered.

The formal discussion of the contract should include:

- Goals or intended outcomes of consultation
- Identity of the consultee
- Confidentiality of service and limits of confidentiality
- Time frame: How long will the service be provided to the organization? To the individual consultee?
- Time(s) the consultant will be available

- Procedures for requesting to work with the consultant
- Ways to contact the consultant if needed
- Possibility of contract renegotiation if change is needed
- Fees, if relevant
- Consultant's access to different sources and types of information within the organization
- Person to whom the consultant is responsible (Brown, Pryzwansky, & Schulte, 1987, p. 137)

Orientation to Consultation

Orientation to consultation requires the consultant to communicate directly with key personnel in the system. Personnel need to know what to expect from the consultant and the consultant relationship. Initially the consultant, in establishing a working relationship, must discuss roles the consultant and consultees will play in the process. This enables all parties to share in the expression of their needs and preferences and creates an atmosphere of open discussion and communication. Typical questions addressed in the orientation include the following:

- What are the consultant's expectations about consultation?
- What roles will the consultant and consultee assume in the consultative effort?
- What are the parameters of the consultant's interventions?
- What are the ethical concerns of the consultee?
- What are the parameters of confidentiality?
- How long will the consultation take?
- What are the procedures governing the gathering of data?
- What are the guidelines for the giving and receiving of feedback?
- What are the procedures used in the assessment of the consultation plan?

Problem Identification

Once the consultant and consultee have oriented themselves to the process of consultation, the consultant needs to identify the problem(s) to be addressed. A first step in problem identification is to meet with the consultee to gather appropriate data. Problem identification begins with establishing goals and objectives to be accomplished in consultation. Specific outcomes to be expected and the format for assessing outcomes is discussed. For example, questions to be considered might include the following:

- What are your general concerns about the problem?
- What needs to be accomplished to overcome your concerns?
- What role will the consultee play in overcoming the problem?
- What aspects of the consultee's problem are most distressing?

Consultation Intervention

Having defined the problem and reviewed the data gathered with the consultee, the consultant proceeds with the development of a specific intervention plan. The plan will include the establishment of objectives, the selection of strategies to be implemented, and the assessment procedures to be followed. Bergan (1977) suggested the following four-point outline as part of implementing a consultation plan:

1. **Make sure that the consultee and consultant agree upon the nature of the problem.** Problem identification during the consultation process is critical to the overall success of consultation and sets the stage for the establishment of the consultant-consultee relationship. During the process,

the consultant's main priority is to assist the consultee in identifying and clarifying the main problem that is experienced by the client. According to Dustin and Ehly (1984), the skills and techniques of focusing, paraphrasing, goal setting, empathy, and genuineness are particularly valuable at this problem identification stage. These skills assist in the development of a plan based upon authenticity and collaborative commitment between the consultant and consultee. According to Meyers et al. (1979), a major task of the consultant is to determine which of four levels of consultation is most appropriate in conceptualizing the problem. The specific consultative techniques will vary depending upon whether the consultant chooses to respond with direct service to the client (level 1), indirect service to the client (level 2), direct service to the teacher (level 3), or direct service to the organization (level 4). Regardless of the level to be addressed, the consultant and consultee must agree upon the nature of scope of the problem.

2. **Complete either the setting and intrapersonal analysis or skills analysis.** One role of the consultant is to help the consultee to accurately estimate the importance of situations, as well as to develop self-efficacy expectations regarding performance. Once performance of a productive behavior has been completed, self-evaluation based on reasonable standards must occur. These processes can be facilitated through modeling and feedback to the consultee. Often, motivation can be enhanced by reminding the consultee about the possible positive outcomes of consultation, helping to set goals and correspond with his or her own standards and developing situations that will build confidence that he or she can perform the skills needed to solve the problem (Brown et al., 1987, p. 284).

3. **Design a plan to deal with the identified problem:**

   (a) establish objectives,
   (b) select interventions,
   (c) consider barriers to implementations, and
   (d) select appropriate procedures.

   Once the problem has been identified, the consultant and consultee work to establish realistic goals—the objectives of the consortium effort. Setting realistic expectations for the outcomes of consultation implies communication about and knowledge of environmental consultee constraints. Further, Bardon (1977) asserted that successful consultation requires consultees who are knowledgable of the consultation process. Without this, understanding discordant expectations between consultant and consultee frequently will lead to resistance (Piersel & Gutkin, 1983). Gutkin and Curtis (1982) asserted that unless consultees actively contribute during consultation interactions, they often will be frustrated by recommendations that are inconsistent with their own thinking, feel little psychological ownership of treatment plans, and fail to expand their own professional skills. This agreement and acceptance of objectives of the consultation plan must be assured before consultation interventions can be planned.

   The selection of intervention strategies should rest with the consultee (Bergan, 1977). The consultee involvement in the selection process will raise the client's awareness of the problem and should enhance motivation by engaging clients in goal setting and evaluation. The major issue in selecting intervention strategies is their appropriateness to the setting and the amount of time needed to monitor strategies. Brown (1985), in his discussion of the training of consultants, suggested that the following questions be asked:

   (a) Is the intervention technically correct?
   (b) Why was the intervention selected over others?
   (c) How much work and change will this intervention cause for the consultee, or if the consultee involves the organization, what structure must change and what are the sources of resistance to this change?
   (d) How will the process and outcomes of the intervention be monitored?
   (e) If this fails what is proposed? (pp. 421-422)

   Reimers, Wacker, and Koepple (1987) suggested that a number of factors influence the selection of interventions. In general, the more severe the problem, the higher the acceptance level of all proposed treatments.

4. **Make arrangements for follow-up sessions with the consultee.** Successful termination of consultation includes the need on the part of the consultant to express an openness to work with the consultee again with other presenting problems. In addition, the collecting of data from the consultee on the outcomes of change efforts can document effective consultation and justify its use in professional practice (Dustin & Ehly, 1984).

Assessing the Impact of Consultation

The success or failure of consultation interventions is determined by assessing the degree to which the results are congruent with the specific objectives. Data for making this determination comes from the observations that began during the entry process and have continued throughout the consultation process. Brown et al. (1987) suggested that steps in the evaluation process are as follows:

1. **Determine the purpose(s) of the evaluation:** The extent to which consultees provide or gather data affects their involvement at this point. The opportunity to make choices that will affect the time that needs to be directed to evaluation as well as the types of information that are collected will contribute to the ownership of the evaluation. A major issue to be considered is the confidentiality of the information to be presented.

2. **Agree on measurements to be made:** The consultant and consultee must agree on methods and procedures of measurement. Measures must specifically address the objective and goals of the intervention plan.

3. **Set a data collection schedule:** the consultant and consultee agree upon a formalized calendar of data collection. The method of collection, the tasks assigned to each party, and the method for summarizing and reporting data are discussed.

4. **Develop a dissemination plan:** The dissemination plan, which includes the format in which data is reported, needs to be carefully considered by both parties. Issues surrounding the reporting of data, the individuals to whom data are reported, and the confidentiality of the data are agreed upon and follow a predetermined plan of action.

5. **Concluding consultation:** The termination of the consultation process is as important as the initial entry into the system. An imperative step is for the consultant to provide the consultee with an open invitation to seek further assistance as the need arises. Follow-up of consultation activities insures that the consultant and consultee have the opportunity to measure the effects of the process over time. The degree to which the termination process is perceived as a smooth transition can determine whether consultation services will be sought in the future (pp. 243-244).

The Consultation Rating Form (Form 9.1) is included in the "Forms" section at the end of this book for use by the site supervisor and university supervisor. This rating form can be used to evaluate consultation activities carried out by the counseling or psychology intern. The form can be used as either an interim or a final evaluation.

Process and Content Models of Consultation

The writings of Schein (1969, 1990) focused upon the need for the helper/consultant to understand the basic assumptions he or she brings to the consultation relationship. Rockwood (1993), in a special issue of the *Journal of Counseling and Development*, discussed Schein's consultation models—examining content versus process components of problems and problem solving. The basic components and major assumptions of the Purchase-of-Expertise Model, Doctor-Patient Model, and Process Consultation Model are outlined here for your consideration.

The Purchase-of-Expertise Model

The Purchase-of-Expertise Model makes the following assumptions:

1. The client has to have made a correct diagnosis of what the real problem is.
2. The client has identified the consultants capabilities to solve the problem.
3. The client must communicate what the problem is.
4. The client has thought through and accepted all the implications of the help that will take place (Schein, 1978).

The Purchase-of-Expertise Model, a content-oriented approach, enables clients to remove themselves from the problem, relying on the skills and expertise of the consultant to "fix" the problem.

The Doctor-Patient Model

The Doctor-Patient Model also focuses upon content and assumes that the diagnosis and prescription for the problem solution rest solely in the hands of the consultant:

1. The client has correctly interpreted the organizational assumptions and knows where the sickness is.
2. The client can trust the diagnosis.
3. The person or group defined as such will provide the necessary information to make the diagnosis.
4. The client will understand and accept the diagnosis, implement the prescription, and think through and accept the consequences.
5. The client will be able to remain healthy after the consultant leaves (Schein, 1978).

The Process Consultation Model

The Process Consultation Model focuses upon how problems are solved in a collaborative effort:

1. The nature of the problem is such that the client not only needs help in making a diagnosis but would also benefit from participating in the making of the diagnosis.
2. The client has constructive intent and some problem-solving abilities.
3. Ultimately, the client is the one who knows what form of intervention or solution will work best in the organization.
4. When the client engages in the diagnosis and then selects and implements interventions, there will be an increase in his or her future problem-solving abilities (Schein, 1978).

Process consultation is systematic in that it accepts the goals and values of the organization as a whole and attempts to work with the client within those values and goals to jointly find solutions that will fit within the organizational system (Rockwood, 1993).

Resistance to Consultation

Resistance in consultative relationships is defined as "What occurs when the consultant is unsuccessful in influencing the consultee to engage actively in the problem solving process" (Piersel & Gutkin, 1983). Berlin (1977) identified four types of resistance to consultation: inertia, active opposition, planned ineptitude, and feared loss of power. Similarly, Parsons and Meyers (1984) discussed four types of organizational resistance:

1. **The desire for systems maintenance:** The entrance of the consultant into the system requires the system to adapt to new input that drains energy and threatens the system. To avoid this pitfall, Parsons and Meyers (1984) suggested that the consultant should be careful not to threaten existing roles or challenge others' jobs or role definitions. The simpler the consultant's entry and the less change in structure, tone, process, or product it entails, the easier it will be for the consultant to avoid resistance based upon system maintenance (p. 102).

2. **The consultant as the outsider:** The consultant often is viewed as an alien in the organization and is treated with suspicion and resistance. The consultant should become familiar with the institution's history, mission, philosophy, and procedures and increase his or her availability to and contact with the staff to reduce this outsider status.

3. **The desire to reject the new as nonnormative:** The desire to maintain status quo by conforming to existing norms in the organization. The consultant must guard against tampering with "time honored" programs, processes, and procedures. Consultant sensitivity to organizational vulnerability is essential.

4. **The desire to protect one's turf or vested interests:** The consultant must recognize that his or her presence is often viewed as an intrusion on the consultee's area of interest or professional responsibility. Involving the consultee in the process would tend to lessen the resistance (pp. 102–106).

Similarly, a number of authors have identified specific variables that increase resistance to consultation. Lin and Zaltsman (1973) suggested that the more complex and involved the intervention, the more likely it is that it will meet with resistance. Kast and Rosenweig (1974) suggested that resistance is tied to the ability to change agents to accurately communicate the nature of interventions to consultees. Reimers, Wacker, and Keppl (1987) suggested that the less time and resources needed to implement interventions, the greater the acceptance. Bardon (1977) asserted that successful consultative interactions require consultees who are knowledgeable of consultation processes. Piersel and Gutkin (1983) maintained that discordant expectations between consultant and consultees will frequently lead to resistance.

■ Contracting and the Forces of Change in the Organization

Kurpius et al. (1993) suggested that an understanding of the cycles of change and the forces of change within the organization are helpful in gaining a better understanding of problems and culture surrounding the problem in the organization. Stages of change include the following:

1. **Development:** Help is needed at an early stage of a new problem or program.

2. **Maintenance:** Things are becoming stagnant and falling behind, needing help to improve. This stage shows signs of consultee desire and motivation for change.

3. **Decline:** Things are worse and consultees recognize that they cannot solve the problem. Consultee may want a quick fix and have high expectations placed in the consultant.

4. **Crisis:** Consultee or consultee system is desperate for help. The consultant may look for dependency first, but it is important that consultees understand that their situation and the investment needs to return to a stable state.

The forces of change within the system need to be understood for consultation to proceed. When the system is closed to change and internal forces vary between being for or against change, there is usually little opportunity for change to occur. When the system recognizes that change is needed but forces for and against change are balanced, progress is possible but slow moving. When the forces for change are external to the members who prefer not to change, one can expect a high degree of conflict and slow change. Finally, when the members recognize the need for help and all want help to improve, then the best chance for successful helping occurs (Kurpius et al., 1993, p. 602).

These models can serve as a test of the feasibility of the consultant's effort and the type of contract the consultant will implement. The formal discussion of the contract between the consultant and the consultee should include a number of critical questions to be answered before a contract is developed and implemented. According to Remley (1993), consultation contracts should do the following:

1. Clearly specify the work to be completed by the consultant.
2. Describe in detail any work products expected from the consultant.
3. Establish a time frame for the completion of the work.
4. Establish lines of authority and the person to whom the consultant is responsible.
5. Describe the compensation plan for the consultant and the method of payment.
6. Specify any special agreement or contingency plans agreed upon by the parties.

Remley (1993) suggested that some individuals complain that written contracts are too legalistic and signify a distrust between the consultant and consultee. Consultation gives a business arrangement and should be entered into in a businesslike fashion. By reducing to written form agreements that have been reached by the parties, misunderstandings can be identified and resolved before further problems arise.

Summary

Consultation in schools and mental health agencies is a highly sought-after skill, and one with which counseling and psychotherapy interns should become familiar. In this chapter, the models and methods of consultation were presented to provide the student with an overview of the ways to organize and establish consultative relationships. The differences between mental health consultation and school consultation have been discussed, along with critical issues such as resistance. Systems and integrative approaches to consultation were chosen as representative samples of consultation strategies, and guidelines for consulting in the school were presented. This chapter also cited a form (Form 9.1) that can be used to assess the intern's consultation activities and that can provide valuable feedback that can help the student to refine and enhance his or her consultation skills.

Suggested Readings

Bergner, R. M. (1998). Characteristics of optimal clinical case formulations. *American Journal of Psychotherapy, 52,* 287–291.

Brack, C. J., & Brack, G. (1996). Mental health counsultation. In defense of merging theory and practice. *Journal of Mental Health Counseling, 18,* 347–358.

Bradley, L. J., & Gould L. T. (1994). Supervisor resistance. ERIC Digest. Greensboro, NC: ERIC Clearing House on Counseling and Student Services.

Freer, P., & Watson, T. S. (1999). A comparison of parent and teacher acceptability ratings of behavioral and conjoint behavioral consultation. *School Psychology Review, 28,* 672–685.

Gable, R. A., & Friend, M. (1990). Interview skills for problem identification in school consultation. *Preventing School Failure, 35,* 1–6.

Leddick, G. R. (1994). Models of clinical supervision. ERIC Digest. Greensboro, NC: ERIC Clearing House on Counseling and Student Services.

Mendoza, D. W. (1993). A review of Gerald Caplan's theory and practice of mental health consultation. *Journal of Counseling and Development, 71,* 629–636.

Riordan, R. J., Matheny, K. B., & Harris, C. W. (1978). Helping counselors minimize client reluctance. *Counselor Education and Supervision, 20,* 6–13.

References

Adler, A. (1930). *The education of children*. South Bend, IN: Gateway Editions, Ltd.

Albee, G. W. (1982). The politics of nature and nurture. *American Journal of Community Psychology, 10,* 1–36.

Albert, L. (1990). *Cooperative discipline: Classroom management that promotes self-esteem*. Circle Pines, MN: American Guidance Service.

Alpert, J. L. (1977). Some guidelines for school consultation. *Journal of School Psychology, 15,* 308–319.

Alpert, J. L., & Meyers, J. (1983). *Training in consultation: Prospectives from mental health, behavioral, and organizational consultation*. Springfield, IL: Charles C. Thomas.

American School Counselor's Association. (1990) *role statement: The school counselor*. Alexandria, VA: ACA Press.

Bardon, J. I. (1977). *The consultee in consultation: Preparation and training*. Paper presented at annual meeting, American Psychological Association, San Francisco.

Bemak, F., Carpenter, L.S., & King-Sears, M.E. (1998). Collaborative counsultant: A new role for counselors serving at-risk youths. *Journal of Counseling and Development, 76,* 123–133.

Bergan. J. R., (1977). *Behavior consultation*. Monterey, CA: Brooks/Cole.

Bergan, J. R., & Tombari, M. L (1975). The analysis of verbal interactions occurring during consultation. *Journal of School Psychology, 13,* 209–226.

Bergan, J. R., & Tombari, M. L (1976). Consultant sell and efficiency and the implementation and outcomes of consultation. *Journal of School Psychology, 14,* 3–14.

Berlin, I. (1977). Resistance to mental health consultation directed as change in public institutions. *Community Mental Health Journals, 15*(2), 119–128.

Blake, R.R., & Mouton, J.S. (1978). Toward a general theory of consultation. *Personnel and Guidance Journal, 56,* 328–330.

Bloom, B. L. (1977). *Community mental health: A general introduction*. Monterey, CA: Brooks/Cole

Brown, D., Pryzwansky, W. B., & Schulte, A. C. (1991). *Psychological consultation: Introduction to theory and practice*. Boston, MA: Allyn & Bacon.

Brown, D. (1985). The preservice training and supervision of consultants. *The Counseling Psychologist, 13,* 410–425.

Brown, D., Pryzwansky, W. B., & Schulte, A. C. (1987). *Psychological consultation: Introduction to theory and practice*. Boston: Allyn & Bacon.

Campbell, C. A. (1992). The school counselor as consultant: Assessing your aptitude. *Elementary School Guidance & Counseling, 26,* 237–250.

Campbell, C. (1993). Strategies for reducing parent resistance to consultation in the schools. *Elementary School Guidance & Counseling, 28,* 83–91.

Campbell, C. A. & Dahir, C. A. (1997). *The national standards for school counseling programs*. Alexandria, VA: ASCA.

Caplan, G. (1970). *The theory and practice of mental health consultation*. New York: Basic Books.

Carkhuff, R. R. (1983). *The art of helping*. Amherst, MA: Human Resource Development Press.

Carroll, B. W. (1993). Perceived roles and preparation experiences of elementary counselors: Suggestions for change. *Elementary School Guidance & Counseling, 27,* 216–227.

Copeland, E. P., & Geil, M. (1996). Applying a solution focus to consultation. *Family Journal, October 1996,* 4, 351–357.

Cormier, W. H., & Cormier, L. S. (1985). *Interviewing strategies for helpers*. Monterey, CA: Brooks/Cole

Costenbader, V., Swartz, J., & Petrix, L. (1992). Consultation in the schools: The relationship between preservice training, perception of consultative skills, and actual time spent in consultation. *School Psychology Review, 21,* 95–108.

Council for the Accreditation of Counseling and Related Educational Programs. (1996). *CACREP accreditation and procedures manual*. Alexandria, VA: Author.

Coyne, R.K. (1987). *Primary prentive counseling: Empowering people and systems*. Muncie, IN: Accelerated Development.

Dinkmeyer, D. Jr., Carlson, J., & Dinkmeyer, D., Sr. (1994). *Consultation: School mental health professionals as consultants*. Muncie, IN: Accelerated Development.

Dinkmeyer, D.C., Dinkmeyer, D. C., Jr., & Sperry, L. (1987). *Adlerian counseling and psychotherapy* (2nd ed.). Columbus, OH: Merrill

Dinkmeyer, D., & Losoncy, L. E. (1980). *The encouragement book*. Englewood Cliffs, NJ: Prentice-Hall.

Dougherty, A. M. (1990). *Consultation practice and perspectives*. Pacific Grove, CA: Brooks/Cole.

Dougherty, A. M. (1992). School consultation in the 1990s. *Elementary School Guidance & Counseling, 26,* 162–164

Dougherty, A. M., Dougherty, L. P., & Purcell, D. (1991). The sources and management of resistance to consultation. *The School Counselor, 38,* 178–186.

Dustin, D., & Ehly, S. (1984, September). Skills for effective consultation. *The School Counselor,* 25–28.

Educational Resources Information Center. (1996). *Welcoming parents at your school: Strategies that work*. Bloomington, IN: ERIC/EDINFO Press.

Egan, G. (1990). *The skilled helper.* Pacific Grove, CA: Brooks/Cole.

Erchul, W. P., & Conoley, C. W. (1991, February). Helpful theories to guide counselors' practice of school based consultation. *Elementary School Counseling and Guidance, 25,* 204–212.

Gallessich, J. (1982). *The profession and practice of consultation.* San Francisco: Jossey-Bass.

Gallessich, J. (1985). Toward a meta-theory of consultation. *The Counseling Psychologist, 13,* 336–354.

Ginter, E. J., Scalise, J. J., & Presse, N. (1990). The elementary counselor's role: Perceptions of teachers. *The school Counselor, 38,* 19–23.

Gladding, S.T. (1998). *Family therapy: History, theory, and practice* (2nd ed.). Upper Saddle River, NJ: Prentice-Hall.

Gladding, S.T. (1996). *Counseling: A comprehensive profession.* Englewood Cliffs, NJ: Prentice-Hall.

Greenfield, L. A. (1996). *Child victimizers: Violent offenders and their victims.* (Department of Justice Publication NO NJC-153258). Annapolis, MD: Department of Justice.

Gutkin, T. B., & Curtis, M. J. (1982). School-based consultation: Theory and techniques. In C. Reynolds & T. B. Gutkin (Eds.), *The handbook of school psychology* (pp. 796–828). New York: Wiley.

Horton, G. E., & Brown, D. (1990). The importance of interpersonal skills in consulate-centered consultation: A review. *Journal of Counseling & Development, 68,* 423–426.

Hutchins, D. F., & Cole, C. G. (1992). *Helping relationships and strategies* (2nd ed.). Monterey, CA: Brooks/Cole.

Jacobson, E., Ravlin, M., & Cooper, S. (1983). Issues in training of mental health consultants in community mental health centers. In J. L. Alpert & J. Meyers (Eds.), *Training in consultation: Prospectives from mental health, behavioral and organizational consultation* (pp. 47–80). Springfield, IL: Charles C. Thomas.

Kast, F. E., & Rosenweig, J. E. (1974). *Organization and management: A system approach* (2nd ed.). New York: McGraw-Hill.

Kirby, J. (1985). *Consultation: Practice and practitioner.* Muncie, IN: Accelerated Development.

Knapp, S., & Salend, S. J. (1984). Maintaining teacher adherence in behavioral consultation. *Elementary School Guidance & Counseling, 18,* 287–294.

Kurpius, D. J. (1978). Consultation theory and process: An integrated model. *Personnel and Guidance Journal, 56,* 335–338.

Kurpius, D. J. (1985). Consultation intervention: Successes, failures, and proposals. *The Counselling Psychologist, 13,* 368–389.

Kurpius, D. J., & Rozecki, T. (1992). Outreach advocacy, and consultation: A framework for prevention and intervention. *Elementary School Guidance & Counseling, 26,* 176–189.

Kurpius, D., Fuqua, R., & Rozecki, T. (1993, July/August). The consulting process: A multidimensional approach. *Journal of Counseling and Development, 71,* 601–606.

Lambert, N. M. (1983). Prospectives on training school-based consultants. In J. L. Alpert & J. Meyers (Eds.), *Training in consultation: Prospectives from mental health, behavioral and organizational consultation* (pp. 29–46). Springfield, IL: Charles C. Thomas.

Lin, N., & Zaltsman, G. (1973). Dimensions and innovations. In G. Zaltsman (Ed.), *Processes and phenomenons of social change* (pp. 93–115). New York: Wiley and Sons.

Maitland, R. E., Fine, M. J., & Tracy, D. B. (1985). The effects of an interpersonally based problem-solving process on consultation outcomes. *Journal of School Psychology, 23,* 337–345.

Martens, B. K., Erchul, W. P., & Witt, J. C. (1992). Qualifying verbal interactions in school-based consultation: A comparision of four coding schemes. *School Psychology Review, 21,* 109–124.

Medway, F. J. (1982). School consultation research: Past trends and future directions. *Professional Psychology, 13,* 422–430.

Medway. F. J., & Updyke, J. F. (1985). Meta-analysis of consultation outcome studies. *American Journal of Community Psychology, 13,* 489–505.

Merriam-Webster. (1991). Webster's ninth new collegiate dictionary. Springfield, MA: Author

Meyers, J., Parsons, R. D., & Martin, R. (1979). *Mental health consultation in the schools.* San Francisco: Jossey-Bass.

Morse, C. L., & Russell, T. (1988). How elementary counselors see their role: An empirical study. *Elementary School Guidance & Counseling, 23,* 54–62.

Muro, J. J., & Kottman, T. (1995). *Guidance and counseling in the elementary and middle schools.* Madison, WI: Brown and Benchmark.

Myrick, R. D. (1993). *Developmental guidance and counseling: A practical approach* (2nd ed.). Minneapolish, MN: Educational Media Corporation.

Noddings, N. (1995, January). A morally defensible mission for schools in the 21st century. *Phi Delta Kappan,* 365–368.

Ohlsen, M. M. (1983). *Introduction to counseling.* Itasca, IL: F.E. Peacock.

Parsons, R. D., & Meyers, J. (1984). *Developing consultation skills.* San Francisco: Jossey-Bass.

Piersel, W. C., & Gutkin, F. B. (1983). Resistance to school based consultation: A behavioral analysis of the problem. *Psychology in the Schools, 20,* 311–320.

Pryzwansky, W. B. (1974). A reconsideration of the consultation model for delivery of school-based psychological services. *American Journal of Orthopsychiartry, 44,* 579–583.

Randolph, D. L., & Graun, K. (1988). Resistance to consultation: A synthesis for counselor-consultants. *Journal of Counseling and Development, 67,* 182–184.

Reimers, T. M., Wacker, D. P., & Keppl, G. (1987). Acceptability of behavioral interventions: A review of the literature. *School Psychology Review, 16,* 212–227.

Remley, T. P. (1993). Consultation contracts. *Journal of Counseling and Development, 72,* 157–158.

Rockwood, G. F. (1993, July/August). Edgar Schein's process versus content consultation models. *Journal of Counseling and Development, 71,* 636–638.

Rogers, C. (1961). *On becoming a person.* Boston, MA: Houghton Mifflin.

Sarason, S. B. (1971). *The culture of the school and the problem of change.* Boston: Allyn and Bacon.

Schein, S. B. (1969). *Process consultation.* Reading, MA: Addison Wesley.

Schein, E. H. (1978). The role of the consultant: Content expert or process facilitator? *The Personnel and Guidance Journal, 56,* 339–345.

Schein, E. H. (1990). Organizational culture. *American Psychologist, 45,* 109–119.

Sherman, R., & Dinkmeyer, D. (1987). *Systems of family therapy: An Adlerian integration.* New York: Brunner/Mazel.

Thompson, C. L., & Rudolph, L. B. (1988). *Counseling Children.* Pacific Grove, CA: Brooks/Cole.

Weinrach, S. G. (1989). Guidelines for clients of private practioners: Committing the structure to print. *Journal of Counseling and Development, 67,* 289–300.

Weissenburger, J. W., Fine, M. J., & Poggio, J. P. (1982). The relationship of selected consultant/teacher characteristics to consultation outcomes. *Journal of School Psychology, 20,* 263–270.

West, J. F., & Idol, L. (1987). School consultation (part I): An interdisciplinary perspective on theory, models, and research. *Journal of Learning Disabilities, 20,* 388–408.

West, J. F., & Idol, L. (1993). The counselor as consultant in the collaborative school. *Journal of Counseling and Development, 71,* 678–683.

White, J., Mullis, F., Earley, B., & Brigman, G. (1995). *Consultation in schools: The counselor's role.* Portland, ME: J. Weston Walch

White, J., & Riordan, R. (1990). Some key concerns in leading parent education groups. *The Journal for Specialists in Group Work, 15,* 201–205.

Wilgus, E., & Shelley, V. (1988). The role of the elementary school counselor: Teacher perceptions, expectations, and actual functions. *The School Counselor, 35,* 259–266.

Wittmer, J. (1993). *Managing your school counseling program: K-12 developmental strategies.* Minneapolis, MN: Educational Media.

John C. Boylan

Internship Preparation

This chapter addresses preparation for the internship component of the student's training program. Emphasis is placed upon the procedures for evaluating and obtaining internship placement in an agency or school setting. This section will provide the student with an overview of what are considered to be the fundamental steps in selecting and evaluating an internship placement.

The material in this section is structured based upon the assumption that the student has completed all or almost all formal coursework at the training institution and is completing his or her internship experience at an approved internship site. An important concept to note is that the internship experience is typically quite different from previous prepracticum and practicum experiences. In the internship, the major responsibility for the supervision of the intern falls upon the site supervisor. Thus, the student needs to formalize the relationship with the site supervisor to ensure that the requirements of the internship are consistent with the goals of the institution and with the student's personal and professional goals.

The transition from practicum to internship can create considerable concern for the student. Selecting an internship site without adequate knowledge of the requirements of both the university training program and the specific internship sites to be considered prevents the student from making an informed decision regarding placement. Although the selection process may be viewed by some students as an opportunity to explore experiences that are available for training and supervisions, other students often feel pressured to make a decision based upon limited information without adequate thought and preparation.

▓ Selection and Evaluation of an Internship Site

A major issue to be addressed by the prospective intern is the appropriateness of the internship experience in relationship to the student's personal and professional goals. A well-recognized fact is that the completion of an internship experience that meets the student's career needs and program needs, in addition to providing good supervision and training, enhances the student's professional viability.

The initial step in the selection of an internship site requires that the student gather as much information as possible about each potential internship site and personnel. In preparation, a number of questions need to be addressed:

- Will the internship site provide me with a wide variety of professional activities in keeping with my training and professional goals?
- Does the internship client or patient population represent the type of population with whom I desire to work?
- Will I be exposed to all the activities that a regular employed staff member would experience?
- Will I be provided with direct supervision by a trained qualified supervisor?
- Have the internship site personnel had experience in working with interns or is this the first time an intern has been placed there?
- Do/will appropriate liaison activities occur between the university training program and the internship staff?

Answers to these questions enable the student to gain an initial overview of the proposed internship experience at one or more different sites. Consulting with university faculty, the internship coordinator, and other professionals is an invaluable source of internship information. Data about the type of setting, the client population, the types of services, and the staff size is in keeping with the student's professional needs. Two forms are provided in the "Forms" section at the end of this book that can be used to gather appropriate information about potential internship sites. The Intern Site Preselection Data Sheet—School (Form 10.1) asks questions appropriate for positions in elementary, middle, secondary, and college level institutions, while the Intern Site Preselection Data Sheet—Clinical (Form 10.2) gathers information relevant to positions in a clinical agency setting. The information needed to complete the forms can be obtained by consulting with professionals familiar with the site, by informally visiting the site, or by writing to the site to obtain available descriptive materials and answers to specific questions.

Once the student has selected several possible internship sites, the next step in the process should be to set up a personal interview at each internship site that holds potential. Taking an interview helps the student to gain first-hand knowledge about the internship site and provides the opportunity to meet with the staff and other professionals. Hersh and Poey (1984) have developed an interviewing guide to assist the intern in preparing for an on-site interview. Their guide is provided in the next section.

A PROPOSED INTERVIEWING GUIDE FOR INTERN APPLICANTS*

Jeffery B. Hersh and Kent Poey

Many internship centers either require or strongly encourage an on-site interview. Some may consider a phone interview. Most only will offer an interview to those applicants who have passed through an initial selection process based on completed written application materials. From our observation, the interview is a critical part of selecting intern candidates. Yet many intern applicants appear unprepared to answer rather standard questions. In the interest of clarifying our expectation and hopefully those of other internship centers, we have outlined a series of questions that interns should consider asking intern directors, because such questions typically indicate initiative and interest. There are, however, some questions that are received in the context of the interview with mixed reactions by intern directors and that may place the intern's evaluation in some negative light. Generally speaking, the best questions are those that reflect motivation to learn and take part in many work activities rather than questions that promote a speculation that the intern may be demanding or complaining.

The listing below is probably more inclusive than encountered in any particular setting, and

* This article appeared in *Professional Psychology: Research and Practice*, 1984, Vol. 15, pp. 3–5. Copyright © 1984 by the American Psychological Association. Reprinted with permission.

should be used as a general preparation guide. It is important that the intern applicant prepare him or herself for the special emphasis of each internship site by anticipating more questions in certain categories than others. For instance, a long discussion of inpatient treatment is unlikely to develop in a training site that primarily provides outpatient services. Our hope is that these lists will be an aid for intern applicants in their preparation for interviews and will be used in conjunction with the published *Survival Guide for Intern Applicants* (Belar & Orgel, 1980). Obviously, preparing for an interview involves more than rehearsing answers to several anticipated questions. We hope the intern candidate will take the opportunity to reflect on his or her learning needs, clinical strengths, and future directions. This contemplative process is invaluable to growth and meaningful challenge in general and will aid the intern candidate in setting his or her priorities for the next year specifically. The intern candidate is advised also to meet with the director of clinical training and other intern applicants for support and feedback.

Common Questions Asked by Internship Directors

General:
1. What interests you in this internship program?
2. Have you worked with client populations similar to those we see here?
3. What are some books or articles that you have read recently?
4. What are some of your specialized skills?

Individual Adult Therapy:
1. What kinds of client problems have you worked with and in what modalities?
2. What experiences have you had doing emergency work and crisis therapy?
3. What kinds of cases do you work well with and what kinds of cases present particular problems?
4. What is your therapeutic orientation?
5. How would you describe your therapeutic style?
6. Describe your conceptualization and treatment of a recent or current case.
7. What are your strengths as a therapist and what areas need improvement?

Group Therapy:
1. Have you led groups?
2. What kinds of groups—therapeutic, educational, etc.—have you led?
3. Have you had co-therapy experience with groups?
4. What in the co-therapy relationship was helpful or difficult?

Child/Family/Couples Therapy:
1. What is your experience with child therapy? Family? Couples?
2. Describe the kinds of cases you have worked with, including your theoretical orientation.
3. What have your co-therapy experience in family and couples work been like?

Inpatient:
1. Have you inpatient experiences? Acute care? Long-term care? Milieu therapy?
2. What are your strengths in this area and what areas do you need to improve?

Psychological Testing:
1. What is your background in testing?
2. With which tests are you familiar?
3. In what specific areas do you want/need further training?

Consultation and Education:
1. What is your background in consultation and education?
2. Have you collaborated with other professional groups including teachers, lawyers, physicians, and nurses?
3. Describe your experiences in conducting workshops.

Supervision:
1. What styles of supervision best facilitate your learning?
2. What styles of supervision tend to inhibit your learning?
3. What theoretical orientation would you be most comfortable with in supervision?
4. Describe a rewarding supervision experience.

Work With Special Populations:
   1. Have you worked with people with physical complaints?
   2. Have you worked with clients who present handicapped, gay, minority, or cross-culture concerns?
Closing:
   1. What areas of your interest are not addressed by this internship?
   2. What areas are especially attractive?
   3. What are your future plans and goals?

Suggested Questions to Ask Internship Directors

   1. How are supervisors assigned? What are their theoretical orientations?
   2. How much opportunity is there for me to pursue special learning interests?
   3. What kind of activities will I be involved in each week?
   4. What is the diversity of the client population?
   5. What is the relationship between disciplines and working relationships among the staff and interns?
   6. Are there any changes in the stipends, vacations, or medical benefits from what is published in the brochure?
   7. What office arrangements are provided for an intern, and what clinical support is available?
   8. Is it possible to speak with a current intern?
   9. Have past interns found jobs available in this area after internship?
   10. How many people are you interviewing? For how many positions? What is the process by which the selection decisions are made? (If there are nonfunded intern positions, ask how decisions are made between funded and nonfunded slots.)
   11. What are the strengths and limits of this program?

Examples of Questions to Avoid Asking Internship Directors

1. How long does an intern work each week?
2. I want to complete by dissertation during my internship year. Could I have time off to do this?
3. Are there any opportunities to earn extra money in private practice during the internship year?
4. Persistent or antagonistic questions and comments showing a lot of interest in a work area that the internship program only minimally provides.
5. Questions and comments indicating a resistance to learning the major theoretical orientation presented by the internship center.

In conclusion, the interview and selection process is highly charged for intern applicants and internship directors. Both want to be evaluated positively. Unfortunately sometimes the pressure is handled by trying to make arrangements contrary to the Association of Psychology Internship Centers guidelines (APIC, 1982). An intern should discuss any procedural or ethical concerns with his or her university director of training. An area that is clearly unethical is encountered when the possibility of "early" acceptance is raised by the internship applicant or internship director. An example of a potentially problematic area is when an intern is asked to rank the internship among his or her potential choices. We hope this question is asked in a flexible and nondemanding way. Our suggestion is for the intern to respond either by saying that more time is needed to sort out his or her priorities or to answer by placing the internship within a range unless it is definitely and unalterably the first choice. Finally, because our remarks reflect our experiences in one internship site, a survey of internship directors regarding their philosophy of interviewing and the questions asked may add subsequential support to our remarks or significantly extend them in important ways. We will conduct such a survey that we hope will benefit both intern applicants and internship setting by clarifying priorities and expectations and by opening the interviewing process to inspection.

A helpful source in obtaining an internship position is Megargee's (1992) *A Guide to Obtaining a Psychology Internship*. This publication provides the doctoral students with advice to survive and succeed in obtaining the best possible internship. It outlines four steps in preparing a professional resume and discusses effective skills for interviewing for internship positions. Suggestions are also provided on what to avoid.

The Internship Agreement

Prior to the start of the internship experience, a formal agreement is made between the student's training program (college or university) and the agency or school in which the internship will take place. In most instances, training programs have internship agreements available that serve as the formal contract between the training program and the agency or school. Copies of an *Internship Contract* (Form 10.3) are included at the end of this chapter, and may be adapted for use by either counseling or psychology interns.

Intern Roles and Responsibilities

The beginning intern approaches the internship experience with much anticipation and anxiety. A contributing factor to the intern's uneasiness can be attributed to lack of familiarity with the role and responsibilities of the organization. Initial confusion and anxiety is lessened when the student makes an early effort to understand the role and responsibilities that interns are expected to perform in the organization. Similarly, the intern needs to "fit" his or her skills and competencies into the structure of the organization. Prior to the start of the internship experience, the intern needs to address a number of critical issues and questions about his or her role:

1. Do I understand the mission, purpose, and goals of the organization?
2. Do I understand the duties and responsibilities required by my university supervisor and my site supervisor?
3. Do I understand my position in the structure of the organization?
4. Am I capable of articulating what I consider to be my assets, strengths, and liabilities?
5. Do I understand the specific objective measures upon which my performance will be evaluated?
6. Do I understand the legal, ethical, and liability issues regarding my work in the organization?
7. Do I have a contract or agreement that delineates my duties and responsibilities? (Form 10.3 is an example of a typical internship contract.)

Individual Performance Plan

Having reviewed his or her professional role and knowing the specific tasks that are required, the intern needs to formulate a tentative plan for carrying out the internship. Egan (1987) pointed to the need for the student to develop an *individual performance plan* when entering a system. Egan's categories have been adapted here to provide suggestions; the intern should use and adapt this list to build an individual performance plan specific to his or her goals.

- **Establish essential linkage.** The intern develops a plan that is linked to the overall mission, strategic plans, and major aims of the organization. The plan is developed in keeping with the university program requirements and the intern's personal training needs.
- **List all personal performance areas.** The intern lists all tasks for which he or she is responsible either alone or with others. Specific behaviors should be identified and planned.

- **Identify key performance areas.** The intern determines the areas in the agency in which he or she can become a major contributor. Consideration is given to the student's perceived strengths and competencies.
- **Set Priorities.** The intern develops objectives in each performance area and determines some of the critical accomplishments in that area. Specific objectives that are attainable in a planned time period are specified.
- **Develop personal performance indicators.** The intern lists the formative and summative measures that can be used to indicate personal progress and accomplishments (Egan, 1987, pp. 9–170).

The completion of an individual performance plan allows the intern to enter into his or her internship armed with information essential to the successful completion of the experience.

In summary, understanding his or her roles and responsibilities in the organization enables the intern to avoid any role conflict and prevent other professionals from having different expectations of the intern. A clear understanding of the division of responsibilities and a well-developed performance plan enables the intern to work collaboratively and cooperatively with other helping professionals in the agency or institution.

Beginning Counselor Supervision

Counselor supervision is an interactional process between an experienced person (supervisor) and a supervised subordinate (supervisee). Hart (1982) defined supervision as an "ongoing educational process in which one person in the role of supervisor helps another person in the role of supervisee acquire appropriate professional behavior through an examination of the supervisee's professional activities" (p. 12). According to Bradley (1989), counselor supervision has three main purposes: "Facilitation of the counselor's personal and professional development, promotion of counselor competencies, and promotion of accountable counseling and guidance services and programs" (p. 8).

To meet these ends, the supervisor must be a serious, committed professional who has chosen counseling and supervision as a long-term career goal (Hart, 1982). Similarly, the supervisor needs to help the new supervisee to "ease" into the process of supervision. The following means of assisting are often accomplished effectively by the supervisor:

1. communicating a caring, empathic, and genuine understanding of the supervisee;
2. providing security to the supervisee as he or she faces training anxieties and vulnerabilities;
3. recognizing typical organizational and role responsibilities required of the supervisee;
4. understanding the supervisee rather than judging the supervisee's behavior in the early stages of supervision;
5. helping the supervisee identify strengths and weakness in an attempt to change or modify these behaviors;
6. attending to and accepting the supervisee's needs;
7. permitting the supervisee to problem solve, experiment, and make mistakes; and
8. helping to foster the development of a professional identity in the supervisee.

Helping the intern "ease" into the process of direct service, while at the same time encouraging the supervisee to test his or her skills and competencies, contributes significantly to development of professional and personal confidence in the supervisee.

Stages of Internship

The intern is reminded that all beginning interns will experience a variety of feelings and emotions as they go through their internship experience. Sweitzer and King (1999) divided the internship experience into five stages, which we discuss below.

Anticipation

The initial stage of the internship is often filled with optimism and energy but also anxiety. This stage is sometimes referred to as the "What If . . . ?" stage. Typically, interns are concerned that they may not be able to handle the situation. "What if they won't listen to me?" and "What if they don't like me?" are questions they frequently ask themselves. The interns may have concerns over what is expected of them, as well as concerns over what their supervisor thinks of them. In this stage task accomplishment is relatively low in that the intern may not be learning the things they want to learn. However, anxiety can be lessened when the intern clearly defines his or her goals and the skills needed to reach them. Setting realistic expectations for their experience and working on being accepted by and developing good relationships with supervisors, coworkers, and staff can help relieve an intern's initial anxiety.

Disillusionment

It is not uncommon for the intern to experience a sense of disappointment or disillusionment about the internship experience once it begins. What the intern anticipates about the internship and what is actually experienced can be quite different. Generally, if the concerns of the anticipation stage have been addressed, the intern will less likely encounter a different reality than was expected. This stage focuses on many of the concerns the student had in the anticipation stage. According to Sweitzer and King (1999, p. 62), this stage is referred to as the "What's wrong?" stage. Feelings associated with this stage can include frustration, disappointment, and sadness. Frequently, these feelings are directed toward the supervisor, coworkers, clients, or even oneself. This stage can be a positive or a negative experience. The feelings associated with it can be quite negative in the sense that the intern may not be learning as effectively as possible, or worse, may find that termination or renegotiation of the internship is required. On the positive side, though, this type of experience is often beneficial in that the working through of these issues encourages the intern to grow both professionally and personally.

Confrontation

The way to get past disillusionment is by acknowledging and confronting problems. According to Sweitzer and King, moving through this stage involves taking a look at your expectations, goals, and skills. Although you may have set goals that seemed reasonable at the time, experience may have shown that some of them are not realistic or the opportunities have changed. This is also a time to reexamine and perhaps take the necessary steps to bolster one's support system (Switzer & King, p. 62). As these issues are resolved, one's morale and efficiency will tend to increase. Keep working at the issues that are raised. As you confront the issues you may feel more independent and more effective. Success is achieved by confronting one's problems, not by ignoring them.

Competence

With the growth of competence comes a higher sense of morale and an increased investment in the internship experience. Trust in yourself, your supervisor, and your coworkers increases to the point where you consider yourself more of a professional than an apprentice. Be aware that stresses of time management may cause you to feel pushed and pulled in many directions. Outside pressures of managing home, school, and internship can become overwhelming if you strive for perfection rather than excellence in these areas.

Culmination

The culmination of the internship experience can give rise to a number of conflicting emotions. Pride in your accomplishments, feelings of guilt about not having more time to give to your clients—these conflicting feelings can be upsetting as well as confusing. Addressing these concerns will enable the intern to focus his or her feelings. Finding satisfying ways to say goodbye to clients, coworkers, and supervisor provides closure to the internship experience.

Internship Experience

The beginning internship student is often unaware of what to expect in clinical supervision. "What will my supervisor expect of me?" "How am I going to be evaluated?" "What is my supervisor's style?" These questions are frequently a source of anxiety and apprehension on the part of the supervisee. Answering these questions can help to alleviate some of the anxiety associated with entering into the supervisory process. This section of the text has been developed to help the intern become familiar with a variety of issues that confront each and every beginning counselor.

Models of Supervision

Leddick (1994) suggested that the focus of early counselor training was on the efficacy of a particular theory of counseling, such as behavioral, psychodynamic, or client centered. Supervision norms were typically conveyed indirectly during the rituals of an apprenticeship. As supervision became more purposeful, however, three types of models emerged. The following is a summary of those three models:

- **Developmental models** suggest that we are continually growing, in growth spurts and patterns, and thus the object of supervision is to maximize growth and identity in the future. Developmental models suggest that attention be directed toward the understanding of the development level of the supervisee. According to Stoltenburg and Delworth (1987) supervisees are grouped as beginning, intermediate, or advanced. Within each level is a trend to begin in a rigid, shallow, imitative way toward more competence, self-reliance and self-assurance. Particular attention is paid to self- and other-awareness, motivation, and autonomy. Beginners tend to rely on their supervisors to diagnose clients and establish therapeutic plans. Intermediate-level supervisees rely on supervisors for help in gaining a better understanding of a difficult client. Advanced-level supervisees tend to function independently and seek consultation when appropriate and to feel a sense of responsibility for their correct and incorrect decisions in therapy.
- **Integrated models of supervision** tend to employ multiple therapeutic orientations. An example by Bernard and Goodyear (1992) is the Discrimination Model, which purports to be atheoretical. This model focuses upon three supervisory roles: (a) teacher, when a supervisor lectures, instructs, or informs supervisees; (b) counselor, when the supervisor assists the supervisee in seeing their "blind spots"; and (c) consultant, when the supervisor acts as a colleague during cotherapy. In addition, the Discrimination Model focuses on three areas of skill building: process (how communication is

conveyed), conceptualization (application of a particular theory to a particular case), and personalization (body language, eye contact, etc).
- **Orientation-specific models of supervision** allows the supervisee to adapt a particular brand of therapy, such as client centered, Adlerian, or cognitive. These models assume the best supervision is the analysis of practice for true adherence to the therapy. (For example, Rogerian, or client-centered, supervisors focusing on the necessary and sufficient conditions of therapy, e.g., empathy, genuineness, etc.)

Regardless of the particular model of supervision employed by supervisors, all effective models address the key components of building a supervisory relationship, structuring for task accomplishment, and multiple supervisory roles and evaluative methods.

Supervisees: What Should I Look for in Supervision?

There are many strategies and methods available to supervisors for use in counseling supervision. It is helpful for the intern to become aware of what approaches or methods their supervisor will use. The intern needs to understand the manner in which he or she is going to be supervised and evaluated. Answers to the following questions will be helpful in understanding what will occur during supervision.

- **Will my supervisor view actual counselor-client interaction?** Assessment of actual counseling behavior with clients allows for corrective measures to be taken and increases the likelihood of successful outcomes. Good supervisors avail themselves of the opportunity to observe their supervisees by examining counselor client sessions by use of audio tape, video tape, and one way mirrors. This provides for immediate feedback and corrective strategies.
- **Does my supervisor know my current developmental level, skill level, and learning style?** Discussing these important issues with the supervisor is essential to becoming comfortable with the supervisory process. The need to be on the same page with the supervisor is essential for effective supervision.
- **What method of supervision is my supervisor using?** Knowledge of and familiarity with the supervisor's methods and strategies can significantly reduce a supervisee's performance anxiety.
- **Is my supervisor empathic? Open? Flexible?** Good supervisors respect their supervisees and are sensitive to individual differences (age, race, gender) and concerns.
- **Does my supervisor seem comfortable with authority and evaluative functions?** Knowing the type and frequency of evaluative methods to be employed is helpful in adjusting to your supervisor and his or her style of supervision.
- **Does my supervisor have the time to provide me with quality supervision?** It is essential that the supervisee feel confident that an appropriate amount of individual supervision is planned.
- **Does my supervisor show enthusiasm about supervising my internship?** Supervisor enthusiasm is an important ingredient in the reduction of supervisee anxiety.

Supervisee: How Am I to Be Evaluated?

Anxiety about the evaluation practices of the supervisor is a realistic concern for the intern. Basically, it is the task of the supervisor to employ a series of informal and formal measurements that result in a judgment that the intern is ready to practice counseling independently (McGahie,1991). Typically, formative evaluations (observation, feedback, modeling, etc.) take place throughout the duration of the supervisor-supervisee relationship and hopefully lead the supervisee toward skill improvement and positive counseling results. Summative evaluations (final evaluation, evaluation of performance objectives), known by the supervisee from the start of supervision, are the supervisor's final statements as to the overall effectiveness of the internship experience.

Harris (1994) summarized sources that reflect requisite skills and knowledge for effective evaluative practices (Bernard & Goodyear, 1992; McGahie, 1991; Stoltenburg & Dilworth, 1987). The following is a summary of those practices:

- The supervisor will clearly communicate criteria to supervisee and develop mutually agreed upon contract.
- The supervisor will identify and communicate strengths and weaknesses of supervisees. Ethical guidelines require ongoing feedback on performance.
- The supervisor will use constructive feedback techniques during evaluations. Corrective feedback is "heard" when a positive supervisory-supervisee relationship is formed.
- The supervisor will utilize specific behavioral, observable feedback dealing with counseling skills and techniques.
- The supervisor will use IPR (Interpersonal Process Recall) to raise supervisee's awareness about personal developmental issues.
- The supervisor will employ multiple measures of supervisee counseling skills (client rating scales, behavioral scales, audio and videotape etc.).
- The supervisor will maintain a series of work samples for use in summative evaluation.
- The supervisor will use a developmental approach that emphasizes progression toward desired goals.

Following this structured approach tends to lessen anxiety for both supervisor and supervisee, while providing a formative and summative means to assess supervisee performance and contributing to the supervisee's sense of effectiveness and worth.

Supervisee Resistance

Supervisee resistance has been thought of as a defensive behavior on the part of the supervisee that serves to reduce supervision induced anxiety. Bradley and Gould (1994) suggested that the goals and objectives of resistant behavior include self-protection against some perceived threat, a concern about not measuring up to supervisory standards, a perception that their skills are superior to those of the supervisor, a power struggle over the supervisee's loss of control, a fear of change, and/or a fear of the evaluative power of the supervisor. In response to these perceived threats, Bradley and Gould (1994) suggested that resistance may take the form of "games" played by supervisees in an attempt to elicit control over the supervisory process. Earlier, Kadushin (1968) defined four categories of games supervisees play:

1. manipulating of the level of demands placed on the supervisee;
2. redefining the relationship by supervisee attempting to make the supervisory relationship more ambiguous;
3. reducing the power disparity by focusing on his or her knowledge base to prove that the supervisor is "not so smart";
4. controlling the situation, directing the supervisor away from the supervisee's performance.

It should be remembered that resistance is quite common in supervision and that resolving the establishment of a positive supervisor-supervisee relationship aids resistance. Resistance can be redirected to provide a positive supervisory relationship. Focusing on the source(s) of resistance coupled with describing and interpreting resistance to the supervisee can help to reduce this common problem.

■ Summary

The essential steps in the process of selecting and evaluating an internship site were discussed in this chapter. Students will benefit from the interview guide presented and should take time to familiarize themselves with the questions presented before meeting with the director of a potential internship site. We also addressed the roles and responsibilities of the internship students and the stages of internship, as well as the types and methods of supervision that they may encounter. It is important for students to understand the various supervision models and the ways in which they, as interns, will be evaluated prior to beginning an internship, as this knowledge will help to reduce anxiety and increase effective learning in the internship setting. The forms cited in this chapter will be of use to students in their preselection planning and will help them to determine if a particular site will be able to meet their educational and professional needs.

■ Suggested Readings

Babad, E., & Solomon, G. (1967). Professional dilemmas of the psychologist in an organizational emergency. *American Psychologist, 33,* 840–846.

Baird, B. B. (1999). *The internship, practicum and field placement handbook.* Upper Saddle River, NJ: Prentice-Hall.

Borders, D. (1994). *The good supervisor.* ERIC Digest. Greensboro, NC: ERIC Clearing House on Counseling and Student Services.

Corless, L. A., & Corless, R. A. (1999). *Advanced practice in human service agencies.* Wadsworth Publishing Company.

Diamond, R. J. (1998). *Instant psychopharmacology: A guide for the nonmedical mental health professional.* New York: Norton.

Faiver, T. L. (1997). *Supervisory relationships.* Pacific Grove, CA: Brooks/Cole.

Friedman, D., & Kaslow, N. (1986). The development of professional identity in psychotherapists: Six stages in the supervision process. In F. Kaslow (Ed.), *Supervision and training: Models, dilemmas, and challenges* (pp. 29–47). New York: Hayworth Press.

Geroski, A. M., & Rodgers, K. A. (1997). Using the DSM IV to enhance collaboration among school counselors, clinical counselors, and primary care physicians. *Journal of Counseling and Development, 75,* 231–240.

Goodyear, R. K., & Bernard, J. M. (1998). Clinical supervision: Lessons from the literature. *Counselor Education and Supervision, 38,* 6–23.

Ivey, A. E., & Ivey, M. B. (1998). Reframing DSM IV: Positive Strategies from Developmental Counseling and Therapy. *Journal of Counseling and Development, 76*(3), 334–351.

Kaiser, T. L. (1997). *Supervisory relationships.* Pacific Grove, CA. Brooks/Cole.

Koslow, N. J., & Rice, D. G. (1985). Developmental stressor of psychology internship training: What training staff can do to help. *Professional Psychology: Research and Practice, 16*(2), 253–261.

Martin, D. G., & Moore, A. E. (1995). *First steps in the art of intervention.* Pacific Grove, CA. Brooks/Cole.

Mead, M. A., Hohenshil, T., et al. (1997). How the DSM system is used by clinical counselors: A national survey. *Journal of Mental Health Counseling, 19*(4), 383–402.

Morran, D. K., & Kurpius, D. J. (1995). A cognitive skills model for counselor training and supervision. *Journal of Counseling and Development, 73*(4), 384–390.

Parsons, R. D., & Wicks, R. J. (1994). *Counseling strategies and intervention techniques for the human services.* Needham Heights, MA: Allyn and Bacon.

Solway, K. S. (1985). Transition from graduate school to internship: A potential crisis. *Professional Psychology: Research and Practice, 16*(1), 50–54.

Stoltenberg, C. D. (1993). Supervising consultants in training: An application model of supervision. *Journal of Counseling and Development, 72,* 131–138.

Werslein, P. G. (1994). *Fostering counselors' development in group supervision.* ERIC Digest. Greensboro, NC: ERIC Clearning House on Counseling and Student Services.

Wilson, S. J. (1980). *Recording guidelines for social workers.* New York: The Free Press.

References

Association of Psychology Internship Centers. (1982). *Directory of internship programs in professional Psychology* (11th ed). Ames, IA: Author.

Belar, C., & Orgel, S. (1980). Survival guide for intern applicants. *Professional Psychology, 11,* 672–675.

Bernard, J. M., and Goodyear, R. K. (1992). *Function of clinical supervision.* Needham Heights, MA: Allyn and Bacon.

Bradley, L. (1989). *Counselor supervision: Principles, process, practice.* Muncie, IN: Accelerated Development.

Bradley, L. J., & Gould, L. J. (1994). *Supervisory resistance.* ERIC Digest. Greensboro, NC: ERIC Clearinghouse on Counseling and Student Services.

Egan, G. (1987). *Change agent skills in helping in human services settings.* Monterey, CA: Brooks/Cole.

Hart, G. (1982). *The process of clinical supervision.* Baltimore, MD: University Park Press.

Harris, M. B. C. (1994). *Supervisory evaluation and feedback.* ERIC Digest. Greensboro, NC: ERIC Clearinghouse on Counseling and Student Services.

Hersh, J., & Poey, K. (1984). A proposed interview guide for intern applicants. *Professional Psychology: Research and Practice, 15,* 305–312.

Kadushin, A. (1968). Games people play in supervision. *Social Work, 13,* 23–32.

Leddick, G. R. (1994). *Models of clinical supervision.* ERIC Digest. Greensboro, NC: ERIC Clearinghouse on Counseling and Student Services.

McGahie, W.C. (1991). Professional competence evaluation. *Educational Researchers, 20,* 3–9.

Stoltenberg, C. D., & Delworth, U. (1987). *Developmental supervision: A training model for counselors and psychotherapists.* San Francisco: Jossey Boss.

Sweitzer, H. F., & King, M. A. (1999). *The successful internship.* Pacific Grove, CA: Brooks/Cole.

CHAPTER

11

John C. Boylan

The Internship Experience

The internship experience is defined by the Council on Standards for Human Services Education (CSHSE), using the terms "fieldwork" and "internship" synonymously, in the following way:

> The advanced or culminating agency based experience which occurs toward the end of the students' college/university experience. This usually requires close supervision from agency personnel and the college/university faculty including regularly scheduled seminars with a faculty member. The experience provides a bridge between the academic experience and later professional employment. (CSHSE, 1995, p.21.)

The Council on Accreditation of Counseling and Related Programs (CACREP) defines the internship in the following way:

> Providing the opportunity for the student to perform all the activities that a regularly employed staff member in the setting would be expected to perform. In each case, a regularly employed staff member is defined as a person occupying the professional role to which the student is aspiring. Internship students generally have a host supervisor at the placement site and also receive supervision at the counselor education department. (CACREP, 1994, p. 64)

Further, the internship experience provides the student with the opportunity to translate what they have learned in their training program into effective methods of counseling. Thus, the focus of the internship is not directed toward the knowledge gained but the application of knowledge in diverse situations. Intern resourcefulness is the key to completion of a successful internship experience.

At the beginning of the internship, most interns will likely question the degree to which their training, background, and experience fits into the internship experience. Most interns will be unfamiliar with some of the typical steps or stages of development that occur in the internship. To help students get a "feel" for what occurs in the internship, the following stages or steps of the internship experience are presented.

Reynolds (1965) identified five learning stages of development that can be applied to the internship experience. An adaptation of those stages follows.

- **Step I:** The acute consciousness of self, of which stage fright is typical. Reactions vary from individual to individual, but it is at this stage that support from supervisors and others is essential.

Interns are encouraged to focus on the strengths and assets and use them as a base from which they can build success.

- **Step II:** The sink or swim adaptation. The intern, in this step, is probably more relaxed and is adapting to their surroundings. The intern may still feel overwhelmed but is less likely to acknowledge it. Being honest with self about fears and anxieties, coupled with continued supervisory support, helps the intern progress through Step II.
- **Step III:** The intern understands the situation without being able to control his or her own activity. Common to this step is frustration over lack of mastery of skills. Interns need to remember that they are still learning skills and should work on honing and refining what they have learned.
- **Step IV:** The intern has mastered skills and can understand and control their own activity. Interns begin to self-evaluate and alter their interventions and behaviors accordingly. The intern is functioning as a competent professional.
- **Step V:** The intern's learning to teach what has been learned. It is not uncommon for interns to reach this stage well after the internship experience has actually been completed.

The steps in the learning process can help the intern recognize that internship experiences follow a learning sequence and thus can be planned for. Kizer (2000), in a text entitled *Getting the Most From Your Human Services Internship: Learning From Experience*, suggests that a knowledge of some of the predictable ways in which internships develop can help the intern master the challenges of each stage. The following is a summary of the stages and challenges of the internship experience.

- **Stage I: Preplacement Stage:** This first stage occurs well before the student begins the internship. As discussed in earlier chapters, this stage consists of all the work that has been previously accomplished by the student and faculty member. Preselection of the internship site, obtaining information about the agency, and preparation for the first day at the internship are characteristics of this stage.
- **Stage II: Initiation (Orientation) Stage:** This is the stage in which the intern becomes familiar with the agency. In this stage, the intern is eager to get started. However, supervisors may suggest an "easing in" period of reading and observation before any direct service is provided. At this time, concerns about the need for more structure and direction may arise. Building a trusting relationship with one's supervisor can enable the intern to approach the supervisor about these types of concerns. Interns need to avoid rushing to judgment about their internship placement. All organizations and agencies have both strengths and weaknesses. It is more appropriate for the intern to determine what can be learned and how to learn it than to be critical of the placement site. In a similar fashion, avoiding early judgments about supervisors is better served by examining one's own behaviors and attitudes about the internship and how they may be affecting the internship experience.
- **Stage III: Working Stage:** Along with the establishment of relationships and the understanding of the intern's roles and responsibilities, this stage is characterized by the achievement of learning goals and the accomplishment of agency work. The intern functions more autonomously and usually feels comfortable in asking questions and receiving constructive feedback. The level of increased comfort and confidence enables the intern to focus on practice skills, learning about the agency, developing professional responsibilities, and learning to use supervision effectively and to handle the everyday tasks of the internship.
- **Stage IV: Termination:** The planning and anticipation of ending the internship begins. Depending on the nature of relationships that have been established, this can be a rather emotional period of time for the intern. Personal reflection by the intern is an important step in the termination process. "How well did I perform?" "What have I learned?" "What do I regret about my internship?" "What do I value about the experience?" These questions are important in reviewing and capturing the internship experience. The manner in which termination occurs speaks to the intern's ability to handle closure. Positive termination requires thoughtful reflection about the internship experience.

Coordination of the Internship

The internship program exists as a quasi-administrative unit within a counselor education department. It is best organized and managed by a designated internship coordinator, who should be a faculty member of the department (Boylan, 1988, Pitts, 1990). The coordinator is responsible for a variety of duties that usually include:

- providing students with a list of approved/appropriate field site placements;
- orienting the internship student to the internship experience;
- maintaining liaison activities between the program, student, and field site supervisor;
- preparing the Internship Contract (Form 10.3) between the university and the placement site supervisor;
- preparing the internship guidelines and program requirements
- contacting the site supervisor and delineating the internship processes and procedures required in the internship program;
- processing student's requests for internship placement;
- familiarizing the intern with the variety of assessment procedures to be used for the evaluation of the student's performance in the internship;
- assigning university supervisors for the on-campus group and individual supervisory sessions;
- coordinating the weekly on-campus group supervision class and the individual supervision sessions held on campus;
- maintaining frequent, direct contact with the site supervisor throughout the internship program.

On-Campus Supervision

CACREP-approved programs and those that follow the CACREP model require mandatory weekly group supervision classes and 1 hour of weekly individual supervision. The group supervision class meets weekly for the purposes of providing the internship student with the opportunity to discuss issues and concerns common to the internship experience, to engage in group supervision activities, and to participate in classroom case presentations and conferencing.

In addition, a variety of other learning activities are routinely provided in these weekly sessions. For example, internship students at Marywood University are provided with short lectures and presentations that focus on topics that are essential for the internship student. Topics that are typically included are models and methods of supervision, crisis intervention strategies, psychopharmacology, and brief therapies. Topics selected for presentation revolve around the areas of counseling that are emphasized at the field site placement.

The following sections of this chapter focus on the strategies and interventions that will likely be the mainstay of what the intern is expected to learn. The first section addresses several models of crisis intervention. The second section provides the student with a brief overview of the types of medications encountered in mental health and agency settings. Finally, the last section of the chapter focuses on the use of brief therapy as a time-limited, cost-effective strategy appropriate for both schools and mental health agencies.

Crisis Intervention

Crisis intervention first appeared in the literature in the 1940s. Eric Lindeman studied the grief reactions of victims in the famous fire at the Coconut Grove in Boston, Massachusetts. Later,

Lindeman and Gerald Caplan established a community based-mental health program in Cambridge, Massachusetts that was named the Wellesley Project (Kanel, 1999).

Crisis intervention, along with the movement aimed at providing mental health services support, evolved with the passage of the Community Mental Health Centers Act of 1963. The Act was designed to serve chronic mental health patients. The Lanterman Petris Short Bill of 1968 established specific requirements for the provision of mental health services in the community. The focus of the bill was short-term crisis intervention for clients who were not chronically mentally ill. Today, crisis intervention is an established practice in most community agencies.

The following are examples of three models of crisis intervention that will provide a representative sample of crisis intervention models and the critical stages in crisis intervention.

Crisis Intervention: The Kanel Model

The ABC model of crisis intervention (Kanel, 1999) is a method of conducting very brief mental health interviews with clients whose functioning level has decreased following a psychosocial stressor. It is a problem-focused approach and is effectively applied within four to six weeks of the stressor. Kanel's model is designed around three specific stages: (A) developing and maintaining contact, (B) identifying the problem, and (C) developing coping strategies for the client. The following is a summary of the key points of the ABC model.

A. **Developing and maintaining contact:** Essential to the establishment of crisis intervention strategies is the development of rapport with the client. Like any other counseling interview, the client must feel understood and accepted by the counselor before there is a willingness to trust and effectively communicate. It is in this phase that counselors are reminded of the effectiveness of the basic attending skills learned early in their training programs. These skills include eye contact, body posture, vocal style, warmth, empathy, and genuineness. Skill in the use of open and closed questions, along with the skills of clarifying, reflecting, and summarizing are all used to develop and maintain contact with the person in crisis.

B. **Identifying the problem:** By identifying the precipitating event, the counselor can gain information regarding the trigger(s) of the client's crisis. The actual cause of the crisis can vary from a recent event to an event that occurred several weeks or even months ago. The time of the event—the beginning of the crisis—is important to determine.

    Kanel uses the following diagram to illustrate the process of crisis formulation:

Precipitating Event ———— Perception ———— Subjective Distress ———— Lowered Functioning

- **Perception of the event:** How the individual views the stressful situation causes him or her to be in a stressful state. The meaning and assumptions the person makes about the crisis event serve to color and magnify the meaning for the client. Careful perception checking of the client's view of the precipitating event must be thoroughly considered.

- **Subjective distress:** The level of distress experienced by the client is an essential area of inquiry. Symptoms can effect academic, behavioral, occupational, social, and family functioning. Discussing the affected functional area(s) and the degree to which the crisis event effects them is crucial (Kanel, 1999, pp. 64–82).

- **Lowered functioning:** It is essential that pre- and post-levels of functioning are understood so that the counselor can ascertain the client's realistic level of coping and the severity of the crisis to the person.

C. **Coping strategies of the client:** The counselor assesses the past, present, and future coping behaviors of the client. Included in such an assessment are the client's unsuccessful coping strategies so that alternate coping strategies can be developed. Clients are encouraged to propose their own coping strategies in addition to new or alternative strategies proposed by the counselor.

Crisis Intervention: The Gilliland and James Model

Gilliland and James (1997), in their textbook *Crisis Intervention Strategies*, defined crisis as a perception of an event or situation as an intolerable difficulty that exceeds the person's resources and coping mechanisms. Unless the person obtains relief, the crisis has the potential to cause severe affective, cognitive, and behavioral malfunctioning.

Gilliland and James suggested that the three models of crisis intervention discussed by Leitner (1974) and Belkin (1984) serve as a foundation for most intervention strategies. The following is a summary of those three models:

- **The Equilibrium Model:** This model suggests that people in crisis are in a state of disequilibrium, and as a result the coping mechanisms they usually employ fail to meet their needs. The equilibrium model seems most appropriate in the beginning of a crisis, when the person is out of control, disoriented, and unable to make good choices. The focus is on stabilizing the individual (Gilliland & James, p. 22).
- **The Cognitive Model:** This model maintains that crises are rooted in faulty thinking about the events or situations that surround the crisis. The major point is that people can gain control of their lives by correcting this faulty thinking. The model's tenets are found in the works of rational-emotive and cognitive therapists.
- **The Psychosocial Model:** This model assumes that individuals are products of their heredity endowment coupled with the learning they have absorbed from their social environment. The goal is for the therapist to collaborate with the individual in their assessment of the internal and external difficulties contributing to the crisis and to obtain workable alternatives to problems.

The following is a summary of the six-step model of crisis intervention developed by Gilliland and James (1997):

1. **Build a helping relationship:** The counselor needs to develop an understanding of the events that precipitated the crisis and the meaning that it has for the client. It is therefore essential that a helping relationship be established. The use of basic attending skills with empathy, positive regard, and concreteness, coupled with the counselor's calm and direct approach can help the client see that something is being done to alleviate the problem.
2. **Assure safety:** Assessing how dangerous the client is to himself or herself or to others is one of the first concerns in crisis intervention (Aguilera, 1998). The myriad reasons why the client comes to the counseling office need to be explored. Suicidal ideation, homicidal ideation, danger from a third party, or fear of being harmed are potential reasons. It is essential that direct questioning focus on these possible motivators. Having determined the client's risk, the counselor can then, if needed, involve others, seek the support of family and friends, hospitalize the client, and protect intended victims. In conducting an assessment, the counselor inquires as to the event that precipitated the crisis, the meaning it has for the client, the support systems available to the client, and the level of functioning prior to the crisis (Aguilera, 1998). Aguilera further suggests that the assessment process begins with a direct question that elicits the client's reasons for coming to counseling, such as "What happened today?" and "Why today?" The counselor needs to determine what may have been the "last straw" for the client. Proceeding with the techniques of concreteness, leading, structuring, and questioning, the counselor can narrow the focus to the precipitating event. Determining what the client is feeling (rage, confusion, anger, hopelessness) gives the counselor an understanding of the meaning that the crisis event had for the client. Once the meaning is understood, it is necessary, according to Roberts (1990, p. 12), to listen for and to note cognitive distortions, overgeneralizations, misconceptions, and irrational belief statements. Attention should focus on the client's physical appearance, behavior, mood, and any signs of distress. These are keys to recognizing the degree of client preoccupation with the crisis event. In addition, the counselor must assess the client's coping mechanisms, decision-making skills, and stress management skills. A knowledge of the client's precrisis level of coping will help in the selection of strategies and interventions with the greatest potential for success.

3. **Give support:** It is essential to assess the client's support systems. The client who has inadequate support in his or her environment needs support from someone who cares about him or her. Seeking out these individuals is imperative in order to provide the needed environmental support. Unfortunately, if the client lacks supportive people in his or her life, then it is essential that the counselor communicate support to the individual. Providing the client with emergency contacts and phone numbers is critical.

4. **Examine alternatives:** The counselor helps the client explore a wide variety of available options. Often, the client feels as though there are no available options. However, it is not necessary to provide the client with a multitude of options. It is more effective to discuss options that are reasonable, appropriate, and realistic to the client's situation.

5. **Assist with action plan:** The counselor can lessen the client's apprehensions and fears about what can be done to solve or cope with the problem. The counselor must tenaciously hold the client's attention on one problem whose moderation will begin to restore equilibrium. The counselor attempts to get the client to look at possible alternatives or solutions. It is also helpful to elicit from the client precrisis coping strategies that can then be modified. The counselor can help in the selection and generation of positive strategies for the client. Before ending the crisis session, the counselor must assess the degree to which the client understands and can describe the action plan that has been developed. It is important to remember that client ownership of the plan is crucial. Clients need to feel autonomous and powerful in their action planning

6. **Obtain commitment:** The counselor demonstrates the need to carry out the action plan. Commitment should go well if the previous steps have been carried out successfully. Follow-up contact or telephone contact with the client will aid the counselor in determining the client's status, whether or not the action plan has been implemented, and the degree to which the client has progressed toward a resolution.

Crisis Intervention: A Model for Teachers

Callahan (1998) in an article entitled "Crisis Intervention: A Model for Teachers," discussed the need for teachers to engage in crisis intervention. The following is an adaptation of that article.

Callahan felt that teachers are in a unique position to gather information and note danger symptoms of children who are prone to violence. Information and hunches should be passed on to other teachers, counselors and administrators who may be able to observe and take the necessary action when violence is about to erupt (Callahan, p. 227). Accordingly, teachers need to understand acting out and how to manage aggressive behavior. Similarly, the teacher must know that when an individual hits a state of disequilibrium (lack of judgment and control), his or her body is in a defensive state of readiness to attack or flee. Normal processes, such as the ability to hear, think logically, and react normally may be limited and the more upset an individual is, the less likely it is that the individual will be able to respond to others. When a person in crisis becomes alarmed and moves into a resistance stage, the person is closer to acting out and becoming unmanageable (Callahan, p.220). Callahan suggested that teachers need to understand this response and conduct an immediate assessment of the student and the situation. Callahan also cited the suggestions of Greenstone and Leviton (1993) with respect to assessing the situation and problem of a student in crisis. The teacher should:

1. Assess the situation to determine what is troubling the student, at this time, by engaging the student in conversation about what is going on. The teacher needs to keep a reasonable, controlled, matter-of-fact tone during the discussion.

2. Attempt to discover specifically what is leading the student into crisis right at this time.

3. Determine the most pressing problem or need from the student's point of view. Remember to always keep the student's subjective interpretation in mind and never negate or belittle any problems presented by the student in crisis.

4. Outline those problems that can be immediately managed.

5. Think through variables that might hinder the problem-solving process.

6. Ask what can be done most effectively in the least amount of time to diffuse the crisis situation.

7. Understand the similarities between the present situation and previous incidents of stress.

Callahan (1998) suggested further that if a crisis is occurring outside the classroom, the teacher should follow safety guidelines, which include the following:

1. The teacher should intervene with a partner, especially if there is more than one person involved in the crisis.

2. The teacher should approach the crisis situation slowly and judiciously.

3. The teacher should help the student(s) involved in the crisis with the student positioned in front of him or her and should not turn his or her back on the student in crisis.

4. The teacher should visually check out the person to determine if there is any weapon available.

5. The teacher should note any objects that could be used as a weapon.

6. The teacher should be prepared for unexpected behavior.

7. The teacher should note entrances and exits in the area. If the situation turns to violence or becomes dangerous, the teacher may need to escape or herd other students to safety.

8. The teacher should remove audiences from escalating situations where possible. A crowd may be egging on a fight or causing a person to act out or save face. If possible, the teacher should separate any students who are having a problem by establishing authority with onlookers and then moving into a position to catch the attention of the student(s) in crisis.

9. The teacher should know where he or she can find assistance. If possible, before intervening in a crisis situation outside a classroom, the teacher should know where other adults might be so that the teacher will know where to possibly seek assistance.

10. The teacher should remove any objects or clothing that a violent student may use against them (pencils, neckties, earrings) (Callahan, pp. 226–227)

Summary

In summary, crisis intervention strategies provide both agency- and school personnel–specific techniques for dealing with crisis. Many schools and agencies are now developing strategies and programs for coping with potential tragedy. The intern needs to become familiar with crisis interventions and strategies to assure their own safety and the safety of their clients.

Psychiatric Medications

Traditionally, counselor training programs have not focused on psychopharmacology as a major content area of training. Philosophical as well as ethical issues regarding the use of medications are contributing factors in the lack of training in this area.

Unfortunately, today's counselors in both schools and agencies are confronted with the fact that a portion of their clientele may be taking medications or in need of medications to function more effectively. It is, therefore, critical that counselors have at least a rudimentary understanding of the types of medications commonly prescribed and their uses in treating mental health issues. Counselors are expected to consult and cooperate with other mental health professionals in the treatment of clients. Familiarity with medications is especially helpful in understanding the pharmacological treatment regimens prescribed for clients by physicians and psychiatrists.

The following listing of medications, used in the treatment of mental health issues, is provided for the purposes of

- providing interns in schools and agencies with a listing of common psychotropic medications used in the treatment of mental disorders;
- familiarizing the intern with basic pharmacological terms, symbols, and definitions;
- providing interns with suggested readings to help in their understanding of psychopharmacological treatment; and
- encouraging interns to learn more about the use and abuse of medications.

The number and types of medications used for the treatment of mental health issues is vast. The following is a representative sampling of the more commonly used medications in the United States.

Antidepressant Medications

Classes of Antidepressants

Tricyclic Antidepressants (TCAs): All TCAs have the same basic chemical structure and are related to the phenothiazine class of antipsychotics (Olen, Hebel, Dombeck, & Kastrup, 1993). TCAs are 65% to 75% effective in relieving the somatic features associated with depression. TCAs have been shown to be effective in treating both endogenous and exogenous depression (Joyce & Paykel, 1989). TCAs are often prescribed for patients with decreased appetite, weight loss, early morning awakening, lack of interest in people and environment, and a family history of depression (Buelow, Hebert, & Buelow, 2000). Specific effects of TCAs include:

- mood elevation
- increase in physical activity and mental alertness
- improvement in sleep and appetite
- nonelevation of mood in nondepressed subjects (American Medical Association, 1983)

Trade name	Generic name	Daily dosage
Adapin	doxepin	100-200 mg.
Anafranil	clomipramine	150–200 mg.
Asenden	amoxepine	200–300 mg.
Aventyl	nortriptyline	75–150 mg.
Elavil	amitriptyline	100–200 mg.
Norpramin	desipramine	100–200 mg.
Pamelor	desipramine	75–150 mg.
Petrofrane	desipramine	75–150 mg.
Surmontil	trimipramine	100–200 mg.
Tofranil	imipramine	100–200 mg.
Vivactil	protriptyline	100–200 mg.

(Olen et al., 1993)

Serotonin Specific Reuptake Inhibitors (SSRIs): SSRIs, or second generation antidepressants, have fewer side effects than TCAs and monoamin oxidase inhibitors (see below). Generally, SSRIs cause less weight gain and less sedation and hypotension than TCAs. Additionally, SSRIs are less lethal when taken in overdose.

Trade name	Generic name	Daily dosage
Luvox	fluvoramine	100–300 mg.
Paxil	paroxetine	20–50 mg.
Prozac	fluoxetine	10–80 mg.
Zoloft	sertraline	50–200 mg.

(Gitlin, 1996)

New Generation Antidepressants

Trade name	Generic name	Daily dosage
Wellbutrin	bupropion	100–300 mg.
Desyrel	trazodone	150–300 mg.
Serzone	nefazodone	300–600 mg.
Remeron	merlazapine	

Monoamine Oxidase Inhibitors (MAOIs): Monoamine oxidase inhibitors are indicated for some patients who are unresponsive to other antidepressants. Due to their side effects profile and a potential for serious interaction with other drugs and food, MAOIs are not used as a first drug of choice when treating depression (Buelow & Buelow, 2000).

Trade Name	Generic Name	Daily Dosage
Marplan	isocarboxazid	45–90 mg.
Nardil	phenelzine	10–30 mg.
Parnate	tranylcypromine	10–30 mg.

Antianxiety Medications

Anxiolytics or Minor Tranquilizers

Benzodiazepines (BDZs): Benzodiazepines are a group of structurally related compounds that have sedative properties. Because of their greater safety margin, use of BDZs has, for the most part, replaced use of barbituates, a more dangerous class of sedatives (Beulow, Hebert, & Beulow, 2000). BDZs are often the treatment of choice for anxiety.

Trade name	Generic name	Daily dosage
Ativan	lorazepam	1–10 mg.
Centrax	prarepam	20–40 mg.
Klonipin	clonazepam	0.25–1.5 mg.
Dalmane	flurazepam	15–30 mg.
Halcion	triazolam	0.125–0.5 mg.
Librium	chlordiazepoxide	15–300 mg.
Prosom	estazolam	1–2 mg.
Restoril	temazepam	0.15–30 mg.
Serax	oxazepam	30–120 mg.
Tranxene	chlorazepate	15–60 mg.
Valium	diazepam	20–40 mg.
Xanax	alprozolam	0.5–1.5 mg.

Antianxiety Agents Other Than Benzediazepines

Trade name	Generic name	Daily dosage
Adapin	Doxepin	25–499 mg.
Sinequan	Doxepin	25–400 mg.
Atarax	Hydroxyzine	
Buspar	Buspirone	

Antipsychotic Medications

Phenothiazines: Phenothiazines are the oldest type of antipsychotic, and are often referred to as tranquilizers or neuroleptics. Phenothiazines are typically used in the treatment of positive symptoms of schizophrenia. Today, neuroleptic is the term used to describe the phenothiazines and Haldol. These medications induce in schizophrenia a "neuroleptic state" that is characterized by decreased agitation, aggression, and impulsiveness, as well as a decrease in hallucinations and delusions, and, generally, less concern with the external environment (Buelow, Hebert, & Buelow, 2000, p. 66).

Trade name	Generic name	Daily dosage
Mellaril	thioridazine	200–700 mg.
Prolixin	fluphenazine	1–20 mg.
Serentil	mezoridazine	75–300 mg.
Stelazine	trifluoperazine	6–20 mg.
Thorazine	chlorpromazine	300–800 mg.
Tindal	acetophenazine	60–120 mg.
Trilafon	perphenazine	8–40 mg.
Vesprin	triflupromazine	100–150 mg.
(Olen et al., 1993)		

Thioxanthenes: The chemical structure of the thioxanthenes is similar to that of the phenothiazines.

Trade name	Generic name	Daily dosage
Navane	thiothixene	6–30 mg.
Taractan	chlorprothixene	500–400 mg.

Other Antipsychotic Medications

Trade name	Generic name	Daily dosage
Loxitane	loxapine	60–199 mg.
Moban	molindone	

Second Generation Antipsychotics: *These antipsychotic medications are effective without the risk of neuroleptic syndrome (a severe, life-threatening complication of using antipsychotic drugs). Second generation antipsychotic medications are effective for the treatment of the negative symptoms of schizophrenia, such as social withdrawal, blunt affect, decreased motivation, and impoverished speech.*

Trade name	Generic name	Daily dosage
Clorazil	clozapine	400–600 mg.
Risperdal	resperidone	4–6 mg.
Serlect	sertindole	
Seroquel	quietapine	
Zyprexa	olanzapine	

Lithium

Lithium is used predominantly in the treatment of mood disorders. The two most common uses of the drug are for the treatment of acute mania and the preventive treatment of bipolar disorder.

Special Populations: Psychopharmacological Treatments for Children and Adolescents

Disorder	Medications
Major depression	Antidepressants
Bipolar disorder	Lithium

Schizophrenia	Antipsychotics
Autistic disorder	Antipsychotics
Obsessive-compulsive disorder	SSRIs
Separation anxiety disorder	Imipramine and benzodiazepines
Attention deficit hyperactivity disorder (ADHD)	Ritalin, Dexadrine, and Cylert
Conduct disorder	Lithium, beta blockers, and Clonidine
Tourette's syndrome	Haldol and Clonidine
Enuresis	Tricyclics
(Gitlin, 1996)	

Medication Dosage Schedule

Qid: four times a day	ac: before meals	hs: at bedtime
Tid: three times a day	pc: after meals	am: in the morning
Bid: two times a day	qd: every day	pm: in the evening

▇ Brief Therapies

The internship student in mental health agencies is frequently confronted with the reality of having to use treatment methods capable of delivering low-cost quality mental health services. The need to employ brief therapeutic strategies in counseling has exploded onto the scene as a result of our presentday managed care environment. Time-limited interventions and role flexibility in practice are clearly required in an age of managed mental health care (Mash & Hunsley, 1993).

The following sections of the text are designed to provide the internship student with a sampling of the varied approaches to brief therapy. In some cases, students will be familiar with and have training in these models. In other cases, this section may provide their first exposure to models of brief therapy. In any case, students need to become familiar with and skilled in the implementation of brief therapeutic interventions and strategies.

Solution-Focused Brief Therapy

Solution-focused brief therapy is based upon the research of deShazer and associates (deShazer, 1989, 1990; deShazer & Berg, 1985), who developed a model of therapy that was intentionally brief by design and was based on "focused solution development." Some of the guiding principles of solution-focused therapy include:

1. the notion that the power of resistance need not be a part of effective therapy but can be replaced by cooperation;
2. the principle that solution-focused therapy is intended to help clients become more competent at living their lives day by day. Accordingly, this conception involves normalizing behavior and the constructing of new meaning from behavior (Fleming, 1998);
3. the belief that client-therapist interactions are directed by three rules: (a) if it ain't broke, don't fix it; (b) once you know what works, do more of it; and (c) if it doesn't work, don't do it again, do something else (deShazer, 1990, pp. 93–94).

Treatment planning in solution-focused therapy is based on the understanding that clients themselves must be customers for change and the realization of the existence of exceptions to their problems when they occur. Treatment plans become a source of documentation of treatment appropriateness, efficacy, and accountability (Fleming, 1998).

The client-therapist relationship is essential for the development of therapeutic intervention. According to deShazer (1990), clients are visitors, complainants, or customers depending on both their views of themselves in relation to their problem and their willingness to take an active part in doing something to solve the problem. Customers are usually those individuals who are willing to do something about their problems. Customers are asked to do something and follow through by taking an active part in their own improvement. Similarly, what clients do to improve their situation between the time of the telephone call for an appointment and the first session can be important to the therapist in his or her search for exceptions to the problem. According to Fleming (1998), the underlying assumption of the solution-focused model is that clients come to therapy because they have a complaint, a problem or both. Problems do not occur all the time. When clients choose to do something differently, in a way that does not involve the problem, problem behavior is less likely to occur and exception behavior is more likely to be observed (deShazer & Berg, 1985).

Both the client and the therapist construct exception behavior while exploring what happens when the problem does *not* occur (Gingerich, deShazer, & Weiner-Davis, 1988). According to Fleming (1998), another guiding principle of solution-focused therapy is to help the client become more competent at living life day by day. Using the EARS—elicit, amplify, reinforce, and start again—approach, the therapist elicits dialogue about exception behavior and positive thoughts and behaviors that the client reports about himself or herself and others. This process helps the client toward goal attainment. Reinforcing what the client has done to improve the situation by attaching positive thoughts and behaviors to his or her goals helps the client realize that his or her action makes a difference.

DeShazer (1990) employed what he calls the miracle question: "Let's suppose tonight while you're asleep a miracle happens that solves all the problems that brought you here. How would you know that this miracle really happened? What would be different?" The therapist uses exception questions and coping questions to get the client to examine his or her attempts at coping. The therapist believes that by asking solution-focused questions, clients become more aware of their resources and strengths and can use them to make better choices for themselves. Finally, the central focus of brief therapy is centered on specific, concrete, and behavioral goals. Talking about goals and the steps taken to achieve goals is essential for positive outcomes. Both client and therapist need to know where they are going and how they are going to get there in order for brief therapy to be successful.

Strategic Solution–Focused Therapy

"What's the trouble?" "If it works, do more of it." "If it doesn't work, don't do it anymore. Do something different." These are some of the guiding principles of strategic solution–focused therapy. This method, developed by Quick (1998), combines the theories and procedures of brief strategic therapy (Fisch, Weakland, & Segal, 1982) and solution-focused therapy (deShazer, 1988).

"What's the trouble?" and "Do something different." are principles derived from brief strategic therapy, a model developed at the Mental Research Institute in Palo Alto, California in the 1960s and 1970s, which stressed the idea that people generally attempt to solve problems by doing what makes sense to them. In contrast, the "If something works, do more of it" principle comes from a model developed at the Brief Family Therapy Center in Milwaukee, Wisconsin in the 1970s and 1980s.

The strategic solution–focused model integrates these parent models in two main ways: (a) by combining brief strategies of focusing on clarification of the problem with the solution–focused emphasis on elaboration of the solution, and (b) to blend the solution–focused emphasis on maintaining what works with the strategic emphasis on interrupting what doesn't. Strategic solution focused therapy is always tailored to the needs of the client.

The following is a summary of some of the major principles and techniques of strategic solution–focused therapy as presented by Quick (1998).

The initial step in strategic solution focused therapy is the clarification of the client's complaint and identifying the highest priority problem. The highest priority problem is the one problem which, if resolved, would make the biggest positive difference in the client's life. The therapist wants to know the "Who?", "What?", "When?", and "Where?" of what happened. Does the client's complaint result in a behavioral excess or deficit? The therapist's focus is to try to clarify what happened at this particular time that makes this problem an immediate issue. The therapist wants to clarify the client's expectations of how therapy is supposed to be helpful. Clarification of the primary problem is an important consideration throughout therapy. It is the therapist's job to find out from the client about what problems or issues should be the focus in sessions.

The next step is the elaboration of the solution. "What will be different in the client's life?" "What will let the client know that things are moving in the right direction?" "What will be the first signs of change?" A focused inquiry invites the client to amplify the solution scenario, elaborating on what will be different as a result of lasting changes (Quick, pp. 527–529). When the solution has been elaborated, the therapist invites the client to describe how he or she has begun to make the positive changes happen. If the primary problem has been identified, the focus shifts to what will be different when that specific issue is resolved.

The next step is assessing what has already been done and suggested in previous attempts to solve the problem. "What has been done?" "What have you tried?" The therapist focuses on specific attempts at problem solution in the session. The therapist looks for main themes among attempted solutions, particularly unsuccessful ones, in an attempt to avoid trying them again. Near the end of the session, the therapist asks if the client wants feedback or input. The therapist will also compliment the client on realizations that he or she has made in the session. This suggestion component of therapy depends upon what has or has not worked for the client. If things are working out, the suggestion may be to continue and amplify existing behaviors. On the other hand, if attempted solutions are not working, the suggestion may be designed to interrupt the behavior. General or specific suggestions may be offered to the client by the therapist.

Keep doing what works for you or do something different. It is important to remember that the needs of the client and the interval between sessions are highly variable. Termination might include encouragement to continue doing what works or to slowly make additional changes.

Major Approaches to Brief Therapy

Steenbarger (1992), in an article entitled " Toward Science-Practice Integration in Brief Counseling and Therapy," outlined the major approaches to brief therapy. The following is a summation of important features of different approaches to brief therapy.

Psychodynamic Approaches to Brief Therapy

Psychodynamic approaches to brief therapy focus on the therapeutic relationship as a change context. Furthermore, they deemphasize the interpretive content of what the client says as a source of change and strive to produce relationship experiences that have an impact on the client.

Interpersonal Dynamic Brief Therapy

This approach views therapy as an experiential process in which corrective emotional experiences (Alexander & French, 1946) rather than verbal interpretations are the crucial elements for change. The focus in interpersonal dynamic brief therapy is on creating conditions wherein client's maladaptive patterns can be enacted in the helping relationship.

Interpersonal Psychotherapy (IPT)

This approach emphasizes the social origins of the client's complaint (Cornes, 1990). Interpersonal psychotherapy deemphasizes the relationship as a change vehicle and focuses instead on nonjudgmental exploration, encouragement of affect, and direct behavior change techniques (Klerman, Weissman, Rounsaville, & Chevron, 1984).

Cognitive Behavioral Counseling

The cognitive approach comprises several different schools of thought. However, these schools focus on learned cognitive and behavioral patterns as the primary source of distress (Steenbarger, 1992).

Cognitive Restructuring Brief Therapy

This approach emphasizes the acquisition of new beliefs and thought patterns. The central notion is that clients build internal "schemas" of self and the world in order to organize their perceptions (Goldfried, 1988; Moretti, Feldman, & Shaw, 1990). Early experiences can lead to the development of negative schemas, which can effect one's perception of self, world and the future. According to Beck (Beck, Rush, Shaw, & Emery, 1979), the counselor collaboratively helps the client to marshal evidence disconfirmatory to negative schemas.

Rational Emotive Therapy (RET)

According to Steenbarger (1992), Ellis takes a different restructuring approach to brief therapy. The focus in rational emotive therapy is on identifying faulty beliefs as a link between activating events and emotional behavioral consequences. Challenging, confronting, and disputing irrational beliefs is an attempt to reshape irrational thought patterns. Ellis, unlike Beck, relies on confrontation rather than collaborative helping to get at the client's irrational thoughts (Steenbarger, 1992).

Coping Skills Brief Therapy

This method represents a teaching approach to counseling in which clients learn to solve difficult life problems and cope with anticipated stresses (Steenbarger, 1992). The focus of this approach to brief therapy is on the use of cognition and behavioral methods in the development of life skills that promote self-efficacy (Bandura, 1977). Coping skills brief therapy relies heavily on in-session and between-session exercises.

Tactical Brief Therapies

These therapies are derived from systems-based family therapies that use prescribed experiences to affect client functioning. Two major schools of tactical brief therapies are listed below

- **Task-centered therapies:** These therapies focus on the use of structured homework assignments of: (a) observational or monitoring tasks, to enhance client awareness (b) experiential tasks aimed at arousing an emotional state and; (c) incremental tasks geared to alter behavior in a step-by-step fashion. It is the out-of-session tasks that are primarily facilitative of change (Wells, 1982).
- **Strategic brief counseling:** This approach emphasizes prescribed client enactments as change vehicles for the purpose of recontextualizing a problem. Strategic counselors observe that problems

are typically maintained by the "solutions" sought by clients, creating circular patterns of distress. The goal, then, is to interrupt the attempted solution so that a circular pattern of distress cannot be maintained. The goal of therapy is to show clients, through experience, that their problems are artifacts of context.

According to Steenbarger (1992) reviewing the practice literature (Budman & Gurman 1988; Butcher & Koss, 1978; Koss & Butcher, 1986) reveals a number of features common to the various schools of brief therapy. The following is a summary of those features.

- Brief therapies limit change efforts to focal patterns that are identified early in the counseling process.
- Brief counselors are active in their role as interveners, maintaining the therapeutic focus and actively employing confrontations, interpretations, reframings, and direct exercises to instigate change.
- Brief therapies are present centered.
- Brief therapy interventions are designed to facilitate a high level of client experiencing in the session.
- Brief therapists actively encourage client expectations for change.
- Brief therapies are structured around the initial evaluation of the client, the initiation of change-oriented interventions, and efforts to extend initial changes.

Summary

This chapter addressed the coordination and on-campus requirements of the internship experience, introducing students to the responsibilities of the internship coordinator as well as the separate supervision requirements that internship students must fulfill at their educational institutions in addition to those mandated at their internship site. We then discussed the three intervention strategies most commonly employed in agency settings, and those that internship students will be most likely to require in their work with clients. Crisis intervention models, basic psychopharmacological medication, and brief therapy approaches have been presented in an effort to help students familiarize themselves with these common treatment methods. The student will benefit from a thorough understanding of these methods, as they are frequently employed by agencies in the treatment of their client populations and will likely be encountered in the course of the internship experience.

Suggested Readings

Bentley, K. J., & Walsg, J. (1996). *The social worker and psychiatric medication.* Pacific Grove, CA: Brooks/Cole.

Brems, C. (2000). *Dealing with challenges in psychotherapy and counseling.* Pacific Grove, CA: Brooks/Cole.

Buelow, G., & Herbert, S. (1995). *Counselor's resource on psychiatric medications: Issues of treatment and referral.* Pacific Grove, CA: Brooks/Cole.

Diamond, R. (1998) *Instant psychopharmacology.* New York. Norton.

Hutchings, J. B., & Balk, D. E. (1997) Fundamentals of crisis intervention. *Death Studies, 21*(4), 427–431.

Pitts, J. H. (1992). Organizing a practicum and internship program in counselor education. *Counselor Education and Supervision, 31,* 196–207.

References

Aguilera, D. C. (1988). *Crisis intervention: Theory and methodology* (5th ed.). St. Louis, MO: Mosby.

Alexander, F., & French, T. M. (1946). *Psychoanalytic therapy: Principles and applications.* Lincoln: Univeristy of Nebraska.

American Medical Assocation. (1983) Antipsychotic drugs. In *AMA Evaluations.* Philadelphia, PA: WB Saunders.

Bandura, A. (1977) Self efficacy: Toward a unifying theory of behavioral change. *Psychological Review, 84,* 191–215.

Beck, A. T., Rush, A. J., Shaw, B. E., & Emery, G. (1979). *Cognitive therapy for depression.* New York: Guilford.

Belkin, G. S. (1984). *Introduction to counseling* (2nd ed.). Dubuque, IA: William C. Brown.

Budman, S. H., & Gurman, A. S. (1988). *Theory and practice of brief therapy.* New York: Guilford.

Buelow, G., Hebert, S., & Buelow, S. (2000). *Psychotherappist's resource on psychiatric medications: Issues of treatment and referral.* Belmont, CA: Wadsworth.

Butcher, J. N., & Koss, M. P. (1978) *Research on brief and crisis oriented psychotherapies.* In S. I. Garfield & A. E. Bergen (Eds). *Handbook of psychotherapy and behavior change* (Vol. 3, pp. 627–670). New York: Wiley.

Callahan, C. J. (1998) Crisis intervention model for teachers. *Journal of Instructional Psychology, 25,* 226–235.

Cornes, C., (1990). Interpersonal psychotherapy of depression (IPT). In R. A. Wells & V. J. Gianetti (Eds.), *Handbook of brief psychotherapies* (pp. 261–276). New York: Plenum.

Council for Accreditation of Counseling and Related Programs. (1994). *CACREP accreditation standards and procedures manual.* Alexandria, VA: Author.

Council on Standards for Human Service Education and Training. (1995). *National standards for human service worker education and training programs.* Fitchburg, MA: Author.

deShazer, S. (1989). Resistance revisited. *Contemporary Family Therapy, 11*(4), 227–233.

deShazer, S. (1990). What is it about brief therapy that works? In J. K. Zeig & S. G. Gillian (Eds.), *Brief therapy: Myths, methods, and metaphors* (pp. 120–151). New York: Brunner/Mazel.

deShazer, S., & Berg, I. K. (1985). A part is not apart: Working with only one of the partners present. In A. S. Gurman (Ed), *Casebook of marital therapy* (pp. 97–110). New York: Guilford.

Fleming, J. (1998). Solution focused brief therapy: One answer to managed mental health care. *Family Journal, 6*(3), 286–295.

Fisch, R., Weakland, J. H., & Segal, L. (1982). The tactics of change. San Francisco: Jossey-Bass.

Gilliard, B. E., & James, R. K. (1997). *Crisis intervention strategies.* Pacific Grove, CA: Brooks/Cole.

Gingerich, W. J., deShazer, S., & Weiner-Davis (1988). Constructing change: A research view of interviewing. In E. Lipchik (Ed), *Interviewing.* Rockville, MD: Aspen.

Gitlin, M. J. (1996). *Psychotherapist's guide to psychopharmacology.* New York: The Free Press.

Goldfried, M. R. (1988) Application of rational restructuring to anxiety disorders. *Counseling Psychologist, 16,* 50–68.

Greenstone, J. L., & Leviton, S. C. (1993). *Elements of crisis intervention.* Pacific Grove, CA: Brooks/Cole.

Joyce, P. R., & Paykel, E. S. (1989). Predictors of drug response in depression. *Archives of General Psychiatry, 46*(1), 89–99.

Kaiser, T. L. (1997). *Supervisory relationships.* Pacific Grove, CA: Brooks/Cole.

Kanel, K. (1999). *A guide to crisis intervention.* Pacific Grove, CA: Brooks/Cole.

Kizer, P. M. (2000). *Getting the most from your human services internship: Learning from experience.* Belmont, CA: Wadsworth.

Klerman, G. L., Weissman, M. M., Rounsaville, B. J., & Chevron, E. S. (1984) *Interpersonal psychotherapy of depression.* New York: Basic Books.

Koss, M. P., & Bucher, J. W. (1986) *Research on brief psychotherapy.* In S. I. Garfield & A. E. Bergen (Eds.), Handbook of psychotherapy and behavior change (Vol. 3, pp 627–670). New York: Wiley

Leitner, L. A. (1974). Crisis counseling may save a life. *Journal of Rehabilitation, 40,* 19–20.

Mash, E. J., & Hunsley, J. (1993). Behavior therapy and managed mental health care: Integrating effectiveness and economics in mental health practice. *Behavior Therapy, 24*(1), 67–90.

Moretti, M. M., Feldman, L. A., & Shaw, B. F. (1990). *Cognitive therapy: Current issues in theory and practice.* In R. A. Wells & V. J. Giametti (Eds.), *Handbook of brief psychotherapy* (pp. 217–238). New York: Plenum.

Olen, B. R., Hebel, S. K., Dombek, C. E., & Kastrup, E. K. (Eds.). (1993). *Facts and comparison.* New York: Lippincott.

Quick, E. (1998). Doing what works in brief and intermittent therapy. *Journal of Mental Health, 7,* 527–534.

Reynolds, B. (1965). *Learning and teaching in the practice of social work.* New York: Russell and Russell.

Roberts, A. R. (1990). *Crisis intervention handbook: Assessment, treatment, and research.* Belmont, CA: Wadsworth.

Steenbarger, B. N. (1992). Toward science practice integration in brief counseling and therapy. *Counseling Psychologist, 20*(3), 403–451.

Wells, R. A. (1982). *Planned short term treatment.* New York: Free Press.

John C. Boylan

Final Evaluation

The preceding chapters in this text primarily addressed facilitating a student's process through the practicum and internship experiences. Theoretical aspects integral to the counselor's training were integrated with various forms and sample formats in order to maximize the learning process for practicum students and interns.

This chapter is organized to help those involved in the practicum and internship to formally evaluate it. This process will help practicum students and interns determine their strengths and weaknesses. It also serves as a vehicle to help site personnel formally evaluate their training structures.

The Monthly Practicum Log (Form 2.7) permits the student to quantify the number of hours spent in particular counseling areas while in the practicum. The practicum student should detail the time spent in the various training activities. The student should have his or her supervisor sign the practicum log monthly in recognition of these activities.

The function of the remaining evaluation forms (Forms 12.1 through 12.5) is explained in the information that follows:

The Internship Log (Form 12.1) parallels the function of the practicum log and is used by interns.

The Student Evaluation Form (Form 12.2) complements the practicum and internship logs. The supervisor utilizes this form to evaluate the student's work in each relevant and appropriate category.

The Client's Personal/Social Satisfaction With Counseling Assessment (Form 12.3) allows the practicum student's or intern's clients to address the degree of satisfaction experienced during the counseling process. The student should have his or her client fill out and sign the form when counseling has been terminated.

The Student Counselor Evaluation of Supervisor (Form 12.4) is completed by the practicum student or intern at the midpoint and conclusion of the supervisory contract. Both the student and his or her supervisor should sign the form.

A Site Evaluation Form (Form 12.5) is to be used so that site personnel and university program faculty can assess the quality of their training sites.

These final evaluation forms are included because they are similar to those typically used in agencies and schools. The final assessment by the student, supervisor, and client at the culmination of the internship experience is a crucial component of the training process and is an excellent opportunity for these individuals to evaluate the internship as a whole. It is only through a final assessment of the internship that the student is truly able to reflect on the material and skills learned. In the same way, feedback provided by the client and supervisor is instrumental in communicating to the student which skills have been used effectively and which need to be further refined. The student or supervisor might consider adapting these forms to address the specific and particular needs of the internship experience.

Index

LETTER TO PRACTICUM SITE SUPERVISOR

(Letter should be typed on official university stationary)

Date _____

Dear Practicum Site Supervisor,

The enclosed contract is designed to formalize the arrangement between _____ (University Program) and _____ (Practicum Site) for student counselors enrolled in the practicum at _____ (University). The practicum activities have been selected based upon APA and CACREP guidelines, state licensing or certification requirements, and the university and program faculty recommendations.

   If the guidelines, agreements, and practicum activities are followed closely, the student counselor should have the opportunity to demonstrate counseling competencies at an increasing level of complexity in the amount of time contracted. We realize that a practicum site may not be able to provide access for the student to every activity because of the differences that exist in individuals and institutions. The contract for each practicum experience will indicate those activities that can be provided.

   We appreciate and thank you for your interest and cooperation in helping to prepare professional counselors and psychologists.

Sincerely,

_____
(Name of Professor)

Ph. # _____

LETTER TO PRACTICUM SITE SUPERVISOR

(Letter should be typed on official university stationary)

Date _____

Dear Practicum Site Supervisor,

The enclosed contract is designed to formalize the arrangement between
_____ (University Program) and
_____ (Practicum Site) for student counselors enrolled in
the practicum at _____ (University). The practicum
activities have been selected based upon APA and CACREP guidelines, state licensing or
certification requirements, and the university and program faculty recommendations.

If the guidelines, agreements, and practicum activities are followed closely, the
student counselor should have the opportunity to demonstrate counseling competencies at
an increasing level of complexity in the amount of time contracted. We realize that a
practicum site may not be able to provide access for the student to every activity because of
the differences that exist in individuals and institutions. The contract for each practicum
experience will indicate those activities that can be provided.

We appreciate and thank you for your interest and cooperation in helping to prepare
professional counselors and psychologists.

Sincerely,

_____
(Name of Professor)

Ph. # _____

PRACTICUM CONTRACT

This agreement is made on _____ by and between _____
                                          (Date)   (Field site)

and _____. The agreement will be effective for a period
                (University program)

from _____ to _____ for_____ per week for _____.
  (Starting date) (Ending date)   (No. hours)   (Student name)

Purpose

The purpose of this agreement is to provide a qualified graduate student with a practicum experience in the field of counseling/psychology.

The university program agrees

1. to assign a university faculty liaison to facilitate communication between university and site;
2. to provide the site prior to placement of the student the following information
   a. profile of the student named above and
   b. an academic calendar that shall include dates for periods during which student will be excused from field supervision;
3. to notify the student that he/she must adhere to the administrative policies, rules, standards, schedules, and practices of the site;
4. that the faculty liaison shall be available for consultation with both site supervisors and students and shall be immediately contacted should any problem or change in relation to student, size, or university occur; and
5. that the university supervisor is responsible for the assignment of a fieldwork grade.

The practicum site agrees

1. to assign a practicum supervisor who has appropriate credentials, time, and interest for training the practicum student;
2. to provide opportunities for the student to engage in a variety of counseling activities under supervision and for evaluating the student's performance (suggested counseling experiences included in the "Practicum Activities" section);
3. to provide the student with adequate work space, telephone, office supplies, and staff to conduct professional activities;
4. to provide supervisory contact that involves some examination of student work using audio/visual tapes, observation, and/or live supervision; and
5. to provide written evaluation of student based on criteria established by the university program.

Within the specified time frame, _____ (site supervisor) will be the primary practicum site supervisor. The training activities (checked below) will be provided for the student in sufficient amounts to allow an adequate evaluation of the student's

level of competence in each activity. _____ (faculty liaison) will be the faculty liaison with whom the student and practicum site supervisor will communicate regarding progress, problems, and performance evaluations.

Practicum Activities

1. Individual counseling/psychotherapy
   Personal/social nature
   Occupational/educational nature

2. Group counseling/psychotherapy
   Coleading
   Leading

3. Intake interviewing
   Taking social history information

4. Testing
   Administration
   Analysis
   Interpretation of results

5. Report writing
   Recordkeeping
   Treatment plans
   Treatment

6. Consultation
   Referrals
   Professional team collaboration

7. Psychoeducational activities
   Parent conferences
   Outreach

8. Career counseling

9. Individual supervision

10. Group or peer supervision

11. Case conferences or staff meetings

12. Other (please list) _____

_____

_____

Practicum site supervisor _____ Date _____

Student _____ Date _____

Faculty liaison _____ Date _____

PRACTICUM CONTRACT

This agreement is made on _____ by and between _____
                            (Date)   (Field site)

and _____. The agreement will be effective for a period
              (University program)

from _____ to _____ for _____ per week for _____.
  (Starting date) (Ending date)   (No. hours)   (Student name)

Purpose

The purpose of this agreement is to provide a qualified graduate student with a practicum experience in the field of counseling/psychology.

The university program agrees

1. to assign a university faculty liaison to facilitate communication between university and site;
2. to provide the site prior to placement of the student the following information
   a. profile of the student named above and
   b. an academic calendar that shall include dates for periods during which student will be excused from field supervision;
3. to notify the student that he/she must adhere to the administrative policies, rules, standards, schedules, and practices of the site;
4. that the faculty liaison shall be available for consultation with both site supervisors and students and shall be immediately contacted should any problem or change in relation to student, size, or university occur; and
5. that the university supervisor is responsible for the assignment of a fieldwork grade.

The practicum site agrees

1. to assign a practicum supervisor who has appropriate credentials, time, and interest for training the practicum student;
2. to provide opportunities for the student to engage in a variety of counseling activities under supervision and for evaluating the student's performance (suggested counseling experiences included in the "Practicum Activities" section);
3. to provide the student with adequate work space, telephone, office supplies, and staff to conduct professional activities;
4. to provide supervisory contact that involves some examination of student work using audio/visual tapes, observation, and/or live supervision; and
5. to provide written evaluation of student based on criteria established by the university program.

Within the specified time frame, _____ (site supervisor)
will be the primary practicum site supervisor. The training activities (checked below) will be
provided for the student in sufficient amounts to allow an adequate evaluation of the student's

level of competence in each activity. _____ (faculty
liaison) will be the faculty liaison with whom the student and practicum site supervisor will
communicate regarding progress, problems, and performance evaluations.

Practicum Activities

1. Individual counseling/psychotherapy
    Personal/social nature
    Occupational/educational nature

2. Group counseling/psychotherapy
    Coleading
    Leading

3. Intake interviewing
    Taking social history information

4. Testing
    Administration
    Analysis
    Interpretation of results

5. Report writing
    Recordkeeping
    Treatment plans
    Treatment

6. Consultation
    Referrals
    Professional team collaboration

7. Psychoeducational activities
    Parent conferences
    Outreach

8. Career counseling

9. Individual supervision

10. Group or peer supervision

11. Case conferences or staff meetings

12. Other (please list) _____
_____
_____

Practicum site supervisor _____ Date _____
Student _____ Date _____
Faculty liaison _____ Date _____

STUDENT PROFILE SHEET

Directions: The student counselor is to submit this form in duplicate to the university practicum liaison, who will submit one copy to the field site.

Practicum Student Counselor/Psychologist

Name _____

Address _____

_____

Telephone: (Home) _____

(Office) _____

Date _____

I hold the degree of _____ from

_____, and have completed the

following courses as part of the _____ (degree)

program, with a major in _____ from

_____.

Psychology of Human Development _____   Tests and Measurements _____

Psychology of Learning _____   Personality Development _____

Counseling Skills _____   Career Development _____

Intro to Counseling _____   Legal and Ethical Issues _____

Theories of Counseling _____   Process and Techniques of
Group Counseling _____

Other (please specify) _____

_____

_____

Professional and nonprofessional work experience _____

_____

_____

STUDENT PROFILE SHEET

Directions: The student counselor is to submit this form in duplicate to the university practicum liaison, who will submit one copy to the field site.

Practicum Student Counselor/Psychologist

Name _____

Address _____

_____

Telephone: (Home) _____

(Office) _____

Date _____

I hold the degree of _____ from

_____, and have completed the

following courses as part of the _____ (degree)

program, with a major in _____ from

_____.

Psychology of Human Development _____   Tests and Measurements _____

Psychology of Learning _____   Personality Development _____

Counseling Skills _____   Career Development _____

Intro to Counseling _____   Legal and Ethical Issues _____

Theories of Counseling _____   Process and Techniques of
                                            Group Counseling _____

Other (please specify) _____

_____

_____

Professional and nonprofessional work experience _____

_____

_____

STUDENT/PRACTICUM/INTERNSHIP AGREEMENT

Directions: Student is to complete this form in duplicate and submit a copy of this agreement to the university practicum supervisor or internship coordinator.

1. I hereby attest that I have read and understood the American Psychological Association and the American Counseling Association ethical standards (Chapter 6 in this manual) and will practice my counseling in accordance with these standards. Any breach of these ethics or any unethical behavior on my part will result in my removal from practicum/internship and a failing grade, and documentation of such behavior will become part of my permanent record.

2. I agree to adhere to the administrative policies, rules, standards, and practices of the practicum/internship site.

3. I understand that my responsibilities include keeping my practicum/internship supervisor(s) informed regarding my practicum/internship experiences.

4. I understand that I will not be issued a passing grade in practicum/internship unless I demonstrate the specified minimal level of counseling skill, knowledge, and competence and complete course requirements as required.

Signature _____

Date _____

STUDENT/PRACTICUM/INTERNSHIP AGREEMENT

Directions: Student is to complete this form in duplicate and submit a copy of this agreement to the university practicum supervisor or internship coordinator.

1. I hereby attest that I have read and understood the American Psychological Association and the American Counseling Association ethical standards (Chapter 6 in this manual) and will practice my counseling in accordance with these standards. Any breach of these ethics or any unethical behavior on my part will result in my removal from practicum/internship and a failing grade, and documentation of such behavior will become part of my permanent record.

2. I agree to adhere to the administrative policies, rules, standards, and practices of the practicum/internship site.

3. I understand that my responsibilities include keeping my practicum/internship supervisor(s) informed regarding my practicum/internship experiences.

4. I understand that I will not be issued a passing grade in practicum/internship unless I demonstrate the specified minimal level of counseling skill, knowledge, and competence and complete course requirements as required.

Signature _____

Date _____

TAPE CRITIQUE FORM

Student counselor's name _____

Client I.D. & no. of session _____

Brief summary of session content:

_____
_____
_____
_____

Intended goals:

_____
_____
_____
_____

Comment on positive counseling behaviors:

_____
_____
_____
_____

Comment on areas of counseling practice needing improvement:

_____
_____
_____
_____

Concerns or comment regarding client dynamics:

_____
_____
_____
_____

Plans for further counseling with this client:

_____

_____

_____

_____

Tape submitted to _____

Date _____

TAPE CRITIQUE FORM

Student counselor's name _____

Client I.D. & no. of session _____

Brief summary of session content:

_____
_____
_____
_____

Intended goals:

_____
_____
_____
_____

Comment on positive counseling behaviors:

_____
_____
_____
_____

Comment on areas of counseling practice needing improvement:

_____
_____
_____
_____

Concerns or comment regarding client dynamics:

_____
_____
_____
_____

Plans for further counseling with this client:

_____

_____

_____

_____

Tape submitted to _____

Date _____

WEEKLY SCHEDULE

Day of week	Location	Time	Practicum activity	Comment
_____	_____	_____	_____	_____
_____	_____	_____	_____	_____
_____	_____	_____	_____	_____
_____	_____	_____	_____	_____
_____	_____	_____	_____	_____
_____	_____	_____	_____	_____
_____	_____	_____	_____	_____
_____	_____	_____	_____	_____
_____	_____	_____	_____	_____
_____	_____	_____	_____	_____
_____	_____	_____	_____	_____
_____	_____	_____	_____	_____
_____	_____	_____	_____	_____
_____	_____	_____	_____	_____
_____	_____	_____	_____	_____
_____	_____	_____	_____	_____
_____	_____	_____	_____	_____
_____	_____	_____	_____	_____
_____	_____	_____	_____	_____
_____	_____	_____	_____	_____
_____	_____	_____	_____	_____
_____	_____	_____	_____	_____
_____	_____	_____	_____	_____

Student counselor name _____

Week beginning _____ Ending _____

WEEKLY SCHEDULE

Day of week	Location	Time	Practicum activity	Comment
___	___	___	___	___
___	___	___	___	___
___	___	___	___	___
___	___	___	___	___
___	___	___	___	___
___	___	___	___	___
___	___	___	___	___
___	___	___	___	___
___	___	___	___	___
___	___	___	___	___
___	___	___	___	___
___	___	___	___	___
___	___	___	___	___
___	___	___	___	___
___	___	___	___	___
___	___	___	___	___
___	___	___	___	___
___	___	___	___	___
___	___	___	___	___
___	___	___	___	___
___	___	___	___	___
___	___	___	___	___
___	___	___	___	___
___	___	___	___	___

Student counselor name _____

Week beginning _____ Ending _____

MONTHLY PRACTICUM LOG

Name _____

Practicum site _____

Practicum supervisor _____
(Signature)

Month of	Intake interview	Ind. counseling	Group counseling	Testing	Report writing	Consultation	Psycho-educational	Career counseling	Case conference	Other (specify)
Week 1 Dates: Total hours:										
Week 2 Dates: Total hours:										
Week 3 Dates: Total hours:										
Week 4 Dates: Total hours:										

MONTHLY PRACTICUM LOG

Name _____

Practicum site _____

Practicum supervisor _____
(Signature)

Month of	Intake interview	Ind. counseling	Group counseling	Testing	Report writing	Consultation	Psycho-educational	Career counseling	Case conference	Other (specify)
Week 1 Dates: Total hours:										
Week 2 Dates: Total hours:										
Week 3 Dates: Total hours:										
Week 4 Dates: Total hours:										

PARENTAL RELEASE FORM

Parent's name _____

Address _____

Phone _____ (Home) _____ (Office)

The Graduate Department of Counseling and Psychology at _____
College/University conducts a Counseling Practicum Course each semester at the college/university. The Counseling Practicum Course is an advanced course in counseling required

of all degree candidates in the Counseling Program at _____
College/University. Students are required to audio- and/or videotape counseling sessions as part of their course and degree requirements.

Student's name _____ would like to work with your son/
daughter, a student at _____ School.

The counseling sessions conducted with your child will be audio- and/or videotaped and will be reviewed by the student's supervisor _____. All audio- and videotapes made will be erased at the completion of your child's involvement in the program.

We hope that you will take the opportunity to have your child become involved in the Counseling Program. If you are interested in having your child participate, please sign the form where indicated.

Thank you for your cooperation.

Parent's signature _____

Date _____

PARENTAL RELEASE FORM

Parent's name _____

Address _____

Phone _____ (Home) _____ (Office)

The Graduate Department of Counseling and Psychology at _____
College/University conducts a Counseling Practicum Course each semester at the college/
university. The Counseling Practicum Course is an advanced course in counseling required

of all degree candidates in the Counseling Program at _____
College/University. Students are required to audio- and/or videotape counseling sessions as
part of their course and degree requirements.

Student's name _____ would like to work with your son/

daughter, a student at _____ School.

The counseling sessions conducted with your child will be audio- and/or videotaped and will
be reviewed by the student's supervisor _____. All
audio- and videotapes made will be erased at the completion of your child's involvement in
the program.

We hope that you will take the opportunity to have your child become involved in the
Counseling Program. If you are interested in having your child participate, please sign the
form where indicated.

Thank you for your cooperation.

Parent's signature _____

Date _____

CLIENT RELEASE FORM

Graduate Department of Counseling and Psychology

_____
(Name of college/university)

I, _____, agree to be counseled by a practicum/intern student in the Department of Counseling and Psychology at _____ College/University.

I further understand that I will participate in counseling interviews that will be audiotaped, videotaped, and/or viewed by practicum/intern students through the use of one-way observation windows.

I understand that I will be counseled by a graduate student who has completed advanced coursework in counseling/therapy.

I understand that the student will be supervised by a faculty member or site supervisor.

Client's signature _____

Age _____ Date _____

Counselor's signature _____

CLIENT RELEASE FORM

Graduate Department of Counseling and Psychology

_____

(Name of college/university)

I, _____, agree to be counseled by a practicum/intern student in the Department of Counseling and Psychology at _____ College/University.

I further understand that I will participate in counseling interviews that will be audiotaped, videotaped, and/or viewed by practicum/intern students through the use of one-way observation windows.

I understand that I will be counseled by a graduate student who has completed advanced coursework in counseling/therapy.

I understand that the student will be supervised by a faculty member or site supervisor.

Client's signature _____

Age _____ Date _____

Counselor's signature _____

INITIAL INTAKE FORM

Name _____ Date _____

Address _____ City _____ State _____ Zip _____

Telephone (Home) _____ (Work) _____

Therapist name _____ Date _____

Identifying Information

Age _____ Date of Birth _____ / _____ / _____ Place _____

Sex: Male _____   Female _____   Height ____ ft. _____ in.   Weight _____ lbs.

Race: White _____ Black _____ Asian _____ Hispanic _____ Other _____

Marital Status: M _____   S _____   D _____   W _____   Sep _____

If married, spouse's name _____ Age _____

Occupation _____ Employer _____

Occupation (Spouse) _____ Employer _____

Referral source: Self _____ Other _____

Name of referral source _____

Address of referral source _____

Treatment History (General)

Are you currently taking medication?   Yes _____   No _____

If yes, name(s) of the medication(s) _____

Dosage of medication(s) _____

Provider of medication(s) _____

Have you received previous psychiatric treatment?   Yes _____   No _____

If yes, name provider _____

Dates of service _____ Location _____

Reason for termination of treatment? _____

Presenting problem or condition (current) _____

Presenting factors (contributors) _____

Symptoms (describe) _____

_____

Acute _____ Chronic _____

Family History (General)

Father's name _____ Age _____ Living _____ Deceased _____

Occupation _____ Full-time _____ Part-time _____

Mother's name _____ Age _____ Living _____ Deceased _____

Occupation _____ Full-time _____ Part-time _____

Brother(s)/Sister(s)

Name _____ Age _____ Living _____ Deceased _____

Name _____ Age _____ Living _____ Deceased _____

Name _____ Age _____ Living _____ Deceased _____

Educational History (General)

	Name of institution	Location	Dates	Degree
Secondary				
College				
Trade				
Graduate				

Employment History (General)

Title/Description	(From when to when)	Full- or part-time

INITIAL INTAKE FORM

Name _____ Date _____

Address _____ City _____ State _____ Zip _____

Telephone (Home) _____ (Work) _____

Therapist name _____ Date _____

Identifying Information

Age _____ Date of Birth _____ / _____ / _____ Place _____

Sex: Male _____   Female _____   Height _____ ft. _____ in.   Weight _____ lbs.

Race: White _____ Black _____ Asian _____ Hispanic _____ Other _____

Marital Status: M _____   S _____   D _____   W _____   Sep _____

If married, spouse's name _____ Age _____

Occupation _____ Employer _____

Occupation (Spouse) _____ Employer _____

Referral source: Self _____ Other _____

Name of referral source _____

Address of referral source _____

Treatment History (General)

Are you currently taking medication?   Yes _____   No _____

If yes, name(s) of the medication(s) _____

Dosage of medication(s) _____

Provider of medication(s) _____

Have you received previous psychiatric treatment?   Yes _____   No _____

If yes, name provider _____

Dates of service _____ Location _____

Reason for termination of treatment? _____

Presenting problem or condition (current) _____

Presenting factors (contributors) _____

Symptoms (describe) _____

_____

Acute _____ Chronic _____

Family History (General)

Father's name _____ Age _____ Living _____ Deceased _____

Occupation _____ Full-time _____ Part-time _____

Mother's name _____ Age _____ Living _____ Deceased _____

Occupation _____ Full-time _____ Part-time _____

Brother(s)/Sister(s)

Name _____ Age _____ Living _____ Deceased _____

Name _____ Age _____ Living _____ Deceased _____

Name _____ Age _____ Living _____ Deceased _____

Educational History (General)

	Name of institution	Location	Dates	Degree
Secondary				
College				
Trade				
Graduate				

Employment History (General)

Title/Description	(From when to when)	Full- or part-time

ELEMENTARY SCHOOL COUNSELING REFERRAL FORM *

(Confidential information to be supplied by teacher or counselor)

Date referral received _____

Teacher's name _____ Date _____

Principal's name _____ Date _____

Child's name _____ Date _____

Grade _____ Section _____ Date of birth _____ Age _____

Test Results

IQ _____ Present Grade Level _____

Group _____ Individual _____ Math _____ Reading _____

Father's name _____ Mother's name _____

Address _____ Address _____

Phone number _____ Phone number _____

Have you had discussion with the child's parent(s) regarding this referral? Yes ___ No ___

What was the parent's reaction to you referring the child for counseling?

Positive _____ Neutral _____ Negative _____

To your knowledge, has the child received counseling services in the school or out of school?
Yes ___ No ___

If yes, supply counselor or agency name _____

Does the child presently qualify for or receive any special education services? Yes ___ No ___
If so, give dates _____

Have the child's parents requested counseling? Yes ___ No ___

Have you discussed your concerns about the child with the building principal?

Yes ___ No ___

---

* Form developed by Dale Malecki, Elementary Counselor, Abington Heights School District, Clark's Summit, PA. Used with permission.

Have you discussed your concerns about the child with the multidisciplinary team (child study team)?   Yes ___   No ___

Student's Present Functioning
(as you perceive it)

	Excellent	Above average	Average	Below average	Poor
Reading	_____	_____	_____	_____	_____
Mathematics	_____	_____	_____	_____	_____
Language arts	_____	_____	_____	_____	_____
Social studies	_____	_____	_____	_____	_____
General learning rate	_____	_____	_____	_____	_____
On-task behavior	_____	_____	_____	_____	_____
Self-directed learner	_____	_____	_____	_____	_____
Follows directions (oral)	_____	_____	_____	_____	_____
Follows directions (written)	_____	_____	_____	_____	_____
Attention span	_____	_____	_____	_____	_____
Completes assignments	_____	_____	_____	_____	_____
Returns homework	_____	_____	_____	_____	_____
Works well with others	_____	_____	_____	_____	_____
Obeys classroom rules	_____	_____	_____	_____	_____
Motor coordination	_____	_____	_____	_____	_____
Self-image development	_____	_____	_____	_____	_____
Adult relationships	_____	_____	_____	_____	_____
Peer relationships	_____	_____	_____	_____	_____
Attitude toward school	_____	_____	_____	_____	_____
Shows enthusiasm for learning	_____	_____	_____	_____	_____
Participates in class	_____	_____	_____	_____	_____

Possible Evidence of
(check if appropriate)

Daydreams _____

Easily distracted _____

Absenteeism _____

Withdrawn _____

Family problems _____

Preoccupied _____

Worries _____

Lacks assertiveness _____

Impulsive behavior _____

Poorly motivated _____

Inappropriate academic placement _____

_____

Other variables

(check if appropriate)

Vision _____   Stature _____

Hearing _____   Hygiene _____

Speech _____   Other (please specify) _____

Special skills, talents, or competencies child has _____

_____

Reason for referral (based on your observation) _____

_____

What strategies or techniques have you tried with this child? _____

_____

Comments and recommendations _____

_____

Please indicate a time(s) which will be convenient for you to have a conference with me.

Monday	Period	Time
Tuesday	Period	Time
Wednesday	Period	Time
Thursday	Period	Time
Friday	Period	Time

Thank you for taking your time to share this information with me.

Signature _____ Date _____
(Elementary Counselor)

ELEMENTARY SCHOOL COUNSELING REFERRAL FORM*

(Confidential information to be supplied by teacher or counselor)

Date referral received _____

Teacher's name _____ Date _____

Principal's name _____ Date _____

Child's name _____ Date _____

Grade _____ Section _____ Date of birth _____ Age _____

Test Results

IQ _____ Present Grade Level _____

Group _____ Individual _____ Math _____ Reading _____

Father's name _____ Mother's name _____

Address _____ Address _____

Phone number _____ Phone number _____

Have you had discussion with the child's parent(s) regarding this referral? Yes ___ No ___

What was the parent's reaction to you referring the child for counseling?

Positive _____ Neutral _____ Negative _____

To your knowledge, has the child received counseling services in the school or out of school?

Yes ___ No ___

If yes, supply counselor or agency name _____

Does the child presently qualify for or receive any special education services? Yes ___ No___
If so, give dates _____

Have the child's parents requested counseling? Yes ___ No ___

Have you discussed your concerns about the child with the building principal?

Yes ___ No ___

---

* Form developed by Dale Malecki, Elementary Counselor, Abington Heights School District, Clark's Summit, PA. Used with permission.

Have you discussed your concerns about the child with the multidisciplinary team (child study team)?   Yes ___   No ___

Student's Present Functioning
(as you perceive it)

	Excellent	Above average	Average	Below average	Poor
Reading	_____	_____	_____	_____	_____
Mathematics	_____	_____	_____	_____	_____
Language arts	_____	_____	_____	_____	_____
Social studies	_____	_____	_____	_____	_____
General learning rate	_____	_____	_____	_____	_____
On-task behavior	_____	_____	_____	_____	_____
Self-directed learner	_____	_____	_____	_____	_____
Follows directions (oral)	_____	_____	_____	_____	_____
Follows directions (written)	_____	_____	_____	_____	_____
Attention span	_____	_____	_____	_____	_____
Completes assignments	_____	_____	_____	_____	_____
Returns homework	_____	_____	_____	_____	_____
Works well with others	_____	_____	_____	_____	_____
Obeys classroom rules	_____	_____	_____	_____	_____
Motor coordination	_____	_____	_____	_____	_____
Self-image development	_____	_____	_____	_____	_____
Adult relationships	_____	_____	_____	_____	_____
Peer relationships	_____	_____	_____	_____	_____
Attitude toward school	_____	_____	_____	_____	_____
Shows enthusiasm for learning	_____	_____	_____	_____	_____
Participates in class	_____	_____	_____	_____	_____

Possible Evidence of
(check if appropriate)

Daydreams _____   Worries _____

Easily distracted _____   Lacks assertiveness _____

Absenteeism _____   Impulsive behavior _____

Withdrawn _____   Poorly motivated _____

Family problems _____   Inappropriate academic placement _____

Preoccupied _____   _____

Other variables
(check if appropriate)

Vision _____   Stature _____

Hearing _____   Hygiene _____

Speech _____   Other (please specify) _____

Special skills, talents, or competencies child has _____

_____

Reason for referral (based on your observation) _____

_____

What strategies or techniques have you tried with this child? _____

_____

Comments and recommendations _____

_____

Please indicate a time(s) which will be convenient for you to have a conference with me.

Monday	Period	Time
Tuesday	Period	Time
Wednesday	Period	Time
Thursday	Period	Time
Friday	Period	Time

Thank you for taking your time to share this information with me.

Signature _____ Date _____

(Elementary Counselor)

SECONDARY SCHOOL COUNSELING REFERRAL FORM

(Confidential information to be supplied by teacher or counselor)

Date referral received _____

Teacher's name _____ Date _____

Principal's name _____ School _____

Child's name _____

Grade _____ Date of Birth _____

Test Results
IQ _____ Group _____ Individual _____

If the child has ever been retained, indicate grade _____

Father's name _____ Mother's name _____

Address _____ Address _____

Phone number _____ Phone number _____

Have you had discussion with the child's parent(s) regarding this referral? Yes ___ No ___

What was the parent's reaction to you referring the child for counseling?

Positive _____ Neutral _____ Negative _____

To your knowledge, has the child received counseling services in the school or out of school?

Yes ___ No ___

If yes, supply counselor or agency name _____

Does the student presently qualify for or receive any special education services? Yes ___ No___
If so, give dates _____

Has the student had a psychoeducational assessment done? Yes ___ No ___
If so, give date _____

Have student's parents requested counseling? Yes ___ No ___

Have you discussed your concerns about the child with your supervisor/principal?

Yes ___ No ___

Student's Present Functioning
(as you perceive it)

	Excellent	Above average	Average	Below average	Poor
Self-directed learner	_____	_____	_____	_____	_____
Attention span	_____	_____	_____	_____	_____
Quality of writer assessment	_____	_____	_____	_____	_____
Self-image	_____	_____	_____	_____	_____
Attitude toward authority	_____	_____	_____	_____	_____
Peer relationships	_____	_____	_____	_____	_____
Works well with others	_____	_____	_____	_____	_____
Completes assignments	_____	_____	_____	_____	_____
Follows classroom rules	_____	_____	_____	_____	_____

Please Check
(if appropriate)

Aggressive	_____	Personable	_____	Engaging	_____
Assertive	_____	Shy	_____	Ambitious	_____
Noncompliant	_____	Dependent	_____	Impulsive	_____
Disregard for Rights	_____	Depressed	_____	Preoccupied	_____
Self-confident	_____	Avoidant	_____	Motivated	_____
Withdrawn	_____	Friendly	_____	Distractible	_____
Argumentative	_____	Social	_____		

Special skills, talents, competencies student has _____

_____

Reason for referral (based on your observations) _____

_____

What interventions have you tried with this student?_____

_____

Comments and recommendations _____

_____

Signature _____ Date _____

Position _____

SECONDARY SCHOOL COUNSELING REFERRAL FORM

(Confidential information to be supplied by teacher or counselor)

Date referral received _____

Teacher's name _____ Date _____

Principal's name _____ School _____

Child's name _____

Grade _____ Date of Birth _____

Test Results
IQ _____ Group _____ Individual _____

If the child has ever been retained, indicate grade _____

Father's name _____ Mother's name _____

Address _____ Address _____

Phone number _____ Phone number _____

Have you had discussion with the child's parent(s) regarding this referral? Yes ___ No ___

What was the parent's reaction to you referring the child for counseling?

Positive _____ Neutral _____ Negative _____

To your knowledge, has the child received counseling services in the school or out of school?

Yes ___ No ___

If yes, supply counselor or agency name _____

Does the student presently qualify for or receive any special education services? Yes ___ No___
If so, give dates _____

Has the student had a psychoeducational assessment done? Yes ___ No ___
If so, give date _____

Have student's parents requested counseling? Yes ___ No ___

Have you discussed your concerns about the child with your supervisor/principal?

Yes ___ No ___

Student's Present Functioning
(as you perceive it)

	Excellent	Above average	Average	Below average	Poor
Self-directed learner	_____	_____	_____	_____	_____
Attention span	_____	_____	_____	_____	_____
Quality of writer assessment	_____	_____	_____	_____	_____
Self-image	_____	_____	_____	_____	_____
Attitude toward authority	_____	_____	_____	_____	_____
Peer relationships	_____	_____	_____	_____	_____
Works well with others	_____	_____	_____	_____	_____
Completes assignments	_____	_____	_____	_____	_____
Follows classroom rules	_____	_____	_____	_____	_____

Please Check
(if appropriate)

Aggressive	_____	Personable	_____	Engaging	_____
Assertive	_____	Shy	_____	Ambitious	_____
Noncompliant	_____	Dependent	_____	Impulsive	_____
Disregard for Rights	_____	Depressed	_____	Preoccupied	_____
Self-confident	_____	Avoidant	_____	Motivated	_____
Withdrawn	_____	Friendly	_____	Distractible	_____
Argumentative	_____	Social	_____		

Special skills, talents, competencies student has _____

_____

Reason for referral (based on your observations) _____

_____

What interventions have you tried with this student?_____

_____

Comments and recommendations _____

_____

Signature _____ Date _____

Position _____

MENTAL STATUS CHECKLIST

Appearance and Behavior

		Check if applies	Circle	Therapist's Comments
1.	Posture	Normal _____	Limp, rigid, ill at ease	_____ _____ _____
2.	Gestures	Normal _____	Agitated, tics, twitches	_____ _____ _____
3.	Grooming	Neat _____	Well groomed, disheveled, meticulous	_____ _____ _____
4.	Dress	Appropriate _____ Casual _____ Formal _____	Dirty, careless, inappropriate, seductive	_____ _____ _____
5.	Facial expression	Appropriate _____	Poor eye contact, dazed, staring	_____ _____ _____
6.	Speech			
	a. Pace	Normal _____	Retarded, pressured, blocking	_____ _____
	b. Volume	Normal _____	Soft, very loud, monotone	_____ _____
	c. Form	Logical _____ Rational _____	Illogical, rambling, incoherent, coherent	_____ _____
	d. Clarity	Normal _____	Garbled, slurred	_____ _____
	e. Content	Normal _____	Loose, associations, rhyming, obscene	_____ _____

Attention/Affect/Mood

		Check if applies	Circle	Therapist's Comments
1.	Attention	Normal _____	Short span, hyper,	_____
		Alert _____	alert, distractible	_____
2.	Mood	Normal _____	Elated, euphoric,	_____
			agitated, fearful,	_____
			hostile, sad	_____
3.	Affect	Appropriate _____	Inappropriate,	_____
			shallow, flat,	_____
			intense	_____

Perception and Thought Content

		Check if applies	Description
1.	Hallucination		
	a. Auditory	_____	_____
	b. Visual	_____	_____
	c. Tactile	_____	_____
	d. Gustatory	_____	_____
	e. Olfactory	_____	_____

2. Delusion

a. Paranoid	_____	b. Persecutory	_____
c. Gradiose	_____	d. Reference	_____
e. Control	_____	f. Thought	_____
g. Insertion	_____	h.Broadcasting	_____
i. Thought withdrawal	_____		

3. Illusions

a. Visual _____

b. Auditory _____

Describe _____

_____

4. Other derealization
   a. Phobias   _____   b. Obsessions   _____
   c. Compulsions   _____   d. Ruminations   _____
   Describe   _____

_____

5. Suicide/homicide
   Ideation   _____   Plans   _____
   Describe   _____

_____

Orientation   Oriented × 3 _____
   Disoriented to: Time _____   Place _____   Person _____

Judgment   Intact _____   Impaired _____
   Describe   _____

_____

Concentration/Memory

1. Memory   Intact _____   Impaired _____
2. Immediate recall   Good _____   Poor _____
3. Reversals   Good _____   Poor _____
4. Concentration   Good _____   Poor _____

Abstract ability

1. Similarities   Good _____   Poor _____   Bizarre _____
2. Absurdities   Recognized _____   Not recognized _____
3. Proverbs   Appropriate _____   Literal _____   Concrete _____   Bizzare _____

Insight   Good _____   Fair _____   Poor _____   Absent _____

MENTAL STATUS CHECKLIST

Appearance and Behavior

		Check if applies	Circle	Therapist's Comments
1.	Posture	Normal _____	Limp, rigid, ill at ease	_____ _____ _____
2.	Gestures	Normal _____	Agitated, tics, twitches	_____ _____ _____
3.	Grooming	Neat _____	Well groomed, disheveled, meticulous	_____ _____ _____
4.	Dress	Appropriate _____ Casual _____ Formal _____	Dirty, careless, inappropriate, seductive	_____ _____ _____
5.	Facial expression	Appropriate _____	Poor eye contact, dazed, staring	_____ _____ _____
6.	Speech			
	a. Pace	Normal _____	Retarded, pressured, blocking	_____ _____
	b. Volume	Normal _____	Soft, very loud, monotone	_____ _____
	c. Form	Logical _____ Rational _____	Illogical, rambling, incoherent, coherent	_____ _____
	d. Clarity	Normal _____	Garbled, slurred	_____ _____
	e. Content	Normal _____	Loose, associations, rhyming, obscene	_____ _____

Attention/Affect/Mood

		Check if applies	Circle	Therapist's Comments
1. Attention	Normal	_____	Short span, hyper,	_____
	Alert	_____	alert, distractible	_____
2. Mood	Normal	_____	Elated, euphoric,	_____
			agitated, fearful,	_____
			hostile, sad	_____
3. Affect	Appropriate	_____	Inappropriate,	_____
			shallow, flat,	_____
			intense	_____

Perception and Thought Content

Check if applies   Description

1. Hallucination
   a. Auditory   _____   _____
   b. Visual   _____   _____
   c. Tactile   _____   _____
   d. Gustatory   _____   _____
   e. Olfactory   _____   _____

2. Delusion
   a. Paranoid   _____   b. Persecutory   _____
   c. Gradiose   _____   d. Reference   _____
   e. Control   _____   f. Thought   _____
   g. Insertion   _____   h. Broadcasting   _____
   i. Thought withdrawal _____

3. Illusions
   a. Visual   _____
   b. Auditory   _____

Describe _____

_____

4. Other derealization

    a. Phobias   _____   b. Obsessions   _____

    c. Compulsions   _____   d. Ruminations   _____

    Describe _____

    _____

5. Suicide/homicide

    Ideation   _____   Plans _____

    Describe _____

    _____

Orientation   Oriented × 3 _____

    Disoriented to: Time _____   Place _____   Person _____

Judgment   Intact _____   Impaired _____

    Describe _____

    _____

Concentration/Memory

1. Memory   Intact _____   Impaired _____

2. Immediate recall   Good _____   Poor _____

3. Reversals   Good _____   Poor _____

4. Concentration   Good _____   Poor _____

Abstract ability

1. Similarities   Good _____   Poor _____   Bizarre _____

2. Absurdities   Recognized _____   Not recognized _____

3. Proverbs   Appropriate _____   Literal _____   Concrete _____   Bizzare _____

Insight   Good _____   Fair _____   Poor _____   Absent _____

PSYCHOSOCIAL HISTORY

Directions: Practicum/internship students should complete this form prior to the initiation of therapy and after completion of the Initial Intake Form.

I. **Identifying Information**

Name _____ Age _____

Address _____ Date of birth _____

Phone _____ Marital status _____

II. **Presenting Problem/Complaint**

Nature of complaint? _____

_____

When did the problem begin (date of onset)?_____

How often does it occur? _____

How does it affect your daily functioning? _____

_____

Are there events, situations, and person(s) that precipitate it? _____

_____

Symptoms:

Acute _____
      (Describe)

_____

Chronic _____
      (Describe)

_____

Previous treatment (List by whom, outcome, and reason for termination of treatment)

_____

_____

Medical:

Physician's name _____

Treatment dates from _____ to _____

Describe _____

_____

Psychiatric

    Therapist's name _____

    Treatment dates from _____ to _____

    Describe _____

    _____

Prescription drugs

    Substance usage _____

    Description/frequency/amount _____

    _____

    _____

III. Developmental History

    Pregnancy _____

    Delivery _____

    Infancy (developmental milestones) _____

    _____

    Middle childhood (developmental milestones) _____

    _____

    Adolescence (developmental milestones) _____

    _____

    Young adulthood, middle adulthood, late adulthood (developmental milestones)

    _____

    _____

IV. Family History

    Parent (names, ages, occupations) _____

    _____

    _____

    Parental description (personality/attitude toward client) _____

    _____

    _____

    Siblings/significant others (names, ages) _____

    _____

    _____

Personality/attitude toward the client _____

_____

_____

V. Educational/Occupational History

Education (highest grade achieved; school performance/special classes/special needs)

_____

_____

_____

Occupational (job status, kinds of jobs, length of employment, vocational interests)

_____

_____

_____

VI. Health History

Childhood disease, prior illnesses, surgery, etc. _____

_____

_____

_____

Current health (description of clinic) _____

_____

_____

_____

Family health (grandparents, children) _____

_____

_____

_____

Current medication (prescribed and over the counter) _____

_____

_____

_____

VII. Marital History

Marital status: Years married, number of children (problems, stressors, enjoyment)

_____

_____

_____

Client's description of the current relationship with spouse _____

_____

_____

_____

Client's perception of sexual relationship (attitudes/behavior) _____

_____

_____

_____

PSYCHOSOCIAL HISTORY

Directions: Practicum/internship students should complete this form prior to the initiation of therapy and after completion of the Initial Intake Form.

I. Identifying Information

Name _____ Age _____

Address _____ Date of birth _____

Phone _____ Marital status _____

II. Presenting Problem/Complaint

Nature of complaint? _____

_____

When did the problem begin (date of onset)?_____

How often does it occur? _____

How does it affect your daily functioning? _____

_____

Are there events, situations, and person(s) that precipitate it? _____

_____

Symptoms:

Acute _____
       (Describe)

_____

Chronic _____
         (Describe)

_____

Previous treatment (List by whom, outcome, and reason for termination of treatment)

_____

_____

Medical:

Physician's name _____

Treatment dates from _____ to _____

Describe _____

_____

Psychiatric

Therapist's name _____

Treatment dates from _____ to _____

Describe _____

_____

Prescription drugs

Substance usage _____

Description/frequency/amount _____

_____

_____

III. Developmental History

Pregnancy _____

Delivery _____

Infancy (developmental milestones) _____

_____

Middle childhood (developmental milestones) _____

_____

Adolescence (developmental milestones) _____

_____

Young adulthood, middle adulthood, late adulthood (developmental milestones)

_____

_____

IV. Family History

Parent (names, ages, occupations) _____

_____

_____

Parental description (personality/attitude toward client) _____

_____

_____

Siblings/significant others (names, ages) _____

_____

_____

Personality/attitude toward the client _____

_____

_____

V. Educational/Occupational History

Education (highest grade achieved; school performance/special classes/special needs)

_____

_____

_____

Occupational (job status, kinds of jobs, length of employment, vocational interests)

_____

_____

_____

VI. Health History

Childhood disease, prior illnesses, surgery, etc. _____

_____

_____

_____

Current health (description of clinic) _____

_____

_____

_____

Family health (grandparents, children) _____

_____

_____

_____

Current medication (prescribed and over the counter) _____

_____

_____

_____

VII. Marital History

Marital status: Years married, number of children (problems, stressors, enjoyment)

_____

_____

_____

Client's description of the current relationship with spouse _____

_____

_____

_____

Client's perception of sexual relationship (attitudes/behavior) _____

_____

_____

_____

THERAPY NOTES

Therapist's name _____ Agency/School _____

Therapist's phone _____

CLIENT IDENTIFYING DATA

Client name _____ Age _____ Sex _____

Date of session _____ Session number _____

Taping: Audio _____ Video _____

Presenting/Current concern

_____

_____

_____

Key issues addressed

_____

_____

_____

Summary of the session

_____

_____

_____

Diagnostic impression(s)

_____

_____

_____

Treatment plan/Objectives

_____

_____

_____

Therapist's comments

_____

_____

_____

Supervisor's comments

_____

_____

_____

Date _____ Therapist's signature _____

Date _____ Supervisor's signature _____

THERAPY NOTES

Therapist's name _____ Agency/School _____

Therapist's phone _____

CLIENT IDENTIFYING DATA

Client name _____ Age _____ Sex _____

Date of session _____ Session number _____

Taping: Audio _____ Video _____

Presenting/Current concern

_____

_____

_____

Key issues addressed

_____

_____

_____

Summary of the session

_____

_____

_____

Diagnostic impression(s)

_____

_____

_____

Treatment plan/Objectives

_____

_____

_____

Therapist's comments

_____

_____

_____

Supervisor's comments

_____

_____

_____

Date _____ Therapist's signature _____

Date _____ Supervisor's signature _____

THERAPEUTIC PROGRESS REPORT

Date _____

Therapist's name _____   Client's name _____

Therapist's phone _____   Client's age _____   Sex _____

Sessions to date with client _____
                                                          (Number)

Client's presenting complaint _____
_____
_____

Therapeutic summary _____
_____
_____

Methods of treatment _____
_____
_____

Duration of treatment _____
_____
_____

Current status _____
_____
_____

Treatment recommendations _____
_____
_____

_____
Therapist's signature

_____
Supervisor's signature

THERAPEUTIC PROGRESS REPORT

Date _____

Therapist's name _____   Client's name _____

Therapist's phone _____   Client's age _____   Sex _____

Sessions to date with client _____
(Number)

Client's presenting complaint _____

_____

_____

Therapeutic summary _____

_____

_____

Methods of treatment _____

_____

_____

Duration of treatment _____

_____

_____

Current status _____

_____

_____

Treatment recommendations _____

_____

_____

_____
Therapist's signature

_____
Supervisor's signature

SELF-ASSESSMENT OF BASIC HELPING SKILLS AND PROCEDURAL SKILLS

Purposes

1. To provide the trainee with an opportunity to review levels of competency in the performance skill areas of basic helping skills and procedural skills.

2. To provide the trainee with a basis for identifying areas of emphasis within supervision.

Directions

Circle a number next to each item to indicate your perceived level of competence.

Basic Helping Skills	Poor		Average		Good
1. Ability to demonstrate active attending behavior	1	2	3	4	5
2. Ability to listen to and understand nonverbal behavior	1	2	3	4	5
3. Ability to listen to what client says verbally, noticing mix of experiences, behaviors, and feelings	1	2	3	4	5
4. Ability to understand accurately the client's point of view	1	2	3	4	5
5. Ability to identify themes in client's story	1	2	3	4	5
6. Ability to identify inconsistencies between client's story and reality	1	2	3	4	5
7. Ability to respond with accurate empathy	1	2	3	4	5
8. Ability to ask open-minded questions	1	2	3	4	5
9. Ability to help clients clarify and focus	1	2	3	4	5
10. Ability to balance empathic response, clarification, and probing	1	2	3	4	5
11. Ability to assess accurately severity of client's problems	1	2	3	4	5
12. Ability to establish a collaborative working relationship with client	1	2	3	4	5
13. Ability to assess and activate client's strengths and resources in problem solving	1	2	3	4	5
14. Ability to identify and challenge unhealthy or distorted thinking or behaving	1	2	3	4	5
15. Ability to use advanced empathy to deepen client's understanding of problems and solutions	1	2	3	4	5
16. Ability to explore the counselor-client relationship	1	2	3	4	5
17. Ability to share constructively some of own experiences, behaviors, and feelings with client	1	2	3	4	5

Basic Helping Skills	Poor		Average		Good
18. Ability to summarize	1	2	3	4	5
19. Ability to share information appropriately	1	2	3	4	5
20. Ability to understand and facilitate decision making	1	2	3	4	5
21. Ability to help clients set goals and move toward action in problem solving	1	2	3	4	5
22. Ability to recognize and manage client reluctance and resistance	1	2	3	4	5
23. Ability to help client's explore consequences of the goals they set	1	2	3	4	5
24. Ability to help clients sustain actions in direction of goals	1	2	3	4	5
25. Ability to help clients review and revise or recommit to goals based on new experiences	1	2	3	4	5

Procedural Skills

	Poor		Average		Good
26. Ability to open the session smoothly	1	2	3	4	5
27. Ability to collaborate with client to identify important concerns for the session	1	2	3	4	5
28. Ability to establish continuity from session to session	1	2	3	4	5
29. Knowledge of policy and procedures of educational or agency setting regarding harm to self and others, substance abuse, and child abuse	1	2	3	4	5
30. Ability to keep appropriate records related to counseling process	1	2	3	4	5
31. Ability to end the session smoothly	1	2	3	4	5

Trainee signature _____

Supervisor signature _____

Date _____

SELF-ASSESSMENT OF BASIC HELPING SKILLS AND PROCEDURAL SKILLS

Purposes

1. To provide the trainee with an opportunity to review levels of competency in the performance skill areas of basic helping skills and procedural skills.

2. To provide the trainee with a basis for identifying areas of emphasis within supervision.

Directions

Circle a number next to each item to indicate your perceived level of competence.

Basic Helping Skills	Poor		Average		Good
1. Ability to demonstrate active attending behavior	1	2	3	4	5
2. Ability to listen to and understand nonverbal behavior	1	2	3	4	5
3. Ability to listen to what client says verbally, noticing mix of experiences, behaviors, and feelings	1	2	3	4	5
4. Ability to understand accurately the client's point of view	1	2	3	4	5
5. Ability to identify themes in client's story	1	2	3	4	5
6. Ability to identify inconsistencies between client's story and reality	1	2	3	4	5
7. Ability to respond with accurate empathy	1	2	3	4	5
8. Ability to ask open-minded questions	1	2	3	4	5
9. Ability to help clients clarify and focus	1	2	3	4	5
10. Ability to balance empathic response, clarification, and probing	1	2	3	4	5
11. Ability to assess accurately severity of client's problems	1	2	3	4	5
12. Ability to establish a collaborative working relationship with client	1	2	3	4	5
13. Ability to assess and activate client's strengths and resources in problem solving	1	2	3	4	5
14. Ability to identify and challenge unhealthy or distorted thinking or behaving	1	2	3	4	5
15. Ability to use advanced empathy to deepen client's understanding of problems and solutions	1	2	3	4	5
16. Ability to explore the counselor-client relationship	1	2	3	4	5
17. Ability to share constructively some of own experiences, behaviors, and feelings with client	1	2	3	4	5

Basic Helping Skills	Poor		Average		Good
18. Ability to summarize	1	2	3	4	5
19. Ability to share information appropriately	1	2	3	4	5
20. Ability to understand and facilitate decision making	1	2	3	4	5
21. Ability to help clients set goals and move toward action in problem solving	1	2	3	4	5
22. Ability to recognize and manage client reluctance and resistance	1	2	3	4	5
23. Ability to help client's explore consequences of the goals they set	1	2	3	4	5
24. Ability to help clients sustain actions in direction of goals	1	2	3	4	5
25. Ability to help clients review and revise or recommit to goals based on new experiences	1	2	3	4	5

Procedural Skills

	Poor		Average		Good
26. Ability to open the session smoothly	1	2	3	4	5
27. Ability to collaborate with client to identify important concerns for the session	1	2	3	4	5
28. Ability to establish continuity from session to session	1	2	3	4	5
29. Knowledge of policy and procedures of educational or agency setting regarding harm to self and others, substance abuse, and child abuse	1	2	3	4	5
30. Ability to keep appropriate records related to counseling process	1	2	3	4	5
31. Ability to end the session smoothly	1	2	3	4	5

Trainee signature _____

Supervisor signature _____

Date _____

COUNSELING TECHNIQUES LIST

Directions

1. First, examine the techniques listed in the first column. Then, technique by technique, decide the extent to which you use or would be competent to use each. Indicate the extent of use or competency by circling the appropriate letter in the second column. If you do not know the technique, then mark an "X" through the "N" to indicate that the technique is unknown. Space is available at the end of the techniques list in the first column to add other techniques.

2. Second, after examining the list and indicating your extent of use or competency, go through the techniques list again and circle in the third column the theory or theories with which each technique is appropriate. The third column, of course, can be marked only for those techniques with which you are familiar.

3. The third task is to become more knowledgeable about the techniques that you do not know—the ones marked with an "X." As you gain knowledge relating to each technique, you can decide whether or not you will use it, and if so, with which kinds of clients and under what conditions.

4. The final task is to review the second and third columns and determine whether or not techniques in which you have competencies are within one or two specific theories. If so, are these theories the ones that best reflect your self-concept? Do those techniques marked reflect those most appropriate, as revealed in the literature, for the clients with whom you want to work?

Key

N = None
M = Minimal
A = Average
E = Extensive

Be = Behavioral Modification (Wolpe)	Ps = Psychoanalytic (Freud)
Cl = Client Center (Rogers)	RE = Rational Emotive Therapy (Ellis)
Co = Conjoint Family (Saur)	TA = Transactional Analysis (Berne)
Ex = Existential (May)	TF = Trait Factor (Williamson)
Ge = Gestalt (Peris)	CT = Cognitive Therapy (Beck)
Lo = Logo (Frankl)	

Technique	Extent Use or Competency	Theory With Which Technique Is Most Appropriate
Acceptance	N M A E	Be Cl Co Ex GE Lo Ps RE TA TF CT
Active imagination	N M A E	Be Cl Co Ex GE Lo Ps RE TA TF CT
Active listening	N M A E	Be Cl Co Ex GE Lo Ps RE TA TF CT
Advice giving	N M A E	Be Cl Co Ex GE Lo Ps RE TA TF CT
Alter-ego	N M A E	Be Cl Co Ex GE Lo Ps RE TA TF CT
Analyzing symbols	N M A E	Be Cl Co Ex GE Lo Ps RE TA TF CT
Analysis	N M A E	Be Cl Co Ex GE Lo Ps RE TA TF CT

Technique	Extent Use or Competency	Theory With Which Technique Is Most Appropriate
Assertiveness training	N M A E	Be Cl Co Ex GE Lo Ps RE TA TF CT
Audiotape recorded models	N M A E	Be Cl Co Ex GE Lo Ps RE TA TF CT
Authoritarian approach	N M A E	Be Cl Co Ex GE Lo Ps RE TA TF CT
Aversion-aversive conditioning	N M A E	Be Cl Co Ex GE Lo Ps RE TA TF CT
Behavior modification	N M A E	Be Cl Co Ex GE Lo Ps RE TA TF CT
Bibliotherapy	N M A E	Be Cl Co Ex GE Lo Ps RE TA TF CT
Break-in, break-out	N M A E	Be Cl Co Ex GE Lo Ps RE TA TF CT
Bumping in a circle	N M A E	Be Cl Co Ex GE Lo Ps RE TA TF CT
Cajoling	N M A E	Be Cl Co Ex GE Lo Ps RE TA TF CT
Case history	N M A E	Be Cl Co Ex GE Lo Ps RE TA TF CT
Catharis	N M A E	Be Cl Co Ex GE Lo Ps RE TA TF CT
Chemotherapy	N M A E	Be Cl Co Ex GE Lo Ps RE TA TF CT
Clarifying feelings	N M A E	Be Cl Co Ex GE Lo Ps RE TA TF CT
Cognitive restructuring	N M A E	Be Cl Co Ex GE Lo Ps RE TA TF CT
Commitment	N M A E	Be Cl Co Ex GE Lo Ps RE TA TF CT
Conditioning techniques	N M A E	Be Cl Co Ex GE Lo Ps RE TA TF CT
Confession	N M A E	Be Cl Co Ex GE Lo Ps RE TA TF CT
Confrontation	N M A E	Be Cl Co Ex GE Lo Ps RE TA TF CT
Congruence	N M A E	Be Cl Co Ex GE Lo Ps RE TA TF CT
Contractual agreements	N M A E	Be Cl Co Ex GE Lo Ps RE TA TF CT
Cotherapist	N M A E	Be Cl Co Ex GE Lo Ps RE TA TF CT
Counterpropaganda	N M A E	Be Cl Co Ex GE Lo Ps RE TA TF CT
Countertransference	N M A E	Be Cl Co Ex GE Lo Ps RE TA TF CT
Crying	N M A E	Be Cl Co Ex GE Lo Ps RE TA TF CT
Decision making	N M A E	Be Cl Co Ex GE Lo Ps RE TA TF CT
Democratic	N M A E	Be Cl Co Ex GE Lo Ps RE TA TF CT
Desensitization	N M A E	Be Cl Co Ex GE Lo Ps RE TA TF CT
Detailed inquiry	N M A E	Be Cl Co Ex GE Lo Ps RE TA TF CT
Diagnosing	N M A E	Be Cl Co Ex GE Lo Ps RE TA TF CT
Doubling	N M A E	Be Cl Co Ex GE Lo Ps RE TA TF CT
Dream interpretation	N M A E	Be Cl Co Ex GE Lo Ps RE TA TF CT
Dreaming	N M A E	Be Cl Co Ex GE Lo Ps RE TA TF CT
Drugs	N M A E	Be Cl Co Ex GE Lo Ps RE TA TF CT
Empathy	N M A E	Be Cl Co Ex GE Lo Ps RE TA TF CT
Encouragement	N M A E	Be Cl Co Ex GE Lo Ps RE TA TF CT
Environmental manipulation	N M A E	Be Cl Co Ex GE Lo Ps RE TA TF CT
Explaining	N M A E	Be Cl Co Ex GE Lo Ps RE TA TF CT
Fading	N M A E	Be Cl Co Ex GE Lo Ps RE TA TF CT
Family chronology	N M A E	Be Cl Co Ex GE Lo Ps RE TA TF CT
Family group counseling	N M A E	Be Cl Co Ex GE Lo Ps RE TA TF CT

Technique	Extent Use or Competency	Theory With Which Technique Is Most Appropriate
Fantasizing	N M A E	Be Cl Co Ex GE Lo Ps RE TA TF CT
Feedback	N M A E	Be Cl Co Ex GE Lo Ps RE TA TF CT
Filmed models	N M A E	Be Cl Co Ex GE Lo Ps RE TA TF CT
First memory	N M A E	Be Cl Co Ex GE Lo Ps RE TA TF CT
Free association	N M A E	Be Cl Co Ex GE Lo Ps RE TA TF CT
Frustration	N M A E	Be Cl Co Ex GE Lo Ps RE TA TF CT
Game theory techniques	N M A E	Be Cl Co Ex GE Lo Ps RE TA TF CT
Group centered	N M A E	Be Cl Co Ex GE Lo Ps RE TA TF CT
Group play	N M A E	Be Cl Co Ex GE Lo Ps RE TA TF CT
Homework	N M A E	Be Cl Co Ex GE Lo Ps RE TA TF CT
Hot seat	N M A E	Be Cl Co Ex GE Lo Ps RE TA TF CT
Identification of an animal, defend it	N M A E	Be Cl Co Ex GE Lo Ps RE TA TF CT
Identification of self as great personage	N M A E	Be Cl Co Ex GE Lo Ps RE TA TF CT
Imagery	N M A E	Be Cl Co Ex GE Lo Ps RE TA TF CT
Inception inquiry	N M A E	Be Cl Co Ex GE Lo Ps RE TA TF CT
Informativity	N M A E	Be Cl Co Ex GE Lo Ps RE TA TF CT
Interpersonal process recall (IPR)	N M A E	Be Cl Co Ex GE Lo Ps RE TA TF CT
Interpretation	N M A E	Be Cl Co Ex GE Lo Ps RE TA TF CT
Irrational behavior identification	N M A E	Be Cl Co Ex GE Lo Ps RE TA TF CT
Laissez faire groups	N M A E	Be Cl Co Ex GE Lo Ps RE TA TF CT
Life space	N M A E	Be Cl Co Ex GE Lo Ps RE TA TF CT
Live models	N M A E	Be Cl Co Ex GE Lo Ps RE TA TF CT
Magic mirror	N M A E	Be Cl Co Ex GE Lo Ps RE TA TF CT
Misinterpretation, deliberate	N M A E	Be Cl Co Ex GE Lo Ps RE TA TF CT
Modeling	N M A E	Be Cl Co Ex GE Lo Ps RE TA TF CT
Multiple counseling	N M A E	Be Cl Co Ex GE Lo Ps RE TA TF CT
Natural consequences	N M A E	Be Cl Co Ex GE Lo Ps RE TA TF CT
Negative practice	N M A E	Be Cl Co Ex GE Lo Ps RE TA TF CT
Negative reinforcement	N M A E	Be Cl Co Ex GE Lo Ps RE TA TF CT
Orientative	N M A E	Be Cl Co Ex GE Lo Ps RE TA TF CT
Paradoxical intention	N M A E	Be Cl Co Ex GE Lo Ps RE TA TF CT
Play therapy	N M A E	Be Cl Co Ex GE Lo Ps RE TA TF CT
Positive regard	N M A E	Be Cl Co Ex GE Lo Ps RE TA TF CT
Positive reinforcement	N M A E	Be Cl Co Ex GE Lo Ps RE TA TF CT
Predicting	N M A E	Be Cl Co Ex GE Lo Ps RE TA TF CT
Probing	N M A E	Be Cl Co Ex GE Lo Ps RE TA TF CT
Problem solving	N M A E	Be Cl Co Ex GE Lo Ps RE TA TF CT

Technique	Extent Use or Competency	Theory With Which Technique Is Most Appropriate
Processing	N M A E	Be Cl Co Ex GE Lo Ps RE TA TF CT
Prognosing	N M A E	Be Cl Co Ex GE Lo Ps RE TA TF CT
Progressive relaxation	N M A E	Be Cl Co Ex GE Lo Ps RE TA TF CT
Projection	N M A E	Be Cl Co Ex GE Lo Ps RE TA TF CT
Psychodrama	N M A E	Be Cl Co Ex GE Lo Ps RE TA TF CT
Punishment	N M A E	Be Cl Co Ex GE Lo Ps RE TA TF CT
Questioning	N M A E	Be Cl Co Ex GE Lo Ps RE TA TF CT
Rational	N M A E	Be Cl Co Ex GE Lo Ps RE TA TF CT
Reality testing	N M A E	Be Cl Co Ex GE Lo Ps RE TA TF CT
Reassurance	N M A E	Be Cl Co Ex GE Lo Ps RE TA TF CT
Recall	N M A E	Be Cl Co Ex GE Lo Ps RE TA TF CT
Reciprocity of affect	N M A E	Be Cl Co Ex GE Lo Ps RE TA TF CT
Reconscience	N M A E	Be Cl Co Ex GE Lo Ps RE TA TF CT
Re-education	N M A E	Be Cl Co Ex GE Lo Ps RE TA TF CT
Reflection	N M A E	Be Cl Co Ex GE Lo Ps RE TA TF CT
Regression	N M A E	Be Cl Co Ex GE Lo Ps RE TA TF CT
Reinforcement	N M A E	Be Cl Co Ex GE Lo Ps RE TA TF CT
Relaxation	N M A E	Be Cl Co Ex GE Lo Ps RE TA TF CT
Release therapy	N M A E	Be Cl Co Ex GE Lo Ps RE TA TF CT
Restatement of content	N M A E	Be Cl Co Ex GE Lo Ps RE TA TF CT
Reward	N M A E	Be Cl Co Ex GE Lo Ps RE TA TF CT
Rocking or cradling above head trust	N M A E	Be Cl Co Ex GE Lo Ps RE TA TF CT
Role playing	N M A E	Be Cl Co Ex GE Lo Ps RE TA TF CT
Role reversal	N M A E	Be Cl Co Ex GE Lo Ps RE TA TF CT
Self-modeling	N M A E	Be Cl Co Ex GE Lo Ps RE TA TF CT
Sensitivity exercises	N M A E	Be Cl Co Ex GE Lo Ps RE TA TF CT
Sensitivity training	N M A E	Be Cl Co Ex GE Lo Ps RE TA TF CT
Shaping	N M A E	Be Cl Co Ex GE Lo Ps RE TA TF CT
Silence	N M A E	Be Cl Co Ex GE Lo Ps RE TA TF CT
Simulation	N M A E	Be Cl Co Ex GE Lo Ps RE TA TF CT
Sociodrama	N M A E	Be Cl Co Ex GE Lo Ps RE TA TF CT
Sociometrics	N M A E	Be Cl Co Ex GE Lo Ps RE TA TF CT
Stimulation	N M A E	Be Cl Co Ex GE Lo Ps RE TA TF CT
Structuring	N M A E	Be Cl Co Ex GE Lo Ps RE TA TF CT
SUD (subjective unit of discomfort)	N M A E	Be Cl Co Ex GE Lo Ps RE TA TF CT
Summarization	N M A E	Be Cl Co Ex GE Lo Ps RE TA TF CT
Supporting	N M A E	Be Cl Co Ex GE Lo Ps RE TA TF CT
Systematic desensitization	N M A E	Be Cl Co Ex GE Lo Ps RE TA TF CT

Technique	Extent Use or Competency	Theory With Which Technique Is Most Appropriate
Termination	N M A E	Be Cl Co Ex GE Lo Ps RE TA TF CT
transference	N M A E	Be Cl Co Ex GE Lo Ps RE TA TF CT
Transparency	N M A E	Be Cl Co Ex GE Lo Ps RE TA TF CT
Trust walk	N M A E	Be Cl Co Ex GE Lo Ps RE TA TF CT
Urging	N M A E	Be Cl Co Ex GE Lo Ps RE TA TF CT
Value clarification	N M A E	Be Cl Co Ex GE Lo Ps RE TA TF CT
Value development	N M A E	Be Cl Co Ex GE Lo Ps RE TA TF CT
Verbal shock	N M A E	Be Cl Co Ex GE Lo Ps RE TA TF CT
Vicarious learning	N M A E	Be Cl Co Ex GE Lo Ps RE TA TF CT
Warmth	N M A E	Be Cl Co Ex GE Lo Ps RE TA TF CT

ADD YOUR OWN:

	Extent Use or Competency	Theory With Which Technique Is Most Appropriate
	N M A E	Be Cl Co Ex GE Lo Ps RE TA TF CT
	N M A E	Be Cl Co Ex GE Lo Ps RE TA TF CT
	N M A E	Be Cl Co Ex GE Lo Ps RE TA TF CT

COUNSELING TECHNIQUES LIST

Directions

1. First, examine the techniques listed in the first column. Then, technique by technique, decide the extent to which you use or would be competent to use each. Indicate the extent of use or competency by circling the appropriate letter in the second column. If you do not know the technique, then mark an "X" through the "N" to indicate that the technique is unknown. Space is available at the end of the techniques list in the first column to add other techniques.

2. Second, after examining the list and indicating your extent of use or competency, go through the techniques list again and circle in the third column the theory or theories with which each technique is appropriate. The third column, of course, can be marked only for those techniques with which you are familiar.

3. The third task is to become more knowledgeable about the techniques that you do not know—the ones marked with an "X." As you gain knowledge relating to each technique, you can decide whether or not you will use it, and if so, with which kinds of clients and under what conditions.

4. The final task is to review the second and third columns and determine whether or not techniques in which you have competencies are within one or two specific theories. If so, are these theories the ones that best reflect your self-concept? Do those techniques marked reflect those most appropriate, as revealed in the literature, for the clients with whom you want to work?

Key

N = None
M = Minimal
A = Average
E = Extensive

Be	= Behavioral Modification (Wolpe)	Ps	= Psychoanalytic (Freud)
Cl	= Client Center (Rogers)	RE	= Rational Emotive Therapy (Ellis)
Co	= Conjoint Family (Saur)	TA	= Transactional Analysis (Berne)
Ex	= Existential (May)	TF	= Trait Factor (Williamson)
Ge	= Gestalt (Peris)	CT	= Cognitive Therapy (Beck)
Lo	= Logo (Frankl)		

Technique	Extent Use or Competency	Theory With Which Technique Is Most Appropriate
Acceptance	N M A E	Be Cl Co Ex GE Lo Ps RE TA TF CT
Active imagination	N M A E	Be Cl Co Ex GE Lo Ps RE TA TF CT
Active listening	N M A E	Be Cl Co Ex GE Lo Ps RE TA TF CT
Advice giving	N M A E	Be Cl Co Ex GE Lo Ps RE TA TF CT
Alter-ego	N M A E	Be Cl Co Ex GE Lo Ps RE TA TF CT
Analyzing symbols	N M A E	Be Cl Co Ex GE Lo Ps RE TA TF CT
Analysis	N M A E	Be Cl Co Ex GE Lo Ps RE TA TF CT

Technique	Extent Use or Competency	Theory With Which Technique Is Most Appropriate
Assertiveness training	N M A E	Be Cl Co Ex GE Lo Ps RE TA TF CT
Audiotape recorded models	N M A E	Be Cl Co Ex GE Lo Ps RE TA TF CT
Authoritarian approach	N M A E	Be Cl Co Ex GE Lo Ps RE TA TF CT
Aversion-aversive conditioning	N M A E	Be Cl Co Ex GE Lo Ps RE TA TF CT
Behavior modification	N M A E	Be Cl Co Ex GE Lo Ps RE TA TF CT
Bibliotherapy	N M A E	Be Cl Co Ex GE Lo Ps RE TA TF CT
Break-in, break-out	N M A E	Be Cl Co Ex GE Lo Ps RE TA TF CT
Bumping in a circle	N M A E	Be Cl Co Ex GE Lo Ps RE TA TF CT
Cajoling	N M A E	Be Cl Co Ex GE Lo Ps RE TA TF CT
Case history	N M A E	Be Cl Co Ex GE Lo Ps RE TA TF CT
Catharis	N M A E	Be Cl Co Ex GE Lo Ps RE TA TF CT
Chemotherapy	N M A E	Be Cl Co Ex GE Lo Ps RE TA TF CT
Clarifying feelings	N M A E	Be Cl Co Ex GE Lo Ps RE TA TF CT
Cognitive restructuring	N M A E	Be Cl Co Ex GE Lo Ps RE TA TF CT
Commitment	N M A E	Be Cl Co Ex GE Lo Ps RE TA TF CT
Conditioning techniques	N M A E	Be Cl Co Ex GE Lo Ps RE TA TF CT
Confession	N M A E	Be Cl Co Ex GE Lo Ps RE TA TF CT
Confrontation	N M A E	Be Cl Co Ex GE Lo Ps RE TA TF CT
Congruence	N M A E	Be Cl Co Ex GE Lo Ps RE TA TF CT
Contractual agreements	N M A E	Be Cl Co Ex GE Lo Ps RE TA TF CT
Cotherapist	N M A E	Be Cl Co Ex GE Lo Ps RE TA TF CT
Counterpropaganda	N M A E	Be Cl Co Ex GE Lo Ps RE TA TF CT
Countertransference	N M A E	Be Cl Co Ex GE Lo Ps RE TA TF CT
Crying	N M A E	Be Cl Co Ex GE Lo Ps RE TA TF CT
Decision making	N M A E	Be Cl Co Ex GE Lo Ps RE TA TF CT
Democratic	N M A E	Be Cl Co Ex GE Lo Ps RE TA TF CT
Desensitization	N M A E	Be Cl Co Ex GE Lo Ps RE TA TF CT
Detailed inquiry	N M A E	Be Cl Co Ex GE Lo Ps RE TA TF CT
Diagnosing	N M A E	Be Cl Co Ex GE Lo Ps RE TA TF CT
Doubling	N M A E	Be Cl Co Ex GE Lo Ps RE TA TF CT
Dream interpretation	N M A E	Be Cl Co Ex GE Lo Ps RE TA TF CT
Dreaming	N M A E	Be Cl Co Ex GE Lo Ps RE TA TF CT
Drugs	N M A E	Be Cl Co Ex GE Lo Ps RE TA TF CT
Empathy	N M A E	Be Cl Co Ex GE Lo Ps RE TA TF CT
Encouragement	N M A E	Be Cl Co Ex GE Lo Ps RE TA TF CT
Environmental manipulation	N M A E	Be Cl Co Ex GE Lo Ps RE TA TF CT
Explaining	N M A E	Be Cl Co Ex GE Lo Ps RE TA TF CT
Fading	N M A E	Be Cl Co Ex GE Lo Ps RE TA TF CT
Family chronology	N M A E	Be Cl Co Ex GE Lo Ps RE TA TF CT
Family group counseling	N M A E	Be Cl Co Ex GE Lo Ps RE TA TF CT

Technique	Extent Use or Competency	Theory With Which Technique Is Most Appropriate
Fantasizing	N M A E	Be Cl Co Ex GE Lo Ps RE TA TF CT
Feedback	N M A E	Be Cl Co Ex GE Lo Ps RE TA TF CT
Filmed models	N M A E	Be Cl Co Ex GE Lo Ps RE TA TF CT
First memory	N M A E	Be Cl Co Ex GE Lo Ps RE TA TF CT
Free association	N M A E	Be Cl Co Ex GE Lo Ps RE TA TF CT
Frustration	N M A E	Be Cl Co Ex GE Lo Ps RE TA TF CT
Game theory techniques	N M A E	Be Cl Co Ex GE Lo Ps RE TA TF CT
Group centered	N M A E	Be Cl Co Ex GE Lo Ps RE TA TF CT
Group play	N M A E	Be Cl Co Ex GE Lo Ps RE TA TF CT
Homework	N M A E	Be Cl Co Ex GE Lo Ps RE TA TF CT
Hot seat	N M A E	Be Cl Co Ex GE Lo Ps RE TA TF CT
Identification of an animal, defend it	N M A E	Be Cl Co Ex GE Lo Ps RE TA TF CT
Identification of self as great personage	N M A E	Be Cl Co Ex GE Lo Ps RE TA TF CT
Imagery	N M A E	Be Cl Co Ex GE Lo Ps RE TA TF CT
Inception inquiry	N M A E	Be Cl Co Ex GE Lo Ps RE TA TF CT
Informativity	N M A E	Be Cl Co Ex GE Lo Ps RE TA TF CT
Interpersonal process recall (IPR)	N M A E	Be Cl Co Ex GE Lo Ps RE TA TF CT
Interpretation	N M A E	Be Cl Co Ex GE Lo Ps RE TA TF CT
Irrational behavior identification	N M A E	Be Cl Co Ex GE Lo Ps RE TA TF CT
Laissez faire groups	N M A E	Be Cl Co Ex GE Lo Ps RE TA TF CT
Life space	N M A E	Be Cl Co Ex GE Lo Ps RE TA TF CT
Live models	N M A E	Be Cl Co Ex GE Lo Ps RE TA TF CT
Magic mirror	N M A E	Be Cl Co Ex GE Lo Ps RE TA TF CT
Misinterpretation, deliberate	N M A E	Be Cl Co Ex GE Lo Ps RE TA TF CT
Modeling	N M A E	Be Cl Co Ex GE Lo Ps RE TA TF CT
Multiple counseling	N M A E	Be Cl Co Ex GE Lo Ps RE TA TF CT
Natural consequences	N M A E	Be Cl Co Ex GE Lo Ps RE TA TF CT
Negative practice	N M A E	Be Cl Co Ex GE Lo Ps RE TA TF CT
Negative reinforcement	N M A E	Be Cl Co Ex GE Lo Ps RE TA TF CT
Orientative	N M A E	Be Cl Co Ex GE Lo Ps RE TA TF CT
Paradoxical intention	N M A E	Be Cl Co Ex GE Lo Ps RE TA TF CT
Play therapy	N M A E	Be Cl Co Ex GE Lo Ps RE TA TF CT
Positive regard	N M A E	Be Cl Co Ex GE Lo Ps RE TA TF CT
Positive reinforcement	N M A E	Be Cl Co Ex GE Lo Ps RE TA TF CT
Predicting	N M A E	Be Cl Co Ex GE Lo Ps RE TA TF CT
Probing	N M A E	Be Cl Co Ex GE Lo Ps RE TA TF CT
Problem solving	N M A E	Be Cl Co Ex GE Lo Ps RE TA TF CT

Technique	Extent Use or Competency	Theory With Which Technique Is Most Appropriate
Processing	N M A E	Be Cl Co Ex GE Lo Ps RE TA TF CT
Prognosing	N M A E	Be Cl Co Ex GE Lo Ps RE TA TF CT
Progressive relaxation	N M A E	Be Cl Co Ex GE Lo Ps RE TA TF CT
Projection	N M A E	Be Cl Co Ex GE Lo Ps RE TA TF CT
Psychodrama	N M A E	Be Cl Co Ex GE Lo Ps RE TA TF CT
Punishment	N M A E	Be Cl Co Ex GE Lo Ps RE TA TF CT
Questioning	N M A E	Be Cl Co Ex GE Lo Ps RE TA TF CT
Rational	N M A E	Be Cl Co Ex GE Lo Ps RE TA TF CT
Reality testing	N M A E	Be Cl Co Ex GE Lo Ps RE TA TF CT
Reassurance	N M A E	Be Cl Co Ex GE Lo Ps RE TA TF CT
Recall	N M A E	Be Cl Co Ex GE Lo Ps RE TA TF CT
Reciprocity of affect	N M A E	Be Cl Co Ex GE Lo Ps RE TA TF CT
Reconscience	N M A E	Be Cl Co Ex GE Lo Ps RE TA TF CT
Re-education	N M A E	Be Cl Co Ex GE Lo Ps RE TA TF CT
Reflection	N M A E	Be Cl Co Ex GE Lo Ps RE TA TF CT
Regression	N M A E	Be Cl Co Ex GE Lo Ps RE TA TF CT
Reinforcement	N M A E	Be Cl Co Ex GE Lo Ps RE TA TF CT
Relaxation	N M A E	Be Cl Co Ex GE Lo Ps RE TA TF CT
Release therapy	N M A E	Be Cl Co Ex GE Lo Ps RE TA TF CT
Restatement of content	N M A E	Be Cl Co Ex GE Lo Ps RE TA TF CT
Reward	N M A E	Be Cl Co Ex GE Lo Ps RE TA TF CT
Rocking or cradling above head trust	N M A E	Be Cl Co Ex GE Lo Ps RE TA TF CT
Role playing	N M A E	Be Cl Co Ex GE Lo Ps RE TA TF CT
Role reversal	N M A E	Be Cl Co Ex GE Lo Ps RE TA TF CT
Self-modeling	N M A E	Be Cl Co Ex GE Lo Ps RE TA TF CT
Sensitivity exercises	N M A E	Be Cl Co Ex GE Lo Ps RE TA TF CT
Sensitivity training	N M A E	Be Cl Co Ex GE Lo Ps RE TA TF CT
Shaping	N M A E	Be Cl Co Ex GE Lo Ps RE TA TF CT
Silence	N M A E	Be Cl Co Ex GE Lo Ps RE TA TF CT
Simulation	N M A E	Be Cl Co Ex GE Lo Ps RE TA TF CT
Sociodrama	N M A E	Be Cl Co Ex GE Lo Ps RE TA TF CT
Sociometrics	N M A E	Be Cl Co Ex GE Lo Ps RE TA TF CT
Stimulation	N M A E	Be Cl Co Ex GE Lo Ps RE TA TF CT
Structuring	N M A E	Be Cl Co Ex GE Lo Ps RE TA TF CT
SUD (subjective unit of discomfort)	N M A E	Be Cl Co Ex GE Lo Ps RE TA TF CT
Summarization	N M A E	Be Cl Co Ex GE Lo Ps RE TA TF CT
Supporting	N M A E	Be Cl Co Ex GE Lo Ps RE TA TF CT
Systematic desensitization	N M A E	Be Cl Co Ex GE Lo Ps RE TA TF CT

Technique	Extent Use or Competency	Theory With Which Technique Is Most Appropriate
Termination	N M A E	Be Cl Co Ex GE Lo Ps RE TA TF CT
transference	N M A E	Be Cl Co Ex GE Lo Ps RE TA TF CT
Transparency	N M A E	Be Cl Co Ex GE Lo Ps RE TA TF CT
Trust walk	N M A E	Be Cl Co Ex GE Lo Ps RE TA TF CT
Urging	N M A E	Be Cl Co Ex GE Lo Ps RE TA TF CT
Value clarification	N M A E	Be Cl Co Ex GE Lo Ps RE TA TF CT
Value development	N M A E	Be Cl Co Ex GE Lo Ps RE TA TF CT
Verbal shock	N M A E	Be Cl Co Ex GE Lo Ps RE TA TF CT
Vicarious learning	N M A E	Be Cl Co Ex GE Lo Ps RE TA TF CT
Warmth	N M A E	Be Cl Co Ex GE Lo Ps RE TA TF CT
ADD YOUR OWN:		
	N M A E	Be Cl Co Ex GE Lo Ps RE TA TF CT
	N M A E	Be Cl Co Ex GE Lo Ps RE TA TF CT
	N M A E	Be Cl Co Ex GE Lo Ps RE TA TF CT

SELF-RATING BY THE STUDENT COUNSELOR*

Suggested Use: The student counselor may use this sheet as a self-evaluation after a therapy session.

Date _____

Student counselor name _____

Client name _____

Directions: The student counselor is to answer each question following a therapy session. The questions serve as a self-rating initiator and may enable the student counselor to determine means for improvement in his/her counseling.

Preparation for the Interview

	Yes	Not sure	No
1. Was I physically in good condition and mentally alert?	___	___	___
2. Did I schedule sufficient time for the interview?	___	___	___
3. Was provision made for privacy and reasonable freedom from interruption?	___	___	___
4. Did I have the physical space arranged where we met so as to suggest welcome and an atmosphere conducive to counseling?	___	___	___
5. Did I have a background of available data about the client that would help me to understand him/her better in the interview but would not prejudice me?	___	___	___
6. Did I have and understand information so as to personalize information processes with the client?	___	___	___
7. Had I previously established a reputation for seeing the client's point of view, being genuinely helpful, and not disclosing confidence?	___	___	___

Comments:

Beginning the Interview

	Yes	Not sure	No
1. Was I sensitive to the client and did I use an appropriate approach?	___	___	___
2. Was I able to create a psychological atmosphere in which the client was stimulated to take responsibility for thinking through the situation?	___	___	___
3. Was I successful in maintaining open communication between us?	___	___	___

Comments:

---

* This material was taken from K. Dimick and F. Krause. *Practicum Manual for Counseling and Psychotherapy.* Accelerated Development, Muncie, IN, 1980. Reprinted with permission.

Development of the Interview

	Yes	Not sure	No
1. Did the client feel freedom to express negative feelings?	_____	_____	_____
2. Did the client have the opportunity to release tension?	_____	_____	_____
3. Was my attitude one of reflecting objectivity while expressing caring?	_____	_____	_____
4. Was I sincere and did I show genuine respect for the client?	_____	_____	_____
5. Was my own attitude, so far as I know, free from bias?	_____	_____	_____
6. Did I follow the leads suggested by the client?	_____	_____	_____
7. Did I help the client to clarify and expand positive feelings?	_____	_____	_____
8. Did the client establish a more forward-looking, positive, hopeful attitude during the interview or series of interviews?	_____	_____	_____
9. Was I able to assist in information processing by the client?	_____	_____	_____
10. Was information provided in a manner which caused the client to move forward realistically in his or her thinking?	_____	_____	_____

Comments:

Planning for Next Session

1. Was I able to identify areas with which to follow through for next session?	_____	_____	_____
2. Was I able to help the client gain a clear view of what might be done in the next session?	_____	_____	_____
3. Did I establish a definite meeting time and place for the next session with the client?	_____	_____	_____
4. Have I identified techniques that might be considered for the next session?	_____	_____	_____
5. Have I identified the materials and/or preparation I will need for the next session?	_____	_____	_____

Comments:

SELF-RATING BY THE STUDENT COUNSELOR*

Suggested Use: The student counselor may use this sheet as a self-evaluation after a therapy session.

Date _____

Student counselor name _____

Client name _____

Directions: The student counselor is to answer each question following a therapy session. The questions serve as a self-rating initiator and may enable the student counselor to determine means for improvement in his/her counseling.

Preparation for the Interview

	Yes	Not sure	No
1. Was I physically in good condition and mentally alert?	____	____	____
2. Did I schedule sufficient time for the interview?	____	____	____
3. Was provision made for privacy and reasonable freedom from interruption?	____	____	____
4. Did I have the physical space arranged where we met so as to suggest welcome and an atmosphere conducive to counseling?	____	____	____
5. Did I have a background of available data about the client that would help me to understand him/her better in the interview but would not prejudice me?	____	____	____
6. Did I have and understand information so as to personalize information processes with the client?	____	____	____
7. Had I previously established a reputation for seeing the client's point of view, being genuinely helpful, and not disclosing confidence?	____	____	____

Comments:

Beginning the Interview

1. Was I sensitive to the client and did I use an appropriate approach?	____	____	____
2. Was I able to create a psychological atmosphere in which the client was stimulated to take responsibility for thinking through the situation?	____	____	____
3. Was I successful in maintaining open communication between us?	____	____	____

Comments:

---

* This material was taken from K. Dimick and F. Krause. *Practicum Manual for Counseling and Psychotherapy.* Accelerated Development, Muncie, IN, 1980. Reprinted with permission.

Development of the Interview

	Yes	Not sure	No
1. Did the client feel freedom to express negative feelings?	_____	_____	_____
2. Did the client have the opportunity to release tension?	_____	_____	_____
3. Was my attitude one of reflecting objectivity while expressing caring?	_____	_____	_____
4. Was I sincere and did I show genuine respect for the client?	_____	_____	_____
5. Was my own attitude, so far as I know, free from bias?	_____	_____	_____
6. Did I follow the leads suggested by the client?	_____	_____	_____
7. Did I help the client to clarify and expand positive feelings?	_____	_____	_____
8. Did the client establish a more forward-looking, positive, hopeful attitude during the interview or series of interviews?	_____	_____	_____
9. Was I able to assist in information processing by the client?	_____	_____	_____
10. Was information provided in a manner which caused the client to move forward realistically in his or her thinking?	_____	_____	_____

Comments:

Planning for Next Session

1. Was I able to identify areas with which to follow through for next session?	_____	_____	_____
2. Was I able to help the client gain a clear view of what might be done in the next session?	_____	_____	_____
3. Did I establish a definite meeting time and place for the next session with the client?	_____	_____	_____
4. Have I identified techniques that might be considered for the next session?	_____	_____	_____
5. Have I identified the materials and/or preparation I will need for the next session?	_____	_____	_____

Comments:

PEER RATING FORM

Purposes 1. To provide trainee with additional sources of feedback regarding skill development.
          2. To provide rater with opportunity to increase knowledge and recognition of positive skill behavior.

Directions 1. Trainee submits this sheet once a week to be completed by peer who reviews the trainee's tapes. The particular skills the counselor is working on are identified by the counselor trainee.
          2. Peer writes remarks once a week on all tapes reviewed rating performance on the targeted skill behavior.
          3. Information is cumulative to aid in review of progress.

Counselor's name _____

Targeted skills (to be identified by counselor) _____
_____
_____
_____

Remarks (based on all tapes reviewed during the week) _____
_____
_____
_____

Signature of rater _____

Date _____

PEER RATING FORM

Purposes 1. To provide trainee with additional sources of feedback regarding skill development.
               2. To provide rater with opportunity to increase knowledge and recognition of positive skill behavior.

Directions 1. Trainee submits this sheet once a week to be completed by peer who reviews the trainee's tapes. The particular skills the counselor is working on are identified by the counselor trainee.
               2. Peer writes remarks once a week on all tapes reviewed rating performance on the targeted skill behavior.
               3. Information is cumulative to aid in review of progress.

Counselor's name _____

Targeted skills (to be identified by counselor) _____

_____

_____

_____

Remarks (based on all tapes reviewed during the week) _____

_____

_____

_____

Signature of rater _____

         Date _____

GOAL STATEMENT AGREEMENT

Directions: The student completes the agreement in duplicate and submits on copy to the supervisor.

Student's name _____ Supervisor's name _____

Date submitted _____

Short-Term Goals

Counseling Performance Skills _____

_____

_____

Cognitive Counseling Skills _____

_____

_____

Developmental Level _____

_____

_____

_____

Long-Term Goals

Counseling Performance Skills _____

_____

_____

Cognitive Counseling Skills _____

_____

_____

Developmental Level _____

_____

_____

GOAL STATEMENT AGREEMENT

Directions: The student completes the agreement in duplicate and submits on copy to the supervisor.

Student's name _____ Supervisor's name _____

Date submitted _____

Short-Term Goals

Counseling Performance Skills _____

_____

_____

Cognitive Counseling Skills _____

_____

_____

Developmental Level _____

_____

_____

_____

Long-Term Goals

Counseling Performance Skills _____

_____

_____

Cognitive Counseling Skills _____

_____

_____

Developmental Level _____

_____

_____

INTERVIEWER RATING FORM*
Rating of a Counseling Session Conducted by a Student Counselor

Client name or identification _____

Student counselor name _____

Check One

___ Audiotape ___ Videotape ___ Observation ___ Other (specify) _____

Signature of supervisor or observer _____

Date of interview _____

Directions: Supervisor or peer of the student counselor marks a rating for each item and as much as possible, provides remarks that will help the student counselor in his/her development.

Specific Criteria	Rating (best to least)	Remarks
1. Opening: Was opening unstructured, friendly, and pleasant? Any role definition needed? Any introduction necessary?	5 4 3 2 1	
2. Rapport: Did student counselor establish good rapport with client? Was the stage set for a productive interview?	5 4 3 2 1	
3. Interview Responsibility: If not assumed by the client, did student counselor assume appropriate level of responsibility for interview conduct? Did student counselor or client take initiative?	5 4 3 2 1	
4. Interaction: Were the client and student counselor really communicating in a meaningful manner?	5 4 3 2 1	
5. Acceptance/Permissiveness: Was the student counselor accepting and permissive of client's emotions, feelings, and expressed thoughts?	5 4 3 2 1	
6. Reflections of Feelings: Did student counselor reflect and react to feelings or did interview remain on an intellectual level?	5 4 3 2 1	

* This material was taken from "Evaluation of Student Counselors and Supervisors," pp. 265–314 in K. Dimick and F. Krause (Eds.), *Practicum Manual for Counseling and Psychotherapy*, Accelerated Development, Muncie, IN, 1980. Reprinted with permission from Gordon Poling, Professor, School of Education, University of South Dakota.

Specific Criteria	Rating (best to least)	Remarks
7. Student Counselor Responses: Were student counselor responses appropriate in view of what the client was expressing or were responses concerned with trivia and minutia? Meaningful questions?	5 4 3 2 1	
8. Value Management: How did the student counselor cope with values? Were attempts made to impose counselor values during the interview?	5 4 3 2 1	
9. Counseling Relationship: Were student counselor–client relationships conducive to productive counseling? Was a counseling relationship established?	5 4 3 2 1	
10. Closing: Was closing initiated by student counselor or client? Was it abrupt or brusque? Any follow-up or further interview scheduling accomplished?	5 4 3 2 1	
11. General Techniques: How well did the student counselor conduct the mechanics of the interview?	5 4 3 2 1	

A. Duration of interview: Was the interview too long or too short? Should interview have been terminated sooner or later?

B. Vocabulary level: Was student counselor vocabulary appropriate for the client?

C. Mannerisms: Did the student counselor display any mannerisms which might have conversely affected the interview or portions thereof?

D. Verbosity: Did the student counselor dominate the interview, interrupt, override, or become too wordy?

E. Silences: Were silences broken to meet student counselor needs or were they dealt with in an effectual manner?

Comments for Student Counselor Assistance: Additional comments that might assist the student counselor in areas not covered by the preceding suggestions.

INTERVIEWER RATING FORM*
Rating of a Counseling Session Conducted by a Student Counselor

Client name or identification _____

Student counselor name _____

Check One

___ Audiotape ___ Videotape ___ Observation ___ Other (specify) _____

Signature of supervisor or observer _____

Date of interview _____

Directions: Supervisor or peer of the student counselor marks a rating for each item and as much as possible, provides remarks that will help the student counselor in his/her development.

Specific Criteria	Rating (best to least)	Remarks
1. Opening: Was opening unstructured, friendly, and pleasant? Any role definition needed? Any introduction necessary?	5 4 3 2 1	
2. Rapport: Did student counselor establish good rapport with client? Was the stage set for a productive interview?	5 4 3 2 1	
3. Interview Responsibility: If not assumed by the client, did student counselor assume appropriate level of responsibility for interview conduct? Did student counselor or client take initiative?	5 4 3 2 1	
4. Interaction: Were the client and student counselor really communicating in a meaningful manner?	5 4 3 2 1	
5. Acceptance/Permissiveness: Was the student counselor accepting and permissive of client's emotions, feelings, and expressed thoughts?	5 4 3 2 1	
6. Reflections of Feelings: Did student counselor reflect and react to feelings or did interview remain on an intellectual level?	5 4 3 2 1	

* This material was taken from "Evaluation of Student Counselors and Supervisors," pp. 265–314 in K. Dimick and F. Krause (Eds.), *Practicum Manual for Counseling and Psychotherapy*, Accelerated Development, Muncie, IN, 1980. Reprinted with permission from Gordon Poling, Professor, School of Education, University of South Dakota.

Specific Criteria	Rating (best to least)	Remarks
7. Student Counselor Responses: Were student counselor responses appropriate in view of what the client was expressing or were responses concerned with trivia and minutia? Meaningful questions?	5 4 3 2 1	
8. Value Management: How did the student counselor cope with values? Were attempts made to impose counselor values during the interview?	5 4 3 2 1	
9. Counseling Relationship: Were student counselor–client relationships conducive to productive counseling? Was a counseling relationship established?	5 4 3 2 1	
10. Closing: Was closing initiated by student counselor or client? Was it abrupt or brusque? Any follow-up or further interview scheduling accomplished?	5 4 3 2 1	
11. General Techniques: How well did the student counselor conduct the mechanics of the interview?	5 4 3 2 1	

A. Duration of interview: Was the interview too long or too short? Should interview have been terminated sooner or later?

B. Vocabulary level: Was student counselor vocabulary appropriate for the client?

C. Mannerisms: Did the student counselor display any mannerisms which might have conversely affected the interview or portions thereof?

D. Verbosity: Did the student counselor dominate the interview, interrupt, override, or become too wordy?

E. Silences: Were silences broken to meet student counselor needs or were they dealt with in an effectual manner?

Comments for Student Counselor Assistance: Additional comments that might assist the student counselor in areas not covered by the preceding suggestions.

SITE SUPERVISOR'S EVALUATION OF STUDENT COUNSELOR'S PERFORMANCE*

Suggested Use: This form is to be used to check performances in counseling practicum. The form may be completed after each supervised counseling session or may cover several supervisions over a period of time. The form is appropriate for individual or group counseling.

Alternate Use: The student counselor may ask a peer to observe a counseling session and mark the evaluation.

Name of student counselor _____

Name of identifying code of client _____

Date of supervision _____ or period covered by the evaluation _____

Directions: The supervisor, following each counseling session that has been supervised or after several supervisions covering a period of time, circles a number that best evaluates the student counselor on each performance at that point in time.

General Supervision Comments	Poor	Adequate	Good
1. Demonstrates a personal commitment in developing professional competencies	1 2	3 4	5 6
2. Invests time and energy in becoming a counselor	1 2	3 4	5 6
3. Accepts and uses constructive criticism to enhance self-development and counseling skills	1 2	3 4	5 6
4. Engages in open, comfortable, and clear communication with peers and supervisors	1 2	3 4	5 6
5. Recognizes own competencies and skills and shares these with peers and supervisors	1 2	3 4	5 6
6. Recognizes own deficiencies and actively works to overcome them with peers and supervisors	1 2	3 4	5 6
7. Completes case reports and records punctually and conscientiously	1 2	3 4	5 6

The Counseling Process			
8. Researches the referral prior to the first interview	1 2	3 4	5 6
9. Keeps appointments on time	1 2	3 4	5 6
10. Begins the interview smoothly	1 2	3 4	5 6
11. Explains the nature and objectives of counseling when appropriate	1 2	3 4	5 6
12. Is relaxed and comfortable in the interview	1 2	3 4	5 6
13. Communicates interest in and acceptance of the client	1 2	3 4	5 6
14. Facilitates client expression of concerns and feelings	1 2	3 4	5 6
15. Focuses on the content of the client's problem	1 2	3 4	5 6
16. Recognizes and resists manipulation by the client	1 2	3 4	5 6

*Reprinted by permission from Dr. Harold Hackney, Assistant Professor, Purdue University. This form was designed by two graduate students based upon material from *Counseling Strategies and Objectives* by H. Hackney and S. Nye, Prentice-Hall, Englewood Cliffs, NJ, 1973. This material was taken from "Evaluation of Student Counselors and Supervisors," pp. 265–274, in K. Dimick and F. Krause (Eds.), *Practicum Manual for Counseling and Psychotherapy*, Accelerated Development, Muncie, IN 19800.

	Poor	Adequate	Good
17. Recognizes and deals with positive affect of the client	1 2	3 4	5 6
18. Recognizes and deals with negative affect of the client	1 2	3 4	5 6
19. Is spontaneous in the interview	1 2	3 4	5 6
20. Uses silence effectively in the interview	1 2	3 4	5 6
21. Is aware of own feelings in the counseling session	1 2	3 4	5 6
22. Communicates own feelings to the client when appropriate	1 2	3 4	5 6
23. Recognizes and skillfully interprets the client's covert messages	1 2	3 4	5 6
24. Facilitates realistic goal setting with the client	1 2	3 4	5 6
25. Encourages appropriate action-step planning with the client	1 2	3 4	5 6
26. Employs judgment in the timing and use of different techniques	1 2	3 4	5 6
27. Initiates periodic evaluation of goals, action-steps, and process during counseling	1 2	3 4	5 6
28. Explains, administers, and interprets tests correctly	1 2	3 4	5 6
29. Terminates the interview smoothly	1 2	3 4	5 6

The Conceptualization Process

	Poor	Adequate	Good
30. Focuses on specific behaviors and their consequences, implications, and contingencies	1 2	3 4	5 6
31. Recognizes and pursues discrepancies and meaning of inconsistent information	1 2	3 4	5 6
32. Uses relevant case data in planning both immediate and long-range goals	1 2	3 4	5 6
33. Uses relevant case data in considering various strategies and their implications	1 2	3 4	5 6
34. Bases decisions on a theoretically sound and consistent rationale of human behavior	1 2	3 4	5 6
35. Is perceptive in evaluating the effects of own counseling techniques	1 2	3 4	5 6
36. Demonstrates ethical behavior in the counseling activity and case management	1 2	3 4	5 6

Additional comments and/or suggestions _____

_____

_____

_____

_____

_____

Date _____ Signature of supervisor _____

                           or peer _____

My signature indicated that I have read the above report and have discussed the content with my site supervisor. It does not necessarily indicate that I agree with the report in part or in whole.

Date _____ Signature of student counselor _____

COUNSELOR COMPETENCY SCALE*

For the Analysis and Assessment of Counselor Competencies

Counselor Competency	Analysis Skill value to interview			Assessment Proficiency	
	Nonessential	Important	Critical	+	−
Personal Characteristics					
1. Social responsibility: The counselor states, and his/her past experiences show, that he/she is interested in social change.	___	___	___	___	___
2. People Oriented: The counselor is people oriented as demonstrated by his/her past experiences and by his/her present social interactions.	___	___	___	___	___
3. Fallibility: The counselor recognizes that he/she is not free from making errors.	___	___	___	___	___
4. Personal problems: The counselor's personal problems are kept out of the counseling session.	___	___	___	___	___
5. Modeling: The counselor models appropriate cognitive processes, behaviors, and feelings during the counseling session.	___	___	___	___	___
6. Nondefensive: The counselor gives and receives feedback to and from his/her clients, peers, and supervisor without making excuses or justifications.	___	___	___	___	___
Other _____	___	___	___	___	___
Other _____	___	___	___	___	___
Other _____	___	___	___	___	___
7. Evaluation: The counselor's theoretical frame of reference includes a means for describing the cognitive, behavioral, and/or affective change(s) that take place in determining the effectiveness of the selected counseling strategy.	___	___	___	___	___
8. Diagnosis: Regardless of his/her theoretical orientation, the counselor can identify maladaptive symptomatology consistent with his/her theoretical frame of reference.	___	___	___	___	___
9. Theory: The counselor states his/her assumptions about human behavior, through which he/she will incorporate or abstract his/her empirical findings and through which he/she will make predictions concerning his/her client.	___	___	___	___	___

*This scale is an altered version of the "Survey of Counselor Competencies" developed by Dennis B. Cogan, Department of Counselor Education, Arizona State University, Tempe, Arizona. This material was taken from Appendix A, pp. 482–490, in J. Boyd (Ed.), *Counselor Supervision,* Accelerated Development, Muncie, IN, 1978.

10. Theory: The counselor explains human behavior from at least two theories of personality.   _____ _____ _____   _____ _____

11. Prioritizing: The counselor decides on which problem, when presented with more than one, to deal with first according to his/her theoretical frame of reference.   _____ _____ _____   _____ _____

12. Interpretation: The counselor provides the client with a possible explanation for, or relationships between, certain behaviors, cognitions, and/or feelings.   _____ _____ _____   _____ _____

13. Prognosis: The counselor can make an evaluation of the client's potential for successful treatment consistent with theoretical frame of reference.   _____ _____ _____   _____ _____

14. Interactions: The counselor describes the interactions that take place between the counselor and client consistent with his/her theoretical frame of reference.   _____ _____ _____   _____ _____

15. Defense Mechanisms: The counselor is aware of the defense mechanisms used by the client as well as the purpose they serve, and can help the client substitute more appropriate ones.   _____ _____ _____   _____ _____

16. Catharsis: The counselor understands the concept of catharsis.   _____ _____ _____   _____ _____

17. Natural consequences: The counselor understands the concept of "natural consequences."   _____ _____ _____   _____ _____

18. Environmental Manipulation: The counselor understands the concept of environmental manipulation.   _____ _____ _____   _____ _____

19. Test Selection: The counselor selects an appropriate test(s) according to his/her theoretical frame of reference.   _____ _____ _____   _____ _____

20. Inferences: The counselor provides an explanation for and the functional use of the client's behaviors, cognitions, and/or feelings consistent with his/her theoretical frame of reference and how they might influence the counseling process.

    Other _____   _____ _____ _____   _____ _____

    Other _____   _____ _____ _____   _____ _____

    Other _____   _____ _____ _____   _____ _____

21. Open-Ended Question: The counselor asks the client a question that cannot be answered by a yes or no, and the question does not provide the client with the answer.   _____ _____ _____   _____ _____

22. Minimal Verbal Response: The counselor uses "mmmh, oh, yes" to communicate to the client that he/she is listening without interrupting the client's train of thought or discourse.   _____ _____ _____   _____ _____

23. Genuineness: The counselor's responses are sincere and appropriate.   _____ _____ _____   _____ _____

24. Positive Regard: Without interjecting his/her own values, the counselor communicates respect and concern for the client's feelings, experiences, and potentials.   ____ ____ ____   ____ ____

25. Language: The counselor uses terminology that is understood by the client.   ____ ____ ____   ____ ____

26. Clarification: The counselor has the client clarify ambiguous cognitions, behaviors, and/or feelings.   ____ ____ ____   ____ ____

27. Paraphrasing: Without changing the meaning, the counselor states in fewer words what the client has previously stated.   ____ ____ ____   ____ ____

28. Summarizes: The counselor combines two or more of the client's cognitions, feelings, and/or behaviors into a general statement.   ____ ____ ____   ____ ____

29. Restatement: The counselor conveys to the client that he/she has heard the content of the client's previous statement(s) by restating in exactly or near exact words that which the client has just verbalized.   ____ ____ ____   ____ ____

30. Empathic Understanding: The counselor's responses add noticeably to the expressions of the client in such a way as to express feelings at a level deeper than the client was able to express for himself/herself.   ____ ____ ____   ____ ____

31. Reflection: From nonverbal cues the counselor accurately describes the client's affective state.   ____ ____ ____   ____ ____

32. Perceptions: The counselor labels his/her perceptions as perceptions.   ____ ____ ____   ____ ____

33. Confrontation: The counselor confronts the client by stating the possible consequences of his/her behaviors, cognitions, feelings.   ____ ____ ____   ____ ____

34. Supportive: The counselor makes statements that agree with the client's cognitions, accepts the client's behavior, and/or shares with the client that his/her feelings are not unusual.   ____ ____ ____   ____ ____

35. Probing: The counselor's statement results in the client providing additional information about his/her cognitions, providing behaviors, and/or feelings.   ____ ____ ____   ____ ____

36. Disapproval: The counselor makes a statement that conveys disapproval of one or more of the client's cognitions, behaviors, and/or feelings.   ____ ____ ____   ____ ____

37. Advice Giving: The counselor shares with the client which alternative he/she would select if it were his/her decision to make.   ____ ____ ____   ____ ____

Other _____   ____ ____ ____   ____ ____

Other _____   ____ ____ ____   ____ ____

Other _____   ____ ____ ____   ____ ____

Counseling Skills

38. Voice: The counselor's tone of voice and rate of speech is appropriate to the client's present state and/or counseling session.   ___ ___ ___   ___ ___

39. Eye Contact: The counselor maintains eye contact at a level that is comfortable for the client.   ___ ___ ___   ___ ___

40. Initial Contact: The counselor greets the client in a warm and accepting manner through some accepted form of social greeting (handshake, nod of head, etc.).   ___ ___ ___   ___ ___

41. Activity Level: The counselor maintains a level of activity appropriate to the client during the counseling session.   ___ ___ ___   ___ ___

42. Physiological Presence: The counselor's body posture, facial expressions, and gestures are natural and congruent with those of the client's.   ___ ___ ___   ___ ___

43. Counselor Disclosure: The counselor shares personal information and feelings when it is appropriate in facilitating the counseling process.   ___ ___ ___   ___ ___

44. Silence: The counselor does not speak when appropriate in facilitating client movement.   ___ ___ ___   ___ ___

45. Accenting: From the client's previous statement, behavior, and/or feeling, the counselor repeats or accentuates the same, or has the client repeat or accentuate the statement, behavior, and/or feeling.   ___ ___ ___   ___ ___

46. Objectivity: The counselor has sufficient control over his/her feelings and does not impose his/her values on the client.   ___ ___ ___   ___ ___

47. Probing: The counselor avoids bringing up or pursuing areas that are too threatening to the client.   ___ ___ ___   ___ ___

48. Resistance: The counselor is able to work through the client's conscious opposition to the counseling process.   ___ ___ ___   ___ ___

49. Verbosity: The counselor speaks when it is necessary, does not inappropriately interrupt the client or verbally dominate the counseling session.   ___ ___ ___   ___ ___

50. Attending: The counselor's attention is with the client's cognitions, behaviors, and/or feelings during the counseling session in accord with his/her stated theoretical frame of reference.   ___ ___ ___   ___ ___

51. Transference: The counselor is able to work through feelings directed at him/her by the client which the client originally had for another object or person.   ___ ___ ___   ___ ___

52. Counter Transference: The counselor is aware of and is able to correct his/her placing his/her own wishes on the client.   ___ ___ ___   ___ ___

53. Manipulation: The counselor recognizes the client's attempt at influencing the counselor for his/her own purpose.

54. Factors: The counselor explores and is aware of socioeconomic, cultural, and personal factors that might affect the client's progress.

55. Dependency: The counselor encourages the client to be independent, does not make decisions for the client or accept responsibility for the client's behaviors, cognitions, and/or feelings.

56. Theory: The counselor can work with clients from at least two theories of counseling.

57. Alternative Exploration: The counselor, with the client, examines the other options available and the possible consequences of each.

58. Implementation: The counselor helps the client put insight into action.

59. Distortions: The counselor explains to the client his/her previously distorted perceptions of self and the environment.

Personal Characteristics

60. Motivation: The counselor can verbally confront the client with his/her lack of goal-directed behavior.

61. Case History Taking: The counselor obtains factual information from the client that will be helpful in developing a course of action for the client consistent with his/her theoretical frame of reference.

62. Insight: The counselor helps the client become more aware of his/her cognitive, behavioral, affective, and spiritual domain.

63. Structure: The counselor structures the ongoing counseling sessions so there is continuity from session to session.

64. Inconsistencies: The counselor explores with the client contradictions within and/or between client behaviors, cognitions, and/or affect.

65. Refocusing: The counselor makes a statement or asks a question that redirects the client to a specific behavior, cognition, or feeling.

66. Goals: The counselor, with the client, establishes short and long-range goals that are congruent with societal goals and are within the client's potential.

67. Reinforcement: The counselor identifies and uses reinforcers that facilitate the identified client goals. _____ _____ _____   _____ _____

68. Flexibility: The counselor changes long- and short-term goals within a specific session or during the overall counseling process as additional information becomes available. _____ _____ _____   _____ _____

69. Behavioral Game: The counselor can develop specific plans, which can be observed and/or counted, for changing the client's behavior(s). _____ _____ _____   _____ _____

70. Strategy: The counselor's course of action is consistent with the counselor's stated theory of counseling. _____ _____ _____   _____ _____

71. Termination: The counselor resolves the client's desire for premature termination. _____ _____ _____   _____ _____

72. Emergencies: The counselor can handle emergencies that arise with the client. _____ _____ _____   _____ _____

73. Termination: The counselor ends each session and the counseling relationship on time or at a point at which the client is comfortable with the issues that have been explored. _____ _____ _____   _____ _____

74. Termination: The counselor advises the client that he/she may return in the future. _____ _____ _____   _____ _____

75. Periodic Evaluation: With the client, the counselor periodically evaluates the progress made toward the established goals. _____ _____ _____   _____ _____

76. Fantasy: The counselor has the client use his/her imagination to gain insight and/or move toward the client's established goals. _____ _____ _____   _____ _____

77. Homework: The counselor appropriately assigns work to the client that is to be completed outside the counseling session. _____ _____ _____   _____ _____

78. Problem Solving: The counselor teaches the client a method for problem solving. _____ _____ _____   _____ _____

79. Test Interpretation: The counselor interprets test(s) according to the procedures outlined in the test manual. _____ _____ _____   _____ _____

80. Role Playing: The counselor helps the client achieve insight by acting out conflicts and/or situations unfamiliar to him/her. _____ _____ _____   _____ _____

81. Desensitization: The counselor can apply a purposeful technique to reduce the level of anxiety that the client is experiencing. _____ _____ _____   _____ _____

82. Dreams: The counselor works with client's dreams in a manner his/her stated theoretical frame of reference. _____ _____ _____   _____ _____

83. Contracts: The counselor makes a contractual agreement
    with the client.

    Other _____ ____ ____ ____   ____ ____

    Other _____ ____ ____ ____   ____ ____

    Other _____ ____ ____ ____   ____ ____

    Adjunctive Activities

84. Case Notes: The counselor is able to communicate in a   ____ ____ ____   ____ ____
    clear concise manner initial, ongoing, and summary
    case notes.

85. Staffing: The counselor can staff a case in a clear and   ____ ____ ____   ____ ____
    concise manner by presenting an objective description
    of the client, significant information, goals for the client,
    strategy to be used, and a prognosis for the client.

86. Test Administration: The counselor can administer   ____ ____ ____   ____ ____
    test(s) according to the procedures in the test manual.

87. Diagnosis: The counselor identifies cognitions, behaviors,   ____ ____ ____   ____ ____
    and/or feelings in the client important in making a
    diagnosis according to the *Diagnostic and Statistical
    Manual of Mental Disorders.*

88. Appointments: The counselor is on time for his/her   ____ ____ ____   ____ ____
    appointments with clients, peers, and supervisors.

89. Informs: The counselor provides the client with factual   ____ ____ ____   ____ ____
    information.

90. Organized: The counselor effectively organizes and   ____ ____ ____   ____ ____
    completes the assigned work within the prescribed
    time limits of the setting in which he/she is employed.

91. Dress: The counselor's attire is appropriate to the client   ____ ____ ____   ____ ____
    population and work setting being served.

92. Responsibilities: The counselor can clarify the role   ____ ____ ____   ____ ____
    responsibilities he/she and the client have in the
    counseling relationship according to his/her theoretical
    frame of reference.

93. Atmosphere: Within the limits of his/her work setting,   ____ ____ ____   ____ ____
    the counselor provides an atmosphere that is physically
    and psychologically comfortable for the client.

94. Cancellations: The counselor notifies the client as soon   ____ ____ ____   ____ ____
    as possible when he/she will be unable to keep an
    appointment.

95. Competency: The counselor is aware of and does not go   ____ ____ ____   ____ ____
    beyond his/her counseling abilities.

    Other _____ ____ ____ ____   ____ ____

    Other _____ ____ ____ ____   ____ ____

    Other _____ ____ ____ ____   ____ ____

Ethical Standards

96. Professionalism: The counselor maintains a professional relationship with the client in accord with APA and/or APGA ethical standards. ___ ___ ___ ___ ___

97. Ethics: The counselor adheres to the ethical standards outlined by the APA and/or APGA. ___ ___ ___ ___ ___

98. Confidentiality: The counselor adheres to the ethical standards of confidentiality as outlined by the APA and/or APGA. ___ ___ ___ ___ ___

Other _____ ___ ___ ___ ___ ___

Other _____ ___ ___ ___ ___ ___

Other _____ ___ ___ ___ ___ ___

COUNSELOR COMPETENCY SCALE*

For the Analysis and Assessment of Counselor Competencies

Counselor Competency	Analysis Skill value to interview Nonessential / Important / Critical ↓ ↓ ↓	Assessment Proficiency + −
Personal Characteristics		
1. Social responsibility: The counselor states, and his/her past experiences show, that he/she is interested in social change.	____ ____ ____	____ ____
2. People Oriented: The counselor is people oriented as demonstrated by his/her past experiences and by his/her present social interactions.	____ ____ ____	____ ____
3. Fallibility: The counselor recognizes that he/she is not free from making errors.	____ ____ ____	____ ____
4. Personal problems: The counselor's personal problems are kept out of the counseling session.	____ ____ ____	____ ____
5. Modeling: The counselor models appropriate cognitive processes, behaviors, and feelings during the counseling session.	____ ____ ____	____ ____
6. Nondefensive: The counselor gives and receives feedback to and from his/her clients, peers, and supervisor without making excuses or justifications.	____ ____ ____	____ ____
Other _____	____ ____ ____	____ ____
Other _____	____ ____ ____	____ ____
Other _____	____ ____ ____	____ ____
7. Evaluation: The counselor's theoretical frame of reference includes a means for describing the cognitive, behavioral, and/or affective change(s) that take place in determining the effectiveness of the selected counseling strategy.	____ ____ ____	____ ____
8. Diagnosis: Regardless of his/her theoretical orientation, the counselor can identify maladaptive symptomatology consistent with his/her theoretical frame of reference.	____ ____ ____	____ ____
9. Theory: The counselor states his/her assumptions about human behavior, through which he/she will incorporate or abstract his/her empirical findings and through which he/she will make predictions concerning his/her client.	____ ____ ____	____ ____

*This scale is an altered version of the "Survey of Counselor Competencies" developed by Dennis B. Cogan, Department of Counselor Education, Arizona State University, Tempe, Arizona. This material was taken from Appendix A, pp. 482–490, in J. Boyd (Ed.), *Counselor Supervision*, Accelerated Development, Muncie, IN, 1978.

10. Theory: The counselor explains human behavior from at least two theories of personality. ___ ___ ___   ___ ___

11. Prioritizing: The counselor decides on which problem, when presented with more than one, to deal with first according to his/her theoretical frame of reference. ___ ___ ___   ___ ___

12. Interpretation: The counselor provides the client with a possible explanation for, or relationships between, certain behaviors, cognitions, and/or feelings. ___ ___ ___   ___ ___

13. Prognosis: The counselor can make an evaluation of the client's potential for successful treatment consistent with theoretical frame of reference. ___ ___ ___   ___ ___

14. Interactions: The counselor describes the interactions that take place between the counselor and client consistent with his/her theoretical frame of reference. ___ ___ ___   ___ ___

15. Defense Mechanisms: The counselor is aware of the defense mechanisms used by the client as well as the purpose they serve, and can help the client substitute more appropriate ones. ___ ___ ___   ___ ___

16. Catharsis: The counselor understands the concept of catharsis. ___ ___ ___   ___ ___

17. Natural consequences: The counselor understands the concept of "natural consequences." ___ ___ ___   ___ ___

18. Environmental Manipulation: The counselor understands the concept of environmental manipulation. ___ ___ ___   ___ ___

19. Test Selection: The counselor selects an appropriate test(s) according to his/her theoretical frame of reference. ___ ___ ___   ___ ___

20. Inferences: The counselor provides an explanation for and the functional use of the client's behaviors, cognitions, and/or feelings consistent with his/her theoretical frame of reference and how they might influence the counseling process. ___ ___ ___   ___ ___

    Other _____ ___ ___ ___   ___ ___

    Other _____ ___ ___ ___   ___ ___

    Other _____ ___ ___ ___   ___ ___

21. Open-Ended Question: The counselor asks the client a question that cannot be answered by a yes or no, and the question does not provide the client with the answer. ___ ___ ___   ___ ___

22. Minimal Verbal Response: The counselor uses "mmmh, oh, yes" to communicate to the client that he/she is listening without interrupting the client's train of thought or discourse. ___ ___ ___   ___ ___

23. Genuineness: The counselor's responses are sincere and appropriate. ___ ___ ___   ___ ___

24. Positive Regard: Without interjecting his/her own values, the counselor communicates respect and concern for the client's feelings, experiences, and potentials. _____ _____ _____ _____ _____

25. Language: The counselor uses terminology that is understood by the client. _____ _____ _____ _____ _____

26. Clarification: The counselor has the client clarify ambiguous cognitions, behaviors, and/or feelings. _____ _____ _____ _____ _____

27. Paraphrasing: Without changing the meaning, the counselor states in fewer words what the client has previously stated. _____ _____ _____ _____ _____

28. Summarizes: The counselor combines two or more of the client's cognitions, feelings, and/or behaviors into a general statement. _____ _____ _____ _____ _____

29. Restatement: The counselor conveys to the client that he/she has heard the content of the client's previous statement(s) by restating in exactly or near exact words that which the client has just verbalized. _____ _____ _____ _____ _____

30. Empathic Understanding: The counselor's responses add noticeably to the expressions of the client in such a way as to express feelings at a level deeper than the client was able to express for himself/herself. _____ _____ _____ _____ _____

31. Reflection: From nonverbal cues the counselor accurately describes the client's affective state. _____ _____ _____ _____ _____

32. Perceptions: The counselor labels his/her perceptions as perceptions. _____ _____ _____ _____ _____

33. Confrontation: The counselor confronts the client by stating the possible consequences of his/her behaviors, cognitions, feelings. _____ _____ _____ _____ _____

34. Supportive: The counselor makes statements that agree with the client's cognitions, accepts the client's behavior, and/or shares with the client that his/her feelings are not unusual. _____ _____ _____ _____ _____

35. Probing: The counselor's statement results in the client providing additional information about his/her cognitions, providing behaviors, and/or feelings. _____ _____ _____ _____ _____

36. Disapproval: The counselor makes a statement that conveys disapproval of one or more of the client's cognitions, behaviors, and/or feelings. _____ _____ _____ _____ _____

37. Advice Giving: The counselor shares with the client which alternative he/she would select if it were his/her decision to make. _____ _____ _____ _____ _____

Other _____ _____ _____ _____ _____ _____

Other _____ _____ _____ _____ _____ _____

Other _____ _____ _____ _____ _____ _____

Counseling Skills

38. Voice: The counselor's tone of voice and rate of speech is appropriate to the client's present state and/or counseling session. _____ _____ _____ _____ _____

39. Eye Contact: The counselor maintains eye contact at a level that is comfortable for the client. _____ _____ _____ _____ _____

40. Initial Contact: The counselor greets the client in a warm and accepting manner through some accepted form of social greeting (handshake, nod of head, etc.). _____ _____ _____ _____ _____

41. Activity Level: The counselor maintains a level of activity appropriate to the client during the counseling session. _____ _____ _____ _____ _____

42. Physiological Presence: The counselor's body posture, facial expressions, and gestures are natural and congruent with those of the client's. _____ _____ _____ _____ _____

43. Counselor Disclosure: The counselor shares personal information and feelings when it is appropriate in facilitating the counseling process. _____ _____ _____ _____ _____

44. Silence: The counselor does not speak when appropriate in facilitating client movement. _____ _____ _____ _____ _____

45. Accenting: From the client's previous statement, behavior, and/or feeling, the counselor repeats or accentuates the same, or has the client repeat or accentuate the statement, behavior, and/or feeling. _____ _____ _____ _____ _____

46. Objectivity: The counselor has sufficient control over his/her feelings and does not impose his/her values on the client. _____ _____ _____ _____ _____

47. Probing: The counselor avoids bringing up or pursuing areas that are too threatening to the client. _____ _____ _____ _____ _____

48. Resistance: The counselor is able to work through the client's conscious opposition to the counseling process. _____ _____ _____ _____ _____

49. Verbosity: The counselor speaks when it is necessary, does not inappropriately interrupt the client or verbally dominate the counseling session. _____ _____ _____ _____ _____

50. Attending: The counselor's attention is with the client's cognitions, behaviors, and/or feelings during the counseling session in accord with his/her stated theoretical frame of reference. _____ _____ _____ _____ _____

51. Transference: The counselor is able to work through feelings directed at him/her by the client which the client originally had for another object or person. _____ _____ _____ _____ _____

52. Counter Transference: The counselor is aware of and is able to correct his/her placing his/her own wishes on the client. _____ _____ _____ _____ _____

53. Manipulation: The counselor recognizes the client's attempt at influencing the counselor for his/her own purpose.   ____ ____ ____   ____ ____

54. Factors: The counselor explores and is aware of socioeconomic, cultural, and personal factors that might affect the client's progress.   ____ ____ ____   ____ ____

55. Dependency: The counselor encourages the client to be independent, does not make decisions for the client or accept responsibility for the client's behaviors, cognitions, and/or feelings.   ____ ____ ____   ____ ____

56. Theory: The counselor can work with clients from at least two theories of counseling.   ____ ____ ____   ____ ____

57. Alternative Exploration: The counselor, with the client, examines the other options available and the possible consequences of each.   ____ ____ ____   ____ ____

58. Implementation: The counselor helps the client put insight into action.   ____ ____ ____   ____ ____

59. Distortions: The counselor explains to the client his/her previously distorted perceptions of self and the environment.   ____ ____ ____   ____ ____

Personal Characteristics

60. Motivation: The counselor can verbally confront the client with his/her lack of goal-directed behavior.   ____ ____ ____   ____ ____

61. Case History Taking: The counselor obtains factual information from the client that will be helpful in developing a course of action for the client consistent with his/her theoretical frame of reference.   ____ ____ ____   ____ ____

62. Insight: The counselor helps the client become more aware of his/her cognitive, behavioral, affective, and spiritual domain.   ____ ____ ____   ____ ____

63. Structure: The counselor structures the ongoing counseling sessions so there is continuity from session to session.   ____ ____ ____   ____ ____

64. Inconsistencies: The counselor explores with the client contradictions within and/or between client behaviors, cognitions, and/or affect.   ____ ____ ____   ____ ____

65. Refocusing: The counselor makes a statement or asks a question that redirects the client to a specific behavior, cognition, or feeling.   ____ ____ ____   ____ ____

66. Goals: The counselor, with the client, establishes short and long-range goals that are congruent with societal goals and are within the client's potential.   ____ ____ ____   ____ ____

67. Reinforcement: The counselor identifies and uses reinforcers that facilitate the identified client goals.

   ____ ____ ____   ____ ____

68. Flexibility: The counselor changes long- and short-term goals within a specific session or during the overall counseling process as additional information becomes available.

   ____ ____ ____   ____ ____

69. Behavioral Game: The counselor can develop specific plans, which can be observed and/or counted, for changing the client's behavior(s).

   ____ ____ ____   ____ ____

70. Strategy: The counselor's course of action is consistent with the counselor's stated theory of counseling.

   ____ ____ ____   ____ ____

71. Termination: The counselor resolves the client's desire for premature termination.

   ____ ____ ____   ____ ____

72. Emergencies: The counselor can handle emergencies that arise with the client.

   ____ ____ ____   ____ ____

73. Termination: The counselor ends each session and the counseling relationship on time or at a point at which the client is comfortable with the issues that have been explored.

   ____ ____ ____   ____ ____

74. Termination: The counselor advises the client that he/she may return in the future.

   ____ ____ ____   ____ ____

75. Periodic Evaluation: With the client, the counselor periodically evaluates the progress made toward the established goals.

   ____ ____ ____   ____ ____

76. Fantasy: The counselor has the client use his/her imagination to gain insight and/or move toward the client's established goals.

   ____ ____ ____   ____ ____

77. Homework: The counselor appropriately assigns work to the client that is to be completed outside the counseling session.

   ____ ____ ____   ____ ____

78. Problem Solving: The counselor teaches the client a method for problem solving.

   ____ ____ ____   ____ ____

79. Test Interpretation: The counselor interprets test(s) according to the procedures outlined in the test manual.

   ____ ____ ____   ____ ____

80. Role Playing: The counselor helps the client achieve insight by acting out conflicts and/or situations unfamiliar to him/her.

   ____ ____ ____   ____ ____

81. Desensitization: The counselor can apply a purposeful technique to reduce the level of anxiety that the client is experiencing.

   ____ ____ ____   ____ ____

82. Dreams: The counselor works with client's dreams in a manner his/her stated theoretical frame of reference.

   ____ ____ ____   ____ ____

83. Contracts: The counselor makes a contractual agreement with the client.

Other _____   ____ ____ ____   ____ ____

Other _____   ____ ____ ____   ____ ____

Other _____   ____ ____ ____   ____ ____

Adjunctive Activities

84. Case Notes: The counselor is able to communicate in a clear concise manner initial, ongoing, and summary case notes.   ____ ____ ____   ____ ____

85. Staffing: The counselor can staff a case in a clear and concise manner by presenting an objective description of the client, significant information, goals for the client, strategy to be used, and a prognosis for the client.   ____ ____ ____   ____ ____

86. Test Administration: The counselor can administer test(s) according to the procedures in the test manual.   ____ ____ ____   ____ ____

87. Diagnosis: The counselor identifies cognitions, behaviors, and/or feelings in the client important in making a diagnosis according to the *Diagnostic and Statistical Manual of Mental Disorders.*   ____ ____ ____   ____ ____

88. Appointments: The counselor is on time for his/her appointments with clients, peers, and supervisors.   ____ ____ ____   ____ ____

89. Informs: The counselor provides the client with factual information.   ____ ____ ____   ____ ____

90. Organized: The counselor effectively organizes and completes the assigned work within the prescribed time limits of the setting in which he/she is employed.   ____ ____ ____   ____ ____

91. Dress: The counselor's attire is appropriate to the client population and work setting being served.   ____ ____ ____   ____ ____

92. Responsibilities: The counselor can clarify the role responsibilities he/she and the client have in the counseling relationship according to his/her theoretical frame of reference.   ____ ____ ____   ____ ____

93. Atmosphere: Within the limits of his/her work setting, the counselor provides an atmosphere that is physically and psychologically comfortable for the client.   ____ ____ ____   ____ ____

94. Cancellations: The counselor notifies the client as soon as possible when he/she will be unable to keep an appointment.   ____ ____ ____   ____ ____

95. Competency: The counselor is aware of and does not go beyond his/her counseling abilities.   ____ ____ ____   ____ ____

Other _____   ____ ____ ____   ____ ____

Other _____   ____ ____ ____   ____ ____

Other _____   ____ ____ ____   ____ ____

Ethical Standards

96. Professionalism: The counselor maintains a professional relationship with the client in accord with APA and/or APGA ethical standards.   _____ _____ _____   _____ _____

97. Ethics: The counselor adheres to the ethical standards outlined by the APA and/or APGA.   _____ _____ _____   _____ _____

98. Confidentiality: The counselor adheres to the ethical standards of confidentiality as outlined by the APA and/or APGA.   _____ _____ _____   _____ _____

Other _____   _____ _____ _____   _____ _____

Other _____   _____ _____ _____   _____ _____

Other _____   _____ _____ _____   _____ _____

SUICIDE CONSULTATION FORM

Directions: Student will complete this form when working with potentially suicidal client. The student will take this information to his/her supervisor for consultation, collaborate on a treatment plan, and place in client's file.

Part I

Name of institution _____

Intern's name _____ Supervisor's name _____

Supervisor's professional degree _____

Supervisor is licensed in _____ Supervisor is certified in _____

Client name _____ Client's age _____

If the client is a minor, has the parent signed a consent form? _____

When was the counseling initiated? Month _____ Day _____ Year _____

Where was counseling initiated? _____

Number of times you have seen this client _____

Part II

Check the presenting symptoms often associated with a suicidal client.

Client is between the ages of 14 and 19. Yes _____ No _____

Client is depressed. Yes _____ No _____

If yes, include a description of the client's depressive behavior:

_____

_____

_____

_____

_____

_____

Has a previous attempt of suicide occurred? Yes _____ No _____

If yes, how long ago was the attempt?_____

Is the client abusing alcohol? Yes _____ No _____

If yes, how much does he/she drink?_____

_____

Is the client abusing some other substance? Yes _____ No _____

If yes, what other substance?_____

_____

Is rational thinking lost? Yes _____ No _____

If yes, explain how this behavior is manifested:_____

_____

_____

_____

_____

_____

Does the client have little social support? Yes _____ No _____

How does the client spend his/her time?_____

_____

_____

_____

_____

_____

Does the client have an organized suicide plan? Yes _____ No_____

If yes, what is the plan?_____

_____

_____

_____

_____

_____

If a plan, does it seem irreversible, e.g. gunshot? Yes _____ No _____

Is the client divorced, widowed, or separated? Yes _____ No_____

Is the client physically sick? Yes _____ No _____

If yes, describe the symptoms: _____

_____

_____

_____

_____

Does the client have sleep disruption? Yes _____ No _____

If yes, describe the disruption: _____

_____

_____

_____

_____

_____

_____

Has the client given his/her possessions away? Yes _____ No _____

Does the client have a history of previous psychiatric treatment or hospitalization?

   Yes _____ No _____

If yes, describe for what the client was hospitalized: _____

_____

_____

_____

_____

_____

_____

_____

_____

Does the client have anyone near him/her to intervene? Yes _____ No _____

Part III

Describe and summarize your interactions with the client. What are his/her basic problems? What is your goal with the client? What techniques are you using?

_____

_____

_____

_____

_____

_____

_____

_____

_____

Describe your supervisor's reaction to the problem:

_____
_____
_____
_____
_____
_____
_____
_____
_____
_____
_____

_____
Supervisor's signature

What are your plans for the client?_____

_____
_____
_____
_____
_____
_____
_____
_____
_____
_____
_____
_____
_____
_____
_____
_____
_____

SUICIDE CONSULTATION FORM

Directions: Student will complete this form when working with potentially suicidal client. The student will take this information to his/her supervisor for consultation, collaborate on a treatment plan, and place in client's file.

Part I

Name of institution _____

Intern's name _____ Supervisor's name _____

Supervisor's professional degree _____

Supervisor is licensed in _____ Supervisor is certified in _____

Client name _____ Client's age _____

If the client is a minor, has the parent signed a consent form? _____

When was the counseling initiated? Month _____ Day _____ Year _____

Where was counseling initiated? _____

Number of times you have seen this client _____

Part II

Check the presenting symptoms often associated with a suicidal client.

Client is between the ages of 14 and 19. Yes _____ No _____

Client is depressed. Yes _____ No _____

If yes, include a description of the client's depressive behavior:

_____

_____

_____

_____

_____

_____

Has a previous attempt of suicide occurred? Yes _____ No _____

If yes, how long ago was the attempt?_____

Is the client abusing alcohol? Yes _____ No _____

If yes, how much does he/she drink?_____

_____

Is the client abusing some other substance? Yes _____ No _____

If yes, what other substance?_____

_____

Is rational thinking lost? Yes _____ No _____

If yes, explain how this behavior is manifested:_____

_____

_____

_____

_____

_____

Does the client have little social support? Yes _____ No _____

How does the client spend his/her time?_____

_____

_____

_____

_____

_____

Does the client have an organized suicide plan? Yes _____ No_____

If yes, what is the plan?_____

_____

_____

_____

_____

_____

_____

If a plan, does it seem irreversible, e.g. gunshot? Yes _____ No _____

Is the client divorced, widowed, or separated? Yes _____ No_____

Is the client physically sick? Yes _____ No _____

If yes, describe the symptoms: _____

_____

_____

_____

_____

_____

Does the client have sleep disruption? Yes _____ No _____

If yes, describe the disruption: _____

_____

_____

_____

_____

_____

_____

Has the client given his/her possessions away? Yes _____ No _____

Does the client have a history of previous psychiatric treatment or hospitalization?

  Yes _____ No _____

If yes, describe for what the client was hospitalized: _____

_____

_____

_____

_____

_____

_____

_____

_____

Does the client have anyone near him/her to intervene? Yes _____ No _____

Part III

Describe and summarize your interactions with the client. What are his/her basic problems? What is your goal with the client? What techniques are you using?

_____

_____

_____

_____

_____

_____

_____

_____

_____

Describe your supervisor's reaction to the problem:

_____
_____
_____
_____
_____
_____
_____
_____
_____
_____
_____

                                        _____
                                              Supervisor's signature

What are your plans for the client?_____

_____
_____
_____
_____
_____
_____
_____
_____
_____
_____
_____
_____
_____
_____
_____
_____

SUICIDE CONTRACT*

1. I, _____, agree not to kill myself, attempt to kill myself, or cause harm to myself during the next period of time, from _____ to _____, the time of my next appointment.

2. I agree to get enough sleep and to eat well.

3. I agree to get rid of things I could use to kill myself (e.g., my guns, pills, etc.).

4. I agree that if I have a bad time, and if I feel that I might hurt myself, I will call _____, my counselor, immediately at #_____, or the Crisis Center (or Suicide Prevention Center), at #_____.

5. I agree that these conditions are part of my counseling contract with_____.

Signed _____ Date _____

Witnessed _____ Date _____

---

*This material is based on W. L. Get et al., in L. E. Fugimura, D. M. Weis, and J. R. Cochran, Suicide: Dynamics and implications for counseling. *Journal of Counseling and Development*, Vol. 63, 1985, p. 614.

SUICIDE CONTRACT*

1. I, _____, agree not to kill myself, attempt to kill myself, or cause harm to myself during the next period of time, from _____ to _____, the time of my next appointment.

2. I agree to get enough sleep and to eat well.

3. I agree to get rid of things I could use to kill myself (e.g., my guns, pills, etc.).

4. I agree that if I have a bad time, and if I feel that I might hurt myself, I will call _____ _____, my counselor, immediately at #_____, or the Crisis Center (or Suicide Prevention Center), at #_____.

5. I agree that these conditions are part of my counseling contract with_____.

Signed _____ Date _____

Witnessed _____ Date _____

---

*This material is based on W. L. Get et al., in L. E. Fugimura, D. M. Weis, and J. R. Cochran, Suicide: Dynamics and implications for counseling. *Journal of Counseling and Development*, Vol. 63, 1985, p. 614.

HARM TO OTHERS FORM

Directions: Student completes the form prior to supervisory sessions and records, supervisor's comments and reactions; student and supervisor then sign the completed form. The student should keep the form in his/her confidential records.

1. Student's name _____

   Client's name _____

2. Number of times the client has been seen _____

3. Dates client has been seen _____

   _____

   _____

   _____

   Client's presenting problem _____

   _____

   _____

   _____

   _____

   _____

   _____

4. Type of therapy given _____

   _____

   _____

   _____

   _____

   _____

   _____

5. What did the client do or say to make the counselor concerned that he/she could represent a "harm to others"? _____

   _____

   _____

   _____

   _____

   _____

6. Was a specific victim(s) named? _____

7. If the victim was not named, what was the relationship of the client to the victim?
    _____

8. If the victim was not named, did the counselor suspect who the person was?
    _____

9. Was a clear threat made? _____

10. Is serious danger present? _____
    _____
    _____

11. Is the danger believed to be imminent? _____

    If so, why? _____
    _____
    _____
    _____

    If not, why not? _____
    _____
    _____
    _____

13. Supervisor's reaction/advice? _____
    _____
    _____
    _____

    What plan of action is to be taken? _____
    _____
    _____
    _____

    _____
    Student's signature

    _____
    Supervisor's signature

    _____
    Date of conference

HARM TO OTHERS FORM

Directions: Student completes the form prior to supervisory sessions and records, supervisor's comments and reactions; student and supervisor then sign the completed form. The student should keep the form in his/her confidential records.

1. Student's name _____

   Client's name _____

2. Number of times the client has been seen _____

3. Dates client has been seen _____

   _____

   _____

   _____

   Client's presenting problem _____

   _____

   _____

   _____

   _____

   _____

   _____

4. Type of therapy given _____

   _____

   _____

   _____

   _____

   _____

   _____

5. What did the client do or say to make the counselor concerned that he/she could represent a "harm to others"? _____

   _____

   _____

   _____

   _____

   _____

6. Was a specific victim(s) named? _____

7. If the victim was not named, what was the relationship of the client to the victim?
    _____

8. If the victim was not named, did the counselor suspect who the person was?
    _____

9. Was a clear threat made? _____

10. Is serious danger present? _____
    _____
    _____

11. Is the danger believed to be imminent? _____

    If so, why? _____
    _____
    _____
    _____

    If not, why not? _____
    _____
    _____
    _____

13. Supervisor's reaction/advice? _____
    _____
    _____
    _____

    What plan of action is to be taken? _____
    _____
    _____
    _____

    _____
    Student's signature

    _____
    Supervisor's signature

    _____
    Date of conference

CHILD ABUSE REPORTING FORM

Praticum counselor and position _____

Date and time _____

Alleged perpetrator _____ DOB _____

    Address _____ S.S. # _____

Alleged victim _____ DOB _____

    Address _____ S.S. # _____

Information obtained from _____ DOB _____

    Address _____

    Relationship to alleged perpetrator _____

    Relationship to alleged victim _____

Brief description of incident or concern _____

_____

_____

_____

Incident(s) ongoing?_____ Or specific date _____

Reported to immediate supervisor on _____

    Supervisor's name and position _____

Reported to children and youth services on _____ Time _____

    Children and youth worker name _____

Alleged perpetrator aware of report?   Yes _____   No _____

Alleged victim aware of report?   Yes _____   No _____

Alleged perpetrator in counseling?   Yes _____   No _____

    Where _____

Alleged victim in counseling?   Yes _____   No _____

    Where _____

Results _____

_____

_____

Student counselor signature _____

Field supervisor signature _____

cc: Client's file
     Agency file

CHILD ABUSE REPORTING FORM

Praticum counselor and position _____

Date and time _____

Alleged perpetrator _____ DOB _____

    Address _____ S.S. # _____

Alleged victim _____ DOB _____

    Address _____ S.S. # _____

Information obtained from _____ DOB _____

    Address _____

    Relationship to alleged perpetrator _____

    Relationship to alleged victim _____

Brief description of incident or concern _____

_____

_____

_____

_____

Incident(s) ongoing?_____ Or specific date _____

Reported to immediate supervisor on _____

    Supervisor's name and position _____

Reported to children and youth services on _____ Time _____

    Children and youth worker name _____

Alleged perpetrator aware of report? Yes _____ No _____

Alleged victim aware of report? Yes _____ No _____

Alleged perpetrator in counseling? Yes _____ No _____

    Where _____

Alleged victim in counseling? Yes _____ No _____

    Where _____

Results _____

_____

_____

Student counselor signature _____

Field supervisor signature _____

cc: Client's file
      Agency file

SUBSTANCE ABUSE ASSESSMENT FORM

Directions: Student asks the client the specific questions addressed on the form. Student, client, and supervisor should sign the form. The completed form is kept in the student's confidential file.

1. What substances do you or have you used? _____
    _____
    _____
    _____
    _____

2. How long have you used (beginning with experimentation)?_____
    _____
    _____
    _____
    _____

3. How often are you high in a week?_____
    _____
    _____
    _____

4. How many of your friends use?_____
    _____
    _____
    _____
    _____

5. Are you on medication?_____
    _____

6. Do you have money for chemicals? How much?_____
    _____

7. How much do you spend for chemicals in a month (if you were to pay for all the
    chemicals)? _____
    _____

8. Who provides if you are broke? _____
    _____
    _____

9. Have you ever been busted (police, school, home, DWIs)? _____

   _____

10. Have you lost a job because of your use? _____

   _____

   _____

11. What time of day do you use? _____

   _____

   _____

   _____

12. Do you use on the job or in school? _____

   _____

   _____

   _____

13. Does it take more, less, about the same amount to get you high? _____

   _____

   _____

   _____

14. Have you ever shot up? What substance? Where on your body? _____

   _____

   _____

15. Do you sneak using? How do you do it? _____

   _____

   _____

   _____

16. Do you hide stuff? _____

   _____

17. Do you have rules for using? What are they? How did they come about? _____

   _____

   _____

   _____

   _____

   _____

   _____

   _____

   _____

18. Do you use alone? _____

_____

_____

_____

19. Have you ever tried to quit? _____

_____

_____

_____

20. Have you had any withdrawal symptoms? _____

_____

_____

_____

21. Have you lost your "good time highs"? _____

_____

_____

_____

22. Have you ever thought about suicide? _____

_____

_____

_____

23. Do you mix your chemicals when using? _____

_____

_____

_____

24. Do you ever shift from one chemical to another? Yes _____ No _____

    What happened that made you decide to shift? _____

_____

_____

_____

25. Do you avoid people who don't use? _____

_____

_____

_____

26. Do you avoid talking about chemical dependency? _____

_____

_____

27. Have you done things when using that you are ashamed of? Yes _____   No _____

What happened? _____

_____

_____

_____

28. Who is the most important person in you life, including yourself?_____

_____

29. How are you taking care of him/her?_____

_____

_____

30. On a scale of 1 (low) to 10 (can't use 5), how is your life going?_____

Explain _____

_____

31. Are there any harmful consequences you are aware of in your chemical use other than

those touched upon?_____

_____

_____

_____

_____

32. Do you think your chemical is harmful to you? Yes _____   No _____

Do you think you have a chemical problem? Yes _____   No _____

Explain _____

_____

_____

_____

_____

_____
Student's signature

_____
Client's signature

_____
Supervisor's signature

_____
Date

CONSENT FOR THE RELEASE OF CONFIDENTIAL INFORMATION

I, _____, authorize _____ (name or general designation of program making disclosure) to disclose to _____ (name of person or organization to which disclosure is to be made) the following information: _____ (nature of the information, as limited as possible).

The purpose of the disclosure authorized herein is to _____ (purpose of disclosure, as specific as possible).

I understand that my records are protected under the federal regulations governing Confidentiality of Alcohol and Drug Abuse Patient Records, 42 CFR Part 2, and cannot be disclosed without my written consent unless otherwise provided for in the regulations. I also understand that I may revoke this consent at any time except to the extent that action has been taken in reliance on it, and that in any event, this consent expires automatically as follows: _____ (specification of the date, event, or condition upon which this consent expires).

Date _____

Signature of participant _____
Signature of parent, guardian,
or authorized representative when required _____

CONSULTATION RATING FORM

Directions: For each of the following questions please rate the degree to which you feel consultation was successful on the following scale:

1. Highly successful
2. Moderately successful
3. Neutral
4. Not successful

The consultant clearly defined his/her role to the staff. _____

The consultant emphasized the importance of the services offered on a request or voluntary basis. _____

The consultant explained the rationale for his/her consultative approach. _____

The consultant encouraged open discussion of any problems or observations about the process of consultation. _____

The consultant was open to suggestions and recommendations from the consultee. _____

The consultant explained and described the steps in the consultation process. _____

The consultant spent time carefully gathering data from the consultee. _____

The consultant intervened with direct services to the consultee. _____

The consultant intervened with indirect services to the consultee. _____

The consultant was successful in identifying the problem. _____

The consultant defined the problem in terms of the person in the environment. _____

The consultant defined the problem in terms of lack of skill, lack of knowledge. _____

The consultant defined the problem in terms of broader organizational problems or issues. _____

The consultant made specific recommendations for change. _____

The consultant provided a variety of interventions and strategies in problem solving. _____

The consultant evaluates the impact of his/her consultation efforts in a formal manner. _____

The consultant provides feedback to the consultee about the assessment of the consultation process. _____

The consultant encouraged follow-up of the consultation relationship. _____

The consultant encouraged independent problem solving by the consultee. _____

CONSULTATION RATING FORM

Directions: For each of the following questions please rate the degree to which you feel consultation was successful on the following scale:

1. Highly successful
2. Moderately successful
3. Neutral
4. Not successful

The consultant clearly defined his/her role to the staff.   _____

The consultant emphasized the importance of the services offered on a request or voluntary basis.   _____

The consultant explained the rationale for his/her consultative approach.   _____

The consultant encouraged open discussion of any problems or observations about the process of consultation.   _____

The consultant was open to suggestions and recommendations from the consultee.   _____

The consultant explained and described the steps in the consultation process.   _____

The consultant spent time carefully gathering data from the consultee.   _____

The consultant intervened with direct services to the consultee.   _____

The consultant intervened with indirect services to the consultee.   _____

The consultant was successful in identifying the problem.   _____

The consultant defined the problem in terms of the person in the environment.   _____

The consultant defined the problem in terms of lack of skill, lack of knowledge.   _____

The consultant defined the problem in terms of broader organizational problems or issues.   _____

The consultant made specific recommendations for change.   _____

The consultant provided a variety of interventions and strategies in problem solving.   _____

The consultant evaluates the impact of his/her consultation efforts in a formal manner.   _____

The consultant provides feedback to the consultee about the assessment of the consultation process.   _____

The consultant encouraged follow-up of the consultation relationship.   _____

The consultant encouraged independent problem solving by the consultee.   _____

INTERN SITE PRESELECTION DATA SHEET—SCHOOL

Name of school _____

Address _____

_____

Level: Elementary _____ Middle _____ Secondary _____ College _____

Student population _____ Staff size _____

Type of Direct Service Provided

Individual counseling	Yes_____	No_____
Group counseling	Yes_____	No_____
Classroom guidance	Yes_____	No_____
Adaptive programs	Yes_____	No_____
Career counseling	Yes_____	No_____
Psychological services	Yes_____	No_____
Social services	Yes_____	No_____

Intern Experience Provided (Direct Service)

Individual counseling	Yes_____	No_____
Group counseling	Yes_____	No_____
Classroom guidance	Yes_____	No_____
Adaptive programs	Yes_____	No_____
Career counseling	Yes_____	No_____
Psychological services	Yes_____	No_____
Social services	Yes_____	No_____

Administrative Experience

Intake interviewing	Yes_____	No_____
Testing	Yes_____	No_____
Scoring	Yes_____	No_____
Interpreting	Yes_____	No_____
Report writing	Yes_____	No_____
Treatment planning	Yes_____	No_____
Consultation	Yes_____	No_____
Referral	Yes_____	No_____
Case summaries	Yes_____	No_____
SAP program	Yes_____	No_____
Staff meetings	Yes_____	No_____
Scheduling	Yes_____	No_____
Parent conferencing	Yes_____	No_____

Supervision Provided

Direct experience   Yes_____   No_____

Individual supervision   Yes_____   No_____

Group supervision   Yes_____   No_____

Education Provided

Professional training seminars   Yes_____   No_____

In-service training   Yes_____   No_____

Research opportunities   Yes_____   No_____

INTERN SITE PRESELECTION DATA SHEET—SCHOOL

Name of school _____

Address _____

_____

Level: Elementary _____ Middle _____ Secondary _____ College _____

Student population _____ Staff size _____

Type of Direct Service Provided

Individual counseling	Yes_____	No_____
Group counseling	Yes_____	No_____
Classroom guidance	Yes_____	No_____
Adaptive programs	Yes_____	No_____
Career counseling	Yes_____	No_____
Psychological services	Yes_____	No_____
Social services	Yes_____	No_____

Intern Experience Provided (Direct Service)

Individual counseling	Yes_____	No_____
Group counseling	Yes_____	No_____
Classroom guidance	Yes_____	No_____
Adaptive programs	Yes_____	No_____
Career counseling	Yes_____	No_____
Psychological services	Yes_____	No_____
Social services	Yes_____	No_____

Administrative Experience

Intake interviewing	Yes_____	No_____
Testing	Yes_____	No_____
Scoring	Yes_____	No_____
Interpreting	Yes_____	No_____
Report writing	Yes_____	No_____
Treatment planning	Yes_____	No_____
Consultation	Yes_____	No_____
Referral	Yes_____	No_____
Case summaries	Yes_____	No_____
SAP program	Yes_____	No_____
Staff meetings	Yes_____	No_____
Scheduling	Yes_____	No_____
Parent conferencing	Yes_____	No_____

Supervision Provided

Direct experience	Yes_____	No_____
Individual supervision	Yes_____	No_____
Group supervision	Yes_____	No_____

Education Provided

Professional training seminars	Yes_____	No_____
In-service training	Yes_____	No_____
Research opportunities	Yes_____	No_____

INTERN SITE PRESELECTION DATA SHEET—CLINICAL

Name of agency _____

Address _____

_____

Type of agency _____ Staff size _____

Client/patient population _____

Type of Direct Service Provided

Inpatient therapy	Yes_____	No_____
Outpatient therapy	Yes_____	No_____
After care	Yes_____	No_____
Addiction therapy	Yes_____	No_____
Individual therapy	Yes_____	No_____
Group therapy	Yes_____	No_____
Marital therapy	Yes_____	No_____
Occupational therapy	Yes_____	No_____
Physical therapy	Yes_____	No_____

Intern Experience Provided (Direct Service)

Inpatient therapy	Yes_____	No_____
Outpatient therapy	Yes_____	No_____
Addiction therapy	Yes_____	No_____
Individual therapy	Yes_____	No_____
Group therapy	Yes_____	No_____
Marital therapy	Yes_____	No_____
Family therapy	Yes_____	No_____

Administrative Experience

Intake interviewing	Yes_____	No_____
Testing	Yes_____	No_____
Scoring	Yes_____	No_____
Interpreting	Yes_____	No_____
Report writing	Yes_____	No_____
Record keeping	Yes_____	No_____
Treatment planning	Yes_____	No_____
Consultation	Yes_____	No_____
Referral	Yes_____	No_____
Case summaries	Yes_____	No_____
Staff meetings	Yes_____	No_____

Supervision Provided

Direct supervision	Yes_____	No_____
Individual	Yes_____	No_____
Group	Yes_____	No_____

Education Provided

Professional training seminars	Yes_____	No_____
In-service training	Yes_____	No_____
Research opportunities	Yes_____	No_____

INTERN SITE PRESELECTION DATA SHEET—CLINICAL

Name of agency _____

Address _____

_____

Type of agency _____ Staff size _____

Client/patient population _____

Type of Direct Service Provided

Inpatient therapy	Yes_____	No_____
Outpatient therapy	Yes_____	No_____
After care	Yes_____	No_____
Addiction therapy	Yes_____	No_____
Individual therapy	Yes_____	No_____
Group therapy	Yes_____	No_____
Marital therapy	Yes_____	No_____
Occupational therapy	Yes_____	No_____
Physical therapy	Yes_____	No_____

Intern Experience Provided (Direct Service)

Inpatient therapy	Yes_____	No_____
Outpatient therapy	Yes_____	No_____
Addiction therapy	Yes_____	No_____
Individual therapy	Yes_____	No_____
Group therapy	Yes_____	No_____
Marital therapy	Yes_____	No_____
Family therapy	Yes_____	No_____

Administrative Experience

Intake interviewing	Yes_____	No_____
Testing	Yes_____	No_____
Scoring	Yes_____	No_____
Interpreting	Yes_____	No_____
Report writing	Yes_____	No_____
Record keeping	Yes_____	No_____
Treatment planning	Yes_____	No_____
Consultation	Yes_____	No_____
Referral	Yes_____	No_____
Case summaries	Yes_____	No_____
Staff meetings	Yes_____	No_____

Supervision Provided

Direct supervision   Yes_____   No_____

    Individual   Yes_____   No_____

    Group   Yes_____   No_____

Education Provided

Professional training seminars   Yes_____   No_____

In-service training   Yes_____   No_____

Research opportunities   Yes_____   No_____

INTERNSHIP CONTRACT

This agreement is made this _____ day of _____, by and between

_____

(hereinafter referred to as the AGENCY/INSTITUTION/SCHOOL) and _____

_____ (hereinafter referred to as the

UNIVERSITY). This agreement will be effective for a period from _____

to _____ for student _____.

Purpose

The purpose of this agreement is to provide a qualified graduate student with an internship experience in the field of counseling/therapy.

The UNIVERSITY shall be responsible for the following:

1. Selecting a student who has successfully completed all of the prerequisite courses and the practicum experience.
2. Providing the AGENCY/INSTITUTION/SCHOOL with a course outline for the supervised internship counseling that clearly delineates the responsibilities of the UNIVERSITY and the AGENCY/INSTITUTION/SCHOOL.
3. Designating a qualified faculty member as the internship supervisor who will work with the AGENCY/INSTITUTION/SCHOOL in coordinating the internship experience.
4. Notifying the student that he/she must adhere to the administrative policies, rules, standards, schedules, and practices of the AGENCY/INSTITUTION/SCHOOL.
5. Advising the student that he/she should have adequate liability and accident insurance.

The AGENCY/INSTITUTION/SCHOOL shall be responsible for the following:

1. Providing the intern with an overall orientation to the agency's specific services necessary for the implementation of the internship experience.
2. Designating a qualified staff member to function as supervising counselor/therapist for the intern. The supervising counselor/therapist will be responsible, with the approval of the administration of the AGENCY/INSTITUTION/SCHOOL, for providing opportunities for the intern to engage in a variety of counseling activities under supervision and for evaluating the intern's performance. (Suggested counselor/therapist experiences are included in the course outline.)

Equal Opportunity

It is mutually agreed that neither party shall discriminate on the basis of race, color, nationality, ethnic origin, age, sex, or creed.

Financial Agreement

Financial stipulations, if any, may vary from one AGENCY/INSTITUTION/SCHOOL to another. If a financial stipulation is to be provided, the agreement is stipulated in a separate agreement and approved by the intern, the AGENCY/INSTITUTION/ SCHOOL, and the UNIVERSITY.

Termination

It is understood and agreed by and between the parties hereto that the AGENCY/INSTITUTION/SCHOOL has the right to terminate the internship experience of the student whose health status is detrimental to the services provided the patients or clients of the AGENCY/INSTITUTION/SCHOOL. Further, it has the right to terminate the use of the AGENCY/INSTITUTION/SCHOOL by an intern if, in the opinion of the supervising counselor/therapist, such person's behavior is detrimental to the operation of the AGENCY/INSTITUTION/SCHOOL and/or to patient or client care. Such action will not be taken until the grievance against any intern has been discussed with the intern and with UNIVERSITY officials.

The names of the responsible individuals at the two institutions charged with the implementation of the contract are as follows:

_____   _____
Internship supervisor at the UNIVERSITY   Agency supervising counselor/therapist
at the AGENCY/INSTITUTION/SCHOOL

In witness whereof, the parties hereto have caused this contract to be signed the day and year first written above.

_____   _____
AGENCY/INSTITUTION/SCHOOL (Administrator)   Witness

_____   _____
UNIVERSITY (Representative)   Witness

INTERNSHIP LOG

Directions:
1. Record the dates of each week at the site where indicated.
2. Record the total number of hours per week for each activity under the appropriate column.
3. Total the number of hours for the week at the bottom of the week's column.
4. At the end of the month, total the hours spent in each activity by adding the hours across each activity; indicate the total in the monthly totals column.
5. Get the supervisor's signature. Keep this in your file to be submitted to the university internship coordinator at the completion of the internship.

Activities	Week 1 From: To:	Week 2 From: To:	Week 3 From: To:	Week 4 From: To:	Monthly totals
Intake interview					
Individual counseling					
Group counseling					
Family counseling					
Consulting/ intervention					
Psychoeduction					
Community work					
Career counseling					
Report writing					
Case conference					

Supervision
  Peer
  Individual
  Group					

Other					
Weekly totals					

Intern's name _____   Date _____

Address _____   Address _____

INTERNSHIP LOG

Directions:
1. Record the dates of each week at the site where indicated.
2. Record the total number of hours per week for each activity under the appropriate column.
3. Total the number of hours for the week at the bottom of the week's column.
4. At the end of the month, total the hours spent in each activity by adding the hours across each activity; indicate the total in the monthly totals column.
5. Get the supervisor's signature. Keep this in your file to be submitted to the university internship coordinator at the completion of the internship.

Activities	Week 1 From: To:	Week 2 From: To:	Week 3 From: To:	Week 4 From: To:	Monthly totals
Intake interview					
Individual counseling					
Group counseling					
Family counseling					
Consulting/ intervention					
Psychoeduction					
Community work					
Career counseling					
Report writing					
Case conference					
Supervision Peer Individual Group					
Other					
Weekly totals					

Intern's name _____   Date _____

Address _____   Address _____

STUDENT EVALUATION FORM

Directions: The site supervisor is to complete this form in duplicate. One copy is to go to the student; the other copy is sent to the faculty liaison.

The areas listed below serve as a general guide for the activities typically engaged in during counselor/psychologist training. Please rate the student on the activities in which he or she has engaged using the following scale:

A – Functions extremely well and/or independently.
B – Functions adequately and/or requires occasional supervision.
C – Requires close supervision in this area.
NA – Not applicable to this training experience.

_____   _____
Student name   Supervisor signature

_____   _____
Site   Date

Training Activities

_____   1. Intake interviewing

_____   2. Individual counseling/psychotherapy

_____   3. Group counseling/psychotherapy

_____   4. Testing: Administration and interpretation

_____   5. Report writing

_____   6. Consultation

_____   7. Psychoeducational activities

_____   8. Career counseling

_____   9. Family/couple counseling

_____   10. Case conference or staff presentation

_____   11. Other (please list) _____

_____

_____

_____

Compared with other graduate students in counseling at this level of training and experience, this student performs at the following level (check) one:

☐	☐	☐	☐	☐
99th %ile	80th %ile	60th %ile	40th %ile	20th %ile

Additional comments

Please use the additional space for any comments that would help us evaluate the student's progress. Student may comment upon exceptions to ratings, if any.

STUDENT EVALUATION FORM

Directions: The site supervisor is to complete this form in duplicate. One copy is to go to the student; the other copy is sent to the faculty liaison.

The areas listed below serve as a general guide for the activities typically engaged in during counselor/psychologist training. Please rate the student on the activities in which he or she has engaged using the following scale:

> **A –** Functions extremely well and/or independently.
> **B –** Functions adequately and/or requires occasional supervision.
> **C –** Requires close supervision in this area.
> **NA –** Not applicable to this training experience.

_____	_____
Student name	Supervisor signature
_____	_____
Site	Date

Training Activities

_____   1. Intake interviewing

_____   2. Individual counseling/psychotherapy

_____   3. Group counseling/psychotherapy

_____   4. Testing: Administration and interpretation

_____   5. Report writing

_____   6. Consultation

_____   7. Psychoeducational activities

_____   8. Career counseling

_____   9. Family/couple counseling

_____   10. Case conference or staff presentation

_____   11. Other (please list) _____

_____

_____

_____

Compared with other graduate students in counseling at this level of training and experience, this student performs at the following level (check) one:

☐　　　☐　　　☐　　　☐　　　☐

99th %ile　　80th %ile　　60th %ile　　40th %ile　　20th %ile

Additional comments

Please use the additional space for any comments that would help us evaluate the student's progress. Student may comment upon exceptions to ratings, if any.

CLIENT'S PERSONAL/SOCIAL SATISFACTION
WITH COUNSELING ASSESSMENT*

Client name _____ Counselor name _____

Client ID number _____ Counselor ID number _____

Date _____

Directions: Please read each of the following questions carefully and **circle** the response for each one that most nearly reflects your honest opinion.

1. How much help did you get with your concern?
   1. None
   2. A little
   3. Some
   4. Much
   5. All I needed

2. How satisfied are you with the relationship with your counselor?
   1. Not at all
   2. Slightly
   3. Some
   4. Pretty well
   5. Completely

3. How much help have you received with concerns other than your original reasons for entering counseling?
   1. None
   2. A little
   3. Some
   4. Much
   5. All I needed

4. How do you feel now compared to when you first came to counseling?
   1. Much worse
   2. A little worse
   3. The same
   4. Quite a bit better
   5. Greatly improved

5. How much has counseling helped you in understanding yourself?
   1. None
   2. A little
   3. Moderately
   4. Quite a bit
   5. Greatly

6. How willing would you be to return to your counselor if you wanted help with another concern?
   1. Unwilling
   2. Reluctant
   3. Slightly inclined
   4. Moderately willing
   5. Very willing

---

* Used by permission from Dr. Roger Hutchinson, Professor of Psychology-Counseling and Director, Counseling Practicum Clinic, Department of Counseling Psychology and Guidance Services, Ball State University. This form originally was printed in Chapter 10 of the *Practicum Manual for Counseling and Psychology* by K. Dimick and F. Krause, Accelerated Development, Muncie, IN, 1980.

7. How willing would you be to recommend your counselor to one of your friends?

1 Unwilling
2 Reluctant
3 Slightly inclined
4 Moderately willing
5 Very willing

8. How much did your counselor differ from what you might consider to be an ideal counselor?

1 Greatly
2 In many ways
3 Somewhat
4 A little
5 Not at all

9. Based on your experience at this clinic, how competent did you judge the counselors to be?

1 Incompetent
2 Little competence
3 Moderately competent
4 Competent
5 Highly competent

10. To what extent could the relationship you had with your counselor have been improved?

1 Greatly
2 Quite a bit
3 Moderately
4 Slightly
5 Not at all

11. How sensitive was your counselor to the way you felt?

1 Insensitive
2 Slightly insensitive
3 Sometimes sensitive
4 Usually sensitive
5 Very sensitive

12. To what extent do you still lack self-understanding about things that trouble you?

1 Great
2 Quite a bit
3 Moderate
4 Slight
5 Not at all

13. If counseling were available only on a fee-paying basis, how likely would you be to return if you had other concerns?

1 I would not return
2 It would be unlikely for me to return
3 I might return
4 I probably would return
5 I would return

14. In general, how satisfied are you with your counseling experience?

1 Not satisfied
2 Moderately dissatisfied
3 Slightly satisfied
4 Moderately satisfied
5 Completely satisfied

15. What was the technique most used by your counselor?

1 Left it to me
2 Interested listener
3 Gave opinions and suggestions
4 Gave interpretations
5 Counselor was vague and unclear

16. Give your reactions while being counseled.

1 Found it unpleasant and upsetting at times
2 Found it very interesting, enjoyed it
3 Got angry often at my counselor
4 Often felt discouraged at lack of progress
5 Felt relaxed and looked forward to sessions
6 Felt that I could not get my story across, that I couldn't get the counselor to understand me

CLIENT'S PERSONAL/SOCIAL SATISFACTION
WITH COUNSELING ASSESSMENT*

Client name _____ Counselor name _____

Client ID number _____ Counselor ID number _____

Date _____

Directions: Please read each of the following questions carefully and **circle** the response for each one that most nearly reflects your honest opinion.

1. How much help did you get with your concern?

   1 None
   2 A little
   3 Some
   4 Much
   5 All I needed

2. How satisfied are you with the relationship with your counselor?

   1 Not at all
   2 Slightly
   3 Some
   4 Pretty well
   5 Completely

3. How much help have you received with concerns other than your original reasons for entering counseling?

   1 None
   2 A little
   3 Some
   4 Much
   5 All I needed

4. How do you feel now compared to when you first came to counseling?

   1 Much worse
   2 A little worse
   3 The same
   4 Quite a bit better
   5 Greatly improved

5. How much has counseling helped you in understanding yourself?

   1 None
   2 A little
   3 Moderately
   4 Quite a bit
   5 Greatly

6. How willing would you be to return to your counselor if you wanted help with another concern?

   1 Unwilling
   2 Reluctant
   3 Slightly inclined
   4 Moderately willing
   5 Very willing

---

* Used by permission from Dr. Roger Hutchinson, Professor of Psychology-Counseling and Director, Counseling Practicum Clinic, Department of Counseling Psychology and Guidance Services, Ball State University. This form originally was printed in Chapter 10 of the *Practicum Manual for Counseling and Psychology* by K. Dimick and F. Krause, Accelerated Development, Muncie, IN, 1980.

7. How willing would you be to recommend your counselor to one of your friends?

1. Unwilling
2. Reluctant
3. Slightly inclined
4. Moderately willing
5. Very willing

8. How much did your counselor differ from what you might consider to be an ideal counselor?

1. Greatly
2. In many ways
3. Somewhat
4. A little
5. Not at all

9. Based on your experience at this clinic, how competent did you judge the counselors to be?

1. Incompetent
2. Little competence
3. Moderately competent
4. Competent
5. Highly competent

10. To what extent could the relationship you had with your counselor have been improved?

1. Greatly
2. Quite a bit
3. Moderately
4. Slightly
5. Not at all

11. How sensitive was your counselor to the way you felt?

1. Insensitive
2. Slightly insensitive
3. Sometimes sensitive
4. Usually sensitive
5. Very sensitive

12. To what extent do you still lack self-understanding about things that trouble you?

1. Great
2. Quite a bit
3. Moderate
4. Slight
5. Not at all

13. If counseling were available only on a fee-paying basis, how likely would you be to return if you had other concerns?

1. I would not return
2. It would be unlikely for me to return
3. I might return
4. I probably would return
5. I would return

14. In general, how satisfied are you with your counseling experience?

1. Not satisfied
2. Moderately dissatisfied
3. Slightly satisfied
4. Moderately satisfied
5. Completely satisfied

15. What was the technique most used by your counselor?

1. Left it to me
2. Interested listener
3. Gave opinions and suggestions
4. Gave interpretations
5. Counselor was vague and unclear

16. Give your reactions while being counseled.

1 Found it unpleasant and upsetting at times
2 Found it very interesting, enjoyed it
3 Got angry often at my counselor
4 Often felt discouraged at lack of progress
5 Felt relaxed and looked forward to sessions
6 Felt that I could not get my story across, that I couldn't get the counselor to understand me

STUDENT COUNSELOR EVALUATION OF SUPERVISOR*

Suggested Use: The practicum or internship supervisor can obtain feedback on the supervision by asking student counselors to complete this form. The evaluation could be done at midterm and/or final. The purposes are twofold: (1) to provide feedback for improving supervision and (2) to encourage communication between the supervisor and the student counselor.

Directions: The student counselor is to evaluate the supervision received. Circle the number that best represents how you, the student counselor, feel about the supervision received. After the form is completed, the supervisor may suggest a meeting to discuss the supervision desired.

Name of practicum/Internship supervisor:_____

Period covered: from _____ to _____

		Poor	Adequate	Good
1.	Gives time and energy in observations, tape processing, and case conferences.	1 2	3 4	5 6
2.	Accepts and respects me as a person.	1 2	3 4	5 6
3.	Recognizes and encourages further development of my strengths and capabilities.	1 2	3 4	5 6
4.	Gives me useful feedback when I do something well.	1 2	3 4	5 6
5.	Provides me the freedom to develop flexible and effective counseling styles.	1 2	3 4	5 6
6.	Encourages and listens to my ideas and suggestions for developing my counseling skills.	1 2	3 4	5 6
7.	Provides suggestions for developing my counseling skills.	1 2	3 4	5 6
8.	Helps me understand the implications and dynamics of the counseling approaches I use.	1 2	3 4	5 6
9.	Encourages me to use new and different techniques when appropriate.	1 2	3 4	5 6
10.	Is spontaneous and flexible in the supervisory sessions.	1 2	3 4	5 6
11.	Helps me define and achieve specific concrete goals for myself during the practicum experience.	1 2	3 4	5 6
12.	Gives me useful feedback when I do something wrong.	1 2	3 4	5 6
13.	Allows me to discuss problems I encounter in my practicum setting.	1 2	3 4	5 6

---

* Printed by permission from Dr. Harold Hackney, Assistant Professor, Purdue University. This form was designed by two graduate students based upon material drawn from *Counseling Strategies and Objectives* by H. Hackney and S. Nye, Prentice-Hall, Englewood Cliffs, NJ, 1973. This form originally was printed in Chapter 10 of the *Practicum Manual for Counseling and Psychotherapy* by K. Dimick and F. Krause, Accelerated Development, Muncie, IN, 1980.

14. Pays appropriate amount of attention to both me and my clients.	1 2	3 4	5 6
15. Focuses on both verbal and nonverbal behavior in me and in my clients.	1 2	3 4	5 6
16. Helps me define and maintain ethical behavior in counseling and case management.	1 2	3 4	5 6
17. Encourages me to engage in professional behavior.	1 2	3 4	5 6
18. Maintains confidentiality in material discussed in supervisory sessions.	1 2	3 4	5 6
19. Deals with both content and effect when supervising.	1 2	3 4	5 6
20. Focuses on the implications, consequences, and contingencies of specific behaviors in counseling and supervision.	1 2	3 4	5 6
21. Helps me organize relevant case data in planning goals and strategies with my client.	1 2	3 4	5 6
22. Helps me to formulate a theoretically sound rationale of human behavior.	1 2	3 4	5 6
23. Offers resource information when I request or need it.	1 2	3 4	5 6
24. Helps me develop increased skill in critiquing and gaining insight from my counseling tapes.	1 2	3 4	5 6
25. Allows and encourages me to evaluate myself.	1 2	3 4	5 6
26. Explains his/her criteria for evaluation clearly and in behavioral terms.	1 2	3 4	5 6
27. Applies his/her criteria fairly in evaluating my counseling performance.	1 2	3 4	5 6

ADDITIONAL COMMENTS AND/OR SUGGESTIONS

_____

_____   _____
Date   Signature of practicum student/intern

My signature indicates that I have read the above report and have discussed the content with my supervisee. It does not necessarily indicate that I agree with the report in part or in whole.

_____   _____
Date   Signature of supervisor

STUDENT COUNSELOR EVALUATION OF SUPERVISOR*

Suggested Use: The practicum or internship supervisor can obtain feedback on the supervision by asking student counselors to complete this form. The evaluation could be done at midterm and/or final. The purposes are twofold: (1) to provide feedback for improving supervision and (2) to encourage communication between the supervisor and the student counselor.

Directions: The student counselor is to evaluate the supervision received. Circle the number that best represents how you, the student counselor, feel about the supervision received. After the form is completed, the supervisor may suggest a meeting to discuss the supervision desired.

Name of practicum/Internship supervisor:_____

Period covered: from _____ to _____

		Poor	Adequate	Good
1.	Gives time and energy in observations, tape processing, and case conferences.	1 2	3 4	5 6
2.	Accepts and respects me as a person.	1 2	3 4	5 6
3.	Recognizes and encourages further development of my strengths and capabilities.	1 2	3 4	5 6
4.	Gives me useful feedback when I do something well.	1 2	3 4	5 6
5.	Provides me the freedom to develop flexible and effective counseling styles.	1 2	3 4	5 6
6.	Encourages and listens to my ideas and suggestions for developing my counseling skills.	1 2	3 4	5 6
7.	Provides suggestions for developing my counseling skills.	1 2	3 4	5 6
8.	Helps me understand the implications and dynamics of the counseling approaches I use.	1 2	3 4	5 6
9.	Encourages me to use new and different techniques when appropriate.	1 2	3 4	5 6
10.	Is spontaneous and flexible in the supervisory sessions.	1 2	3 4	5 6
11.	Helps me define and achieve specific concrete goals for myself during the practicum experience.	1 2	3 4	5 6
12.	Gives me useful feedback when I do something wrong.	1 2	3 4	5 6
13.	Allows me to discuss problems I encounter in my practicum setting.	1 2	3 4	5 6

* Printed by permission from Dr. Harold Hackney, Assistant Professor, Purdue University. This form was designed by two graduate students based upon material drawn from *Counseling Strategies and Objectives* by H. Hackney and S. Nye, Prentice-Hall, Englewood Cliffs, NJ, 1973. This form originally was printed in Chapter 10 of the *Practicum Manual for Counseling and Psychotherapy* by K. Dimick and F. Krause, Accelerated Development, Muncie, IN, 1980.

14. Pays appropriate amount of attention to both me and my clients.	1 2	3 4	5 6
15. Focuses on both verbal and nonverbal behavior in me and in my clients.	1 2	3 4	5 6
16. Helps me define and maintain ethical behavior in counseling and case management.	1 2	3 4	5 6
17. Encourages me to engage in professional behavior.	1 2	3 4	5 6
18. Maintains confidentiality in material discussed in supervisory sessions.	1 2	3 4	5 6
19. Deals with both content and effect when supervising.	1 2	3 4	5 6
20. Focuses on the implications, consequences, and contingencies of specific behaviors in counseling and supervision.	1 2	3 4	5 6
21. Helps me organize relevant case data in planning goals and strategies with my client.	1 2	3 4	5 6
22. Helps me to formulate a theoretically sound rationale of human behavior.	1 2	3 4	5 6
23. Offers resource information when I request or need it.	1 2	3 4	5 6
24. Helps me develop increased skill in critiquing and gaining insight from my counseling tapes.	1 2	3 4	5 6
25. Allows and encourages me to evaluate myself.	1 2	3 4	5 6
26. Explains his/her criteria for evaluation clearly and in behavioral terms.	1 2	3 4	5 6
27. Applies his/her criteria fairly in evaluating my counseling performance.	1 2	3 4	5 6

ADDITIONAL COMMENTS AND/OR SUGGESTIONS

_____   _____

Date   Signature of practicum student/intern

My signature indicates that I have read the above report and have discussed the content with my supervisee. It does not necessarily indicate that I agree with the report in part or in whole.

_____   _____

Date   Signature of supervisor

SITE EVALUATION FORM

Directions: Student completes this form at the end of the practicum and/or internship. This should be turned in to the university supervisor or internship coordinator as indicated by the university program

Name _____ Site _____

Dates of placement _____ Site supervisor _____

Faculty liaison _____

Rate the following questions about your site and experiences with the following scale:

A. Very satisfactory   B. Moderately satisfactory   C. Moderately unsatisfactory   D. Very unsatisfactory

1. _____ Amount of on-site supervision
2. _____ Quality and usefulness of on-site supervision
3. _____ Usefulness and helpfulness of faculty liaison
4. _____ Relevance of experience to career goals
5. _____ Exposure to and communication of school/agency goals
6. _____ Exposure to and communication of school/agency procedures
7. _____ Exposure to professional roles and functions within the school/agency
8. _____ Exposure to information about community resources
9. _____ Rate all applicable experiences that you had at your site:

   _____ Report writing
   _____ Intake interviewing
   _____ Administration and interpretation of tests
   _____ Staff presentation/case conferences
   _____ Individual counseling
   _____ Group counseling
   _____ Family/couple counseling
   _____ Psychoeducational activities
   _____ Consultation
   _____ Career counseling
   _____ Other _____

10. _____ Overall evaluation of the site

Comments: Include any suggestions for improvements in the experiences you have rated moderately (C) or very unsatisfactory (D).

SITE EVALUATION FORM

Directions: Student completes this form at the end of the practicum and/or internship. This should be turned in to the university supervisor or internship coordinator as indicated by the university program

Name _____ Site _____

Dates of placement _____ Site supervisor _____

Faculty liaison _____

Rate the following questions about your site and experiences with the following scale:

A. Very satisfactory   B. Moderately satisfactory   C. Moderately unsatisfactory   D. Very unsatisfactory

1. _____ Amount of on-site supervision
2. _____ Quality and usefulness of on-site supervision
3. _____ Usefulness and helpfulness of faculty liaison
4. _____ Relevance of experience to career goals
5. _____ Exposure to and communication of school/agency goals
6. _____ Exposure to and communication of school/agency procedures
7. _____ Exposure to professional roles and functions within the school/agency
8. _____ Exposure to information about community resources
9. _____ Rate all applicable experiences that you had at your site:

   _____ Report writing
   _____ Intake interviewing
   _____ Administration and interpretation of tests
   _____ Staff presentation/case conferences
   _____ Individual counseling
   _____ Group counseling
   _____ Family/couple counseling
   _____ Psychoeducational activities
   _____ Consultation
   _____ Career counseling
   _____ Other _____

10. _____ Overall evaluation of the site

Comments: Include any suggestions for improvements in the experiences you have rated moderately (C) or very unsatisfactory (D).